Spirit Heart Soul

Origins & Destinies

J. R. Thomas

© 2013 by J. R. Thomas.

All rights reserved. No part of this book may be used or reproduced by any means, graphic, electronic, or mechanical, including photocopying, recording, taping or by any information storage retrieval system without the written permission of the publisher except in the case of brief quotations embodied in critical articles and reviews.
1st Edition published 2012. 2nd edition 2013.

Published by:
Origins and Destinies
Australia
Contact: www.jrthomas.com.au

Copies of this book are available through all good booksellers. For further information contact the publisher directly through the above website.

Because of the dynamic nature of the Internet, any web addresses or links contained in this book may have been changed since publication and may no longer be valid. The views expressed in this work are solely those of the author and do not necessarily reflect the views of the publisher, and the publisher hereby disclaims any responsibility for them.

Cover imagery © Thinkstock

ISBN: 978-0-9923014-0-8 (sc)
ISBN: 978-0-9923014-1-5 (e)

Spirit Heart Soul—Origins and Destinies
by J. R. Thomas 1968-

The main category of this book – Religion/Spirituality
Secondary subject category – Christianity

2nd Edition 2013

Unless otherwise stated, all Scripture is taken from The Holy Bible, English Standard Version® (ESV®), copyright © 2001 by Crossway, a publishing ministry of Good News Publishers. Used by permission. All rights reserved.

Scripture quotations marked "NKJV™" are taken from the New King James Version®. Copyright © 1982 by Thomas Nelson, Inc. Used by permission. All rights reserved.

Scripture quotations marked "NIV" are taken from the Holy Bible, NEW INTERNATIONAL VERSION®. Copyright © 1973, 1978, 1984 by Biblica, Inc. All rights reserved worldwide. Used by permission.

NEW INTERNATIONAL VERSION® and NIV® are registered trademarks of Biblica, Inc. Use of either trademark for the offering of goods or services requires the prior written consent of Biblica US, Inc.

Scripture quotations marked "GIB" are from *The Interlinear Bible—Hebrew Greek English*, by Jay P. Green, Sr., 2nd Edition copyright ©1986 by Hendrickson Publishers, Peabody, Massachusetts. Used by permission. All rights reserved.

Scripture quotations marked "YLT" are taken from Young's Literal Translation of the Holy Bible by Robert Young, 1862, Public Domain.

Written in honour of my parents
Keith and Claire Lawson,
for your faithfulness to God in passing on
the truth of the gospel
to the next generation; and

With thanks to my husband David,
for your encouragement and support
in writing this book . . .

For my children
Angela, Adam, Angus, and Amy,
with the confidence that you will pass on
the truth of the gospel
to the next generation.

Contents

ACKNOWLEDGEMENTS..XI
INTRODUCTION...XIII

Part One—You

CHAPTER ONE—THE PHYSICAL WORLD—THE BEGINNING......................3
    The Origin, The Fall, The Consequences, The Tree, The Garden, Here's What We Need
CHAPTER TWO—THE SPIRIT...20
    The Origin, The Nature, The Destiny, Here's What We Need
CHAPTER THREE—THE SOUL..33
    The Origin, The Nature, The Heart, The Mind, The Destiny, Here's What We Need
CHAPTER FOUR—THE HEART..53
    The Origin, The Nature, The Conscience, The Destiny, Here's What We Need

Part Two—The Others

CHAPTER FIVE—ANGELS..73
    The Origin, The Nature, The Role of Angels, Here's What We Need
CHAPTER SIX—SATAN AND DEMONS..81
    The Origin, The Nature, The Tempter, The Infiltrator, The Accuser, The Destroyer, The Deceiver, The Danger, The Counterfeiter, The Victims, The Name, Here's What We Need

Part Three—God

CHAPTER SEVEN—THE CREATOR..105
    The Origin, The Nature of God, The Creation, Ancient Words—New Discoveries, The Plan, The Family Tree, The Flood, The Call, The Chosen, The Law, The Whole World in His Hands, The Holy Spirit in the Old Testament, Here's What We Need

CHAPTER EIGHT—THE PROMISE...133
    The Son in Eternity Past, The Son in the Old Testament, The Promise of the Messiah

CHAPTER NINE—THE WAY—TWO WORLDS COLLIDE......................141
    Preparing the Way of the Lord, Mary and Joseph Are Proud to Announce the Birth of a Son, The Life and Teachings of the Messiah, I AM, The Mission

CHAPTER TEN—THE SAVIOUR...155
    The Night Before, The Crucifixion, The Resurrection, The Ascension, Pentecost, The Spreading of the Good News

CHAPTER ELEVEN—A LOOK BEHIND THE SCENES...........................168
    A Look at the Death and Resurrection of Jesus with Spiritual Eyes

Part Four—You (Again)

CHAPTER TWELVE—THE LIFE..185
    What Really Matters ... A Message to the Reader, Eating Fruit, What We Needed, The Options, The Ransom, The Importance of Being 'In', To Believe ... A New Heart and a New Spirit, ... Or Not to Believe, Family News, Being the Chosen, The Helper, Your New Destiny—The Hope of Heaven

CHAPTER THIRTEEN—THE PATH..204
    Stone Buildings, Freedom, Love and Obedience, Sin and Holiness, Identifying with Christ, Seeking, Praising, Praying, Giving, Staying on the Path, Joining Others on the Path, Going and Taking the Path with You, Telling Others about the Path

Part Five—You (Yet Again), The Others, and God

CHAPTER FOURTEEN—PATH'S END—THE NEW BEGINNING...............237
    The Day of the Lord, The Return of the King, The Beginning is Nigh

WEB INFORMATION AND OTHER BOOKS BY J R THOMAS.................269
NOTES..271
BIBLIOGRAPHY..274

Acknowledgements

It would be impossible to acknowledge all those who have had an influence on my life and faith over the years. It would have to include family, friends, pastors, and teachers of Scripture. In addition, it would have to include the many authors of books whose writing has assisted me in my understanding of the Word of God and songwriters, whose talent and ability to present the truth of the gospel in music have strengthened and encouraged my walk with the Lord.

I would, however, like to thank my family for their patience while I was writing this book. I have written it at a time in my life when my 'spare time' was inadequate to devote to writing a book. Time had to come from somewhere though, and I would be the first to admit that some things have undoubtedly suffered a little. Hopefully my family would agree that the temporary 'neglect' was for a good cause. I 'finished the manuscript' so many times that my family was probably under the impression that I had been writing many books, not just one! Thanks David, Angela, Adam, Angus, and Amy for putting up with the inconvenience of the journey!

I am indebted to my parents for the blessing of being brought up in a home where there was love, where we were taught the things of God, and where my parents demonstrated their faith with integrity and genuineness, giving myself and my siblings—Andrea, Mark, and Kym, a solid foundation on which to build and an excellent example to follow. Thanks Mum and Dad!

Finally, I am grateful to two people in particular for their willing assistance in the proof-reading and review of the manuscript for this book. Firstly, I wish to thank Keith Lawson, whom I was confident would find missing commas, superfluous punctuation, grammatical errors, and words that were not really words at all but only existed in my imagination. I was not disappointed!

I would also like to thank Peter Grice, whose passion for apologetics and willingness to share his knowledge and understanding of Scripture I have greatly appreciated. You have encouraged me to think deeper about some of the issues that are explored in this book.

Thank you both for giving your valuable time to the reading and correction of the final draft and for your advice and suggestions for improvement.

Introduction

origin—*n.* starting point; source

destiny—*n.* fate

There are now billions of people living on the earth—every one of whom has a spirit, a heart, and a soul. Of these, probably the majority are vaguely *aware* that they have a spirit, a heart, and a soul, but very few people actually know or understand the *origin* of their spirit, heart, and soul. Some may not even care about where they came from and perhaps have not even given it any thought; they're here and that's all that matters! However, it is a very rare person who does not yearn to know their *destiny*—what will happen to them when they die.

This book will tell you both your origin *and* your destiny. It is the book I wanted to read but could not find! After searching for it for many years, I began the process of writing it myself:

> With many questions, I began a journey
> I found the truth within a Book
> I found the clues within the truth
> I wove the clues together
> And found . . . the answers

This book contains the answers to the questions of life and death—answers found in *the* Book that contains the ancient words of *eternal* life. This book will tell you where you came from and where you are going. It will tell you where heaven is, where hell is, and how to get to one and avoid the other!

It is a book written for:

—those who go about their lives in quiet desperation in the hope that when they die, they will somehow end up in the right place;

—those who believe there is a God; but who are not really sure what to *do* about that belief, or if, in fact, they need to do *anything*;

—those who *don't* believe in God, or who suspect they might believe the wrong thing, and are living with a mild anxiety about the possibility that they themselves may be mistaken and that this may have eternal consequences;

—those who once had faith, but have somehow *left* the path; and

—those who *have* faith, but are not sure of the answers to some of the issues of life and death and the reasons for what they believe, and who have a desire for deeper understanding and clarity.

In fact, this book is for *all* those who are seekers of truth. It is a book for you!

Why have I searched the Bible for answers? Because therein lies the truth; for "the words of the Lord are flawless, like silver refined in a furnace of clay, purified seven times" (Ps. 12:6 NIV). The Word of God has been given to inform us, to inspire us, to bring us out of darkness and into the light, and to give us life and hope. The Holy Scriptures have been preserved from ancient times through the sacrifice of many and by the grace of God, so that in these times in which we live, we can know the truth that will set us free.

The Bible is not one, but sixty-six books written by about forty different authors over a period of some fifteen hundred years. God, through His Spirit, guided the writers of the books of the Bible to write down His words—His message for mankind, and yet each writer retains his own distinctive style: "The Lord announced the word, and great was the company of those who proclaimed it" (Ps. 68:11 NIV). The Bible contains history, prophecy, poetry, wisdom, law, and instruction for right living. Its words give hope and its message brings good news that is just as relevant today as it was when it was written many centuries ago.

Can we find out the answers to everything? No. God reveals only what He wants to reveal to man, for "the secret things belong to the LORD our God, but the things revealed belong to us and our children for ever" (Deut. 29:29 NIV). God promises, however, that if we seek, we will find. As I have sought answers to our origin and our destiny in the Word of God, He has brought much to light.

Even the most diligent Bible scholar is limited by the length of his or her lifetime in the seeking and understanding of the Scriptures, and subsequently being able to share his or her understanding of them with others. We can start 'from scratch' in our investigation of God's Word, or we can build on the knowledge and understanding of those who have gone before us, trusting that *they* have understood and interpreted Scripture correctly. This book is a combination of both approaches in that I have investigated, to an extent, the interpretations of those who have gone before, but at the same time I have recognized that, like myself, they are only human and it is unlikely that any one person will have an absolutely correct interpretation of *all* of Scripture. It would, in fact, be a very confident (or perhaps disillusioned) scholar who would presume that all of *his or her* interpretations were correct! To that end, I have chosen not to automatically assume that every interpretation that I have read is correct, and indeed they cannot *all* be correct. Nor am I assuming every interpretation that *I* have come up with is correct. I have also allowed for the possibility that the correct interpretation of something has *not* yet come to light, based on the understanding that God often reveals the meaning of Scripture progressively.

It is likely that others will build on, or even come up with reasons for challenging, conclusions that I have reached, and they are most welcome to do this! I am aware that, like other writers, there will be points in this book that some will disagree with (hopefully graciously) and interpret differently. I am quite willing to categorise some of my conclusions as theory, albeit theory that I believe makes sense and has scriptural support!

> **Theory** /theer-ree/ *n.* (pl.—ies) 1 supposition or system of ideas explaining something, esp. one based on general principles independent of the particular things to be explained.[1]

Theories are ideas that explain something, but are yet to be proven. Unlike theories involving the physical world however, it is not possible to quantify *spiritual* data to prove or disprove a spiritual theory. Therefore, it would be reasonable to say that a spiritual theory is perhaps unable to be proven or disproven conclusively. I believe, however, that the spiritual theories presented in this book are compatible with Scripture.

I have referred to the Nicene Creed during my investigation of Scripture, to ensure that my interpretations of the fundamentals of Scripture are within the boundaries of this generally accepted orthodox statement of beliefs. The Nicene Creed was formulated in AD 325 as a profession of faith by the first ecumenical council which met in the city of Nicaea. It has generally been adopted as a profession of faith among the church body and is the most widely used creed among orthodox Christianity today. Having said this, it should be emphasized strongly that a creed is *not* authoritative, nor are doctrines authoritative, both being subject to amendment. Indeed, historically, creeds and doctrines *have* been amended. This book is not authoritative; the books or articles of other writers are not authoritative. *Only Scripture is authoritative*: "The word of the LORD endures forever" (1 Pet. 1:25 NKJV). I would encourage you to read this book with the Bible by your side, checking the Scriptures for yourself as you read.

The Nicene Creed

I believe in one God, the Father Almighty, Maker of heaven and earth, and of all things visible and invisible.

And in one Lord Jesus Christ, the only-begotten Son of God, begotten of the Father before all worlds; God of God, Light of Light, very God of very God; begotten, not made, being of one substance with the Father, by whom all things were made.

Who, for us men and for our salvation, came down from heaven, and was incarnate by the Holy Spirit of the virgin Mary, and was made man; and was crucified also for us under Pontius Pilate; He suffered and was buried; and the third day He rose again, according to the Scriptures; and ascended into heaven, and sits on the right hand of the Father; and He shall come again, with glory, to judge the quick and the dead; whose kingdom shall have no end.

And I believe in the Holy Ghost, the Lord and Giver of Life; who proceeds from the Father and the Son; who with the Father and the Son together is worshipped and glorified; who spoke by the prophets.

And I believe in one holy catholic and apostolic Church. I acknowledge one baptism for the remission of sins; and I look for the resurrection of the dead, and the life of the world to come. Amen.

It is a blessing to be able to share what I have found with others who are also seeking answers, which are to be found only in the:

Ancient Words
... of the Ancient of Days
... of the man who was God
... of kings, prophets, and priests
To show you the way if you are lost
To reveal the truth in a world filled with lies
To bring life in the shadow of death
To refresh your spirit with new life
To fill your heart with peace
To find rest for your soul

I pray that the Lord will open your heart to the truth in His Word, and that He will bless you with understanding. If this book changes only one life and that life is yours, it will have been worth writing.

J. R. Thomas

Dear Reader,

Embark on a journey with me,
And as you travel through the pages of this book,

You will uncover the truth about
You . . . God . . .
Angels & Demons . . . Heaven & Hell

You will discover the way to
Forgiveness . . . Restoration . . . Eternal life

You will discover the path of life that has no end.

Beginnings—Endings—Beginnings

Let us begin . . .

Part One

You

Chapter One
The Physical World
—The Beginning

> In the beginning God created the heavens and the earth.
>
> —Gen. 1:1

This one verse would probably be the most well-known verse in the whole Bible. This is where we will start on our examination of the *physical* world—the world that is tangible, measureable, and visible. This first verse in the book of Genesis tells of the Creator bringing into existence the space-time-matter universe—the building blocks on which His grand design would take shape.

The Hebrew word for 'created' used in this verse, is the word *bara*.

Bara—(absolutely) to *create*.[1]

This act of creation pertains only to God. It is the calling into existence something that has had no previous existence. In other words, God created *something* from *nothing*. The heavens (space) and the earth (matter) were not previously in existence. God created them from nothing. "The universe was created by the word of God, so that what is seen was not made out of things that are visible" (Heb. 11:3). In contrast to God, human beings, whilst able to be creative, cannot create in *this* way. We can only build, fashion, form, or make from what is already in existence, using matter previously created by God.

God creates through His Word. "He commanded and they were created" (Ps. 148:5). He *spoke* the earth into existence. Jeremiah tells us that God "made the earth by his power . . . established the world by his wisdom, and by his understanding stretched out the heavens" (Jer. 10:12), and God said: "It is I who by my great power and outstretched arm have made the earth, with the men and animals that are on the earth" (Jer. 27:5).

How old is the earth? Although the exact age of the earth is unable to be accurately determined, there are a number of factors which point to a 'young' earth, that is, thousands, rather than millions, or even billions, of years old.

These factors include:
1. Before God created light and began the processes of separation and the ordering of the elements, starting with the separation of light and dark, He spoke the heavens and the earth into existence—the raw materials if you like. God is all-powerful and is more than able to speak something into existence in an instant. There would be no logical purpose for doing this over a vast period of time. The reason He created the earth was for it

"to be inhabited" (Isa. 45:18). Why would He delay the bringing about of the pinnacle of Creation—the inhabitation of the earth by mankind, by slowly forming the earth over millions, or even billions, of years?
2. The account in Genesis states that God made the world in six days.
3. The book of Genesis tells us that each of these days consisted of evening and morning, implying a *literal* six days.
4. The Bible contains a record of genealogy. The age of fathering the next generation as well as the age of death of those in the list of generations is given in the Bible and, although there may be some generations that were omitted between the names listed, these genealogy lists give some basis for calculating the approximate timeframe of man's occupation on the earth.
5. God is perfectly capable of making things in a state of maturity. For example, God can make an *adult* human being—the first man Adam, a *fully grown* horse, a *mature* tree, a butterfly, and a chicken. He does not *need* to create everything from a single cell and then wait billions of years for His design to finally come together.

Imagine for a moment, if the human eye had to evolve over millions of years. There are many components which allow us to see that make up the physiology of the eye. Light must be collected through the iris—a diaphragm that regulates its intensity. It then passes through a series of lenses. The image is then sent via the optic nerve to the visual cortex in the brain. If just one of those components is missing or not formed we would be blind. If mankind was blind for thousands or perhaps millions of years waiting for all of those components to evolve, surely we would have come to great harm through predators or accidents and become extinct long ago. Instead of this occurring, the population has exploded to billions of people!

Likewise, imagine the consequences if the many components in the blood which cause the blood to clot had not been created at the same time but came about through a lengthy process of evolution. The process of blood clotting after a cut requires that platelets form a plug at the site of the injury and that proteins in the blood plasma form fibrin strands which strengthen the platelet plug. There are at least thirty known coagulation factors and related substances, each of which has a function in the clotting of blood. If just one of these clotting factors were not present in the human body right from the very beginning, early man would have bled to death well before the earth had been populated. God—the designer and Creator, knew exactly what He was doing!

Before God formed the earth into a habitable place, it was featureless and dark. It is described as having been "without form and void, and darkness was over the face of the deep" (Gen. 1:2). The earth was covered in water "and the Spirit of God was hovering over the face of the waters" (Gen. 1:2). It is the Spirit of God that brings life and movement to Creation by the power of God.

We now have five elements in the 'Creation equation'—two are the *source* of Creation and three are the *components* of Creation:

Time—"In the beginning"
Power—"God created"
Space—"the heavens"
Matter—"and the earth"
Life—"and the Spirit of God was hovering over the face of the waters".

After the creation of these building blocks, there followed four days of separation, or bringing the components of Creation into order, to prepare the earth for habitation. On the first day of Creation God spoke light into the physical universe and separated the darkness from the light. On the second day He separated the waters above from the waters below to create the sky. On the third day He separated the waters below to let dry land and sea appear. Also on the third day God called vegetation to sprout forth from the earth. The vegetation was designed to yield seed and to continue to produce more plants after their kinds. On the fourth day God made the sun, moon, and stars.

Now the earth was ready for the purpose for which God had created it—to be inhabited, "for thus says the LORD, who created the heavens (he is God!), who formed the earth and made it (he established it; he did not create it empty, he formed it to be inhabited!)" (Isa. 45:18).

On the fifth day of Creation God made creatures to swim in the sea and birds to fly in the sky. God gave them His creative blessing by commanding them to "be fruitful and multiply and fill the waters in the seas, and let birds multiply on the earth" (Gen. 1:22). On the sixth day of Creation God said: "Let the earth bring forth living creatures according to their kinds—livestock and creeping things and beasts of the earth according to their kinds" (Gen. 1:24), again speaking His creative blessing over the creatures He had created.

THE ORIGIN

On the sixth day of Creation, not only did God create animals, He also created the first man. In fact the *whole* of mankind had their beginnings when God created the first man, Adam.

> Then God said, "Let us make man in our image, after our likeness. And let them have dominion over the fish of the sea and over the birds of the heavens and over the livestock and over all the earth and over every creeping thing that creeps on the earth." So God created man in his own image, in the image of God he created him; male and female he created them. And God blessed them and God said to them, "Be fruitful and multiply and fill the earth and subdue it and have dominion over the fish of the sea and over the birds of the heavens and over every living thing that moves on the earth."
>
> —Gen. 1:26-28

God was speaking His creative blessing over mankind by commanding them to 'be fruitful and multiply and fill the earth'.

Who was God talking to when He said: "Let us make man in *our* image, after *our* likeness" (Gen 1:26) (Italics added)? In the very first verse in the Bible, the Hebrew word used for 'God' is *Elohiym*.

> **Elohiym—plu. of *gods* in the ordinary sense; but spec. used (in the plur. thus, espec. with the art.) of the supreme God.**[2]

This title for God means that He is one, yet more than one. God has existed and will exist eternally in God the Father, Son, and Holy Spirit. Father, Son, and Holy Spirit are one and equally God and were working together as one in creating the heavens and the earth.

Human beings are the only part of Creation to be made in the image of God. We have the ability to think, reason, decide, ponder, and reflect. We have emotions, a conscience, and the ability to make moral choices. We have a heart, a spirit, and a soul. We are not just physical matter controlled by the processes of the brain. Nor did we evolve over millions of years from a single cell organism or more recently from the ape family. We were created by a loving God in His image.

The Bible tells us that "Jehovah God formed the man out of dust from the ground, and blew into his nostrils the breath of life; and man became a living soul" (Gen. 2:7 GIB). In Hebrew, the word 'formed' used in this verse is *yatsar*.

> **Yatsar—(through the *squeezing* into shape) . . . to *mould* into a form; espec. as a *potter* . . . earthen, fashion, form, frame, make.**[3]

Yatsar means to form or fashion. This means that God was using something which He had already created—earth or dust, to form something else—man. Adam, the first man, was formed from the dust of the earth. Our physical bodies are made up of elements that exist in the earth. God did not add anything new. The physical elements that compose the human body, including gases which come from the air we breathe, are oxygen, carbon, hydrogen, nitrogen, calcium, phosphorous, potassium, sulphur, chlorine, sodium, magnesium, iron, cobalt, copper, zinc, iodine, selenium, fluorine, and trace quantities of some other elements.

The human body also contains a unique code called DNA.

> **DNA *abbr.* deoxyribonucleic acid, the self-replicating material (present in nearly all living organisms, esp. as a constituent of chromosomes) which is the carrier of genetic information.**[4]

Within the cells, the DNA is organized into string-like structures called chromosomes which are duplicated during the process of cell division allowing DNA replication. This means that each new cell will then have its own complete set of chromosomes. Human cells have twenty-three pairs of chromosomes. One of these pairs of chromosomes is the sex chromosomes and determines whether the person is male or female. Each person has unique DNA inherited from both their parents and contains the genetic information that determines that individual's physical characteristics such as hair colour, eye colour, and skin tone.

Even though Adam's physical body had been formed, at this stage he did not have life. After Adam's body had been formed from the dust of the earth, God blew into his nostrils the 'breath of life'. By breathing into Adam, God began in him the physical processes of life—the intake of air and oxygen, the pumping of the heart, the exchange of gases, the circulation, and so on. He was literally bringing Adam's lifeless body to life.

When God created Adam from the dust of the earth, the whole human race was there in Adam's body. This is quite an amazing concept to ponder. The entire DNA that was to be passed down through the generations that followed Adam existed in the body of Adam. The genetic blueprint for the whole of mankind was created when God created Adam. When God created Adam, He created *mankind*.

Eve, the first woman, was also present in the body of Adam, although not yet brought forth. In fact, in the first chapter of Genesis, on day six, when only Adam was visible and not Eve, we read: "Male and female he created them" (Gen. 1:27). This verse is not just talking about *Adam*. Nor is it only talking about *Adam and Eve*. It is talking about the moment in history when God created the *whole* of mankind. This was the moment in time when God called "forth the generations from the beginning" (Isa. 41:4 NIV). There in the body of Adam was *our* physical beginning, yet to be called forth by God's creative blessing to Adam to "be fruitful and multiply" (Gen. 1:28).

The book of Hebrews speaks of the concept of being present in the body of one's ancestor: "When Melchizedek met Abraham, Levi was still in the body of his ancestor" (Heb. 7:10 NIV). Physically we began our existence when Adam was created but we were yet to be brought forth. Our soul, however, was not in existence until our conception. We therefore were not conscious of existence prior to this because our soul, which includes our consciousness, our personality, and so on, did not pre-exist.

At the end of the sixth day of Creation, God's work of creating was complete. He "saw everything that he had made, and behold, it was very good. And there was evening and there was morning, the sixth day. Thus the heavens and the earth were finished, and all the host of them. And on the seventh day God finished his work that he had done, and he rested on the seventh day from all his work that he had done" (Gen. 1:31–2:2).

First, God created a beautiful place called 'Earth' on which man was to dwell. Then He made the first man and called him Adam. Then God set about establishing a relationship with Adam, first of all by putting him in a special place that He had made on the earth for him to live. "The LORD God planted a garden in Eden, in the east, and there he put the man whom he had formed. And out of the ground, the LORD God made to spring up every tree that is pleasant to the sight and good for food" (Gen. 2:8-9).

It has been suggested that the likely location of this ancient garden was in Mesopotamia, as this area would correspond to the description of the rivers given in Genesis. This may or may not be the case as the landscape would have changed dramatically following the catastrophic flood in the time of Noah. Ancient Mesopotamia is, however, thought of by archaeologists as the 'cradle of civilisation'. It was located around the area of modern-day Iraq, north-eastern Syria, south-eastern Turkey, and south-western Iran.

In this beautiful garden in Eden, there were rivers, gold and precious jewels, lush ferns, beautiful flowers, shady trees, and good food to eat. "The LORD God took the man and put him in the garden to work it and keep it" (Gen. 2:15). It was an ideal existence but it certainly wasn't an idle existence that God had planned for man! He had a job to do. God knew that work and having purpose and responsibility was for man's good.

Although the Bible does not tell us how much time passed from when Adam was created until God made Eve, it would be assumed that there was very little time. God knew that men could not survive too long without women! "The LORD God said, 'It is not good that the man should be alone; I will make him a helper fit for him'" (Gen. 2:18), or "as his counterpart" (Gen. 2:18 YLT). Men and women were created to be complementary to each other. "The LORD God caused a deep sleep to fall upon the man, and while he slept took one of his ribs and closed up its place with flesh. And the rib that the LORD God had taken from the man he made into a woman and brought her to the man" (Gen 2:21-22). This was the first general anaesthetic and the first recorded operation! God took a part of Adam that would regrow—the rib. Ribs can regenerate if the periosteum, or membrane, surrounding the rib is left intact. Adam's rib would likely have regrown quickly, if not instantly, because his body was in a state of perfect health and because of the access that Adam had to the fruit of the Tree of Life which would have aided his body in the healing and regeneration process.

This concludes the account of the creation of the heavens and the earth, and of the physical creation of mankind. In the Scriptures there are many passages that tell of The Creation apart from the book of Genesis. God wants us to understand how everything was created and He wants us to have faith in the *biblical* account of The Creation. He invites us to "ask now of the days that are past, which were before you, since the day that God created man on the earth, and ask from one end of heaven to the other, whether such a great thing as this has ever happened or was ever heard of" (Deut. 4:32).

THE FALL

Before Adam and Eve sinned they lived in perfect bodies in a perfect world. When God's work of creation was complete, He "saw everything that he had made, and behold, it was very good" (Gen. 1:31). Looking around at the world, at our fellowman, and certainly at ourselves, we must wonder at the contrast between those first days in the Garden of Eden and the world we know today. Why does it seem so very different? What could possibly have gone wrong? We constantly hear of wars, famine, suffering, and political unrest. Our own lives are touched by ill health, troubled relationships, and hardship. Prisons are bursting at the seams, hospitals are full, and unemployment is high.

The answer to what went wrong is found in the same place as the answers to *all* the big questions in life—God's Word. In the book of Genesis, immediately after the account of our origin or beginning, we find out exactly what went wrong.

God did not make mankind like robots with no ability to make decisions, no freewill, and no initiative. He made us to think, to feel, to decide, and to choose. He made us in His image! Without these abilities, for example, we could not love, trust, or obey.

Love is a choice. We could not love our Creator or each other if we had no choice. We were created to love and to be loved by God, but it would be impossible for us to love someone if there was no other alternative. That would not be love. True love is given freely.

Trust is also a choice. You have the ability to decide whether or not to put your trust in another person. Likewise, you are free to decide whether or not to trust what God says, and you have the choice whether or not to put your faith in God.

Obedience is also a choice. There was only *one* thing that God commanded Adam, and therefore Eve, not to do. He did not need to give them any other prohibitions. *If* they were going to choose to disobey God and go their own way, they would only need *one* command or rule that would put them to the test, and that one thing involved food; one food in particular; food that they thought would make them more like God. It appealed to their appetite and their pride.

"And the LORD God commanded the man, saying, 'You may surely eat of every tree in the garden, but of the tree of the knowledge of good and evil you shall not eat, for in the day that you eat of it you shall surely die'" (Gen. 2:16-17). There would be immediate consequences if they chose to disobey, and they were warned about this beforehand. To 'die' would mean to be cut off from the source of life, and God told them that this was the consequence that would happen the very day they disobeyed.

It is unlikely that the fruit from this tree in itself had any particular qualities that would cause something to happen, such as a physiological reaction or response in the bodies of Adam and Eve or even a spiritual change. It was more likely that the *action* of disobedience would cause some kind of a change to take place. It was probably of no consequence *what* God chose to prohibit them from doing but rather the fact that there *was* something that they were not to do. In other words, it was the action of *disobedience* that would cause the consequences rather than the *object* (the fruit) itself. If God had prohibited them from doing something else, say, walking backwards while whistling, and they did *this*, it would more than likely have had the same effect, as it was the doing of what God had told them *not* to do that would result in the consequences.

Enter—the deceiver. Since the beginning of time, Satan has tried to deceive mankind and turn us away from God, our loving heavenly Father. At this point in the history of the world, Satan had already chosen to rebel and turn away from God. This was the perfect opportunity to tempt Adam and Eve to do this also. In the book of Genesis, Satan is referred to, or represented as, a serpent:

> Now the serpent was more crafty than any other beast of the field that the LORD God had made. He said to the woman, "Did God actually say, 'You shall not eat of any tree in the garden'?" And the woman said to the serpent, "We may eat of the fruit of the trees in the garden, but God said, 'You shall not eat of the fruit of the tree that is in the midst of the garden, neither shall you touch it, lest you die.'"
>
> —Gen. 3:1-3

It is obvious from what Eve said to the serpent, that her conscience was telling her that it would be wrong to do what God had forbidden. It is also interesting to note that Eve *added* to what God had said. He told them that they were not to *eat* of this tree. He did not say they could not *touch* it. She embellished the facts a little! The dialogue continues:

> But the serpent said to the woman, "You will not surely die. For God knows that when you eat of it your eyes will be opened, and you will be like God, knowing good and evil."
>
> —Gen. 3:4-5

Satan's ploy has always been to get man to question whether God's rules are really in man's best interests, whether God really means what He says, whether perhaps we misunderstand what God says and He is really saying, or meaning, something quite different. Satan tried to deceive Adam and Eve into believing that, although God had told them that the consequence of disobedience was death, He did not really intend to carry this punishment out. In other words, Satan wanted them to think that God was just 'calling their bluff'. Finally, Satan appealed to their pride. Are they content with their place in the universe? Wouldn't they like to be like God? Satan, of course, would be only too familiar with the desire to be like God. Knowing that this is what led *him* to rebel gave him confidence that this line of temptation would more than likely appeal to Adam and Eve.

This whole line of deceit sounds very familiar. How about paralleling this to some of Satan's schemes today to get people to turn away from God or disobey God:

— God's rules are archaic and irrelevant in today's 'enlightened' or 'post-modern' world;

— God doesn't have *our* interests at heart. He is just trying to spoil our fun and stop us from having a good time;

- Surely in today's modern society God would accept *other* forms of marriage, not just that of husband and wife;
- God probably wasn't counting tax avoidance when He said: 'Do not steal'. He just meant *big* thefts like robbing banks;
- God was probably excluding the taking of the life of unborn children and the taking of one's own life when He said: 'Do not murder';
- If God is a God of love, surely this means that *everyone* will go to heaven when they die; and how about
- We ourselves are actually God, or one day we might attain god-like status, therefore, there is no one to whom we are answerable; no one to be accountable to!

Satan excels at the art of deception. He has been around a very long time and he knows what works!

So ... what happened next in the garden? "When the woman saw that the tree was good for food, and that it was a delight to the eyes, and that the tree was to be desired to make one wise, she took of its fruit and ate, and she also gave some to her husband who was with her, and he ate" (Gen. 3:6).

We now have a chain of events happening here in the garden:

1. God prohibited Adam and Eve from eating the fruit; therefore
2. Adam and Eve knew in their consciences what they should or should not do.
3. Satan tempted and deceived Eve; then
4. Eve went against her conscience and yielded to temptation.
5. Eve disobeyed God and ate of the fruit of The Tree of the Knowledge of Good and Evil; then
6. Eve tempted Adam by giving some of the fruit to him.
7. Adam went against his conscience and yielded to temptation; then
8. Adam disobeyed God and ate of the fruit of the tree also.

Although Adam and Eve could have resisted temptation because they had the ability to choose, they didn't. They went against their consciences and against God's command and they chose to disobey God. The Bible calls this *sin*. Sin is measured against God's standards.

> **Sin—***n.* **1** *a.* **breaking of divine or moral law esp. deliberately.** *b.* **such an act. 2 offence against good taste or propriety etc .—***v.* **(-nn-) 1 commit a sin. 2 (foll. by against) offend.**[5]

Adam and Eve both sinned by breaking God's command. If there was no command, then eating this fruit would not have been a sin. Sin is doing the things that we should *not* do, and omitting to do the things that we *should* do. It is the assertion of spiritual autonomy—declaring independence from God and going your own way. Sin causes disconnection and alienation from God because God is holy and cannot dwell with sinful man.

What happened after Adam and Eve sinned?

> The eyes of both were opened, and they knew that they were naked. And they sewed fig leaves together and made themselves loincloths. And they heard the sound of the LORD God walking in the garden in the cool of the day, and the man and his wife hid themselves from the presence of the LORD God among the trees of the garden. But the LORD God called to the man and said to him, "Where are you?" And he said, "I heard the sound of you in the garden, and I was afraid, because I was naked, and I hid myself." He said, "Who told you that you were naked? Have you eaten of the tree of which I commanded you not to eat?" The man said, "The woman whom you gave to be with me, she gave me fruit of the tree, and I ate." Then the LORD God said to the woman, "What is this that you have done?" The woman said, "The serpent deceived me, and I ate."
>
> —Gen. 3:7-13

This sin led to some immediate consequences in Adam and Eve:
— They felt *shame* and tried to hide their nakedness. They became *self-conscious;*
— They felt *guilt* for doing what God had told them not to do. They felt *self-reproach;* and
— They felt *fear*—fear of punishment; fear of facing up to God. They felt the need for *self-preservation.*

Adam and Eve's 'self' had become the centre of their lives in place of God. They had chosen to be *self-reliant, self-sufficient,* and *self-determining.* Now they had to live with the consequences. They had not felt shame, guilt, or fear before, because they had previously had nothing to feel ashamed, guilty, or fearful about.

God knows and sees everything. He knows the future. He knew that this would happen and He saw it happen. It did not come as a surprise to Him. God knew where Adam and Eve were in the garden and yet He sought them out. Although He knew what they had done, He still required a confession from them. Confessing sins is part of the process of forgiveness and of the cleansing of the heart. It was not for His *own* benefit that God required Adam and Eve to confess their sins. It was for *their* benefit. Forgiveness was not for God's benefit either, but for the benefit of Adam and Eve to cleanse their hearts from the guilt of sin. Sin is an action that takes place at a particular time and, once committed, it is in the past. It is not the *sin* that remains. It is the *guilt* of that sin that remains and contaminates the heart making it unclean.

As is typical of human nature, Adam tried to blame Eve and Eve tried to blame Satan. This was their attempt at cleansing their hearts from a guilty conscience; again a product of their drive for self-sufficiency (I can fix this myself!). They thought that if they could convince themselves, and perhaps even God, that it was not really their fault, maybe everything would be all right and things could return to the way they were. Perhaps they were now thinking that it had all been a bit of a mistake and that they hadn't really meant to do this. They did not want to be held accountable for their sin and they tried to make excuses. God knew their hearts and, although Satan was also held responsible and consequently punished, He held Adam and Eve accountable for their own actions. They had been forewarned of the consequences of disobeying God—that they would 'surely die', and now they would find out just how devastating and far reaching those consequences were, not only in the moments immediately following their disobedience, but also in the effect that this event would have on the rest of their lives and on the lives of the generations to come.

THE CONSEQUENCES

God is holy and just. Because of His holiness He cannot dwell with sinful man. Because He is just He cannot allow sin to go unpunished. God, because of His nature, needed to bring Adam and Eve to justice.

What had Adam and Eve done? They had been led into temptation by Satan. They had sinned. They had deliberately chosen to go their own way. But what they had really done was to damage the relationship that they had with God. They had broken the connection they had to their heavenly Father. They were unfaithful to God. God had given them eternal life but that was dependant on their connection to God and their faith in Him. They only had eternal life *in Him*. Because all humanity was represented both physically and spiritually in Adam, the connection to God for all generations to follow was broken.

Picture an open air court scene in a beautiful garden with God presiding over the court, Satan slinking around in the background perhaps smirking, and Adam and Eve standing in front of their Creator, heads hung in shame awaiting their sentence. One could imagine the whole host of angels attending court holding their breath awaiting the delivery of the sentence. It was a sad day for a loving God.

With the court now in session, God begins by pronouncing the sentence upon Satan, followed by the sentence upon Eve, and finally the sentence upon Adam:

> So the LORD God said to the serpent: "Because you have done this, you are cursed more than all cattle, and more than every beast of the field; on your belly you shall go, and you shall eat dust all the days of your life. And I will put enmity between you and the woman, and between your seed and her Seed; He shall bruise your head, and you shall bruise His heel." To the woman He said: "I will greatly multiply your sorrow and your conception; in pain you shall bring forth children; your desire shall be for your husband, and he shall rule over you."
>
> Then to Adam He said, "Because you have heeded the voice of your wife, and have eaten from the tree of which I commanded you, saying, 'You shall not eat of it': Cursed is the ground for your sake; in toil you shall eat of it all the days of your life.

Both thorns and thistles it shall bring forth for you, and you shall eat the herb of the field. In the sweat of your face you shall eat bread till you return to the ground, for out of it you were taken; for dust you are, and to dust you shall return."

—Gen. 3:14-19 NKJV

For the woman, the pains of childbearing are rather self-explanatory. Many readers would have no argument that *this* part of the sentence is a reality! The man ruling over the woman has generally played itself out throughout history in most cultures in the prevalence of male dominance in the home, workplace, and community. God had originally made the woman to be man's counterpart, but this relationship changed due to the fall of man. Possibly due to the fact that Eve was the first deceived and then she offered the fruit to Adam, God placed the husband in a role of dominance over the wife.

The curse that God placed upon the ground has caused man to be in a constant struggle for food, necessitating back-breaking labour and often a battle against the elements just to put food on the table. Droughts, floods, bushfires, and other disasters have frequently devastated crops and destroyed livestock. Much of the land on the earth is hostile to the growth of crops and the support of livestock, with vast areas of desert and large areas of land covered in ice. Other places are simply too hot or too cold to successfully grow food or provide fodder for animals. The curse on the ground meant that Adam and Eve could no longer just wander around the Garden of Eden gathering their food. It would now require hard toil on their part just to survive. Today many people are in starvation and poverty because of the curse that is on the land as a consequence of sin.

Furthermore, in the pronouncement of their punishment, the Lord makes it clear to Adam and Eve that not only did they experience immediate *spiritual* death when they sinned, by being cut off from the life of God—the source of spiritual life, but *physical* death, although not immediate, was now inevitable. God told them that one day they would return to dust.

Their physical death, it seems, was something that God only made them aware would happen *after* they had sinned. If they had known that this would occur as a result of their disobedience, they may not so readily have chosen to take of the fruit, as they would have been motivated by self-preservation. They took the fruit however, because of their misguided belief that they would become like God and because of their desire to be in control—self-determining. God wanted them to obey Him purely because they loved and trusted Him, rather than because they were afraid of physical death. Physical death meant that they would not live in their physical bodies on this earth indefinitely, but that they would now have a limited lifespan. One day their bodies would die and return to dust.

Was there death in the world before Adam and Eve sinned? The Scriptures do not clearly tell us whether or not *animals* were subject to a limited lifespan before The

Fall, although it seems that the Tree of Life was purely for the partaking of by humans, and only humans were directly connected to God's Spirit. This does not necessarily mean though, that animals died before The Fall. There may or may not have been death in the animal kingdom prior to sin entering the world and, as it was likely a very short period of time from The Creation until The Fall, most animals would not have lived out their lifespan even if they did have a limited life.

Adam and Eve did not eat meat. It was not until after the flood that God allowed meat to be eaten, so they would not have had to kill an animal to eat it. Plants were eaten by Adam and Eve however, and for a plant to be eaten, implies the death of that plant. The plant may have had to be removed from the soil or part of the plant cut off the parent plant in order for it to be consumed. Furthermore, for many plants to reproduce plants 'after their kinds' they would need to die in order for the seed to be released and new plants to grow. It is logical therefore, to assume that plants *were* subject to death prior to The Fall as part of their continuing lifecycle, but not to disease. If this was the case, Adam and Eve would perhaps have had an idea of what death meant *before* their 'sentence' was carried out. They would have observed that the death of a plant meant the disconnection of that plant from its life source, namely, the soil or the parent plant. They were not in *total* ignorance about the implications and consequences of choosing to sin.

When God pronounces the sentence on Satan we see a glimmer of hope. God warned Satan: "I will put enmity between you and the woman, and between your offspring and hers; he will crush your head, and you will strike his heel" (Gen. 3:15 NIV). This is the very first prophecy in Scripture. God was announcing that, one day, a man would be born who, although Satan would wound Him, He would crush Satan. This One who was to come would be unique in that He would be the offspring of the woman only, not of the man. Adam and Eve were given a message of hope for their salvation and the salvation of mankind.

After God had spoken to them, He "made for Adam and for his wife garments of skins and clothed them" (Gen. 3:21). To make garments of skins required that a life or lives first had to be sacrificed. You cannot remove animal skin unless the animal first dies. The slaughter of an innocent animal—the taking of the life of another living being, had to take place. The skin from this animal or animals and therefore the losing of life, would cover the shame that Adam and Eve felt because of their nakedness, which was a consequence of having become sinners. It is significant that *God* demonstrated His mercy for them by doing this.

Sin is costly. The Bible tells us that "the wages of sin is death" (Rom. 6:23).

> **Wage** /wayj/—*n. 1 (in sing. or pl.)* **fixed regular payment to an employee, esp. a manual worker (cf. SALARY). 2** (*in sing. Or pl., with the pl. sometimes treated as sing.*) requital (*the wages of sin is death*).[6]

The 'wages' means the payment that has to be made. The payment for sin was, and still is, death.

THE TREE

There were two trees growing in the Garden of Eden that were specifically mentioned in the account of The Creation. One of these trees was the Tree of the Knowledge of Good and Evil which Adam and Eve chose to disobey God and eat from. There is a reference in the book of Hosea to 'eating the fruit of deception'. The people of Israel were told that this was what they were doing in their wickedness by depending "on their own strength" (Hosea 10:13 NIV). When Adam and Eve ate the fruit from this tree, they were deceived. They thought that they could be independent from God and depend 'on their own strength'. They deceived themselves into thinking that they did not *need* God. That is not how we were designed!

When God told Adam not to eat of the Tree of the Knowledge of Good and Evil, He said that the consequences of this would be that: "In the day of your eating from it surely you shall die" (Gen. 2:17 GIB). This tells us that death would immediately follow. Clearly they did not drop dead on biting into this fruit in a similar fashion to Snow White on biting into the poisoned apple! After the event they were still alive and breathing.

What was this immediate death that God was speaking of that would occur in the day that they ate of the fruit? What is death? Death is a separation from life. When Adam and Eve sinned, they were choosing to separate themselves from God and go their own way. This meant that they became separated from the source of spiritual life—their Creator. From that moment on, it was as if they were spiritually dead. This is the death that was immediate. Because of this, their relationship with God, which was meant to be that of a loving Father and child, had become marred and damaged and was now distant. But there was more death to come...

The other tree in the garden was the Tree of Life. Adam and Eve were no longer allowed access to this tree from which they had previously been allowed to eat:

> Then the LORD God said, "Behold, the man has become like one of us in knowing good and evil. Now, lest he reach out his hand and take also of the tree of life and eat, and live forever—" therefore the LORD God sent him out from the garden of Eden to work the ground from which he was taken. He drove out the man, and at the east of the garden of Eden he placed the cherubim and a flaming sword that turned every way to guard the way to the tree of life.
>
> —Gen. 3:22-24

It seems that the Tree of Life had sustained the physical bodies of Adam and Eve so that, by the eating of its fruit, they would not experience cellular degeneration, ageing, and finally death. It indefinitely suspended their bodies in a state of health and youthfulness. The Tree of Life, and therefore the fruit from this tree, must have contained the properties the human body needed in order to be maintained in this youthful, healthy state—properties that prevented cellular degeneration.

It makes perfect sense that enduring *spiritual* life came from the continuing connection to a *spiritual* source—God, and that enduring *physical* life came from the continued access to a *physical* source—the fruit of the Tree of Life, which had been created by God for man's benefit. Our physical health is largely dependent on what we eat and drink. That is how God designed us. This tree with its fruit was God's design—a source that was able to be withdrawn if necessary.

Just as it was only when Adam and Eve were connected to God's Spirit that they had *spiritual* life, it was only for as long as they ate from the Tree of Life that Adam and Eve's *bodies* would live for ever. The eating of the fruit of this tree had enabled them to maintain the life and health of their bodies. Now that they had sinned, they were no longer allowed access to this tree. This was a big problem. They would now experience cellular degeneration, gradual breakdown of their bodies, and finally physical death, returning to the dust from which they were formed.

Why did God not allow sinful man to live forever? If this happened, man could then potentially become more and more wicked and drift further and further away from God. It is because of God's mercy and wisdom that He limited man's life.

So what happened to the two trees that were in the middle of the garden? Well, the Tree of the Knowledge of Good and Evil is not mentioned again. This further confirms the likelihood that it may have been just an ordinary tree and that it was the actual act of sin by the disobedience of Adam and Eve in the eating of the fruit of this tree that was the catalyst, or cause, of spiritual death rather than anything pertaining to the tree or the fruit itself. The Bible certainly speaks volumes about the issues of good and evil though.

The Tree of Life is referred to a number of times throughout Scripture following the account of The Creation. In the book of Proverbs, which is a collection of wise sayings by King Solomon, there are several references where the writer likens things to a tree of life. These are metaphors and he is not referring to the original Tree of Life spoken of in Genesis. The things for which he uses a tree of life as a metaphor for are:

— "The fruit of the righteous" (Prov. 11:30);
— "A longing fulfilled" (Prov. 13:12 NIV) as opposed to "hope deferred";
— "The tongue that brings healing" (Prov. 15:4 NIV); and
— "Wisdom" (Prov. 3:18 NIV).

Throughout the centuries people of all races and religions have embarked on the quest to find eternal youth, the fountain of youth, or some sort of elixir to prevent ageing. Foods are analysed, drugs are created, locations are studied, and those who have outlived the average life span or perhaps look younger or have a lesser 'biological age' than their years suggest they should have, are interrogated and their 'secrets' prised out of them, but to no avail. No one has yet found anything that will *significantly* add years to life or halt the progression of old age. Perhaps we can live a few extra years by eating the right foods, exercising, avoiding activities which are damaging to the body such as smoking, alcohol, drug-taking, and contact with high voltage power lines, but in the end everybody dies.

If, as the saying goes, there are two things certain in life—death and taxes, then why do we try so hard to avoid both? Why not just accept the inevitable? Okay, maybe some people *are* highly skilled in the art of tax avoidance but not in the art of death avoidance! Why? Because the source of continued physical life, health, the maintenance of youth, and the prevention of ageing does not exist on the earth at this moment in time. It did in the beginning, it will in the end, but in the meantime our bodies will continue to breakdown. We will be subject to illness and pain. There will be times when we will not experience healing and, of course, we will age and at some point we will die. We are not going to find a remedy in a bottle or on a mountain top. Nor will we one day tune in to a news broadcast and find that scientists have found the amazing scientific breakthrough they have been looking for.

It is at the end of the Bible in the very last book of The Revelation that we discover the whereabouts of the Tree of Life. It is seen in a vision by the apostle John to be "in the paradise of God" (Rev. 2:7) and the promise is given that those who are faithful and overcome, or endure in faith to the end, will be given the right to eat from this tree.

There is nothing you can do to indefinitely extend the physical life of your body. The Tree of Life is temporarily out of reach! The same however, cannot be said about eternal *spiritual* life. The psalmist said of God: "With you is the fountain of life" (Ps. 36:9). That is within your reach right now and that is certainly a quest worth embarking on!

Interestingly, there are two prophets of God spoken of in the Old Testament who did *not* die an earthly physical death. "Enoch walked with God, and he was not, for God took him" (Gen. 5:24). The letter to the Hebrews in the New Testament tells us that "by faith Enoch was taken up so that he should not see death, and he was not found, because God had taken him" (Heb. 11:5). The other prophet was Elijah who, in full sight of his understudy Elisha, was taken away *bodily* by God without dying: "As they still went on and talked, behold, chariots of fire and horses of fire separated the two of them. And Elijah went up by a whirlwind into heaven" (2 Kings 2:11).

To sustain physical life in a physical body, it is likely that these two godly men would need to have access to something that would prevent their bodies from cellular degeneration, ageing, and death. It would therefore be logical that, unless there was some other way of preserving their bodies, they would need access to the Tree of Life so that, just as the fruit of this tree prevented Adam and Eve's bodies from cellular degeneration and death in the Garden of Eden originally, it would do the same for these two men. It is therefore likely that they were transported to the location of the Tree, or Trees, of Life, wherever that may have been at the time when the men were taken from the earth; likely paradise.

THE GARDEN

What happened to the Garden of Eden after The Fall? The prophet Isaiah makes reference to the "garden of the Lord" (Isa. 51:3) and Ezekiel speaks of the "garden of God" (Ezek. 31:9). *Paradise* means 'the king's garden'. The word is believed to be of Persian origin and a place of blessedness, delight, and happiness. The apostle John wrote of an occasion when he was "caught up into paradise and heard inexpressible words" (2 Cor. 12:4 NIV) in a place he also referred to as the 'third heaven'. The similarity of both the Garden of Eden and paradise suggests that perhaps part of heaven came down to earth at the time of The Creation and the heavenly paradise—the king's garden, became the Garden of Eden on earth at the time when God walked with Adam and Eve 'in the cool of the day', before sin entered the world. When man sinned, heaven then moved further away taking the Garden of Eden, or paradise, with it.

It appears that this beautiful garden is not lost to mankind forever though. In the book of Revelation, we read that overcomers will be given the right to eat from "the tree of life, which is in the paradise of God" (Rev. 2:7). This 'paradise of God', along with trees of life, will descend from heaven to earth when the earth is made new.

HERE'S WHAT WE NEED:

It is clear from the account of The Creation and The Fall, that all is not how God intended it to be. The curse on the earth needs to be broken. The earth needs to be renewed.

We feel a certain injustice in the knowledge that our life is limited. Death does not seem fair. We have, built in to us, the desire to live for ever. However, our bodies at present are subject to what the apostle Paul refers to as "the law of sin and death" (Rom. 8:2 NKJV); that is, the curse of death that was placed on mankind when sin entered the world through Adam.

This curse of death upon mankind needs to be broken. We need our bodies to be renewed and restored to the state of health and perfection that Adam's body was prior to The Fall. If we had restored bodies we would possibly also need access to the Tree of Life, or at least a way of sustaining our bodies in a state of health and eternal youthfulness.

We need a 'return to Eden'—a return to the way God intended man to live!

Chapter Two
The Spirit

The physical world is measurable and quantifiable. Physical elements and compositions are subject to laws and their actions and functions are generally able to be determined based on their known properties. They may be visible and able to be touched, smelt, heard, and tasted by the physical senses.

The human being is made up of two very different 'substances'. One of these substances is physical, or matter. The other substance is spiritual. The spiritual body is comprised of the spirit and the soul.

The previous chapter focussed mainly on the *physical* Creation; in particular, the creation of the first man and woman. This chapter will examine in greater detail how the first man was created, particularly in regard to his spirit, as well as how we received *our* spirits.

THE ORIGIN

"God is spirit" (John 4:24). God is eternal. He had no beginning and will have no end. Directly from God's Spirit came the breath of life that formed the human spirit. Without the spiritual to impart life, the physical *has* no life.

Adam was created when "Jehovah God formed the man out of dust from the ground, and blew into his nostrils the breath of life; and man became a living soul" (Gen. 2:7 GIB). God created the *physical* substance of Adam from the dust of the earth and breathed into him His own Spirit—the breath or Spirit of life, forming the spirit of man.

Because Adam received this Spirit of life from God, he is referred to in the genealogy list in the book of Luke as "the son of God" (Luke 3:38). All other generations are referred to as sons of the previous generation; for example, "Seth, the son of Adam" (Luke 3:38).

God's *breath,* or Spirit, formed man's spirit. The book of Job confirms that "there is a spirit in man, the breath of the Almighty gives him understanding" (Job 32:8 NIV). God is "the God of the spirits of all flesh" (Num. 16:22) and He is "the Father of spirits" (Heb. 12:9 NKJV). Our bodies are created. Our spirits are *not* created. They are given to us by our heavenly Father. Before God breathed the breath of life, or spirit, into Adam's nostrils there was no life in his body because "the body apart from the spirit is dead" (James 2:26). Life is a gift from the Creator.

When referring to God as the Creator of the earth, the book of Isaiah tells us that He "gives breath to the people on it, and spirit to those who walk on it" (Isa. 42:5). With regard to man's spirit and also to his dependence on God to sustain his life, the Lord said that if He was continually angry with man because of his wickedness that "the spirit would grow faint before me, and the breath of life that I made" (Isa. 57:16).

If God did not sustain the spirit of life within mankind, the Bible makes it very clear as to the result: "If he should set his heart to it and gather to himself his spirit and his breath, all flesh would perish together, and man would return to dust" (Job 34:14-15). Our life therefore, is sustained by the Spirit of God.

The human spirit is *not* the fullness of God. According to Scripture, God in His fullness also has a Soul. For example, God said: "My Soul shall not abhor you" (Lev. 26:11 NKJV). Even Adam in his original sinless perfection did not receive the *fullness* of God. Adam received *life* from the Spirit of God—the giver and sustainer of life, and this life became his human spirit.

As Adam was the first human created, he was unique in the way in which he came into being, not only in a physical sense, but also in a spiritual sense. To understand the unique creation of Adam, try to picture Adam's body lying there on the ground having just been formed out of the dust of the earth. Now picture the Lord God his Creator lovingly leaning over Adam and gently breathing into his nostrils the breath of life—His own breath—His own Spirit, to give life to Adam and form Adam's spirit within him. Adam's lungs immediately inflate, his heart starts beating, and blood starts flowing throughout his body.

Once God breathed into Adam's nostrils, what happened to his spirit? Did it stay in his lungs? Did it go to a small place in him that was reserved for his spirit, perhaps in his heart or his brain? As a breath in the nostrils does not remain in the nostrils but goes down into the lungs, that would likely be the path that Adam's spirit took. With the physical breath there is an infusion of oxygen from the lungs into the bloodstream. The first place this oxygenated blood travels to is the heart. From there it is pumped throughout the entire body. When God breathed life or spirit into Adam, it is likely that this spirit went immediately into Adam's heart and then permeated the whole of Adam's body along the same pathway, and at the same time, as his physical breath—via his blood. This would allow the spirit to permeate the entire person.

Although the components required by the *body* are carried in the blood, as 'life' is *spirit* and the entire body has life in it, it would make sense that the spirit would also be carried throughout the entire body along the same pathway as the blood; in fact, in the blood itself, enabling the spirit to permeate our entire body. It would not, of course, be possible to prove or disprove this, as spirit is not able to be studied and examined under a microscope as matter is able to be. It would also be likely that, at the point of the blood being removed from the body to examine it, or at least a short time later, the spirit would no longer be there anyway. There would be a period of viability after which there would remain no life, or spirit, in the blood.

How did Eve receive her spirit? Eve was made in a unique way also, although in a different way to Adam. The account in Genesis, which tells of God bringing Eve into being, tells us that "Jehovah caused a deep sleep to fall on the man, and he slept. And He took one of his ribs, and closed up the flesh underneath. And Jehovah God formed the rib which He had taken from the man into a woman, and brought her to the man" (Gen. 2:21-22 GIB). Imagine Adam's surprise to wake up and see the perfect woman. No man has ever done that since!

The Bible does not tell us that God breathed the breath of life into Eve. God did not *need* to do this because Adam's rib came complete with a blood supply and therefore had spirit and life in it already. In other words, God gave Eve *her* spirit through Adam. In this way Adam's spirit was passed on to Eve.

What about you? How did you receive *your* spirit? There are various beliefs and ideas about this. Some people believe that a baby does not have a spirit until it takes its first breath. This may be due to the knowledge that Adam received spirit at *his* first breath and so they assume this to be the case for all of mankind. Some believe that God must individually give the baby spirit at the point of conception or perhaps at the moment of the implantation of the embryo in the womb. Others believe that God gives spirit to the baby at some other stage during the baby's development in the womb, but they are a bit unsure as to exactly when. Perhaps this belief allows people to justify abortion. They could then try to convince themselves and others that this little life is just a group of cells and is not a complete human being, or not really a baby, until it reaches a certain period of gestation.

If, for argument's sake, a baby is not really a person until twelve weeks, then what about a baby at eleven weeks, six days, twenty-three hours, fifty-nine minutes, and fifty-nine seconds? What mysteriously happens to the baby one second later? There is no scientific or biblical reason to justify the treatment of an unborn child as a 'non-person'. There are no 'grey areas', particularly once you understand the way the whole baby—spirit, soul, and body, is formed.

God knows about a person before they are born and in His eyes the unborn are people too. He sees and loves them in the same way that He sees and loves those who have already been born. God planned your life even *before* you were conceived. He even knew about you before your *parents* were born; even before Adam was formed and given life! This is because God knows everything before it happens. David says that "future generations will be told about the LORD. They will proclaim his righteousness to a people yet unborn" (Ps. 22:30-31 NIV).

There is a beautiful Psalm written by King David reminding us of just how unique and how precious to God the life of each person is:

> Oh LORD, you have searched me and known me! You know when I sit down and when I rise up; you discern my thoughts from afar. You search out my path and my lying down and are acquainted with all my ways. Even before a word is on my tongue, behold, Oh LORD, you know it altogether. You hem me in, behind and before, and lay your hand upon me. Such knowledge is too wonderful for me; it is high; I cannot attain it.
>
> Where shall I go from your Spirit? Or where shall I flee from your presence? If I ascend to heaven, you are there! If I make my bed in Sheol, you are there! If I take the wings of the morning and dwell in the uttermost parts of the sea,

even there your hand shall lead me, and your right hand shall hold me. If I say, "Surely the darkness shall cover me, and the light about me be night," even the darkness is not dark to you; the night is bright as the day, for darkness is as light with you.

For you formed my inward parts; you knitted me together in my mother's womb. I praise you, for I am fearfully and wonderfully made. Wonderful are your works; my soul knows it very well. My frame was not hidden from you, when I was being made in secret, intricately woven in the depths of the earth. Your eyes saw my unformed substance; in your book were written, every one of them, the days that were formed for me, when as yet there was none of them.

How precious to me are your thoughts, O God! How vast is the sum of them! If I would count them, they are more than the sand. I awake, and I am still with you.

—Ps. 139:1-18

To the prophet Jeremiah God said: "Before I formed you in the womb I knew you, before you were born I set you apart" (Jer. 1:5 NIV). God is never surprised that any one of us is born! He is the giver and sustainer of life and He loves us individually.

When God created Adam from the dust of the ground, you were there too. No new genetic information has been added to the human race since Adam was formed. God lovingly forming Adam from the dust of the ground and breathing His Spirit into him was really your beginning too. The Spirit of life breathed into Adam and passed on down the generations to you is eternal. It is from the very breath of God, for "He himself gives to all mankind life and breath" (Acts 17:25). Your spirit comes from the breath of your Creator! This spirit is the gift of life that you need to cling to and not lose. Life is your connection to your loving Creator—your heavenly Father.

A search of the Scriptures confirms that babies in the womb have spirit. The writer of Ecclesiastes, believed to be King Solomon, wrote: "As you do not know the way the spirit comes to the bones in the womb of a woman with child, so you do not know the work of God who makes everything" (Eccl. 11:5).

When and how does a baby receive his or her spirit in the womb? Right from the moment of conception there is no doubt that this tiny human being is alive, or has life. There is a definite process of growth and formation occurring right from this moment that can only come about if this new human being has life, or spirit, because, as we have noted, the body without the spirit is dead. Clearly the baby, right from the very beginning, is alive. Therefore, this little human being must have received life or spirit at the point of conception, as the moment of conception is the point at which the new human being begins life, at the uniting of sperm and egg.

Having established that spirit is present in a baby from the moment of conception, there are two possibilities for the way in which this spirit is given. Either:

1. God individually puts spirit into that little person right at that point, and does this at that exact moment in the life of each new individual; or
2. The spirit is part of what is transferred from either one or both parents.

An important point to remember when determining the most logical possibility is that, when God finished creating the universe and all that was in it, He rested from His work of creating. When He created mankind, He blessed mankind with His creative blessing, telling them to "be fruitful and multiply" (Gen. 1:28). Part of God's design of mankind, and in fact of all of Creation, is that we would reproduce after our own kind. He made the 'complete package' right from the beginning. Although God is involved in bringing a new life into being and, according to the psalmist 'knits us together in our mothers' wombs', He did not have to continually add spirit each time a new life was conceived. God's creative blessing to reproduce was a *perpetual* blessing. God's design was one that contained processes, both physical *and* spiritual, which allowed mankind to continually replenish and reproduce—truly an amazing and complex design. The Bible refers to that which life originates from as 'seed'. There is *physical* seed (sperm and egg), and there is *spiritual* seed. God's creative blessing upon mankind encompassed both the physical *and* the spiritual being, and it was upon both the physical seed *and* the spiritual seed.

In light of the above, it seems reasonable to draw the conclusion that spirit must be passed on, or inherited, from one or both parents at the same time that the genetic information contained within the DNA is passed on.

When analysing the possible origin of the inheritance of the spirit, whether from the father or the mother or from both parents, it seems that the most logical conclusion is that the spirit is passed on through the male—the father. Again, this conclusion is unable to be verified by examination under the microscope or by scientific data. However, there are several reasons for reaching this conclusion:
1. Sperm production is a continual process and it takes approximately sixty-four days for sperm to pass through the production cycle. The initial stages of sperm production, or spermatogenesis, take place in the seminiferous tubules within the testes. These seminiferous tubules have walls that are adjacent to the blood supply. It would perhaps be possible for spirit to be transferred from the blood stream into the seminiferous tubules and pass through the cell membrane of the sperm. This spirit could then be passed on at conception at the same time as the DNA contributed by the father.
2. Ova production is *not* continual. In fact, a baby girl is born with her quota of ova or eggs already present, awaiting maturity. Nothing is added to them. The formation of ova, or oocytogenesis, occurs in the female unborn baby. This process is complete by around twenty week's gestation when approximately seven million primary oocytes have been created. This number will have dropped to around one to two million by

birth. As there is not a continual production of ova, it seems unlikely that it is the mother who contributes spirit to the new human being at conception. It is likely that, during formation in the unborn foetus, the ova would have had spirit in them, being in contact with the blood supply at that stage, but once formed and detached from the ovary walls, ova would become 'self-contained' and would likely enter a stage of dormancy without spirit. The maturation of ova is triggered by the action of hormones from the time of puberty.

3. The spirit would not be passed on from the mother at a later stage. Nor would the mother's spirit be in contact with the baby because, although the mother's spirit is in her blood, the blood of the mother does not come in contact with the developing foetus.

4. If the spirit *was* in the ovum, we would expect it to be a frequent occurrence that unfertilised ovum would implant and develop in the womb, or even begin to develop while still in the ovary, once they reach maturity. It is, in fact, possible for the full complement of genetic information to come from the mother. Half of your chromosomes come from each of your parents. The features that you inherit from them depend on whether they pass on dominant or recessive genes. If both genes from your parents for a feature such as hair colour are dominant genes, then that will be *your* hair colour. If there is one dominant and one recessive gene, then the dominant gene will be the one that determines your hair colour. If they are both recessive genes, then *that* will determine your hair colour. If, in a very rare case, the mother had all dominant genes for all characteristics and the father had all recessive genes then, although you would still receive DNA from the father *and* the mother, all of your genes, and therefore your inherited features, would come from the mother. A new life needs both physical matter *and* spirit, therefore, if spirit was in the ovum, because the DNA from the mother is capable of contributing the complete genes needed to form a new life, this would then mean that the soul would be formed too—a complete human (the formation of the soul will be discussed further in the following chapter). All that would be necessary would be for this embryo to implant in the womb, or in fact anywhere in the woman's reproductive system. Clearly this does not happen, and further confirms that the spirit is *not* passed on through the mother.

5. A rather sordid tale is recorded in the book of Genesis which took place at a very 'dark' point in the history of mankind. It seems, however, to give further confirmation that it *is* possible that all *physical* matter for a new life can come from the female, but spirit needs to come from *elsewhere*, that is, the father. In the time of Noah, immediately before

The Flood, there were fallen angels who procreated with human women. It appears that these women provided the full complement of genes for the baby that was formed as there was no other human contribution. The fallen angels, therefore, must have contributed spirit. Spirit from the 'father', in this case a fallen angel, in combination with the DNA from the human mother, formed a new life—a 'blend of two seeds'—the physical seed from the human mother and the spiritual seed from the fallen angel. This was a union that was *not* sanctioned by God and was against the natural created order.

6. In the lists of generations in the Bible, it is the line of the *father* that is given, rather than the mother. It is likely to be more than just because of tradition that the father's heritage is important. It would also be because of the spiritual inheritance that is passed down through the generations. The Bible generally speaks of the father as the one who 'gave you life'. Life, as we have established, comes from spirit. If the father gives life, he must therefore be giving spirit. The mother is generally referred to as the one who 'gave birth to you'. In the book of Isaiah, for example, God said: "Woe to him who says to his father, 'What have you begotten?' or to his mother, 'What have you brought to birth?'" (Isa. 45:10 NIV).

7. Lastly, the Scriptures state that it is through *Adam* that we have all sinned, and that sin entered the world through *Adam*. If we inherited our sinful nature through *both* Adam and Eve, that is, if the fallen and disconnected spirit was passed on through both, then it would be expected that this would be *attributed* to both in the Scriptures. Eve would likely be included in the verses that explain the entry of sin into the human race. Instead of reading that sin entered the world through *one man*, we might read that sin entered the world through *one woman and one man*. There is no doubt that Eve sinned. She was even ahead of Adam in this! The passing on of the fallen spirit through Adam though, seems to be reflected in the fact that the Bible says that 'in Adam' all sinned.

When a new life is formed from the union of husband and wife, these two separate lives effectively become as one new life. The DNA from both parents and the spirit, likely from the father, combine to form this new life. As the spirit is likely passed on through the male, Adam's spirit was inherited in the form of a spiritual seed to form the spirit of the next generation, and so on, through subsequent generations.

If the spirit that was originally breathed into Adam through his nostrils then permeated his entire being, then it follows that our spirit permeates *our* entire being. It does not seem logical that our spirit would be in just one part of our being and not anywhere else. The apostle Paul writes: "For what man knows the things of a man except the spirit of the man which is in him?" (1 Cor. 2:11 NKJV). In order for our spirit to 'know' these things, the spirit would have to have access to the *entire* man, not just to one part. Additionally, the entire person has *life*. If I look at my little finger, for instance, it certainly seems to be alive. It therefore must have life in it. It would seem then, that it must be infused with spirit, as spirit *is* life. If life is carried by the blood and the blood flows to my extremities, then, although I cannot see it, my spirit must too, permeating my entire body. It makes sense, therefore, that if we were only to see our *spiritual* body, which includes our soul, it might look much the same as our *physical* body although of a different substance. We would expect the spiritual body to take the same form or shape as our physical body, as we would expect our spirit to be within the boundaries of our body.

Where does the spirit originate from within the person? Is there a central point? The writer of Proverbs tells us that out of the heart flow the 'springs of life'. He cautions the reader to "keep your heart with all vigilance, for from it flow the springs of life" (Prov. 4:23). As life is spirit, it seems that the spirit proceeds, or flows from, the heart. This, of course, would be referring to our *spiritual* heart, but it seems likely that our spiritual heart is located in the same place as our physical heart. The following passage of Scripture refers to the clothing that Moses' brother Aaron wore in representing the people of Israel before God as their priest:

> So Aaron shall bear the names of the sons of Israel on the breastplate of judgement over his heart, when he goes into the holy place, as a memorial before the Lord continually. And you shall put in the breastplate of judgement the Urim and the Thummim, and they shall be over Aaron's heart when he goes in before the Lord. So Aaron shall bear the judgement of the children of Israel over his heart before the Lord continually.
>
> —Exod. 28:29-30 NKJV

'Heart', in this passage, seems to be referring to Aaron's spiritual heart *and* his physical heart, as a breastplate is worn on the chest in such a position as to protect the *physical* heart, but it would be assumed that it is the *spiritual* heart over which the breastplate of *judgement* would be worn, as it would be expected that Aaron would be bearing judgement over his *spiritual* rather than his *physical* heart. It can be reasoned from this that both the physical *and* the spiritual heart are under this breastplate, likely in the same place.

Just as our physical heart is the centre of our physical body and it is the pump that distributes blood and therefore nutrients to our body, the spiritual heart is the wellspring of life that distributes our spirit throughout our body.

Is our spirit static, unchanging, unchangeable? No. We are not 'stuck with' what is passed on. The father will inherit spirit from his father as a spiritual seed, and then what changes in that spirit during the new father's lifetime is the spirit that forms the seed that is then passed on to the following generation.

Just as the condition of a person's physical heart affects his physical body, so the condition of a person's spiritual heart affects his spirit. For example, Solomon writes that "by sorrow of heart, the spirit is broken" (Prov. 15:13 NKJV). The spirit is directly affected by the state of our spiritual heart because the heart is the wellspring of life from which our spirit flows.

Zechariah, when describing God as Creator, said: He "formed the spirit of man within him" (Zech. 12:1). The word 'formed' used here in Hebrew is *yatsar*. It means to form, fashion, or mould something from what already exists. Over our lifetime, our spirit can be moulded and changed as our heart changes or is changed by God. This, in turn, can affect our soul and even our physical being.

The heart, which will be discussed in greater depth in a later chapter, is referred to in the Scriptures much more than is the spirit or the soul, because the state of the heart is what most affects our relationship with God.

THE NATURE

What can the spirit do? The Bible gives us some understanding as to the actions and qualities of our spirit. According to Scripture, the spirit can seek God, worship God, serve, and glorify God. Your spirit can compel you to do something. You can perceive something in your spirit, make diligent search with your spirit, rejoice in your spirit, and bless with your spirit. You can sing or pray with your spirit and you can 'walk' in the spirit. Your spirit can hasten to be angry with someone or rise against someone. It can groan, fail, have no rest, sustain you in sickness, depart from your body at death, and return to your body if brought back to life.

When the prophet Elijah was taken up to heaven in a whirlwind, Elisha, his understudy or assistant, requested to inherit a double portion of his spirit, and his request was granted. In this instance, there was a transfer of spirit. Spirit can increase. For example, a spiritual seed becomes the full human spirit, and Elijah's spirit was doubled.

What can God do to, or with, your spirit? Your spirit can be moved by God, weighed by God, preserved by God's care, stirred up by God, and hardened by God. You can harden your own spirit against God, probably as a consequence of hardening your heart. Your spirit can be faithful or unfaithful to God. It can be ruled by yourself. It can be made new by God and it can be preserved blameless by God. God knows us through the spirit that is in our hearts. King Solomon wrote: "The spirit of a man is the lamp of the Lord, searching all the inner depths of his heart" (Prov. 20:27 NKJV). There is nothing you can do that is hidden from Him.

Your spirit can be an example to others. The Bible refers to the 'life' of your spirit and the 'heat' of your spirit, and cautions us to take heed to our spirit. There are many adjectives that are used to describe the human spirit in the Bible including troubled, in anguish, willing, jealous, sorrowful, sullen, deceitful (or not deceitful), contrite, steadfast, overwhelmed, haughty, humble, calm, patient, proud, perverse, grieved, anxious, excellent, false, willing, strong, provoked, fervent, filthy, gentle, and quiet. That's quite a list! Many of these are emotions that spring from the heart but, carried by the spirit, affect the soul and the body. Obviously some of those qualities are desirable and some are best avoided!

There seems to be a difference in the quality of one human spirit over another, perhaps the spirit with the more desirable traits being the better quality spirit. It would be assumed, for example, that Elijah's spirit exuded a certain quality that was highly desired by Elisha.

THE DESTINY

We have investigated the origin of the spirit, the inheritance of the spirit, and the location of the spirit, as well as the actions and qualities of the spirit. What about the destiny of the spirit?

Originally, before Adam sinned, his spirit was pure, having been breathed into him from the breath of God. The Holy Spirit gives life and forms connections. Adam's spirit was originally connected to, and continually renewed by, the Spirit of God through his heart which was open to God. After Adam sinned, his heart closed to God's Spirit and he became disconnected from the source of life. His spirit was then within a 'closed circuit'. Adam's spirit was passed on to the next generation *in the state that it had become* due to Adam sinning, and this was the state in which it continued to be passed on, down through the whole human race. This inheritance we received from Adam was therefore that of a spirit disconnected from the life source—God. We received a spirit with *self* at the centre.

Originally, Adam's spirit was *not* subject to the law of sin and death but was under the law of the spirit of *life*, and that is how God originally intended us to inherit *our* spirit—a pure spirit forever in connection with, and communion with, God our Father. Our spirit was also intended to remain within perfect physical bodies which were not subject to death and decay. It was in this state of perfection, free from sin and death, that we were designed to live here on this earth in *its* original perfect state. But due to the sin of one man, the spirit we inherited means that we are born with a sinful nature. This is how 'in Adam' we all sinned. The spirit that the human race has inherited is a spirit that is subject to the spiritual law of sin and death. This means that the inevitable consequence of sin is death. The apostle Paul tells us that "many died through one man's trespass" (Rom. 5:15), and that "sin came into the world through one man, and death through sin, and so death spread to all men because all sinned" (Rom. 5:12). We are all sinners. It is our nature, our inheritance.

Down through the generations since Adam and Eve, every child was conceived in the same way—by the uniting of DNA from the mother with DNA and spirit from the father, resulting in a new human being that inherited a body that was subject to physical death, and a spirit that was under the law of sin and death, separated from God. When we die, our bodies return to dust. At the moment of death, a separation occurs—the soul and spirit depart from the body. At the end of physical life here on earth, the same 'rule' applies to the body as it did to Adam's body *before* he was given spirit. That is, without the spirit the body is dead.

Author Alexander McCall Smith's description of death is an excellent word picture of the result of the absence of this life from the human body:

> It was very peaceful, almost as if somebody had silently gone away, somewhere else, had left the room. How strange is the human body in death—so still, and so vacated. That vitality, that spark, which makes for life, is simply not there. The tiny movements of the muscles, the sense of there being somebody keeping the whole physical entity orchestrated in space—that goes so utterly and completely. It is no longer there.[1]

The moment of physical death is the moment when a person breathes their last breath and their heart stops beating and is no longer circulating blood around the body. Other physiological functions will cease shortly after this. In addition to the cessation of these physical functions, the spiritual heart will no longer circulate the spirit throughout the body, and the spirit and soul will depart. The writer of Psalms says that the breath *and* spirit depart. He says of man that "his spirit departs, he returns to his earth" (Ps. 146:4 NKJV). The *English Standard Version* uses the word *breath* and the passage reads: "When his breath departs, he returns to the earth" (Ps. 146:4). 'Spirit' and 'breath' are sometimes used interchangeably in Scripture.

Just as the spirit entered through the nostrils of Adam, it is likely that the spirit also *departs* through the breath. The human spirit was passed down through all the generations that have ever lived, from Adam to you. If you are a father, you will have passed on a spiritual seed to your children. If you are a father and also have grandchildren, the spirit that was in you will be passed on to them through *your* sons as a spiritual seed, and so on. The spirit that is in you when you die will pass out with your last breath.

In the instance of a person having died then being made alive again through a miracle or through modern methods of resuscitation, the return of the spirit to the body is the moment of the return of life. If the spirit returns, it would likely return through the nostrils or the mouth, either of which are entry points for the breath. There is an account in the Old Testament in the book of Second Kings of a young boy who had died. God brought him back to life through the prophet Elisha. As the boy's spirit returned to him he sneezed seven times, possibly due to the sensation of his spirit returning through his nostrils. The account of the boy's spirit returning, implies that this spirit that return is the same as that which originally left him; that is, his own spirit.

The spirit, according to God's Word, returns to God. The writer of Ecclesiastes wrote that "the dust will return to the earth as it was, and the spirit will return to God who gave it" (Eccl. 12:7 NKJV). The spirit of life originated from God, and therefore as our spirit departs our body it returns to its origin, that is, where God is. God's dwelling place is in heaven. There is no differentiation made in this passage of

Scripture between the spirit of the 'righteous' and the 'unrighteous', the believer and the unbeliever. It implies that *all* spirit returns to God because God gave it.

> **Righteousness—holy and upright living in accordance with God's standard . . . Righteousness is a moral concept. God's character is the definition and source of all righteousness . . . Therefore, the righteousness of human beings is defined in terms of God's.** [2]

The Bible makes it clear, however, that it is only the *spirit* of all men that returns to God upon death, not the *soul*. The spirit and the soul are not one and the same. The soul is the conscious 'you'—the part of you that has awareness of 'being'. Where your soul is, that is where you are aware of being. The destiny of the soul will be discussed in the following chapter.

The length of our days on the earth is not ours to decide, it is God's. God said: "I put to death and I bring to life" (Deut. 32:39 NIV). You do not know when you will take your final breath and when your spirit will depart. "No man has power to retain the spirit, or power over the day of death" (Eccl. 8:8). David wrote: "My times are in your hand" (Ps. 31:15), and Job tells us that in God's hand "is the life of every creature and the breath of all mankind" (Job 12:10 NIV). His "days are determined, and the number of his months is with you, and you have appointed his limits that he cannot pass" (Job 14:5).

The Bible tells us that "the wages of sin is death" (Rom. 6:23). In other words, eternal separation from the source of eternal spiritual life is the payment that is required for our sin. Right from the beginning, when God told Adam that death would be the price paid for his sin, until today, that payment is still required. You can pay this price yourself. After all, it is *your* sin that you would be paying for; a very high price to pay nevertheless. That is an option that has always been there and, tragically, most people *will* pay this price. But is this necessary? Is there some way that the price might be paid on your behalf? Could you somehow receive a *new* spirit that is *not* subject to the law of sin and death?

HERE'S WHAT WE NEED:

Because of the curse on mankind due to sin, we are under the law of sin and death. This means that the payment for sin is death—eternal separation from the source of life, our heavenly Father.

It seems that we need a new spirit—one that reconnects us to God—the source of eternal life. This new spirit would have to be *exempt* from the law of sin and death. It would need to be able to remain with our soul at the moment of our physical death, so that our soul would return to God along with the spirit.

The only spirit that would qualify is a *pure* spirit that has *not* been passed down through the generations from Adam. If this perfect and pure new spirit flowed throughout our entire bodies, then it follows that our bodies would be restored to the state that Adam and Eve's bodies originally were.

Clearly, if our fallen spirit is the only spirit we have, we do *not* have eternal life. We need a spirit in us that has come from a source in which there is *no* sin.

Chapter Three
The Soul

The spiritual body is comprised of the spirit and the soul. We have examined in detail the origin, the nature, and the destiny of the spirit. Now we will examine what the Bible has to say about the *soul*.

The most logical place to begin in order to gain an understanding of what the Scriptures mean by the word 'soul' would be right at the beginning of Creation, on day six. In the book of Genesis, we read that "Jehovah God formed the man out of dust from the ground, and blew into his nostrils the breath of life; and man became a living soul" (Gen. 2:7 GIB). This is the moment when the breath of God entered Adam's newly formed body. This is also the moment when Adam's soul was formed. As the breath of God formed Adam's spirit within him, the action of the spirit on his physical body formed his soul. Likewise, when spirit which had been passed on from Adam through the line of the male interacted with the physical seed which was contributed by both of your parents at conception, *your* soul was formed.

The soul is part of the spiritual body. It is made of spiritual substance and is brought into existence by the imprint of the spirit on the physical body. Within the soul is the life of the spirit. The physical body is superimposed over the form of the spiritual body.

In the same way that the physical body is brought life and nutrients by the blood, so the soul is continually supplied with life by the spirit. As the blood is to the physical body, so the spirit is to the soul, each bringing life, sustaining life, and preventing death for as long as they are flowing through the body. The spirit and soul combined are therefore in essence, the one spiritual body within the shape and boundary of the physical body. The whole person then, is made up of body (natural or physical body), and spirit and soul (spiritual body), with the spirit giving life to the soul.

The soul is not pre-existing as some believe. Your soul did not previously exist in the body of another. You have not had a 'past life' as Joan of Arc or William the Conqueror! The spirit which was given by God and which gave life to your soul and body is eternal in origin as God is eternal, and your spirit was formed from His breath. Your DNA has existed from the moment God formed Adam from the dust of the earth. Your soul though, only came into existence at the moment that your spirit and physical matter met.

In a similar way, a cake does not exist until all the ingredients are put together in a certain way. Think about the making of a cake. You could not call it a cake and it would not *be* a cake when the ingredients are separate even though all the components of the cake pre-exist. Certain processes must occur to form the ingredients into a cake, just as there are processes that must occur, both physical and spiritual, in the bringing forth of a new life.

Because the soul is formed when the spirit interacts with the body, the soul is individual and unique to each person. Your soul has the imprint of your unique DNA on it and includes your personality. Even though your spirit and DNA were present in Adam, you were not conscious of existing until your soul was formed and existed and you were 'brought forth'. Awareness of 'being' (or where and when you are aware of being) is in the soul.

Just as the physical body is made up of parts, so it seems is the spiritual body. For example, there are many references in the Bible to our spiritual eyes and ears. One would assume that these are in the same location as our *physical* eyes and ears. Sometimes God allows or enables a person to see or to hear with their spiritual eyes or ears, such as the time when the Lord opened Balaam's eyes and enabled him to see in the spiritual realm: "The spirit of God came upon him, and he uttered his oracle: 'The oracle of Balaam the son of Beor, the oracle of the man whose eye is opened, the oracle of him who hears the words of God, who sees the vision of the Almighty, falling down with his eyes uncovered'" (Num. 24:2-4).

As our physical body is superimposed on our spiritual body, if we were to see just a person's spiritual body, we would more than likely recognize that person. However, they would be of a different substance, that is, spirit, and would likely have some different abilities or capabilities from those of their physical bodies. For example, we would, if seeing through our spiritual eyes, be able to see things of a spiritual nature such as angels. With our spiritual ears, we would be able to audibly hear God speaking to us. It is likely that this was the experience of Adam and Eve prior to The Fall.

Because the spirit and soul are of spiritual substance and the body is of physical substance, the interaction between them would need to have a surface at the boundary where the two systems meet, possibly at cellular level, that is a compatible *interface* which allows communication and interplay between the two systems.

> **Interface—***n.* **/in-tuh-fays/ 1 surface forming a boundary between two regions. 2 means or play of interaction between two systems etc.**[1]

In chemistry, for example, an interface forms the surface between two liquids or two chemical phases. In computer science it might be the point of interaction between a computer and a printer, or even between the human operator and the computer.

As a result of The Fall, it seems that we lost much of our spiritual function ... or did we? There seems to be *two* possibilities:
1. We lost the *function* of our spiritual bodies, for example, the use of our spiritual eyes and ears; or
2. We did not actually lose the use of these and they are still functioning but rather, we no longer have a fully functioning *connection* between our

spiritual and our physical bodies which were designed to work in harmony with each other. This diminution in connection would mean that, generally speaking, we are unable to perceive what our spiritual eyes and ears are seeing or hearing, and our current limited brain capacity is unable to translate or process this.

The second possibility is the more likely one for the following reasons:
1. The Fall resulted in a number of disconnections. Adam and Eve became disconnected from the source of ongoing physical life and vitality—the Tree of Life. They were no longer allowed access. They became disconnected from the source of spiritual life—God. Their spirit and soul were to become disconnected from their body at physical death. Their spirit was to become disconnected from their soul at this point also.
2. It is believed that we only use about ten to twenty percent of our brain capacity. It may be that the other eighty to ninety percent of our brain would have originally been active in processing input from the spiritual body, for example, from the spiritual eyes and ears, in a similar way that the nervous system receives, processes, and sends signals.
3. There are examples in Scripture where the Holy Spirit took a person to other places where they were able to see and hear the spirit world. If they had been taken out of their bodies, as some instances imply, then it seems that, without the constraints of their bodies, the person was able to see, hear, speak, and interact in the location to which they had been taken. In other words, they were functioning in their *spiritual* bodies independently of their *physical* bodies. This would mean that, if we were *out* of our physical bodies, we would have full awareness of the function of our spiritual bodies, but when *in* our physical bodies, we do not have a fully functioning connection and are therefore generally not aware of them.
4. After our spiritual bodies (spirit and soul) leave our physical bodies at death, our souls are portrayed as being fully functional. An example of this is found in a story that Jesus told of a rich man and a poor beggar named Lazarus. The constraints of their bodies had been lifted and they were seeing, hearing, and talking in the abode of the dead as well as feeling 'in anguish' and experiencing thirst. Clearly these abilities and sensations were possible without their physical bodies.

It may be that it is the diminution in function of the *interface* between the spiritual and the physical system that has resulted in the reduction in awareness and function of our spiritual bodies. It is also likely that the only way that we would have the *full* use of our spiritual bodies whilst still in our physical bodies is if our spirits were the pure Spirit of life from God, like the spirit that Adam originally had, rather than a disconnected spirit. Perhaps it is only this pure spirit that is fully and perfectly compatible with the interface between the two systems, and therefore with the physical body.

This loss of connection is for our own good. Imagine if, in man's current sinful state, his spiritual capabilities were enhanced, say, tenfold. Imagine if history's most evil dictators could easily liaise with demons, for example. What would the consequences of that be? One shudders to think!

THE NATURE

Now that we have investigated the *origin* of the soul, we will examine the *nature* of the soul.

Factors that affect the soul, both in the initial forming of the soul and in the process of development of the facets of the soul over the life of the person, include:
— The type, quality, and characteristics of the spirit that forms the spiritual seed that is passed on at conception which forms the new human spirit;
— The genetic inheritance from both parents, as the soul is taking on the imprint of the physical which comes from both parents;
— The development of the spirit over the course of a person's life which gives life to the soul;
— The state of the spiritual heart which is the wellspring of life from which the spirit proceeds and gives life to the soul.

Many of the actions and the descriptions found in God's Word of the nature of the soul share something in common with those of the heart and the spirit. This is to be expected, as the heart is the wellspring from which the spirit flows throughout the soul.

According to Scripture, the soul can seek, love, and follow God. It is known by the Lord. With your soul you can serve God, return to God, turn to God, trust in God, lay up God's words in it, walk before Him in truth, and obey His voice. Your soul can be set to seek God, and can observe His statutes and judgements. It can be restored, converted, saved, and preserved.

The soul can be in anguish, afflicted, discouraged, bitter, tormented, grieved, and troubled. It can be lifted up to the Lord or lifted up to an idol. It can be joyful, sorrowful, downcast, satisfied or unsatisfied, cast off by the Lord, or delighted by the Lord's comfort. It can be strengthened, unsettled, or discouraged.

Your soul can desire, hate, mourn, loathe life, wait for the Lord, boast in the Lord, rejoice, thirst for God, faint, melt, rest, long for God, praise the Lord, and magnify the Lord. It can feed on violence and desire evil. It can desire and have nothing, or be made rich. The soul can have knowledge, crave, delight, and loathe. The soul can sin.

The soul can be calmed and quieted, troubled and brought out of trouble, righteous, generous, refreshed, weary, satisfied, hungry, delighted, empty, lost, and fearful. Knowledge is pleasant to your soul. You can do 'good' to your soul. He who gets wisdom loves his own soul. Your soul can be preserved blameless at the Lord's coming and be saved from death. Now that *is* good news!

This is by no means a complete description of the nature of the soul, but it gives an idea of the vast array of actions the soul is capable of and of the characteristics of the soul, both good and bad.

THE HEART

The heart, while being within the boundaries of your soul and formed in the same way as your soul, that is, by the spirit of life imprinting the matter of your physical being (in this case the physical heart), is referred to in Scripture separately from the soul. There are at least twenty-four references in the Bible where, in the same verse, the heart and soul are said to be doing the same thing as each other, for example, loving the Lord. This would suggest that God sees these two parts of our spiritual being as distinct yet interrelated. The heart plays a specific role in the body and will be discussed in greater detail in the following chapter.

THE MIND

It is generally agreed that the soul is comprised of mind, will, and emotions, which, in combination, make up your personality, and you can see from the extensive description of some of the soul's capabilities that, what are generally accepted as attributes of the mind, will, and emotions fit into those biblical descriptions of the soul. The spirit flows through, and gives life to, the mind. The book of Job says that "the spirit of my understanding causes me to answer" (Job 20:3 NKJV), and in the letter to the Ephesians, Paul implores believers to "be renewed in the spirit of your mind" (Eph. 4:23 NKJV).

So just what is the mind? If the spirit of life flows throughout our entire physical being and brings our soul into being by imprinting the physical, and if the physical body is superimposed on the spiritual body and that spiritual body has structure and function in similar fashion to the physical, then it follows that the physical brain has a spiritual counterpart, namely, the mind.

The mind would be formed in the same way as the entire soul, being a part of the soul, but, like the heart, the mind gets special mention in the Scriptures because of the unique and important role that it plays within the person.

Being made in the image of God, man has the capability of intelligence and is able to design, improve on previous designs, reason, contemplate, invent new things, and formulate solutions to problems. Man has invented many complex machines, medicines that save lives, and methods of harnessing energy to convert to power, as well as composing beautiful music, writing poetry, putting together a seemingly unlimited variety of culinary treats, and beautifying his environment with works of art.

Intelligence is not something that has evolved. Whilst *knowledge* has increased, because knowledge is cumulative and therefore man's ability to do *more* because of that widening knowledge base has increased, man was intelligent right from the beginning. Cain, for example, who was the firstborn son of Adam and Eve, even built a city (probably a small one!), and according to the book of Genesis, the eighth generation named in the list of generations was playing harps and flutes and making all kinds of tools out of bronze and iron. Archaeological evidence shows that early man made beautiful jewellery and pottery as well as sculptures, and the children had toys and games to play with. A monetary system and systems of government and law were established within a relatively short period of time. In Abraham's day, in the city of Ur where he came from, there were flushing toilets and an extensive system of pipework providing water to the city. All of these innovations and inventions came about through the thoughts and plans in the minds of men.

In the mind decisions are made, ideas are formulated, memories are called to mind, and thoughts are processed. This is then *actioned* in the processes of the brain. The brain is part of the nervous system which, along with the spinal cord and nerves, acts to serve as a system of communication and co-ordination for the body. The nerves and spinal cord carry information *to* the brain and relay instructions *from* the brain. The brain however, needs a *spiritual* input to its physiological function. This is the role of the mind. The brain, while being an amazingly capable organ, still needs to be told what to do.

Thoughts do not start in the brain, they start in the mind. A computer is sometimes used as an analogy to help understand the mind-brain relationship. Computers are amazingly complex machines which are capable of many complicated tasks through a system of data processing. They still, however, need a human being to tell them what to do. It is like this with the relationship between the mind and the brain. The following study, although obviously limited by subject availability due to the number of patients whose brain needed exposing for surgery, is one that seems to demonstrate this mind-brain relationship:

> Californian physiologist Benjamin Libet did a series of experiments on human patients whose brains had been exposed for surgery. Patients indicated when they decided to move their wrist. There is a fair amount of wiring between the brain and the wrist, and, unsurprisingly, the wrist moved about 200 milliseconds after this decision was apparently made. But here's the really, really odd thing. The brain processes involved in planning the movement could be detected using electrodes. And they seemed clearly to have begun more than a third of a second before the patient became aware of the decision to move. In other words, the decision to move seemed not to have been made by the conscious 'I' at all. More recent work has suggested that this period might in fact be as long as ten seconds.[2]

The results from this series of experiments would seem to suggest that there is a process occurring whereby:

1. 'Something' communicates the decision to move the wrist to the brain; however,

2. The patient is not yet consciously aware of this decision.
3. Approximately one third of a second later the brain begins the processes of *planning* the movement still before the patient is even aware of this decision to move.
4. The patient now becomes aware of the decision to move their wrist; and
5. The impulse is sent down the nerve pathway from the brain to the wrist; then
6. About 200 milliseconds later the wrist moves.

This unidentified 'something' in the experiment that communicates to the brain the decision to move the wrist, would be the mind.

Possible objections to this interpretation, and also some exceptions whereby this order of events may not occur, may be:

1. There are circumstances whereby the mind is *not* involved in a decision, such as when you rest your hand on something very hot and promptly withdraw it. This would be a reflex action involving a signal travelling along the nerve pathway to the spinal cord relaying the message to the spinal cord that you have touched something hot, and a message travelling back along the nerve pathway telling you to withdraw your hand. In this case, the mind does not *need* to be involved in making a decision. It is a natural reflex.

    In a reflex, the impulse is relayed from one nerve to another by a shortcut that produces a reaction without involving the brain. The kneejerk is an example of the simplest sort of reflex reaction. When the knee is tapped, the impulse travels through the sensory nerve that receives the tap, crosses a single synapse, and activates the motor nerve that controls the quadriceps muscle in the thigh, causing the leg to jerk up automatically.[3]

    In the case of the hot object, the brain and the mind would soon receive the message that you touched something hot and had withdrawn your hand but only *after* the event transpired, rather than for the purpose of decision-making.

2. What about repetitive activities? Would your mind have to continually make a decision to tell your brain what to do each time? Take, for example, walking up the stairs. Would your mind have to tell your brain to walk up each stair individually? No.

    A very different sort of reflex is the conditioned reflex. Conditioning is the process of building links or pathways in the nervous system. When an action is done repeatedly the nervous system becomes familiar with the situation and learns to react automatically. A new reflex has been built into the system. Hundreds of daily actions are conditioned reflexes. Walking, running, going up and down stairs, and even buttoning a shirt all involve great numbers of muscle co-ordinations that have become automatic.[4]

This is not to say that the mind would not make the *original* decision to walk up the stairs. It would not, however, need to send continual messages to the brain in order to orchestrate each individual move.

3. In the case of having to make a quick judgement such as the slamming on of brakes to avoid hitting the car in front of you, if you had to wait for your mind to make a decision and send this message to your brain to process and then wait for your brain to send impulses along the nerve pathway to your foot telling it to hit the brakes, would this be too late? Well, from the experiment cited above, it appears that the mind-brain delay can be as little as one third of a second. That is probably a relatively insignificant delay and it is likely that it would make little or no difference to the outcome. Alternatively, the reaction of hitting the brakes may be similar to that of the conditioned reflex in that, without actually thinking about the problem and deciding to act, the hitting of the brakes is an automatic response to seeing the bumper of the car in front looming large in your view; or perhaps the noise of the squealing of brakes in front of you triggers the conditioned reflex to hit your own brakes without first having to contemplate in your mind to do this and then put that thought into action in the brain.

4. What about a similar example of having to take instant action, but action that is planned rather than unplanned? Take, for example, a race scenario. If you were at the beginning of a race waiting for the starter gun and could only begin to take off from the starting line when the starter gun was fired, would you then have to wait for your mind to send the message to your brain to send the message to your legs? No; although you would not be at a disadvantage if you did because all the other competitors would have this same delay! However, your mind would have already sent the message to your brain that, when you hear the noise of the starter gun, it needs to send the signal to your legs via the nerve pathways to take off. In other words, the mind would have already informed the brain that the *trigger* for sending this message to the legs is the sound of the starter gun.

The mind would be able to interact with the brain through the interface that serves as a link for communication or interplay between the two systems.

Does God have access to your mind? In the book of Psalms, we read that "the righteous God tests the hearts and minds" (Ps. 7:9 NKJV). The writer of the letter to the Hebrews tells us that the Lord will put His "law into their hearts, and in their minds I will write them" (Heb. 10:16 NKJV). In the book of Daniel, we read that God put thoughts into the mind of the king: "As for you O king, thoughts came to your mind while on your bed, about what would come to pass after this; and He who reveals secrets has made known to you what will be" (Dan. 2:29 NKJV). These thoughts may have come while the king was awake or while he was sleeping, in the form of a dream.

An analysis of what the Scriptures say about our mind reveals that it can be willing, vexed, anxious, sound, ready, futile, shaken, lowly, fully convinced, defiled, enraged, spiteful, corrupt, or pure. Paul describes the mind of the unbeliever as corrupted, saying that "they profess to know God, but they deny him by their works" (Titus 1:16), demonstrating by a lack of evidence that they do not genuinely know God or have a relationship with Him.

The mind can be set on earthly things or on things above. It can be guarded by the peace of God. Your mind can keep a matter in it (memory) and you can call something to mind (remember). You can have a plan in your mind to do something and you can have a 'mind to work'. You can be renewed in the spirit of your mind. You can have wisdom in your mind put there by God and you can love and serve God with your mind.

The New Testament gives an account of demon possession of a man. After the demons were commanded to leave the man, he was then said to be in his 'right' mind. This would imply that demon possession affects the mind and puts a person in a 'wrong' mind.

THE DESTINY

Originally, God created mankind to live forever. The body was not subject to sickness, pain, the ravages of old age, and finally death. The soul was designed to remain infused by the spirit, connected through the heart to God's Spirit—the source of life, giving life to the soul for eternity. The soul and spirit were also designed to remain in perfect physical bodies. Due to sin entering the world though, our physical bodies will die and return to dust. After Adam sinned, God said that, at the end of his life, he would "return to the ground. For you have been taken out of it; for you are dust, and to dust you shall return" (Gen. 3:19 GIB). We learnt from Scripture that "the spirit will return to God who gave it" (Eccl. 12:7 NKJV). So, after our bodies die, what then becomes of the soul—the part of us within which we have awareness of being?

The soul, being formed by the imprint of the physical body on the spirit, belongs to God. God said: "Behold, all souls are Mine" (Ezek. 18:4 NKJV). The destiny of the soul is therefore in God's hands. Jesus said: "Do not fear those who kill the body but cannot kill the soul" (Matt. 10:28). Like the spirit, the soul is of *spiritual* substance. The soul cannot break down or be killed in the way that the physical body can. Because the soul is not composed of matter like the body is, the soul does not remain with the body and break down to dust as matter will. It will endure after physical death. As awareness of 'being' is with the soul, the location of the soul rather than that of the spirit or body after death, is where the person will be aware of being.

King David describes God as "he who has kept our soul among the living" (Ps. 66:9). This implies an alternative then, in that, if our soul is *not* amongst the living, the only other alternative for it to be *would* be amongst the dead.

As a result of sin entering the world, death also entered the world. The two go hand in hand. There is a spiritual 'law' referred to in Scripture as 'the law of sin and death'; the essence of that law being that "the wages of sin is death" (Rom. 6:23), both physical and spiritual. This means that death is the payment required for sin.

The Bible tells us that "the soul who sins will die" (Ezek. 18:4 NKJV) and that "it is appointed for man to die once, and after that comes judgement" (Heb. 9:27). We know what the death of the body means; that is, for life to depart and for the body to return to dust. But what does the death of the soul mean? When we die our spirit, by default, is destined to become separated from our soul and return to God. The spirit is what gives life to our soul. Without life or spirit then, what happens to your soul? As it cannot cease to exist because it is of spiritual substance, it must go somewhere after it departs the body.

Matthew asks: "For what profit is it to a man if he gains the whole world, and loses his own soul? Or what will a man give in exchange for his soul?" (Matt. 16:26 NKJV). What does it mean to *lose* your soul? If you are still alive here on earth living in your physical body could you have already lost your soul? No. It means that when you die, your soul, which is in essence 'you', would become separated from your spirit. As it is your spirit that gives life to your soul, and on physical death that spirit returns to God, this would mean that your spirit and soul would become separated at death. You would lose the *life* from your soul. If you were *eternally* separated from life and therefore from the giver of life—God, your Creator, that would be the greatest tragedy to befall you. Once that happens, it is too late. To be *eternally* separated from the source of eternal life is what it means to 'lose your soul'. Is this outcome the only alternative? Is there some way that, upon death, our soul could return to God with our spirit?

You could have everything on earth that you desire, or think that you desire, such as riches, fame, friends, an exciting career, or a fantastic social life but if, when you die, you become forever separated from the source of life, nothing that you had on this earth will matter and you will wish that you could exchange all of that for the saving of your soul. That is the tragedy that Matthew speaks of when he wrote of the futility of gaining the whole world but losing your soul. Matthew was one of Jesus' disciples. Before Jesus met him he was a despised tax collector who amassed great earthly riches for himself by taking much more than he should when collecting taxes from the people. After he met Jesus, he understood the folly of earthly wealth, left his life of dishonesty, and followed Jesus.

This life here on earth that you are living right now is the *only* chance that you have for the saving of your soul. After death there is no second chance. This, therefore, should be the single most important issue to you or to anyone. The saving or the losing of the soul has eternal consequences. The loss of the soul equates to the loss of eternal life.

Because the soul continues to exist after the body dies it must always have a location, including after the death of the body. There must be a place for the soul to go at the moment of death. In the Old Testament, in the record of the young boy who had died, the prophet Elisha prays for the boy to come back to life. He asks the Lord to "let this child's soul come back to him" (1Kings 17:21 NKJV). Clearly, the child had already died and his soul had departed. It could not 'come back' unless it had first gone somewhere else.

The soul does not remain with the body. It goes to another destination or abode. It does not remain on the earth floating around keeping company with the living, sneakily moving hands of clocks, finding lost wedding rings, and appearing to so-called psychics or mediums with messages for the loved ones they have left behind such as: "Aunt Mary wants you to know that she forgives you for not visiting her last year while she was in hospital"; or :"Someone who was close to you and is now on the other side wants you to know that they have a small fortune hidden under the rose bush in the backyard beside the tank stand and they would like you to have it"! If not attributed to natural phenomenon, these occurrences can certainly be attributed to the work of demons, who seek to deceive people into believing untruths rather than the truth of God's Word and therefore keep people alienated from God in their unbelief. If the truth in God's Word is not known or believed, then people will cling to all manner of misunderstandings about the soul after death, hoping that their loved ones are still with them here on earth, watching over them and perhaps trying to communicate with them through these mediums who, not surprisingly, benefit financially from their grief, their guilt, and their misplaced hope.

In the Bible, the destination of the soul was referred to using several names or terms. The Hebrew word *Sheol* is used in the Old Testament and the Greek word *hades* in the New Testament. This place is also called the pit, the pit of corruption, the abode of the dead, the grave, or prison. *Hades*, which means 'the unseen world' was generally translated as *hell* in the New Testament and was believed to be a place of punishment for the unrighteous.

Where is this place? The location of the place where we will go when we die must have real co-ordinates. Just as our soul is in an actual place at this present moment in time, that is, in our physical bodies, it will have an actual place where it will be *after* it leaves the body. It will travel from 'point A' to 'point B'.

The grave, the pit, hades, Sheol, hell, or whatever name the place of the dead is called, is always referred to in the Bible as 'down'. Down, no matter where you are standing on the earth means into the *depths* of the earth. This is the location of the abode of the dead. In the book of Numbers there is an account of a rebellion that took place against Moses and Aaron. The rebels were punished by God in an unusual way: "The ground under them split apart. And the earth opened its mouth and swallowed them up, with their households and all the people who belonged to Korah and all their goods. So they and all that belonged to them went down alive into Sheol, and the earth closed over them" (Num. 16:31-33). No doubt their bodies did not survive too long!

Even though the soul is of *spiritual* substance, there is no reason why this place of the dead needs to be of a spiritual nature—invisible, and unable to be seen by the physical eye if, say, it were in an *accessible* place in the depths of the earth. After all, if angels exist in our physical world on the *surface* of the earth without us being able to see them, it is comprehensible that the human soul can exist in a physical place *below the surface*.

In the book of Amos, God says of the unfaithful Israelites that "if they dig into Sheol, from there my hand shall take them" (Amos 9:2). The upper chambers of Sheol may therefore not be all that deep below the surface of the earth. If we were able to dig deep enough down into the depths of the earth and knew *where* to dig it would perhaps, as this passage suggests, be possible to dig into Sheol but you would not see or hear any of the souls of the dead. This is because you would be aware of seeing or hearing only with *physical* eyes and ears, rather than *spiritual*. You may, however, be able to see the actual physical *place* where the departed are.

Originally, this place in the depths of the earth was not used for the purpose of 'housing' the departed. No place was originally needed and, at the end of the sixth day of creation, God pronounced that all that He had made was 'very good'. If a place was created specifically to accommodate the souls of the dead it could not be described as 'very good'. After He had finished His Creation, God did not later create an *additional* place to use for the purpose of the dwelling of souls. When God had finished His works of Creation at the end of day six He really *had* finished. As God has foreknowledge, He *knew* that Adam and Eve would sin. He knew that one day they would depart their bodies and that they would need somewhere to go. He used something that He had already created, but not specifically *for* that purpose—a place within the existing Creation that would *serve the purpose* that was now required of it—to house the souls of those who had died. The first to go to this place of the dead was Abel, the son of Adam and Eve, who was killed by his brother Cain.

It is possible that the spirit and soul remain within a person while they are alive because of the *viability* of the physical person, possibly on a cellular level. In other words, the person has physical life; therefore the spirit and soul remain. Once that physical life ceases, the spirit and soul depart. This would be a system of cause and effect involving the spiritual and the physical. This would mean, perhaps, that there is some factor, substance, or process within the living person, likely within the cells, that, whilst it remains or is active, the interface between the spiritual and the physical functions, thus retaining the spirit and the soul. Once this viability or physical life is no longer there, the interface between the physical and spiritual ceases to function, and the spiritual body—the spirit and soul, depart.

How does the soul get from the body to the abode of the dead? The spirit and soul separate from the body. The body returns to dust. Scripture tells us that the spirit returns to God who gave it. In the time before Christ, *all* souls would become separated from their spirits and descend into this place of the dead. This is a result of the law of sin and death—the soul that sins must die.

The Bible says of the Old Testament saints that, upon death, they were 'gathered'. When Abraham died, for example, the Bible tells us that he "breathed his last and died a good old age, an old man and full of years, and was gathered to his people" (Gen. 25:8). For something to be gathered implies that there is a *gatherer*. This 'gathering' is one of the many roles of angels. They would gather the souls of the righteous and escort them to the abode of the dead where they would be in the company of the righteous who had died before them. Jesus confirms that the gathering of righteous souls is one of the roles of angels by the telling of the story of the poor beggar called Lazarus, who was carried by the angels to Abraham's side when he died. 'Abraham's side' was the name that the people of Israel referred to as the place of the righteous after death. Jesus referred to this place of the righteous as 'paradise' when speaking to the thief on the cross. Here the faithful believed that they would find comfort and peace in the company of the 'fathers of their faith'—Abraham, Isaac, and Jacob. The Bible does not say that the souls of the unrighteous were gathered. Likely the souls of the unrighteous simply went by default to the abode of the dead *without* angelic escort.

There are angels assigned to the management of the place of the dead and to the care of the righteous, as confirmed in the story of the beggar, Lazarus. These angels would be under God's instruction and would be held accountable to God.

Does God have access to this place? The psalmist certainly believed this to be the case. He asks: "Where shall I go from your spirit? Or where shall I flee from your presence? If I ascend into heaven, you are there! If I make my bed in Sheol, you are there!" (Ps. 139:8), "for God is present in the company of the righteous" (Ps. 14:5 NIV). Job says that "Sheol is naked before God" (Job 26:6). In other words, it is not hidden from the eyes of God, for "he does not withdraw his eyes from the righteous" (Job 36:7). God is fully aware of what is going on in the abode of the dead. This is not to suggest though, that this is the actual *dwelling place* of the Lord God. His dwelling place is in heaven.

Who goes to this place of the dead? If you had lived in the time before Christ, this place of the dead, be it the place of rest or turmoil, would be your destination immediately upon death. Your spirit and soul would depart from your body, your spirit would separate from your soul and return to God, and your soul would go to this place within the earth. That is where you would be aware of being.

The abode of the dead is not an 'everyone in together' affair. There are punishments received and rewards enjoyed. The nature of God's grace towards the righteous and His wrath against the wicked is evident in the dialogue He had with Abraham in an account in the Old Testament that tells of Abraham pleading with God to spare the city of Sodom, whose wickedness was great. Abraham wanted to know if

God would spare the city for the sake of any righteous that might be there and says: "Far be it from you to do such a thing, to put the righteous to death with the wicked, so that the righteous fare as the wicked! Far be that from you! Shall not the Judge of all the earth do what is just?" (Gen. 18:25). It is God's nature to be just and fair.

King David pleaded with God: "Do not gather my soul with sinners, Nor my life with bloodthirsty men" (Ps. 26:9 NKJV). This implies that there is *another* place where his soul could go, a far preferable place—with the righteous. The righteous would arrive at the place of comfort, peace, and rest, at 'Abraham's side', and the unrighteous would arrive at a place of punishment, darkness, and torment with *no* rest for their souls.

What is the place of departed souls like? According to Old Testament writers, the abode of disembodied souls is 'shadowy'. Job pictured it as a place where "the wicked cease from troubling, and there the weary are at rest. There the prisoners are at ease together; they hear not the voice of the taskmaster. The small and the great are there, and the slave is free from his master" (Job 3:17-19). Job also pictures it to be a "place of no return . . . the land of gloom and deep shadow . . . the land of deepest night . . . of deep shadow and disorder, where even the light is like darkness" (Job 10:21-22 NIV). The occupants are conscious although their existence, at least in some areas, may be dull and inactive compared to their former existence on the earth.

In the story that Jesus told about the two men who had died, the rich man begged Lazarus to dip his finger in water to cool his tongue for him, as he was 'in anguish' in the flame. These men were clearly in two separate areas, but close enough for the rich man to see Abraham with Lazarus by his side, and therefore to have the hope that this request might be possible. Jesus said, however, that a great chasm has been fixed so that neither can cross over to the other side. It is also apparent from this, that the spiritual body can feel pain, discomfort, and thirst.

In the place of departed souls then, there is a place of peace and a place of punishment, both in fairly close proximity but inaccessible to each other. It is interesting to note that the rich man lifted up his eyes to see the poor man Lazarus. This suggests that the place of punishment was lower down in the earth than the place of rest.

In the book of Job, there is a description given of the destiny of the wicked. He says that "fire resides in his tent; burning sulphur is scattered over his dwelling . . . He is driven from light into darkness and is banished from the world . . . surely such is the dwelling of an evil man; such is the place of one who knows not God" (Job 18:15, 18, 21 NIV). God said: "A fire is kindled by my anger, and it burns to the depths of Sheol" (Deut. 32:22). This tells us that the unrighteous part of the place of the dead includes darkness, fire, and burning sulphur.

The apostle Peter speaks of 'dungeons' in hell where angels who sinned are currently being held. He says that "God did not spare angels when they sinned, but cast them into hell and committed them to chains of gloomy darkness to be kept until the judgment" (2 Pet. 2:4). Some of the unrighteous are also being held in this part of the abode of the dead that has dungeons, whilst at the same time being punished. Peter writes that "the Lord knows how to . . . hold the unrighteous for the day of judgement, while continuing their punishment. This is especially true of those who follow the corrupt desire of the sinful nature and despise authority . . . blackest darkness is reserved for them" (2 Pet. 2:9-10, 17 NIV), again suggesting degrees of punishment and degrees of darkness.

There is then, in the abode of the dead:
— Places of rest, peace, and reward;
— Separation of the righteous and the unrighteous;
— Varying levels or depth; the abode of the righteous being in the upper chambers; the abode of the unrighteous being in the lower chambers;
— A variation in the amount of light and darkness;
— Dungeons;
— Degrees of punishment in the abode of the unrighteous; and
— Fire and burning sulphur.

At the point of death, the soul would travel, or be gathered and escorted by angels, to the abode of the dead and either stop at the place reserved for the righteous, or continue on down to the place of the unrighteous.

As well as separate areas for the righteous and the unrighteous, there is also an area that is presently unoccupied but reserved for the future, following judgement. In the book of Psalms we read of the wicked returning to Sheol after judgement: "The Lord has made himself known; he has executed judgement; the wicked are snared in the work of their own hands. The wicked shall return to Sheol, all the nations that forget God" (Ps. 9:16-17). This would imply that they went to Sheol *after* death and then at some later stage would be brought up and judged and then *returned* to Sheol.

What is this currently unoccupied place in Sheol that Scripture says the wicked will be returned to after judgement? There is a place deep in the earth called the 'abyss' which we read of in the book of Revelation. Access to the abyss is through a shaft which is currently locked; the key to which the Bible tells us is now in the possession of Jesus, and will be opened at the end of time:

> And the fifth angel blew his trumpet, and I saw a star fallen from heaven to earth, and he was given the key to the shaft of the bottomless pit. He opened the shaft of the bottomless pit, and from the shaft rose smoke like the smoke of a great furnace, and the sun and the air were darkened with the smoke from the shaft.
>
> —Rev. 9:1-2

Shaft—/shahft/ -*n.* narrow usu. vertical space, for access to a mine, or (in a building) for a lift, ventilation, etc.[5]

Access to the abyss is through a shaft or deep tunnel. It is further down in the earth past the abode of the righteous and the unrighteous. The fact that it must be unlocked with a key in the future suggests that no one is currently in this place and that it is being held in reserve. Although there is punishment in the unrighteous areas of the abode of the dead, the abyss is the place of *final* punishment following judgement. This is the location of the lake of fire. A 'lake' suggests that it consists of a liquid that is permanently ablaze.

In view of the Scripture supporting the concept of levels or different areas in the abode of the dead, it would seem to suggest that:
1. Closer to the surface of the earth where it is shadowy is the place of the righteous dead. Here there is rest and peace;
2. Deeper down is the area where the unrighteous dead are, awaiting judgement. This has degrees of punishment within it and is deeper down into the earth. The deeper the chambers of this place, the darker it is, and the greater the punishment and distress, considering that it would be hotter as you approach the centre of the earth. It would be assumed then, that the lower portions of hell, being deeper down and therefore closer to the abyss or the lake of fire, are the areas that have greater degrees of punishment. Within this area there are also dungeons; and
3. From the lower chambers of this level, a shaft that is at present locked, leads down to the abyss which is the location of the lake of fire—a liquid lake that burns continually. This place is currently not being used, but is being kept in reserve for the future.

The description of the levels in the abode of the dead, correspond with what is believed to be the composition of the earth. What scientists know for certain about the composition of the earth is very limited. From the movement of the earth's tectonic plates, volcanic eruptions and activity, and knowledge about gravity, magnetic fields, and various data, scientists have pieced together a picture of what they believe may be the composition of the layers of the earth:

Crust—the outer layer of the earth including the continents and ocean basins. It is between approximately five and seventy kilometres thick.

Mantle—the middle layer of the earth consisting of the upper mantle and the lower mantle. This is approximately 2, 900 kilometres thick and contains lava which is like a river of hot rock that flows under pressure.

Core—consists of the outer core which is liquid and composed mostly of a nickel-iron alloy and sulphur and is 2, 300 kilometres thick, and an inner core which is solid and is mostly composed of iron and sulphur and is 3, 500 kilometres thick.

It may be that the upper section of the abode of the dead is not all that far below the surface of the earth. There may be hollow places within the outer layers of the earth or the crust—deep cavernous places. The composition of the deeper layers of the earth is certainly consistent with biblical descriptions of burning sulphur and fire, and a lake that constantly burns.

It is understandable that no one would really want to spend one minute in the abode of the unrighteous, let alone contemplate an eternal future in the lake of fire, but what about the abode of the righteous? If the abode of the righteous were the ideal place to go, then why were the writers of the Old Testament so keen to be delivered from there? Let's have a look at what some of these writers have to say...

The Bible describes Job as 'righteous' so we can safely use him as an example of one who would have been a temporary resident of the righteous section of the abode of the dead. Job said that God "keeps back his soul from the pit" (Job 33:18 NKJV), implying that he is not too keen to go there and that to have one's soul kept back from the pit as long as possible would be a good thing. He also says that "his soul draws near the pit" (Job 33:22 NKJV), implying that this was something undesirable that he was not looking forward to, and that he would prefer to delay this journey as long as possible. It paints an image of some kind of great open vortex slowly sucking him in!

God promised the rescue of Job's soul from Sheol and the souls of all those who put their faith in Him. Job, when contemplating God's promise of the future salvation of his soul from the pit, said:

> Oh that you would hide me in Sheol, that you would conceal me until your wrath be past, that you would appoint me a set time, and remember me! If a man dies, shall he live again? All the days of my service I would wait, till my renewal should come. You would call, and I would answer you; you would long for the work of your hands. For then you would number my steps; you would not keep watch over my sin; my transgression would be sealed up in a bag, and you would cover over my iniquity.
>
> —Job 14:13-17

Job is looking forward to being called from the grave by the voice of the Lord, being renewed, united with his heavenly Father, and his sins being remembered no more. Also in the book of Job, we read that God is "wooing you from the jaws of distress to a spacious place free from restriction, to the comfort of your table laden with choice food" (Job 36:16 NIV). This is a contrast of the temporary restricted and confined place of the abode of the dead with the future spacious and comfortable eternal home of the righteous. The 'table laden with choice food' certainly sounds much more welcoming than the 'jaws of distress'.

In the book of Hosea, God promised the people of Israel that He would "ransom them from the power of the grave; I will redeem them from death" (Hosea 13:14 NIV).

> **Ransom—/ran-suhm/ —*n*. 1 money demanded or paid for the release of a prisoner. 2 liberation of a prisoner in return for this. —*v*. 1 buy the freedom or restoration of; redeem. 2 = *hold to ransom* 3 release for a ransom. (Latin: related to REDEMPTION).**[6]
>
> **Redeem—/ruh-deem/ *v*. 1 recover by expenditure of effort or by a stipulated payment. 2 make a single payment to cancel (a loan etc.). 3**

convert (tokens or bonds etc.) into goods or cash. 4 (of Christ) deliver from sin and damnation. 5 make up for; be a compensating factor in (*has one redeeming feature*). 6. (foll. by *from*) save from (a defect). 7 *refl.* Save (oneself) from blame. 8 purchase the freedom of (a person). 9 save (a person's life) by ransom. 10 save or rescue or reclaim. 11 fulfil (a promise).[7]

The Old Testament saints such as David and Job had faith in this promise of redemption from death. David knew that Sheol was only temporary and he believed that God had a better place waiting for him in heaven. He wrote that God would "not abandon my soul to Sheol" (Ps. 16:10).

David referred many times to God's promised salvation of his soul, including in the following Scriptures:

"You will not leave my soul in Sheol" (Ps. 16:10 NKJV); and

"God will redeem my soul from the power of the grave, for he shall receive me" (Ps. 49:15 NKJV).

David leaves no doubt that he does not wish to depart to the place of the dead any sooner than is necessary. Nor does he wish to spend eternity in this place. Why not? Because he would not be in the dwelling place of God his Creator, his heavenly Father who loves him. For him, the dwelling place of God is the ultimate place to be—by his Father's side. He knows that this will happen when he is redeemed from Sheol and he says: "As for me, I shall behold your face in righteousness; when I awake, I shall be satisfied with your likeness" (Ps. 17:15). David expected to see the promised Messiah—the likeness of God, come to redeem and rescue him from Sheol. Even though he knows that, temporarily, he will be in Sheol, he has faith and hope in his future redemption.

In David's well-known Twenty-third Psalm, he writes: "And I shall dwell in the house of the LORD forever" (Ps. 23:6). The 'house of the LORD' is in heaven. That is what David is looking forward to. He knows that, in this place of death where his soul will be gathered with the righteous, he is *not* living with his Father in heaven. He knows that heaven is where he wants to be more than anywhere else. Where his heavenly Father is, that is *home*. His life here on earth is but a pale comparison to the life he is looking forward to in 'the house of the LORD', and the existence of his soul in this shadowy place of the dead is definitely undesirable compared with the glory of heaven. The book of Amos tells us that God "builds his lofty palace in the heavens" (Amos 9:6 NIV). David was looking forward to joining his Father in this 'lofty palace'.

The difference between being in Sheol and being in heaven may be likened to the difference for the Israelites between being slaves in Egypt for four hundred years and being brought by God into the Promised Land. No comparison! In Egypt there was bondage, not freedom, and God did not dwell among them. They were living in the hot dry desert, not the lush and beautiful land 'flowing with milk and honey'. They were there awaiting their liberty, their freedom, clinging to the promises that God had made to them through their forefathers, as the righteous who had died were awaiting God's promise of liberation from Sheol. God's promise to the Israelites was that, "because of the blood of my covenant with you, I will set your prisoners free from the waterless pit" (Zech. 9:11)—the abode of the dead.

If you were to read about the abode of the dead in a travel magazine it would not appeal to you as the ultimate destination, not even as a temporary stopover! You would want to go where there was life and beauty, light and love; somewhere even better than anywhere you had ever been before.

Why couldn't those who died go to heaven? Because God cannot abide sin. God is holy. We are sinful. In His *mercy*, He did not allow mankind to live forever on earth in a sinful state. But, because of His *holiness,* He cannot allow mankind to dwell with Him in heaven in a sinful state. There had to be a place for the righteous to go to await redemption, and there had to be a place for the unrighteous and unrepentant to go to await judgement.

As a result of The Fall, the soul, by default, is destined to become separated at death from the spirit, which gives the soul life. If this happens, the soul will *not* return to God with the spirit. However, God in His abundant grace and mercy has made a way for this to happen—a way to 'reset the default'. We are given hope when we read in the Scriptures that "he who turns a sinner from the error of his way will save a soul from death and cover a multitude of sins" (James 5:20 NKJV). The saving of a person from death therefore, is possible *if* our sins are covered. That is very good news! If our sins are *covered*, we will not have to pay the price for them ourselves.

The psalmist, in speaking of the sure knowledge of the salvation of his soul writes:
> "Truly my soul silently waits for God; from him comes my salvation" (Ps. 62:1 NKJV);
> "Draw near to my soul and redeem it" (Ps. 69:18 NKJV);
> "My soul, which you have redeemed" (Ps. 71:23 NKJV); and
> "For great is your mercy towards me . . . you have delivered my soul from the depths of Sheol" (Ps. 86:13 NKJV).

David knew that he would not have to stay in Sheol and he was looking forward to this redemption by God. He understood that salvation comes from the Lord by faith in the forgiveness of sins through the promised Messiah, and he wrote that God "will revive me again; from the depths of the earth you will bring me up again. You will increase my greatness and comfort me again" (Ps. 71:20-21).

HERE'S WHAT WE NEED:

After examining the Scriptures to investigate the origin, nature, and destiny of the soul, it seems that what we need is a way for the soul, on departing from the physical body, to bypass the default destination—the abode of the dead.

We need some way for the spirit of life to remain infused within the soul, and for the spirit *and* soul to depart to heaven together upon the death of the body. We need a way of avoiding this 'in between' and undesirable state of existence in the abode of the dead, thus avoiding judgement, and certainly avoiding an eternal destiny in the lake of fire! Our souls need *redeeming* from this fate to which we, because of sin, have been condemned.

To *redeem* something means to buy it back. There is an exchange of one thing for another. Scripture makes it very clear that "the redemption of souls is costly" (Ps. 49:8 NKJV). During our quest to find what we need, we will discover just how costly the redemption of souls is.

Chapter Four
The Heart

Scripture has considerably more to say about the heart than about the soul and the spirit. More than any other part of us, the state of our heart indicates the state of our relationship with God and influences and affects the state of our whole being. Although we have already discussed a little about the heart in previous chapters, it might be helpful to review some of these points again before we look at the heart in more detail.

THE ORIGIN

When God created Adam He formed his physical body out of the dust of the earth. He then breathed into his nostrils the breath of life. This breath of God, which was Adam's first breath, activated Adam's lungs and permeated his entire body bringing it to life, beginning the physical processes such as the exchange of oxygen and carbon dioxide through his lungs, the initiation of the beating of his heart, and the circulation. The Spirit of life from God formed Adam's human spirit which, by its interaction with the physical body, formed the soul. The soul took on the imprint of the physical in the same way that plaster would have an imprint if poured into a mould. It would remain the *substance* of plaster, but would take on the *characteristics* of the mould. Souls are unique to the individual and it is within the soul that we have awareness of 'being'. In other words, where the soul is, that is where we are aware of being.

The Spirit of life from God entered Adam's heart forming his spiritual heart. From that point, Adam's spirit circulated around his body. As spirit is life, and it flows throughout the entire person, as does the blood, it is likely that the spirit of life is *in* the blood and follows the same pathway as that of the blood, although it is of spiritual substance rather than physical.

Unlike Adam, who had the breath of life or spirit breathed into his nostrils, our spirit is passed on through the father along with the physical seed. This combines with the physical seed contributed by the mother at conception, immediately forming the beginnings of our spirit, soul, and body. We originated from two *physical* seeds and one *spiritual* seed.

The little group of cells—a tiny human being which has been newly formed, divides and very quickly forms a rudimentary heart and circulatory system. The embryonic structures that become the heart begin to form very early in the process of the development of the baby and from about day twenty-two, the tiny heart begins to beat. In order for the blood to reach all parts of our body, it flows from a single point in our body—our physical heart, which functions as a pump, circulating the oxygenated blood to the extremities and then returning to exchange gases via the lungs and re-oxygenate the oxygen-depleted blood. The fact that the heart of the person is the first part of them that is *physically* formed, gives support to the likelihood that the flow of the spirit originates from the *spiritual* heart.

The spiritual heart is in the same location as the physical heart; the physical being superimposed on the spiritual. Although the heart is referred to separately from the soul in the Bible, it is within the *boundaries* of the soul and is formed in the same way as the soul, that is, by the action of spirit upon matter. In other words, the spiritual heart would be formed in the embryo by the action of the spirit on the physical heart. The heart, although encompassed by the soul and therefore in a sense part of the soul, is unique.

The Scriptures tell us that we have spiritual eyes and ears, we have spirit in our mind, and our spirit affects our bones. Even though the spiritual is not necessarily subject to laws and processes in the same way that the physical is, the conclusion may be drawn that our souls are in fact similar in form and function to our physical bodies. This, in turn, draws the conclusion that our *spiritual* heart, which the Bible says is the 'wellspring of life', has a similar structure and function to that of our *physical* heart in that, just as our physical heart circulates blood around our bodies, the spiritual heart circulates our spirit around our bodies. Right from the minute beginnings of the embryo, the physical and the spiritual hearts function in their crucial role of bringing life to the body and the soul.

The heart would undoubtedly be the most vital organ in our body. The condition of our physical heart affects the circulation of our blood and its ability to bring life to our physical bodies. Similarly, the most vital spiritual 'organ' in our body is our spiritual heart. If our spiritual heart functions as the spiritual equivalent to our physical heart, then as blood flows from the physical heart bringing oxygen to the body and then returns to the heart to be replenished with oxygen via the lungs, so the spirit would proceed from the spiritual heart, flow throughout the body bringing life to the soul and would *return* to the heart before being recirculated.

It is in the heart that the spirit can be renewed and refreshed. The Bible cautions us to keep our "heart with all vigilance, for from it flow the springs of life" (Prov. 4:23)—the spirit. If our heart is not in a healthy state, our spirit is not either. If our spirit is not in a healthy state, our soul, which depends on our spirit to give life, is not going to be in a healthy state. The state of our heart, and therefore our spirit and soul, can also affect our *physical* health as the spirit flows throughout the body. If the heart is in poor condition however, as a result of sin and of not being in a right relationship with the Creator, the spirit flowing from the heart will *not* be filling the soul with renewed life and vitality.

One of the main functions of the Holy Spirit is that of connecting. When God made the first man and woman they were without sin. In fact, "God saw everything that he had made, and behold, it was very good" (Gen. 1:31). Their spiritual hearts were open to God and they had a spiritual connection via their hearts to God's Spirit—

His life. Adam and Eve were connected to God's presence through their hearts by the Holy Spirit. They did not have a 'piece' of God's Spirit that was disconnected from the rest of His Spirit but, rather, God's Spirit was flowing from Him to Adam and Eve while *still being connected* to Him. Adam and Eve were able to communicate directly with God because, having a spirit and soul in a state of perfection, they had full use of their spiritual bodies. They could see God, hear God, and God walked with them "in the garden in the cool of the day" (Gen. 3:8). It was a very close relationship—family, in fact!

In the beginning, Adam and Eve knew only good, not evil. God did, however, make mankind with a free will; that is, the ability to choose. The first man and woman chose to exercise that free will when they sinned. They chose independence from God, or spiritual autonomy. From the account in the book of Genesis, we read that "the LORD God took the man and put him in the garden of Eden to work it and keep it. And the LORD God commanded the man, saying, 'You may surely eat of every tree of the garden, but of the tree of the knowledge of good and evil you shall not eat, for in the day that you eat of it you shall surely die'" (Gen. 2:15-17). They disobeyed God's command and ate of this tree and there were immediate consequences. Sin causes disconnection from, and alienation from, God. When Adam and Eve sinned, their hearts became closed to the Spirit of God and they lost connection with the source of life.

The result of this sin was spiritual death—separation from God. Instead of God's Spirit giving them renewed life through their open hearts, their hearts *closed* and this resulted in a disconnected spirit that simply recirculated through their hearts rather than their hearts being connected directly to God. This was the *not* the way that we were made to function. In a state of independence from God, and *not* connected to the Creator—our source of life, is spiritual death.

After The Fall, Adam and Eve were no longer able to enjoy a close relationship with God. It was this loving relationship with their heavenly Father that they were made for, and there was no substitute for this; nothing else that would fill that gap.

As a result of their disobedience, they no longer had access to the Tree of Life which sustained them physically and prevented their bodies from cellular degeneration and ageing. They were now destined for physical death. It was the mercy of God that mankind would not live on the earth forever in a sinful state. The alternative being the case, that is, to physically live forever in a sinful state, would mean having the potential for compounding evil in a person's life, and the potential for moving further and further away from his or her loving Creator. Imagine some of the most evil dictators or mass murderers living for ever here on earth. That would not be a scenario any of us would like to contemplate!

The Bible not only gives us an idea of what happened to the hearts of Adam and Eve when they sinned, but also of the state of the hearts of all those who have *not* repented of their sins and put their faith in the Lord. Before the flood, we read that "the

LORD saw that the wickedness of man was great in the earth, and that every intent of the thoughts of his heart was only evil continually" (Gen. 6:5 NKJV). Even *after* the flood, God said that "the imagination of man's heart is evil from his youth" (Gen. 8:21 NKJV). God tells us in the book of Jeremiah that "the heart is deceitful above all things, and desperately wicked" (Jer. 17:9-10 NKJV). The Bible certainly paints a bleak picture of the state of the heart of man!

When the Israelites turned away from God and hardened their hearts to Him (referred to in the Scriptures as having a 'heart of stone'), He said: "(I) will circumcise your heart and the heart of your descendants, to love the LORD your God with all your heart and with all your soul, that you may live" (Deut. 30:6 NKJV). He also told the Israelites they were to "circumcise the foreskin of your heart" (Deut. 10:16 NKJV).

In the book of Jeremiah there is reference to the "uncircumcised in heart" (Jer. 9:26 NKJV)—those whose hearts were *not* open to God, and God commands the men of Judah and the inhabitants of Jerusalem to "circumcise yourselves to the LORD, and take away the foreskins of your hearts" (Jer. 4:4 NKJV).

In his New Testament letter to the Romans, Paul describes a true Jew, stating that "he is a Jew who is one inwardly; and circumcision is that of the heart" (Rom. 2:29 NKJV). To have a 'circumcised heart' is to have a heart that is *open* to the Lord. In the book of Acts, Paul chastens the Jews and calls them "stiff-necked and uncircumcised in heart and ears!" and goes on to say: "You always resist the Holy Spirit; as your fathers did, so do you" (Acts 7:51 NKJV). He directly attributes the state of their hearts, that is, uncircumcised, or not open to God, as being a result of resisting the work of the Holy Spirit. Just as it was the Holy Spirit that formed the *connection* that Adam and Eve had to God's presence, it is also the work of the Holy Spirit to *open* hearts to God.

To reconnect to the source of life, that is, to God our heavenly Father, our hearts *must* be open. An open heart comes through the repentance of, and turning away from, sins, and through faith. This faith, through the work of the Holy Spirit, causes the spiritual heart to open to God. This is what is meant by a circumcision of the heart. It is an opening of the heart to God.

THE NATURE

God knows what is in our hearts for "the LORD looks at the heart" (1 Sam. 16:7 NKJV). The writer of the First Book of Kings says of God: "For you alone know the hearts of all the sons of men" (1 Kings 8:39 NKJV), and King David tells us that God "knows the secrets of the heart" (Ps. 44:21 NKJV) and he invites God to "search me, O God, and know my heart, that I might not sin against You!" (Ps. 119:11 NKJV). In the book of First Chronicles we read that "the LORD searches all hearts and understands all the intents of the thoughts" (1 Chr. 28:9 NKJV). The 'intents of the thoughts' would be our motives—the reasons behind what we think and therefore what we do or say.

"The spirit of a man is the lamp of the LORD, searching all the inner depths of his heart" (Prov. 20:30 NKJV). God is able to search our hearts like searching a dark place with a lamp. By looking at man's heart God is, in essence, seeing the true man. The apostle Peter refers to "the hidden person of the heart" (1 Pet. 3:4 NKJV). This 'hidden person' is not hidden from God though!

The book of Proverbs gives an excellent metaphor for the heart: "As in water face reflects face, so a man's heart reveals the man" (Prov. 27:19 NKJV). The state of the heart dictates the state of the whole man. If your heart is in a poor state, then this will be evident in what you say and what you do. It will also be evident to God.

Jesus tells us that "out of the abundance of the heart the mouth speaks" (Matt. 12:34 NKJV). He goes on to say that "those things which proceed out of the mouth come from the heart, and they defile a man. For out of the heart proceed evil thoughts, murders, adulteries, fornications, thefts, false witness, blasphemies" (Matt. 15:18-19 NKJV). Jesus likens what is in the heart to treasure, and says that "a good man out of the good treasure of his heart brings forth good; and an evil man out of the evil treasure of his heart brings forth evil" (Luke 6:45 NKJV). The perception of what is 'treasure' then, seems to depend on the state of the heart of the man. Perhaps this may be the origin of the saying "one man's trash is another man's treasure"!

Interestingly, the Lord "weighs the hearts" (Prov. 21:2 NKJV). This 'weighing' may indicate the quality or worth of the heart of a man. Of men, we read in Psalms that the Lord "fashions their hearts individually" (Ps. 33:15 NKJV). God is able to *change* the heart, *cleanse* the heart, and even make it *new*. As the soul is unique to the individual, so is the heart.

Your heart is capable of many and varied emotions according to Scripture. These include being afraid, anguished, discouraged, sad, heavy, broken, distressed, overwhelmed, sorrowful, grieved, terrified, and spiteful. Your heart can be tender, contrite, glad, joyful, merry, cheerful, concerned, humbled, noble, and good. You can have a heart that is turned by God towards others.

Your heart is capable of a great many other things according to God's Word. It can have God's Law in it, follow God, have visions, cry out to the Lord, and receive the Lord's words into it. You can exalt self in your heart. Your heart can depart from the Lord, and your heart can covet. You can commit adultery in your heart and plan or think evil against someone in your heart. You can consider and reason in your heart. You can have bitter envy and self-seeking in your heart. You can doubt in your heart, ponder things, keep God's commands, acquire knowledge, envy, devise violence in, despise correction in, lust in, and have abominations in your heart.

A fool trusts in his *own* heart. Your heart can yearn, faint, cry out, fear, and gather iniquity (sin) to itself. You can find it in your heart to pray, take delight in the ways of the Lord in your heart, sing for joy in your heart, meditate in your heart, and praise from your heart. Your heart can trust in the Lord and it can stand in awe of God's Word. Your heart can rejoice in God's salvation. God can put the ability to teach into your heart. Your heart can seek, know, love, serve, and obey God. With your heart you can fear God and keep His commandments. Your heart can be turned away from God by wealth or to serve false gods. You can have God's Word hidden in your heart.

The heart can be filled with wisdom and filled with understanding. It can be guided, applied to instruction, and set to seek and search out by wisdom. What is wisdom? What is understanding? "The fear of the Lord, that is wisdom, and to turn away from evil is understanding" (Job 28:28). To have the fear of the Lord in your heart, or to revere Him, is to have wisdom; and "does he not have regard for all the wise in heart?" (Job 37:24 NIV). The book of Isaiah tells us that the fear of the Lord is the key to treasure: "The LORD is exalted, for he dwells on high; he will fill Zion with justice and righteousness, and he will be the stability of your times, abundance of salvation, wisdom, and knowledge; the fear of the LORD is Zion's treasure" (Isa. 33:5-6).

Scripture gives us an indication of the state of a heart that has *not* been restored to God. It is uncircumcised, or closed, to God's Spirit and to the life of God. It is impure, hardened, blind, far removed from the Lord, turned away after false gods, not right in the sight of God, deceived, rebellious, evil, haughty, divided, slow to believe, wicked, bitter, dull, proud, arrogant, in turmoil, inclined to do an evil thing, perverse, stubborn, unmoved, obstinate, deceived, confused, insolent, troubled, darkened, and lost.

In contrast to that list, the Scriptures paint another picture—that of the heart that is *open* to God. It reads much more favourably. That heart is guarded by the peace of God, assured before Him, comforted, purified by faith, lifted to God, upright, circumcised, inclined to God, steadfast, cleansed, strengthened by the Lord, pure, faithful, set to seek the Lord, fixed towards God, revived by the Lord, washed from wickedness, opened by the Lord, refreshed in the Lord, and established by grace.

It sounds like you would need an absolute miracle to switch from the heart of the first description to the heart of the second description. It sounds like you would need a brand new heart!

THE CONSCIENCE

The conscience is a function of the heart. The writer of the letter to the Hebrews confirms this by saying: "Let us draw near with a true heart in full assurance of faith, having our hearts sprinkled from an evil conscience and our bodies washed with pure water" (Heb. 10:22 NKJV).

According to Scripture, the conscience can be weak, defiled, or seared with a hot iron (metaphorically speaking). The conscience can bear witness or bear testimony—like a witness giving evidence against you in a court case, and it can convict you of sin or wrongdoing—like a judge or jury would in a court of law.

The conscience functions to tell us if something is good or evil, right or wrong, and to convict us of wrongdoing if we go against what the conscience is telling us we should or shouldn't do. Sin is doing what we shouldn't do and omitting to do what we should do. There is then, a correlation between the conscience and sin.

In Adam's and Eve's consciences, there was only one thing that God had told them *not* to do. There was nothing else that they were prohibited from. This one thing was the eating of the fruit from the Tree of the Knowledge of Good and Evil. They knew that to do this thing would be wrong. The command not to eat of this tree could have been a command not to do *anything;* the principle of it would have been the same. Their conscience would have told them not to do it. This was where their freewill came in to play. Their freewill meant that they then had to decide what to do:

1. Do what their consciences were telling them *not* to do, that is, to 'eat the fruit'; or
2. Do what their consciences were telling them *to* do, that is, 'don't eat the fruit'.

This is one of the roles of your conscience—conviction of right and wrong, good and evil—a role of discernment.

The conscience is an inbuilt mechanism within the heart. Adam and Eve, up until the point of sinning, depended only on God and were spiritually connected to God. Through lack of faith in God and their desire for independence, Adam and Eve did the thing which their consciences had told them *not* to do. They ate from the fruit of the Tree of the Knowledge of Good and Evil. They went *against* their consciences. Immediately something happened to their spiritual hearts. Their hearts closed to God. They had chosen independence over dependence on God and as a result of this they were no longer connected to God's Spirit.

Our conscience also functions in another role. Paul, in his letter to the Romans, speaks of our "conscience also bearing witness, and between themselves their thoughts accusing or else excusing them" (Rom. 2:15 NKJV). This means that, once you have exercised your freewill and acted upon a matter, you will then have one of two thoughts about the matter. These thoughts will either tell you that you should *not* have done this (accuse) or that you have done the *correct* thing (excuse).

If we go against what our conscience is telling us is the right thing to do, our "heart condemns us" (1 John 3:20) by the action of our conscience. The 'condemning' that our hearts do is to make us feel *guilty* if we have gone against our conscience.

The apostle John said that "if our heart does not condemn us, we have confidence before God" (1 John 3:21). In other words, if we have *not* gone against our conscience in a matter, then we will not have a *guilty* conscience over that matter, and we will therefore be confident that we will *not* stand condemned before God over that matter. Conversely, if we *have* gone against our conscience in a matter, then we *will* have a guilty conscience over that matter, and we *will* stand condemned before God over that matter. Our conscience exists for *our* sake, not God's. It is a checkpoint; a spiritual mechanism that God intended for us to pay attention to.

A conscience then, will not only tell us that something is the *wrong* thing to do or say or even think, but will also tell us if we *should* be doing, saying, or thinking something. For example, you may pass by a person at the shopping centre who has just dropped their bag of groceries. Your conscience might be telling you to stop and help them as that would be a good and morally right thing to do. You could obey your conscience and help, or ignore it and then feel guilt in your heart. Another example of this is that you may notice that someone is working extra hard on something and you know that you should acknowledge that person but you just haven't gotten around to doing it yet. That would be your conscience telling you that you *should* do this good thing and the longer you keep on ignoring it, the longer you will feel guilty for *not* doing it.

Sometimes a person may make a habit of ignoring his or her conscience and then over time, that 'little voice' will seem to get quieter and quieter. The person has become conditioned to ignore his or her conscience and not hear what it is saying. The result of this is that the person does not seem to feel guilt. The guilt is there but the person's sensitivity to that feeling of guilt has become numbed. Some of the most hardened criminals have probably become that way because of this practice of ignoring the conscience.

Are the consciences of all people similar? It appears not. For a start, the consciences of believers and unbelievers are different. Paul says that the minds and the consciences of unbelievers are corrupted for "they profess to know God, but they deny him by their works" (Titus 1:16). In other words, they are only fooling themselves into thinking that they know God, or trying to fool others, but their actions, as evidence of their corrupted minds and consciences, paint a different picture.

A basic knowledge of right and wrong, good and evil, is inbuilt into the conscience of every person. This includes not to murder, steal, lie, cheat, and so on, but as we mature and become more aware of the needs of those around us and of what God requires of us, our conscience does, or at least *should*, develop and become more finely-tuned as to what is the right thing to do or say or think, and also what is wrong. As we mature therefore, we become accountable to God for our thoughts, words, and actions. For example, we should develop a 'social conscience' that gives us a desire to help the poor and needy. As a result of this we might become generous in our giving and kinder to our suffering fellowman. When we were five years old, for example, we might pass a needy person in the street and just stare out of curiosity or not even notice them. We probably would not feel any guilt about doing this because our consciences are not developed sufficiently to feel the need to do anything. When we are older however, we might say 'hello' to them, give them a smile or a word or two, and perhaps give them some money or food. This is because our consciences are telling us that this is what we should do and to ignore this would result in a feeling of guilt. We do not like having a feeling of guilt and this desire to avoid guilt by obeying our conscience would be one of the reasons that we choose to extend this charity or kindness to them (hopefully not the primary reason!).

In the early church, there was concern amongst believers about whether they could eat certain meats. In particular, they were wondering whether to eat meat that had been offered to idols. Paul's answer was that each one should act according to his or her conscience, depending on what *their own individual belief* of what the right thing to do was. There were those who believed they had the liberty or freedom to eat of this meat and those whose conscience told them it would be wrong to eat this meat. Of those who believed that it was okay to eat the meat, they were not to do this *if,* by doing it, they were seen by someone whose conscience told them not to but was so weak that *they* would then be emboldened to eat of this meat also and in this way *they* would be sinning. As a result of seeing the one eating the meat, the weaker person would be going against *their own* conscience by eating the meat also. In other words, you are not only to do what is right according to *your own* conscience, but also be aware of the conscience of your fellowman. In this way you will not be responsible for causing another to stumble in his faith by causing *him* to sin by going against what he believes in *his* conscience to be right. Paul implies that by appearing to be doing the wrong thing in another person's eyes, even though your own conscience may allow you to do this, is wrong.

This understanding of the relationship between the conscience of yourself and that of others is useful with regards to many issues such as drinking alcohol, gambling, using offensive language, and so on. If your conscience is telling you not to do it, don't. If you offend someone else by doing it, don't. If you are a bad example to others by doing it, don't. If you do it, and someone whose conscience is telling *them* not to do it might then do it because of you, don't. If in doubt, don't! Doubt is your conscience 'pricking' you. Learn to listen. This way you will avoid a guilty conscience.

In Paul's letter to the Romans, he speaks about judging others for what they do or don't do. This passage gives us further insight into the function of the conscience and guilt. He writes: "Therefore you have no excuse, O man, every one of you who judges. For in passing judgment on another you condemn yourself, because you, the judge, practice the very same things . . . Do you suppose, O man—you who judge those who practice such things and yet do them yourself—that you will escape the judgment of God?" (Rom. 2:1, 3). As an example, if you condemn another person for claiming an item that is not a legitimate work-related expense against their income and then you do the same thing as them, it is *obvious* that your conscience is telling *you* that this is the wrong thing to do, otherwise you would not have criticised or condemned the other person for doing it. This means that *you* will have sinned because you went against what you had already made it clear was on *your* conscience. Because of your judgement on the other person, you have actually condemned *yourself* for doing this and are, without a doubt, guilty. If *you* set a standard for *others*, then that is the *minimum* standard for yourself.

In Jesus' day there were religious leaders called Pharisees. They studied the Scriptures diligently and claimed to know God and to know the truth. But, Jesus said to them: "If you were blind, you would have no guilt; but now that you say, 'We see,' your guilt remains" (John 9:41). In other words, if they did not know right from wrong, they would not be guilty if they did sin. Because they *claimed* that they could 'see', they were claiming that they *knew* what was right and what was wrong. By *claiming* that they knew right from wrong, when they sinned, they were guilty.

When Jesus was speaking to His disciples of 'the world', He said: "If I had not come and spoken to them, they would not have been guilty of sin, but now they have no excuse for their sin" (John 15:22). In other words, the people *now* knew what was right and what was wrong, what was good and what was evil, because they had now heard the teachings of Jesus. Knowing these teachings meant that they would experience guilt in their hearts for doing the wrong thing. Because they now *knew* that what they were doing was wrong, they had no excuse for what they did. They were guilty.

Your conscience tells you whether something is right or wrong to do or say or think. If you then go ahead and do this thing that your conscience has told you *not* to do, or if you do not do something that your conscience was telling you *to* do, it convicts you of wrongdoing or sin by a feeling of guilt. If you do something contrary to what your conscience is telling you, this guilt that you feel should cause you to feel a sense of remorse, and then you will, or should, feel the need to apologize to someone, ask forgiveness, make amends, and seek to restore a relationship, or make restitution for a wrong. This spiritual 'mechanism' of a guilty conscience should lead you to a desire to rid yourself of the feeling of guilt by asking God for forgiveness and, if you have wronged your fellowman, by asking *them* for forgiveness. It should give you the desire to make amends for the wrong you have done. Your conscience will keep reminding you of the necessity of this until you act on it, and once you have acted on it, your heart will be cleansed from guilt. It should also have the effect of giving you the desire to not commit this sin again in the future.

Guilt is an unpleasant feeling to have in your heart and one that is undesirable. It makes the heart 'unclean'. Adam and Eve experienced this feeling of guilt for the first time when they sinned. They then needed their hearts to be cleansed from the guilt of their sin. The removal of guilt is by the confession of sins, forgiveness by the wronged party (God and perhaps a person or persons), and sometimes a price being paid for restitution, perhaps by compensating the person whom you have wronged.

Job, a man of God who "was blameless and upright . . . feared God and turned away from evil" (Job 1:1), said: "My conscience will not reproach me as long as I live" (Job 27:6 NIV). He was determined to:

1. Always do what his conscience told him was the right thing to do; which would
2. Avoid reproach or accusation from his conscience; which would
3. Keep his heart free from guilt; which meant he
4. Would continue to be 'blameless and upright'.

He was also aware of the deceit that was in the heart of man with regard to the *concealing* of sin, and did not want to conceal his sin "as men do, by hiding the guilt in my heart" (Job 31:33 NIV). Job knew that this would be pointless, as God knows the hearts of men and nothing can be hidden from Him. He also knew the importance of a clean heart brought about by the confession of sins, the seeking of God's forgiveness, and by making restitution for the wrong committed.

Job had three friends who sat with him through his ordeal. God had allowed Satan to test Job's faithfulness to Him by bringing upon him great disasters including the loss of family, loss of wealth, and loss of health. Satan thought that Job's faith was in God only because everything seemed to be going well in his life and because God had put a 'hedge' around him. The three friends thought they were helping Job by trying to get him to confess to sins that he had not even committed in case *this* was the cause of the calamities that befell him. Job, however, maintained that he had a clear conscience, "so these three men ceased to answer Job, because he was righteous in his own eyes" (Job 32:1). Being 'righteous in his own eyes' meant that Job's conscience was clear, because he always did what his conscience told him to do.

King David knew what it was like to feel guilty and he understood the need for forgiveness. He had taken to himself the wife of another and then had her husband placed in the front line of battle so that he would be killed. In the book of Second Samuel chapter twenty-four, we read that he was 'conscience-stricken'. He then confessed his sin to the Lord and asked the Lord to take away his guilt. Until he had done that he suffered greatly, "for day and night your hand was heavy upon me; my strength was dried up as by the heat of summer. I acknowledged my sin to you, and I did not cover my iniquity; I said, 'I will confess my transgressions to the LORD,' and you forgave the iniquity of my sin" (Ps. 32:4-5).

1. David's conscience told him that both adultery and murder were wrong; but
2. He planned to do this even though he *knew* that it was wrong.
3. David went against his conscience and sinned by doing what he knew was wrong.
4. He was 'conscience-stricken'. His conscience accused him of doing the wrong thing; and
5. He felt guilt in his heart and great remorse that he had sinned.
6. His guilt caused him much suffering, including the sapping of his strength and the feeling that God's hand was 'heavy' upon him; so

7. He confessed his sin to the Lord and asked the Lord to take away his guilt; then
8. The Lord forgave David his sin and cleansed his heart from guilt.

When Adam and Eve sinned against God, their consciences accused them and caused them to feel guilty. They tried to cover up their sin and hide from God. God sought them out and required a confession of sin from them. There were consequences for that sin and a price had to be paid, but through God's mercy, grace, and love, there was forgiveness for that sin and the removal of the guilt that was in the hearts of Adam and Eve. Sadly though, the closeness they had experienced before with their Creator was gone and they had entered a state of spiritual separation from God. They had become sinners.

We are all sinners "for all have sinned and fall short of the glory of God" (Rom. 3:23 NKJV). We have all sinned against God's Law and against our consciences. As a result of sin, we have guilt in our hearts and we need to confess our sins to God and ask for forgiveness. Only God can cleanse the heart from guilt. To have the heart cleansed from guilt by the confession of sins and the forgiveness of God is to have a heart at peace.

How about the unborn, babies, children, or the severely intellectually disabled? What is the state of *their* hearts? Do *they* have a conscience? If they are born with a sinful nature because they have inherited the spirit that has been passed on from Adam down through the generations, does this mean that, if they die, no matter what age they are or what their understanding is, they will be subject to God's judgement as an adult would? God is loving and just. We would expect that there would be mercy and grace shown to them by their heavenly Father; and there is.

We have established that, right from the moment of conception, the child is a complete person. They have a body, they have a spirit, and they have a soul. They are as much a person as you or I. Therefore, no matter how long the life of this little person lasts, whether one minute after conception or one hundred years after birth, they, like us, will exist for eternity.

The Bible tells us that children are not born with the *knowledge of good and evil;* that is, their conscience is not fully developed. They do, however, have a sinful nature—the tendency to sin, which has been inherited through the passing on of the spirit from Adam down through the generations.

There are several references in the Bible to children not yet being of the age of 'knowing good and evil'. In the book of Deuteronomy, Moses and the Israelites were told by God that, because of their disobedience and lack of faith, they would not be allowed to enter the Promised Land. He said that only Joshua, Moses' assistant, Caleb (who had maintained faith in God), and "your children, who today have no knowledge of good or evil" (Deut. 1:39) would be allowed to enter. In other words, the children were not held accountable for the actions of the Israelite community as they did not *know* that what was done by the community was wrong. It was the responsibility of the *adults* to determine what was right and wrong on behalf of the children. The children did not have the guilt of wrongdoing in their hearts as they were not *aware* of any wrongdoing, and therefore their consciences had not convicted them of sin.

In the book of Isaiah, there is a passage of Scripture foretelling the birth of the coming Messiah:
> Therefore the Lord himself will give you a sign. Behold, the virgin shall conceive and bear a son, and shall call his name Immanuel. He shall eat curds and honey when he knows how to refuse the evil and choose the good. For before the boy knows how to refuse the evil and choose the good, the land whose two kings you dread will be deserted.
>
> —Isa. 7:14-16

From this passage, it is clear that there comes a point when a person's conscience is mature enough to know 'how to refuse the evil and choose the good'. This knowledge of good and evil is something that develops with time, experience of life, and maturity. *The New International Version* translates this as 'knowing enough to reject the wrong and choose the right'. This knowledge of good and evil then, comes at a point in life when the person 'knows enough'. Through Moses, God gave the Israelites many laws, rules, and regulations to assist them in knowing right from wrong, so that they were without excuse. Knowing these laws meant that their consciences would tell them what was right and what was wrong. The little children would have had little or no knowledge of these laws and their consciences would not have been fully developed or mature.

The physical body has a system of cause and effect. Even though the spiritual body is not visible to our physical eyes, there is no reason why the *spiritual* body should not also have a system of cause and effect, or an actual process or mechanism occurring, such as the closing or opening of the spiritual heart to God.

When God breathed the breath of life into Adam's body creating his soul, a part of which was his heart, Adam's heart was open to God allowing a spiritual connection to God. That was how our hearts were made to be. It is the original design of the heart—open plan if you like!

When the spirit of life infuses the physical substance of the new human being at the point of conception, the soul, and therefore the spiritual heart, is formed in the same way as was Adam's. The difference between Adam and the new life conceived is that Adam's spirit was formed by the breath of God which was breathed in through his nostrils and was pure, whereas a baby's spirit is formed from the spiritual seed that is passed on to them from the previous generation. As Adam and Eve were to reproduce after their own kind, it would be likely that each new generation would begin life with an *open* spiritual heart.

It was only when Adam and Eve ate from the Tree of the Knowledge of Good and Evil, that their hearts became closed to their Creator. This 'knowing of good and evil', this lack of faith in God, this choice of independence from God's Spirit and reliance on self, caused the closing over of Adam and Eve's spiritual hearts.

If the spiritual heart of a child is still open to God up until a certain point in their maturity and understanding, that is, the point in time when they are mature enough to 'know good and evil', their conscience is developed, and they are capable of experiencing the guilt of sin, it is likely that if they then choose to go their own way independent of God, there would be a closing over of the spiritual heart. At a point in the child's life, the child would develop a 'knowledge of good and evil', an understanding of what is right and wrong, a knowledge of accountability to a higher authority—their Creator, and an awareness of being answerable for their actions. Their conscience would become fully functional.

As the closing of the heart is an individual action, it is unlikely that there would be a set age when this would happen. Similarly, a baby can be born and be independent from the mother at a wide range of gestational periods from, say, twenty-four weeks to forty-two weeks. In the case of someone who is intellectually unable to develop this knowledge of good and evil, the closing of the heart may never happen and they would remain under God's grace for the remainder of their lives.

At the point in a person's life when they are old enough to know how to 'refuse the evil and choose the good', one of two things would be possible:
1. Their heart would *close* as they would choose dependence on *self* as did Adam and Eve; or
2. If they had, at some point prior to this, come to faith in God, their hearts would remain *open* to God as they would have become connected to the source of eternal life through the indwelling of the Holy Spirit.

Jesus gave a very strong warning about our responsibility to little ones who do not yet know good and evil. He said that "whoever causes one of these little ones who believe in me to sin, it would be better for him if a great millstone were hung around his neck and he were thrown into the sea" (Mark 9:42). That is pretty drastic! But Jesus was warning us that we have a responsibility to bring up these little ones to know and *continue* to believe in Him so that there would not be a point at which they became lost. To never be lost or out of the protection and care of God at all is better than to *become* lost and then *found again*. To become lost and *never* be found again, and consequently to *never* be connected to the source of life—our Creator and heavenly Father, is the greatest tragedy of all.

Jesus said that the children 'believed in him'. These children that Jesus was referring to at that time were most likely from a variety of backgrounds. Some would have been brought up in a devout Jewish home where the Scriptures were taught, and some would have perhaps been from rough neighbourhoods whose parents were not believers and who did not follow Jewish teachings or meet at the temple or synagogue. Jesus, however, was implying that *all* the little ones there believed.

The writer of Ecclesiastes, believed to have been King Solomon, said that God has "put eternity into man's heart" (Eccl. 3:11). Each person has the knowledge in their hearts that God exists, that they are answerable to Him, and that their lives are not limited to this small period of time here on the earth. This knowledge or understanding is ingrained in the heart of the child. It is only as the child grows and begins to seek independence from God that they may begin to purposefully block out this knowledge. In Paul's letter to the Romans, he writes:

> For the wrath of God is revealed from heaven against all ungodliness and unrighteousness of men, who by their unrighteousness suppress the truth. For what can be known about God is plain to them, because God has shown it to them. For his invisible attributes, namely, his eternal power and divine nature, have been clearly perceived, ever since the creation of the world, in the things that have been made. So they are without excuse. For although they knew God, they did not honour him as God or give thanks to him, but they became futile in their thinking, and their foolish hearts were darkened.
>
> —Rom. 1:18-21

God has made it plain to *all* people that He exists. It is clear to mankind that the earth and the universe did not just happen of their own accord. There is a Creator—a master designer—Someone far greater than themselves to whom they are accountable. Perhaps it is this thought of being accountable to someone that causes people to block out their inherent knowledge of God.

When children or babies die, born or unborn, where do they go? Jesus said to the disciples: "Let the children come to me; do not hinder them, for to such belongs the kingdom of God" (Mark 10:14). If the kingdom of God belongs to the children, it would mean that the children would continue to remain under God's grace and care if they died at this early age. These little ones would *not* come under the judgement of God, as they are *already* part of God's kingdom.

Jesus also said that children have angels watching over them. He said: "See that you do not despise one of these little ones. For I tell you that in heaven their angels always see the face of my Father who is in heaven" (Matt. 18:10). These angels are held accountable for the little ones in their care. They are acting on behalf of God in a protective role as guardians, particularly in regard to the protection of their open heart. As angels are gatherers of souls when people die, should the little one in their care die, his or her soul would be gathered and received into the loving care of the heavenly Father. This should be of great comfort to those who have lost little ones either in the womb or as infants or children. There would be no better place to grow up than in God's care in heaven, and the knowledge of this should help to ease the grief of those they have left behind.

Immediately after Jesus told the disciples that these guardian angels always see the face of His Father in heaven, He began to tell them a story about sheep. Jesus loved to tell parables. These were stories about everyday events and things in the lives of the people that also had a message in them about God, heaven, or certain spiritual truths. He said to the disciples:

> If a man has a hundred sheep, and one of them has gone astray, does he not leave the ninety-nine on the mountains and go in search of the one that went astray? And if he finds it, truly, I say to you, he rejoices over it more than over the ninety-nine that never went astray. So it is not the will of my Father who is in heaven that one of these little ones should perish.
>
> —Matt. 18:12-14

Clearly, this parable is talking about the little children. The sheep in the parable are under the shepherd's care in the same way that children are under God's grace and care. They are safe, they are watched over. Then one of the sheep goes astray in the same way that a child, on reaching the age of knowing enough to choose the good and reject the evil seeks to go his own way, and live a life independent from God. This one sheep was not lost to begin with. It started out in the flock with the other sheep. The shepherd goes in search of this one sheep, finds it, brings it back and rejoices over it, just as God rejoices over a sinner who repents and comes back to Him. Away from the shepherd's care the sheep would have perished, as would the sinner outside of God's care. Once found, it is safe again, back in the sheepfold under the protection of the shepherd.

There is then, a point in a person's life when a he or she may choose independence from God and wander away like the sheep in the parable. The person would then no longer be covered by God's grace. Sadly, this is what most people do. As little children they have been under the grace of God even though they are not fully aware of this, but, if later they choose to go their own way, they will no longer be under the protection of their loving heavenly Father. God seeks to bring them back into His family, into His 'sheepfold' where they will be safe, and if they return to Him, He rejoices greatly over them.

A similar parable to the parable of the sheep is told of a woman with ten silver coins: "What woman, having ten silver coins, if she loses one coin, does not light a lamp and sweep the house and seek diligently until she finds it?" (Luke 15:8). Again, the coin was not lost to begin with. It started out with the other nine silver coins but then *became* lost. God seeks to save those who become lost.

It is immediately after the telling of this parable that Jesus told the story of the prodigal son. It is a story of a man who had two sons. The younger one decided that he wanted his share of the father's fortune. The father gave him half of his property and the son left the family home, went off to a distant land, and squandered the money on wild living, having no regard for his father. It was as if this son were dead. The other son stayed in the family home with his father. After some time the money ran out for the younger son and he realised that he was no longer having a good time and that where he really belonged was at home with his father. He set out to return to his father. His father saw him coming and ran out to embrace him. He celebrated with a great feast in honour of the younger son. The older son was angry that the father had done this for his brother when all along he himself had been loyal and always at the father's side but his father said to him: "Son, you are always with me, and all that is mine is yours. It was fitting to celebrate and be glad, for this your brother was dead, and is alive; he was lost, and is found" (Luke 15:31-32).

Both of these brothers were brought up in the father's care and under the father's protection, being a part of the father's household. One son chose to remove himself from under the father's care and protection and to go his own way, in effect disowning his father and choosing independence. As children, we are safe in our heavenly Father's care. We are under His grace. Many will, like the younger brother, choose not to *remain* in that care. They will choose to seek independence from the Father; to seek the pleasures of the world. They want everything and they want it *now*. They want earthly treasures and good times and whatever this world can offer. They do not want to wait for 'treasures in heaven' or promises of blessings that seem a long way off.

Like the prodigal son, who was as if dead to his father, most people are spiritually dead and are disconnected from God—the source of eternal life. God seeks to connect them to Himself through His Spirit, and to bring them back under His care and protection. When anyone who was dead in their sins and lost to God returns, just like the father of the prodigal son rejoiced, there is great rejoicing in heaven. Jesus tells us that "there is joy before the angels of God over one sinner who repents" (Luke 15:10). That person will be restored to God, just like the prodigal son was restored to *his* father.

THE DESTINY

Upon physical death when the heart ceases to beat and the person breathes their last breath, the soul and the spirit depart the body and, by default, will separate from each other. Scripture tells us that "the spirit returns to God who gave it" (Eccl. 12:7).

From the time of the first human death (that of Abel, the son of Adam and Eve) up to the time of Jesus' death and resurrection, the souls, along with the hearts, of *all* who died would go to the abode of the dead (excepting those who have not yet developed the knowledge of good and evil). This is still the place where *most* people will go when they die, to await judgement.

HERE'S WHAT WE NEED:

We are in need of a new heart—a heart cleansed from the guilt of sin and open to God—our Creator, our heavenly Father, and the source of life. Without a new heart cleansed from the guilt of sin, we cannot have a new spirit, because the new spirit would not be able to dwell in an unclean heart. The spirit we need is one that is *not* subject to the law of sin and death, one that will connect us with the life of God and will therefore save us from death by giving life to our souls—eternal life!

Part Two

The Others

Chapter Five
Angels

Now that we have had a good look at *ourselves*, it is time to learn a little about the other occupants in our space-time-matter universe. It is easy to sometimes forget that we are not the only ones who inhabit the world that God has created. We will now embark on an investigation of the spirit world.

Throughout the centuries, people have been fascinated with angels. Angels are well represented in the world of literature—in prose and poetry and in the arts, often being depicted in paintings and sculptures. They also feature widely on greeting cards and lapel pins. People believe that it is the job of angels to protect them and watch over them as guardians. Bumper stickers, possibly designed by the local highway patrol branch of the law enforcement, warn people not to go faster than their angel can fly!

Angels are generally portrayed as female, winged, and dressed in white, with halos on their heads. Often people imagine angels to be a sort of fairy-like creature—delicate and wispy with long golden hair, or perhaps chubby and cute with short curly hair playing a little harp or shooting an arrow from a bow to make one human fall in love with another. In order to sort out fact from fantasy, let us take a look at what God's Word tells us about the spirit world that He created...

THE ORIGIN

When were angels created? One of the main roles of angels is to minister to the people that God created to inhabit the earth. To fulfil this purpose, they would have had to be created *before* man. The very first verse in the Bible tells us that "in the beginning God created the heavens and the earth" (Gen. 1:1). The heavens are inhabited by the angels, so angels are not likely to have been created *prior* to the heavens being created, however, the book of Job implies that the angels were there to rejoice with God at the ordering of the elements which gave form to the earth. The Lord asked Job: "Where were you when I laid the earth's foundation? . . . On what were its footings set, or who laid its cornerstone—while the morning stars sang together and all the angels shouted for joy?" (Job 38:4, 6 NIV).

This narrows down the likely timeframe for the creation of angels to the period of time between the initial bringing into existence the elements of the space-time-matter universe and the formation of the elements into order. This is confirmed in the book of Ezekiel where Satan, a fallen angel, is described as having been "in Eden, the garden of God; every precious stone was your covering, sardius, topaz, and diamond, beryl, onyx, and jasper, sapphire, emerald, and carbuncle; and crafted in gold were your settings and your engravings. On the day that you were created they were prepared" (Ezek. 28:13). It seems that Satan, and therefore angels, must have been created on the same day as these precious jewels were created.

God is spirit. The psalmist tells us that "by the word of the LORD the heavens were made, and by the breath of his mouth all their host" (Ps. 33:6). Spirit comes from spirit. Angels are spiritual in substance or form. Angels are sometimes referred to in Scripture as starry hosts, celestial beings, hosts of heaven, sons of God, stars, morning stars, or messengers.

The Bible is not specific about the number of angels that God created but, in the letter to the Hebrews the writer tells believers that they have come to "Mount Zion, to the heavenly Jerusalem, the city of the living God. You have come to thousands upon thousands of angels in joyful assembly" (Heb. 12:22 NIV). In the book of Revelation, the apostle John is given a vision of angels around the throne of Jesus in heaven, praising and worshipping Him. They were "numbering thousands upon thousands, and ten thousand times ten thousand" (Rev. 5:11 NIV). It is unlikely that these numbers are the exact number of angels, but rather that the writers were trying to convey the *vastness* of the number of angels—too many to count!

The number of angels is limited to the number originally created. They do not reproduce with each other and, after God finished His work of Creation at the end of day six, no additional angels were made.

THE NATURE

Angels are spirit, therefore they have life. Angels are individuals and have thoughts, personalities, emotions, and feelings, therefore they must have souls.

Angels rejoice. The Bible tells us that "there is rejoicing in the presence of the angels of God over one sinner who repents" (Luke 15:10 NIV). Angels can discern good and evil. They also have free will. They, like humans, can choose to love and obey God or choose not to do so. God loves angels. We read in the book of Zechariah that "the LORD answered gracious and comforting words to the angel" (Zech. 1:13) who came and reported to Him.

Angels are more intelligent and more powerful than humans and they have greater wisdom. The psalmist tells us that God made man "a little lower than the heavenly beings" (Ps. 8:5). Angels can only be in one place at a time, and they do not know everything. They do not have knowledge of the future or knowledge of the time of the end of the ages. They only know what has been revealed to them by God.

Angels are not to be worshipped. When the apostle John fell down at the feet of the angel who had brought him the revelation given to him by Jesus, the angel said to him: "You must not do that! I am a fellow servant with you and your brothers who hold to the testimony of Jesus. Worship God" (Rev. 19:10). In comparing the angels to God their Creator, the psalmist asks: "For who in the skies can be compared to the LORD? Who among the heavenly beings is like the LORD, a God greatly to be feared in the council of the holy ones, and awesome above all who are around him?" (Ps. 89:6-7).

Angels always appear in the Scriptures in *male* form, never female. Certainly the disobedient angels who procreated with human women were male. Although in this 'modern' and 'enlightened' age there are those who prefer to avoid assigning a gender to God or to angels, this does not change the fact that angels in the Bible are portrayed as male and God is always 'He', and has the title of 'Father'.

In heaven angels eat. We are told in the book of Psalms that their food includes manna—also referred to in the Bible as the 'grain of heaven' or the 'bread of angels'. This is the food which God rained down from heaven for the Israelites to eat on their forty-year journey through the desert to the Promised Land. It was described as being sweet like honey.

Although angels are of the *spirit* world, there are four ways that angels can appear in our *physical* world:
1. They are able to appear in physical form by materialising—taking on material or tangible form. Angels may look very similar to humans and may even be mistaken for humans. The writer of Hebrews cautions us: "Do not neglect to show hospitality to strangers, for thereby some have entertained angels unawares" (Heb. 13:2). Angels may appear taller and stronger than the average human. As mentioned, there is no biblical evidence that they appear in female likeness.
2. On occasions, people may be enabled by God to see the spirit world with their spiritual eyes;
3. Angels can appear in dreams and visions; and
4. Angels are able to take over the bodies of people or animals by 'possession' or 'demonization'. This is only done by demons or fallen angels and is prohibited by God.

This chapter and the following one will examine a number of examples given in the Bible of each of these manifestations.

THE ROLE OF ANGELS

Angels have ranks. There are those with greater authority and splendour than others. There are also different roles assigned to different angels including:

FACE TO FACE MESSENGERS—There are angels that have the special task of announcing an important event or bringing news or messages to people. On one occasion, for example, Abraham had the privilege of entertaining angels who had come to bring him a message. They ate food in his presence. The archangel Gabriel appeared to announce to Zechariah that, in their old age, his wife Elizabeth would give birth to a son, John, who would have the task of preparing the way for the promised Messiah. Gabriel later appeared to Mary to give her the news that she would be the mother of God's Son—the promised Messiah, who would save the people from their sins. An angel announced the birth of Jesus to some shepherds who were tending their flock and then there appeared "a multitude of the heavenly host praising God" (Luke 2:13). The last book in the Bible—the book of Revelation, was made known to John through an angel sent to him by Jesus.

MESSENGERS IN DREAMS AND VISIONS—There are a number of examples of angels appearing in dreams and visions to people. An angel appeared to Joseph in a dream to confirm to him that Mary was with child through the Holy Spirit, and later appeared in a dream to warn Joseph to take Jesus to Egypt to flee from King Herod who was seeking to kill the child. Angels appeared in dreams to Jacob. "He dreamed, and behold, there was a ladder set up on the earth, and the top of it reached to heaven. And behold, the angels of God were ascending and descending on it!" (Gen. 28:12). Later we read that Jacob "went on his way, and the angels of God met him" (Gen. 32:1). Angels can appear in visions as one did to King Nebuchadnezzar, who told Daniel: "I saw in the visions of my head as I lay in bed, and behold, a watcher, a holy one, came down from heaven" (Dan. 4:13). Angels are used to explain the meaning of visions or dreams to people. For example, Daniel had a vision of the time of the end and the angel Gabriel explained the meaning of the vision to him.

SERVING GOD—Angels serve and worship God around his throne in heaven. There is a special class of angel called cherubim and seraphim. They are the only ones whom the Bible refers to as having wings. The prophet Isaiah had a dream in which he "saw the Lord sitting upon a throne, high and lifted up; and the train of his robe filled the temple. Above him stood the seraphim. Each had six wings: with two he covered his face, and with two he covered his feet, and with two he flew. And one called to another and said: 'Holy, holy, holy is the LORD of hosts; the whole earth is full of his glory!'" (Isa. 6:1-3). It was cherubim whom God placed in the Garden of Eden to prevent Adam and Eve from accessing the Tree of Life after they had been banished from the garden.

GATHERING SOULS—When the righteous in the Old Testament died, they were said to be 'gathered to their people'. Jesus told a story of two men—a rich man and a beggar, who both died. The beggar was carried or gathered "to Abraham's side" (Luke 16:22). This job of gathering souls and escorting them to the abode of the dead is the task of angels.

Before the time of Jesus' death, angels would escort the souls of the righteous to Sheol. These were those who had faith in God and in the coming Messiah. Although believers will go to heaven when they die because they have the Holy Spirit in their hearts, it is possible that they may also be escorted there by angels as is recorded as happening to the righteous in Old Testament times.

HEAVENLY COUNSEL—God holds counsel with the angels, they are able to make suggestions at this counsel, and it appears that there may be 'planning committees' held in heaven on certain matters, such as in the case of King Ahab:

And Micaiah said, "Therefore hear the word of the LORD: I saw the LORD sitting on his throne, and all the host of heaven standing beside him on his right hand and on his left; and the LORD said, 'Who will entice Ahab, that he may go up and fall at Ramoth-gilead?' And one said one thing, and another said another. Then a spirit came forward and stood before the LORD, saying, 'I will entice him.' And the LORD said to him, 'By what means?' And he said, 'I will go out, and will be a lying spirit in the mouth of all his prophets.' And he said, 'You are to entice him, and you shall succeed; go out and do so.' Now therefore behold, the LORD has put a lying spirit in the mouth of all these your prophets; the LORD has declared disaster for you."

—1 Kings 22:19-23

It is clear that the Lord has control over the decision, yet the angels seem to have a say and are able to express opinions and suggest ideas which may, or may not, be acted upon. Angels are often sent out from the throne of God on a mission for a particular purpose.

COMFORT AND ENCOURAGEMENT—Angels are sometimes sent to comfort and give courage to God's people. The apostle Paul, for example, was visited by an angel who encouraged him prior to his trial before Caesar. Angels can be sent to minister to people. The writer of the book of Hebrews asks: "Are they not all ministering spirits sent out to serve for the sake of those who are to inherit salvation?" (Heb. 1:14). It should be noted that they are only sent to serve *this* particular group of people—not *all* people. When Elijah was in the desert, an angel brought him food to eat. When Jesus was in the Garden of Gethsemane in great anguish the night before He was crucified, "there appeared to him an angel from heaven, strengthening him" (Luke 22:43).

PROTECTION—Angels protect people. Michael is the name of the archangel who is the protector of Israel. The angels who are protectors of children are known as 'guardian angels'. David wrote that "the angel of the LORD encamps around those who fear him, and delivers them" (Ps. 34:7). No such promises are made to those who do *not* fear the Lord no matter how many lapel pins they wear or how many 'I believe in angels' bumper stickers are on their car! God commands angels to guard the *righteous* and protect the *righteous* from harm. David wrote: "He will command his angels concerning you to guard you in all your ways. On their hands they will bear you up, lest you strike your foot against a stone" (Ps. 91:11-12).

RESURRECTION—Angels were involved in the resurrection of Jesus. After Jesus had died, His body was placed in a tomb and a heavy stone was rolled across the entrance. The tomb was guarded by soldiers so that no-one could come and steal His body. On the third day, "there was a great earthquake, for an angel of the Lord descended from heaven and came and rolled back the stone and sat on it. His appearance was like lightning, and his clothing white as snow. And for fear of him the guards trembled and became like dead men" (Matt. 28:2-4). This angel spoke to the two women who had come to the tomb and told them that Jesus was alive! Angels must be very strong, for only *one* was needed to roll the heavy stone away. Angels can be dazzling in appearance and their presence can provoke great fear. Later, Mary returned to the tomb after telling the disciples what she had seen and heard. When she looked inside the tomb she "saw two angels in white, sitting where the body of Jesus had lain, one at the head and one at the feet" (John 20:12).

RESCUE—Angels are experts in the art of 'prison break'! In the book of Acts, there is an account recorded where the apostles were arrested by the authorities and placed in prison, "but during the night an angel of the Lord opened the prison doors and brought them out, and said, 'Go and stand in the temple and speak to the people all the words of this Life'" (Acts 5:19-20).

Another time, the apostle Peter was arrested, bound with chains, and put in prison with guards at the door:

> And behold, an angel of the Lord stood next to him, and a light shone in the cell. He struck Peter on the side and woke him, saying, "Get up quickly." And the chains fell off his hands. And the angel said to him, "Dress yourself and put on your sandals." And he did so. And he said to him, "Wrap your cloak around you and follow me." And he went out and followed him. He did not know that what was being done by the angel was real, but thought he was seeing a vision. When they had passed the first and the second guard, they came to the iron gate leading into the city. It opened for them of its own accord, and they went out and went along one street, and immediately the angel left him. When Peter came to himself, he said, "Now I am sure that the Lord has sent his angel and rescued me from the hand of Herod and from all that the Jewish people were expecting."
>
> —Acts 12:7-11

SPIRITUAL WARFARE—Angels are often engaged in battle on behalf of God's people. There are battles in the heavenly realms in the spirit world that we are totally unaware of. For example, when Joshua was near Jericho he met an angel who was standing in front of him who had a drawn sword in his hand and described himself as "commander of the army of the LORD" (Josh. 5:14).

When soldiers came to arrest Jesus and lead Him to His death, Peter drew his sword and cut off the ear of one of the soldiers. Jesus rebuked him and healed the man's ear, saying to Peter: "Do you think that I cannot appeal to my Father, and he will at once send me more than twelve legions of angels?" (Matt. 26:53).

In the book of Second Kings, there is an account of a servant of Elisha being enabled to see the Lord's army. "Elisha prayed and said, 'O LORD, please open his eyes that he may see.' So the LORD opened the eyes of the young man, and he saw, and behold, the mountain was full of horses and chariots of fire all around Elisha" (2 Kings 6:17). The servant was able to see that there was a mighty army on their side and was then greatly reassured.

An angel was instrumental in the defeat of the Assyrian army. God said: "'I will defend this city to save it, for my own sake and for the sake of my servant David.' And the angel of the LORD went out and struck down 185,000 in the camp of the Assyrians. And when people arose early in the morning, behold, these were all dead bodies" (Isa. 37:35-36).

The army of the Lord is no small battalion. In fact, "the chariots of God are tens of thousands and thousands of thousands" (Ps. 68:17 NIV). When King David was amassing his army, it is recorded that "from day to day men came to David to help him, until there was a great army, like an army of God" (1 Chr. 12:22).

TERRITORIAL ASSIGNMENT—Angels may be assigned to individual churches. We read in the book of Revelation that John was instructed to write messages to the angels of seven churches. The messages were of relevance to the people of those churches and to the church body throughout the following centuries, but they were addressed to the *angels* of the churches. There may also be angels who are assigned a specific territory, town, city, or even a country. There are also demons assigned these places by Satan.

ADMINISTRATION OF GOD'S WRATH—Angels can be used by God to bring punishment and death, such as when the angel of death passed through the houses of the Egyptians killing every firstborn son. In the book of Acts, we read that, "because Herod did not give praise to God, an angel of the Lord struck him down, and he was eaten by worms and died" (Acts 12:23 NIV). In end times, angels are active in administering the wrath of God against mankind in the form of disasters and plagues. They are seen to blow trumpets, open seals to reveal what is about to take place on the earth, and open and read scrolls.

Angels can cause an affliction, for example, blindness. Before God destroyed the cities of Sodom and Gomorrah because of their wickedness, two angels arrived at Sodom and they struck some men with blindness to prevent them from finding the door to a house.

HERE'S WHAT WE NEED:

Angels are part of the spiritual world that we cannot usually see. God created them for a purpose—to minister to humans. God's design was that people and angels should interact with each other in the way in which He had intended, and that together they should honour and glorify Him.

When God created Adam and Eve, they would have been able to see and hear angels and communicate and interact with them all the time, rather than this being the exception. They had the ability to see with spiritual eyes and hear with spiritual ears. This ability was taken away from them when they sinned. Their physical bodies no longer worked in harmony with their spiritual bodies. Their physical eyes were 'opened' and their spiritual eyes were effectively closed. Their world had narrowed.

What we need is a renovation! Imagine seeing and communicating with angels. For this to happen, we would need our spiritual eyes and ears to be 're-opened'. We would need new spirits throughout our entire bodies, and we would need renewed bodies that would function in perfect harmony with our spiritual bodies. We would need a return to the original order of Creation as it was in the beginning when humans were aware of angels and they both lived in harmony in God's beautiful and perfect world without the constraints or the consequences of sin; both praising their maker and enjoying Him forever.

Chapter Six
Satan and Demons

Just as the physical world is no longer in the state in which it was intended to be, neither is the spiritual world. Like mankind, angels were created with a free will. They have the choice to love, trust, and obey God, or to disobey God and remove themselves from under His divine grace and care. Unlike human beings however, angels cannot be saved or redeemed once they have fallen. We will now investigate what the Scriptures tell us about the fall of angels.

THE ORIGIN

Satan was called Lucifer when he was created. He was a guardian cherub, ranking high in the order of angels. Being a cherub he is likely to have wings rather than horns and a pitchfork! He was powerful and beautiful, but he soon became proud and boastful, jealous of God his Creator and discontent with his position. The apostle Paul said that the devil became "conceited" (1 Tim. 3:6 NIV). He wanted to be 'boss'. This was likely brought on by jealousy over the creation of man. Satan wanted to be worshipped.

Angels, like humans, are *not* created to be worshipped. They are *part* of Creation. They are *not* the Creator! The book of Ezekiel gives an account of the creation and fall of Satan, describing his beauty when he was created, his position and ranking, and his pride leading to his rebellion and fall:

> You were the signet of perfection, full of wisdom and perfect in beauty. You were in Eden, the garden of God; every precious stone was your covering, sardius, topaz, and diamond, beryl, onyx, and jasper, sapphire, emerald, and carbuncle; and crafted in gold were your settings and your engravings. On the day that you were created they were prepared. You were an anointed guardian cherub. I placed you; you were on the holy mountain of God; in the midst of the stones of fire you walked. You were blameless in your ways from the day you were created, till unrighteousness was found in you. In the abundance of your trade you were filled with violence in your midst, and you sinned; so I cast you as a profane thing from the mountain of God, and I destroyed you, O guardian cherub, from the midst of the stones of fire. Your heart was proud because of your beauty; you corrupted your wisdom for the sake of your splendour. I cast you to the ground; I exposed you before kings, to feast their eyes on you.
>
> —Ezek. 28:12-17

The prophet Isaiah, in speaking of Lucifer, or Satan, wrote: "You said in your heart, 'I will ascend to heaven; above the stars of God I will set my throne on high; I will sit on the mount of assembly in the far reaches of the north; I will ascend above the heights of the clouds; I will make myself like the Most High'" (Isa. 14:13-14). God, of course, did not allow this to happen, and Satan led a rebellion of angels (one third of them) against God. The book of Revelation tells of a great red dragon, symbolic of Satan, whose "tail swept down a third of the stars of heaven and cast them to the earth" (Rev. 12:4). These fallen angels are also known as 'demons'.

When did the fall of angels occur? At the end of day six of creation, "God saw everything that he had made, and behold, it was very good" (Gen. 1:31). As God made the angels, and at this stage He is proclaiming all of Creation to be 'very good', this would have to include *all* the angels as they are a part of Creation—a part of what God has made. The rebellion and fall of Satan and one third of the angels happened sometime *after* day six of creation but *before* the fall of man as Satan was present in the Garden of Eden in his role as tempter.

THE NATURE

Satan, in contrast to God, can only be in one place at a time. For example, at the time when the vision, which is recorded in the book of The Revelation of Jesus Christ, was given to the apostle John, Satan's location was in a place called Pergamum. John writes to the church in Pergamum: "I know where you dwell, where Satan's throne is" (Rev. 2:13). Satan is limited by the ability of demons to report to him on what is happening in the world based on what *they* see or hear from their various locations. God, in contrast, can be everywhere at the same time through the Holy Spirit. Not only that, but He has double the manpower, or more correctly 'angel-power' that Satan does! Outnumbered two to one!

Satan does not know everything. God does. Satan does not know the future. Only God does. Satan cannot create. Only God can. Satan is a very powerful being but God is *all*-powerful and He is able to do all things. No contest! There is no one greater than God and "he does as he pleases with the powers of heaven and the peoples of the earth" (Dan. 4:35 NIV). Satan has no power over God or over the Lord Jesus whom the apostle Peter tells us "has gone into heaven and is at the right hand of God, with angels, authorities, and powers having been subjected to him" (1 Pet. 3:22). The devil, however, "has the power of death" (Heb. 2:14).

God has power over Satan and demons and can use them for His purposes if He so desires. This could be to teach a lesson to someone, to humble the proud and haughty, to test, or to punish. For example, Paul speaks of some who had been believers but who had then gone on to reject their faith and their good conscience and so have "made shipwreck of their faith, among whom are Hymenaeus and Alexander, whom I have handed over to Satan that they may learn not to blaspheme" (1 Tim. 1:19-20). Paul also writes of a man in the church who, because of his sexual immorality, Paul tells the elders that they are to "deliver this man to Satan for the destruction of the flesh, so that his spirit may be saved in the day of the Lord" (1 Cor. 5:5). It would appear that the Holy Spirit had told Paul that this particular man would only reach the point of repentance after he had sunk even deeper into immorality, influenced by Satan. Only then would he truly see how wretched he had become and seek forgiveness and restoration.

Satan has many facets to his character and therefore is active, along with demons, in many roles, which we will now examine. Being confined to the limitations of one chapter, this is by no means comprehensive or exhaustive.

THE TEMPTER

We have read of Satan's role of tempter in the Garden of Eden leading to the fall of man, but at the very beginning of Jesus' ministry, Satan also tried to tempt Him. After Jesus was baptised by John the Baptist, He went out into the desert for forty days where He had nothing to eat. During this time, the devil came and tried to tempt Jesus with food, earthly kingdoms, earthly authority and power, and independence from God His Father if Jesus would only worship Satan. He also tried to tempt Jesus to test God and quoted Scripture, just as he tempted Eve to test what God had said by quoting, or rather misquoting, God. Same tricks as in the Garden of Eden. Jesus, unlike Adam and Eve, was not drawn into temptation, and quoted back Scripture to the devil—accurately of course, and the devil left Him.

There is an account recorded in the book of Job where Satan came with the angels to present himself before God: "Now there was a day when the sons of God came to present themselves before the LORD, and Satan also came among them. The LORD said to Satan, 'From where have you come?' Satan answered the LORD and said, 'From going to and fro on the earth, and from walking up and down on it'" (Job 1:6-7). Fallen angels and Satan are still accountable to God and are required to report or present themselves to God. Job was a man of great faith whom God described as a "blameless and upright man, who fears God and turns away from evil" (Job 1:8). Satan is of the opinion that this 'blamelessness' and 'uprightness' that Job has in his character would only be there for as long as God protected him, blessed him and his household, and did not allow anything to happen to him. Satan believed that if disaster were to strike Job, he would curse God and lose faith in God. Satan is given permission by God to test this theory and consequently, Job loses his children, his health, and his wealth. Satan uses these disasters to attempt to tempt Job into sinning against God. Satan does *not* get the satisfaction of this happening and Job does *not* curse God.

At the end of the period of testing, throughout which Job continues to honour God with his words and deeds, all things are eventually restored to him. Satan is shown to be wrong in his assumptions about Job's faith, thus proving that he does *not* have the ability to see the future. If he *had* known the end results, it is unlikely that he would have requested permission from God to test Job in the first place. Only God knew what would happen and He knew that Job would remain faithful. Not only that, Job proved that it *is* possible to stand up to the temptations of the devil!

THE INFILTRATOR

Angels are not able to reproduce with each other and their number is limited. They are always referred to in Scripture as being male. However, although they are not able to reproduce with *each other*, in the time immediately before the flood we read of an account of angels, called here 'sons of God', reproducing with human women:

> The sons of God saw that the daughters of man were attractive. And they took as their wives any they chose. Then the LORD said, "My Spirit shall not abide in man forever, for he is flesh: his days shall be 120 years." The Nephilim were on the earth in those days, and also afterward, when the sons of God came in to the daughters of man and they bore children to them. These were the mighty men who were of old, the men of renown.
>
> —Gen. 6:2-4

This was an act of wicked disobedience on the part of the angels and was far from God's plan of the natural order of things. Angels and humans were not created to procreate together. Obviously though, this was possible, and, although the mechanism by which this occurred would be speculative, it seems likely that the angels took on human form, or materialised, for this abomination to occur.

A new human being is formed by the action of spirit on physical matter. This creates the soul. In this instance however, the DNA which formed the physical body must have come *entirely* from the mother, united with spirit from the angel, and formed a soul. Thus a complete 'person' was formed—a sort of hybrid. This meant that they were not entirely human, nor entirely angel.

To get to the root cause of *why* this happened, we have to remember that Satan's goal is to thwart the saving work of God. He knew of God's plan to bring a Saviour into the world and he knew that it would be through the seed of the woman. God had announced this plan when He was telling Adam and Eve of the consequences of *their* sin and Satan of the consequences of *his* role in their temptation and subsequent disobedience. If Satan could possibly prevent this from happening, he would. By contaminating the human race with 'demon seed' he was attempting to destroy the pure genetic line through which the Saviour would be born.

Straight after this account of the union between demons and women resulting in offspring we read that:

> The LORD saw that the wickedness of man was great in the earth, and that every intention of the thoughts of his heart was only evil continually. And the LORD regretted that he had made man on the earth, and it grieved him to his heart. So the LORD said, "I will blot out man whom I have created from the face of the land, man and animals and creeping things and birds of the heavens, for I am sorry that I have made them." . . . Now the earth was corrupt in God's sight, and the earth was filled with violence. And God saw

the earth, and behold, it was corrupt, for all flesh had corrupted their way on the earth.

—Gen. 6:5-7, 11-12

It was likely that the result of this procreation of angels with humans added to the already great wickedness on the earth to the extent that God's heart was filled with pain and He decided to wipe mankind off the face of the earth.

There was one man however, who was unlike the rest of mankind—Noah. He "found favour in the eyes of the LORD . . . Noah was a righteous man, blameless in his generation. Noah walked with God" (Gen. 6:8-9). It is quite possible that, at this point in history, Noah and his family were in the minority by *not* being contaminated by this demon seed. *Young's Literal Translation* says: "These are the births of Noah: Noah is a righteous man, perfect he hath been among his generations" (Gen. 6:9 YLT).

Perfect—/ per-fuhkt/ *adj.* 1 complete; not deficient. 2 faultless (*a perfect diamond*).[1]

The line of Noah had not been corrupted. It was without fault. The line of his three sons, therefore, would not have been corrupt either, and they were yet to have children of their own. God still had a pure lineage through which the Messiah would come.

God brought a devastating flood upon the whole earth destroying "all flesh in which is the breath of life under heaven. Everything that is on the earth shall die" (Gen. 6:17). Noah and his family were the only people who were saved and "from these the nations spread abroad on the earth after the flood" (Gen. 10:32).

The disobedient angels who took women as wives were to be severely punished for their actions. The apostle Peter speaks of angels being *immediately* punished, possibly referring to these angels. He says that "God did not spare angels when they sinned, but cast them into hell and committed them to chains of gloomy darkness to be kept until the judgment" (2 Pet. 2:4), and Jude tells us that "the angels who did not stay within their own position of authority, but left their proper dwelling, he has kept in eternal chains under gloomy darkness until the judgment of the great day" (Jude 1:6).

THE ACCUSER

We read of Satan's self-appointed role as 'accuser' in the book of Zechariah where we see him standing next to the throne of God to accuse Joshua, Israel's high priest. The Lord rebukes him and puts him in his place. He also did his best to accuse Job of being so weak in his faith that he would curse God if bad things were to happen to him. Does Satan still have access to heaven? At this point in time, according to the book of Revelation, he does. He continues to accuse the people of God before the throne day and night, but Jesus is in heaven at the right hand of God and intercedes on behalf of His people. Satan's accusations against the people of God cannot stand when they have Jesus as their advocate.

THE DESTROYER

One thing that Satan does *not* like is forgiveness. To *not* forgive someone who has wronged you or to not *seek* forgiveness when you have wronged another causes much heartache, malice, resentment, and grief in our relationships with other people. To not seek forgiveness from *God* for wrongdoing affects our relationship with Him.

Paul tells the Corinthians that "if you forgive anyone, I also forgive him. And what I have forgiven—if there was anything to forgive—I have forgiven in the sight of Christ for your sake, in order that Satan might not outwit us. For we are not unaware of his schemes" (2 Cor. 2:10-11 NIV). Satan's scheme is to destroy, not heal. Lack of forgiveness is one of the main issues that will destroy relationships and damage the spiritual heart. Satan's aim is to destroy relationships—to alienate us from God and from each other, and cause bitterness to spring up, resulting in lasting grudges and heartache.

THE DECEIVER

Jesus said that the devil was "a murderer from the beginning, and does not stand in the truth, because there is no truth in him. When he lies, he speaks out of his own character, for he is a liar and the father of lies" (John 8:44). How does Jesus know this? He was there *before* the beginning of time and He told the disciples that He "saw Satan fall like lightning from heaven" (Luke 10:18).

One of Satan's ploys is to blind unbelievers to the truth of God's Word. Paul explains that "the god of this world has blinded the minds of the unbelievers, to keep them from seeing the light of the gospel of the glory of Christ, who is the image of God" (2 Cor. 4:4). How are people blinded to the truth of the gospel? By lies, half-truths, and substitutes for the truth. Often the lies are cleverly disguised and hard to distinguish as lies, "and no wonder, for even Satan disguises himself as an angel of light . . . his servants, also, disguise themselves as servants of righteousness" (2 Cor. 11:14-15).

The devil's lies are nothing new! In Jeremiah's time, God said to the people: "You live in the midst of deception; in their deceit they refuse to acknowledge me" (Jer. 9:6 NIV). Some of the lies that Satan would have people believe include:

— There is no God;
— The universe evolved;
— There are many paths to God;
— There is no spiritual world; and
— Choose your own path—your destiny will be the same.

At the core of Satan's mission is the desire to keep as many people as possible from the truth. He does not mind what religion people follow, what belief they have, or even if they have no belief at all, as long as they are not following the only one who can save their souls. Satan loves an atheist. They are not even searching for God! What does the Word of God say about atheists? "The fool says in his heart, 'There is no God'" (Ps. 14:1).

There is plenty of temptation to dabble in other religions and spiritual practices that God has forbidden. There is a whole smorgasbord out there! It's all the same to Satan as the result will be the same. The person will remain separated from the one true living God—the source of life. One of Satan's biggest lies is that all religions lead to God. That is not what God's Word tells us. Jesus said: "I am the way, the truth and the life. No-one comes to the Father except through me" (John 14:6).

An equally effective lie of Satan's is in the half-truths of some religions or cults, even some organizations that call themselves 'Christian'. Some of what they teach may be correct, but thrown in with the truth may be subtle or perhaps not so subtle, lies, to deceive people. They may *add* something to God's free gift of salvation through faith, say, good deeds. They may remove a very important teaching or truth. For example, rather than Jesus being the Son of God, it might be taught that He was just a prophet and a good man, or even an angel. It might be taught that He was created rather than that He has existed eternally. Their 'worship' of God may be "made up only of rules taught by men" (Isa. 29:13 NIV). They may use a Bible that has had bits added or words changed here and there. God warned: "You shall not add to the word that I command you, nor take from it" (Deut. 4:2). They may use the Bible but hold that another book has equal authority to God's Word or that a church leader or a founder of their 'faith' has equal authority to God.

Some of these organizations may have even started out with the truth of the gospel but then, over time, have added or subtracted from the Word of God, distorting the gospel and misleading followers to the point where they have totally wandered off the path. This is nothing new! It was also happening in the *early* days of the Christian church. Paul wrote to the Galatians:

> I am astonished that you are so quickly deserting him who called you in the grace of Christ and are turning to a different gospel—not that there is another one, but there are some who trouble you and want to distort the gospel of Christ. But even if we or an angel from heaven should preach to you a gospel contrary to the one we preached to you, let him be accursed. As we have said before, so now I say again: If anyone is preaching to you a gospel contrary to the one you received, let him be accursed.
>
> —Gal. 1:6-9

Paul is addressing this part of his letter to those who had once walked in the truth. If Paul had to repeat his warning, then he must have considered it a major problem! Paul also urged believers to "watch out for those who cause divisions and create obstacles contrary to the doctrine that you have been taught; avoid them. For such persons do not serve our Lord Christ, but their own appetites, and by smooth talk and flattery they deceive the hearts of the naïve" (Rom. 16:17-18).

Being the master of deceit, Satan will try to tempt people with riches on earth and a comfortable life, where they rely on 'self' instead of on God. "They spend their days in prosperity, and in peace they go down to Sheol. They say to God, 'Depart from us! We do not desire the knowledge of your ways. What is the Almighty, that we should serve him? And what profit do we get if we pray to him?'" (Job 21:13-15). These are the people whom King David referred to as "men of this world whose reward is in this life" (Ps. 17:14 NIV). They may enjoy position, riches, and earthly power, which might fill them with a sense of their own importance, "but God drags away the mighty by his power; though they become established, they have no assurance of life. He may let them rest in a feeling of security, but his eyes are on their ways" (Job 24:22-23 NIV).

David says that "in his pride the wicked does not seek him; in all his thoughts there is no room for God" (Ps. 10:4 NIV). If there is no room in their thoughts for God, what are they busy thinking of then? How to make money, how to get out of work where possible, what to do in their leisure time that might give them maximum happiness, how to accumulate wealth for their retirement, how to accumulate more property and possessions, their next holiday destination, perhaps the opposite sex (even the same sex!).

This complacency or total disdain for God is not new. In fact, the path is old. Job painted a picture of this disdain for God in *his* day and likened it to the total disregard that people had towards God in the time of the flood, asking of them: "Will you keep to the old way that wicked men have trod? They were snatched away before their time; their foundation was washed away. They said to God, 'Depart from us,' and 'What can the Almighty do to us?'" (Job 22:15-17). Thousands of years later, not much has changed!

Not only does Satan try to keep people *from* the truth, his mission is also to draw away those who are already on the path of salvation and turn them *away* from the truth. One of the biggest deceptions of recent times is the belief that, once you come to faith in the Lord Jesus, no matter what you do, no matter the future state of your heart and no matter whether you continue to believe or not, you can be assured that you will still be saved and go to heaven. Scripture is full of verses and passages that tell us otherwise, and they are difficult to ignore (unless, of course, you don't read them!).

In several places in the Bible, we read about a book called 'the book of life'. This book of life is a record of all those who are to inherit eternal life. Is it possible to have your name in the book and then have it removed? According to Scripture, this *can* happen. Your name *can* be blotted out. A person can come to faith at a point in their lives and then later reject that faith.

Paul writes that "the Spirit expressly says that in later times some will depart from the faith by devoting themselves to deceitful spirits and teachings of demons" (1 Tim. 4:1). Later in this same letter, Paul says that "some have already strayed after Satan" (1 Tim. 5:15). Clearly these people had faith in the first place otherwise they would have had nothing to 'depart from' or 'stray from'. The early church did not take their faith lightly and they certainly did not believe that no matter what a person did after coming to faith, including whether or not they maintained that faith, their salvation was assured. The two issues that are raised by Paul in these passages are that of initially *coming* to faith and then that of either *continuing in* that faith or *turning away from* that faith. These two issues are treated differently in Scripture because they are just that—two *different* issues! The 'modern' church is full of reassurances to those who have fallen away from their faith, giving them a false sense of hope and security.

Jesus often warned about the dangers of going to hell. Who was He addressing these warnings to? A careful examination of the gospels reveals that most of His warnings were given to gatherings of *believers*, often just His disciples. Clearly, if Jesus thought that the danger of *them* turning away from their faith and wandering off the path of life was very real, how much more so the danger to those who are *weak* in their faith.

It is easy for the busyness of day to day life to distract people and draw them away from God, so that at first they may become complacent in their faith and then, over a period of time, forget about God, no longer believe, and eventually lose faith altogether. In their complacency, it is also easy for them to slip back into their old ways, and for their hearts to become so corrupted and unclean with the stain of sin that the Holy Spirit can no longer dwell within them. That is the resultant tragedy of the lie that Satan would have people believe. Most vulnerable to this lie are those who do not have a sound knowledge and understanding of the Scriptures and are listening to those who tell them what their ears want to hear, that is—'all is fine, don't worry, your salvation is assured'.

The best way to be sure that someone falls out of a boat is to convince him that there is nothing that he can do that will cause him to fall out of the boat! Satan loves the 'once saved always saved' deception as it plays right into his hand. We are seeing this deception gain magnitude as the end of the ages approaches because the devil knows that "his time is short" (Rev. 12:12).

God, by His very nature, is loving and gracious. He is a forgiving God—the God of second chances! He knows that we are frail and fickle human beings and that there will be times when our faith is weak and He is able to carry us. He knows that there will be days of doubt and times when we will sin. That is part of the weakness that we have as human beings and part of the consequences of The Fall.

God offers forgiveness and the cleansing of our hearts from sin if we repent and He gives the Holy Spirit to believers to counsel and guide them in their walk. However, God created us with a free will. God never forces faith and belief on anyone or forces them to continue to have faith.

Satan would have people believe that the path of life is wide and edged with guard rails and that there is no chance of slipping off it. Jesus tells us that it is a *narrow* path and faith and diligence is needed to stay on the path. Do not be deceived!

THE DANGER

Demons are instrumental in the practice of magic and witchcraft. They have impressed the easily led with their 'tricks' for thousands of years and have it down to a fine art! For example, when Moses sought to obtain freedom for the Israelites in Egypt, God showed Pharaoh that His power was with Moses through various signs. On seeing this demonstration of the power of God, "Pharaoh summoned the wise men and the sorcerers, and they, the magicians of Egypt, also did the same by their secret arts" (Exod. 7:11).

There are magicians who are genuinely very clever illusionists. They thrill the audience with a sleight of hand. Their skill is their own and has been perfected through years of practice and hard work, turning their abilities into an art form. Then there are imposters who employ the use of demons. These demons are particularly involved in feats such as levitation whereby an object or person is seemingly suspended in mid-air or may move without any visible means to do so. The audience, of course, cannot see the demons that are supporting or moving this person or object. This is also how Ouija board pointers move. Demons are also the force behind automatic writing. Spirit can animate and mobilize matter.

The Israelites were warned that there must be no one among them who "burns his son or his daughter as an offering, anyone who practices divination or tells fortunes or interprets omens, or a sorcerer or a charmer or a medium or a necromancer or one who inquires of the dead" (Deut. 18:10-11). Demons are actively involved in all of these dark practices.

Angels and demons do *not* know the future. A medium, fortune teller, or clairvoyant though, may be able to tell a person certain things that the person would not expect them to know. This may impress the person who is consulting them as it gives the client the illusion that the person they have consulted actually knows things before they happen and knows things about them. They will not realise *how* it is that this person seems to know so much about them or about their family, their deceased loved ones and so on, but the explanation for this is a very simple one if you are aware of how the world of demons operates to deceive the vulnerable.

All angels were created right at the beginning of the creation of the world. There have not been any additional angels created since this time, therefore, all angels, and consequently all demons, are as old as the earth. Because of this, they have seen much—all there is under the sun! Add this to the fact that they are superior in knowledge, understanding, and power to humans and you will begin to get an appreciation of how they are able to 'predict' things through these mediums.

Mediums or psychics receive information from demons to pass on to the person. Demons would pass this on by either speaking to the psychic audibly, but externally, in such a way that the client is unable to hear this, causing various 'signs' to occur such as controlling a roll of the dice, or by speaking through the medium's vocal chords as in the case of demon possession, where the demon actually inhabits the medium's body. They may tell the person that the spirit of their deceased father wants them to know that he is with them and ask something like: 'Does the number eighty-four and the colour blue have any significance to you?' 'Oh yes' the person will exclaim, 'Dad was eighty-four when he died and his favourite colour was blue'! The person goes away from the consultation after handing over a large sum of money, satisfied and believing that 'dear old Dad' is with them. What they do not understand though, is that the psychic did not know this information themselves but was told this information by demons, who have an extensive network and who knew this information about the deceased person.

Satan is the master of deception. He lures many because of the natural curiosity that people have about the future. Habakkuk, an Old Testament prophet, refers to him as the 'wicked foe' who "brings all of them up with a hook; he drags them out with his net; he gathers them in his dragnet; so he rejoices and is glad" (Hab. 1:15).

Not only will psychics claim to know information about someone who has passed away, they will also claim to know the future. Fortune-telling is nothing new. In the New Testament, the apostles encountered just such a person—"a slave girl who had a spirit of divination and brought her owners much gain by fortune-telling" (Acts 16:16). In this case, the fortune-teller was what we would term as being 'possessed' by a demon (a demon dwelt within her).

Fortune-tellers may predict that someone you love is going to have a car accident, for example. This event then becomes a reality, leading the person consulting them to believe that the psychic really does know what is going to happen. Demons have spoken of this event to the psychic and then have caused the event to happen.

Psychics may predict something about someone's health. They may say, for example, that 'someone close to you has a problem with their lungs and will experience a period of ill health'. You may not be aware of any problem and that person may not either but, as these demons have seen everything under the sun, they may have observed a certain subtle sign or symptom in the person that the person themselves may not have even detected. The demons may have seen this symptom enough times in other people over thousands of years to safely predict that there is a disease process going on. They then pass this on to the psychic who amazes the person who is paying and consulting them with their knowledge. Some weeks or months later, they find out that Aunt Bessie has emphysema! The person is very impressed and returns to the psychic for even more readings. This has the effect of emptying the person's pockets, lining the pockets of the psychic, and giving the demons great satisfaction. Why? Because the person is putting their faith in something, or someone, other than God. That is Satan's goal!

Only God knows the future. God says of those who choose to consult demons:
> Let them bring them, and tell us what is to happen. Tell us the former things, what they are, that we may consider them, that we may know their outcome; or declare to us the things to come. Tell us what is to come hereafter, that we

may know that you are gods; do good, or do harm, that we may be dismayed and terrified. Behold, you are nothing, and your work is less than nothing; an abomination is he who chooses you.

—Isa. 41:22-24

THE COUNTERFIETER

In Bible times, people used to worship false gods. Invariably these were not just statues. There were powerful demons behind these religions or practices that even required that people sacrifice to them; often human sacrifice—even their own sons and daughters.

In the book of Second Kings, we read of the messengers of the king of Samaria "going off to consult Baal-Zebub, the god of Ekron" (2 Kings 1:3 NIV). You would not be able to 'consult' a lump of stone or wood. This was a demon that they were consulting. Isaiah wrote in an oracle concerning Egypt: "Behold, the LORD is riding on a swift cloud and comes to Egypt; and the idols of Egypt will tremble at his presence" (Isa. 19:1). These are clearly demons the people are worshipping. Lumps of wood and stone don't tremble. Okay—maybe you could shake them, but that doesn't count!

Demons themselves are under no illusions about the fact that they are false 'gods' and are deceiving people. James says: "You believe that God is one; you do well. Even the demons believe—and shudder!" (James 2:19). Why don't these demons and Satan repent and return to God? Because they know that, for them, there is no salvation. There are no second chances. Unlike man, angels did not *inherit* a sinful nature. Those that rebelled against God individually chose to rebel long ago and they knew the consequences. "The gods who did not make the heavens and the earth shall perish from the earth and from under the heavens . . . They are worthless, a work of delusion; at the time of their punishment they shall perish" (Jer. 10:11, 15). Perhaps they are deceiving themselves into thinking that they have a chance of victory over God. That's not how the 'story' ends, and all of the prophecies in the Bible have so far come to pass. That's a perfect track record!

Many times the Israelites, God's chosen people, turned away from God and served these false gods. Other nations often had their own gods and goddesses, and the people of Israel would become unfaithful to God and serve them instead. They "bowed down to all the starry hosts, and they worshipped Baal" (2 Kings 17:16 NIV). Their unfaithfulness resulted in punishment and banishment from the Promised Land for the Israelites.

The worship of idols or false gods continues today in various guises, some religions having hundreds of 'gods'. But the Bible says: "Ignorant are those who carry about idols of wood, who pray to gods that cannot save" (Isa. 45:20). The book of Habakkuk says: "Woe to him who says to a wooden thing, Awake; to a silent stone, Arise! Can this teach? Behold, it is overlaid with gold and silver, and there is no breath at all in it. But the LORD is in his holy temple; let all the earth keep silence before him" (Hab. 2:19-20). That puts them in their place!

In the end times, God warns that He will bring destruction upon mankind who "did not repent of the works of their hands nor give up worshiping demons and idols of gold and silver and bronze and stone and wood, which cannot see or hear or walk" (Rev. 9:20).

Gold, silver, bronze, iron, or wood, false gods, angels, or demons—none of these can save. Only the one true living God through His Son has the power to save. Paul wrote:

> We know that "an idol has no real existence," and that "there is no God but one." For although there may be so-called gods in heaven or on earth—as indeed there are many "gods" and many "lords"—yet for us there is one God, the Father, from whom are all things and for whom we exist, and one Lord, Jesus Christ, through whom are all things and through whom we exist.
>
> —1 Cor. 8:4-6

Satan has the ability to produce "all kinds of counterfeit miracles, signs and wonders, and . . . every sort of evil that deceives those who are perishing" (2 Thess. 2:9-10 NIV). Demons can cause 'religious' phenomenon to occur, causing statues to weep, blood to pour from wounds, or apparitions to appear. If these phenomenon result in people flocking to and worshipping the statue or the apparition, then the purpose of the demons has been fulfilled; that is, that people are worshipping an *image* rather than the living God.

Another deception of Satan and demons is that of 'aliens'. There is no evidence in the Bible that God created other intelligent life to inhabit other planets or galaxies. God tells us *what* He created and *on which day* of Creation. God's Word only speaks of angels and human beings. Adam is always referred to as the *first* man, Eve is "the mother of all living" (Gen. 3:20), and the Bible clearly says that only the descendants of *Adam* can be saved.

So why do some people claim that they have seen phenomenon in space? Why do some claim that they were abducted by aliens? Demons can take on physical form and deceive people into believing that they are 'aliens'. They have the ability to even take people places, as the spiritual can cause the physical to move (the opposite does not seem to be the case). They can cause strange sights to appear in the sky—lights and shapes that deceive people into believing that they have seen spacecraft.

What would be the purpose of this deception? To call into question our origin and to question the truth and reliability of the Bible. If people believe that we originated from 'aliens', they will not believe the truth of what the Bible says about our origin. You cannot believe both. If people believe that 'aliens' exist and are perhaps a more intelligent form of life, this may lead them to seek out these 'beings', base their lives around hoping for sightings or signs and make this their 'religion'. They become followers. The 'aliens' are then a substitute for God.

Satan loves to be worshipped. That was the reason he rebelled in the first place. He wanted to set himself up in the place of God. Whether people are consciously worshipping Satan or worshipping a *substitute* for God—perhaps a false god, religious leader, aliens, or even themselves, he will be satisfied, as long as people are not worshipping the one true Living God.

THE VICTIMS

In the Bible, there are many accounts of evil spirits, or demons, indwelling people. This is one of the consequences of living in a fallen world where evil exists. Demons can gain entry to a person through various routes including the mouth, the eyes, the ears, and the sexual organs, and they can also be passed on at conception, for example, through generational curses. Often the entry point depends on the cause of the person being open to this demonic entry. For example, demonic entry through pornography may be through the eyes, because it is with the eyes that these images are viewed. Demonic entry through involvement in homosexuality, or other sexual practices apart from that which God intended, that is, between a husband and wife, is likely to be through the sexual organs. Demonic entry through involvement in false religions is likely to be through the heart because the heart is related to faith and belief.

Although there are many activities that can lead to the entry of a demon into a person, due to the vastness of the topic of demonization and demonic oppression, we will primarily focus on that which comes about through false belief systems.

The most common entry point for a demon, or demons, which have entered a person because of false beliefs, is through the heart, likely via the mouth or breath. There are a number of activities that can open a person's heart to this kind of demonic entry. These include, but are not limited to, involvement with the occult and witchcraft, consulting mediums, clairvoyants, witchdoctors, fortune tellers, spiritists, psychics, astrology and consultation of horoscopes, involvement in idol worship, false religions, practices such as mysticism, hypnotism, various forms of meditation, some alternative 'health' practices, astral travel, divination, involvement in cults, use of Ouija boards, or even drug use that involves out of body experiences or alterations in perception. These are very dangerous practices with evil undercurrents and usually people dabbling in these things do not understand just how dangerous they are.

What is it that opens a person's heart to these things? Faith! If someone believes in something that is of a spiritual nature—something or someone that they believe in as being higher spiritually than themselves and they put their faith and trust in this thing, person, or entity, their spiritual heart may open. Their heart was closed in dependence on self. Through faith, albeit *misplaced* faith, their heart will open as they put their trust and belief in a 'higher' spirit. If a person's heart opens because they put their faith and belief in something other than in the truth, then they are very vulnerable to demonic entry. A demon may enter through their breath, through their lungs, and into their body via the heart. This is not to say that *all* who have consulted or been involved with practices of this kind will have demons in them, but by being involved in these practices they will have made themselves very vulnerable to demonic entry.

What about putting your faith in another human being because you believe that that person has special powers, say, in healing? Some people put their faith in 'saints', or people of history that are long dead and pray to them, believing that this departed 'saint' might hear their prayers and answer them or at least speak to God on their behalf, perhaps performing some miracle for them. Although these saints may have been highly respected, perhaps 'religious' people, even those who had genuine faith in God, they are just that ... people. Some people may put their faith in 'aids' to worship—icons, beads, relics or statues; even religious rituals. Others may put their faith in various 'healers' whose 'powers' come from Satan, or in practices linked to false 'religions' and idol worship. Some put their faith in angels. Angels, while used by God as messengers, warriors, and protectors, are *created* beings. They are not to be worshipped. Faith in anything other than the one true living God, the Creator and sustainer of the universe, is *misplaced* faith!

Demons are opportunistic. If faith in these people or angels as substitutes for God opens a person's heart, then that person may be vulnerable to demonic entry, even if these demons are not linked in any way to the people or the angels that the person has put their faith in. It is just the fact that their hearts may *open* that makes them vulnerable.

According to the book *Healing Through Deliverance* (Horrobin 2008), in addition to misplaced faith, demons can enter a person if that person (usually unknowingly) gives them the 'right' to do this through sinful practices such as sexual sin and pornography. Horrobin explains that demons can enter a person through unforgiveness that leads to bitterness and resentment, through curses, addictions, protracted grieving, abuse, and various other avenues. As already mentioned, demons can indwell a person from the point of conception (implying that the right has been given to the demon to enter by a previous generation).

Demons can only be in one place at a time and they will enter the person as a *complete* entity. There will not be a part of a demon in one person and a part of that same demon in another person. If a person has a demon in them you cannot 'catch' this demon simply by contact with the person as you might catch measles. Demons can, however, transfer from one person to another as a complete entity if the other person is vulnerable to this. There is nothing a demon likes better than to inhabit the body of a person and, upon the death of a host, the demon or demons will seek a new host.

Demons can inhabit a part of a person, for example, the mouth, such as in the 'lying spirit' in the mouths of the prophets of King Ahab. They can also inhabit the entire body and can often see out through the person's eyes. This sometimes makes the victims eyes look darker than normal, as the demon can affect the normal response of the eye to light. Demons may also cause the person to hear voices in their head. This can lead the person to behave irresponsibly or dangerously to themselves and others and they may attempt to cause harm to themselves or others, acting under instruction from the demon, although people are certainly capable of causing harm in their own right without demonic influence! After the Holy Spirit had departed from King Saul and an evil spirit came upon Saul, he would become violent and throw his spear at David, who had come to soothe Saul by playing the harp for him. Demons can cause the person to exhibit great strength and power, usually manifested in violence. The book of Acts for example, gives an account of a man with an evil spirit who had jumped on some other men, and "mastered all of them and overpowered them, so that they fled out of that house naked and wounded" (Acts 19:16).

Even without actually indwelling a person, demons can make themselves heard from outside a person, therefore people may say they hear voices in their ear, as Job's friend Eliphaz did:

> Now a word was brought to me stealthily; my ear received the whisper of it. Amid thoughts from visions in the night, when deep sleep falls on men, dread came upon me, and trembling, which made all my bones shake. A spirit glided past my face; the hair of my flesh stood up. It stood still, but I could not discern its appearance. A form was before my eyes; there was silence, then I heard a voice.
>
> —Job 4:12-16

Often these voices are heard over the person's shoulder.

Demons can speak through a person using the vocal chords of the person. They can cause the person to exhibit a second, or even multiple, personalities. This is because the person has their *own* spirit which has formed their own soul and includes *their* personality, but also has the *demonic* spirit or spirits which have brought their *own* personality. The personality that is active or playing out at any given time is the one whose 'person' is at that moment active or dominant. They can switch from one personality to the other in a matter of seconds. These 'personalities' can have different voices, likes and dislikes, talents, and ability to relate to others. The person may even refer to themselves in the third person as if they are separate entities and, technically, they are. The person may not be fully aware of these other 'personalities' and they may experience a degree of amnesia for the period of time when another entity takes over and may not take responsibility for the actions and words of the other, or others, as if a completely different person was responsible.

Demons can cause disabilities such as blindness, deafness, and muteness in a person. They can cause physical manifestations such as foaming at the mouth and the making of animal noises. Demons can cause fits and convulsions and can cause the body to contort and be in an unnatural position, or even levitate. In Mark' gospel, for example, we read the story of a man who came to Jesus for help. His son was afflicted by "a spirit that makes him mute. And whenever it seizes him, it throws him down, and he foams and grinds his teeth and becomes rigid . . . the spirit saw him, immediately it convulsed the boy, and he fell on the ground and rolled about, foaming at the mouth" (Mark 9:17-18, 20).

It is not unusual for a person to begin with one demon and then for that demon to invite other demons in. In the New Testament, we read of a woman known as Mary Magdalene "from whom seven demons had gone out" (Luke 8:2). Demons or evil spirits often work as a 'family' and may have a hierarchy, some being more authoritative and powerful than others.

The manifestations of demonization obviously fit the description of the signs and symptoms of some mental illnesses. Although mental illness can certainly be caused by environmental factors, chemical imbalance, hereditary factors, and even the actions or side effects of certain drugs, demonic indwelling is a cause that should not be, although usually is, overlooked. Health professionals tend to concentrate on the physical and the psychological, even the social causes of mental illness, but not the spiritual. Most health care workers would be unaware of spiritual issues or at least feel uncomfortable with suggesting that this may be the cause of some mental illnesses, and the real issues may go untreated.

Demonic influence in a person may also manifest itself in more subtle signs rather than as an obvious mental illness. According to the book *Healing Through Deliverance* (Horrobin 2008), sometimes the person affected by demonization may experience manifestations such as nightmares, phobias, addictions, physical illness, social issues such as difficulty interacting with other people or maintaining healthy relationships, sexual deviations such as homosexual tendencies, or emotional disturbances such as depression, anger, sadness, or mood swings. Some of the *causes* of demonization can be similar to some of the *manifestations or signs.*

Medication can sometimes mask or reduce the signs and symptoms, or manifestations, of the demon in the person by dulling the person's perception of, and response to, the foreign entity, but will not remove it. It is a *spiritual* problem. The only cure is to remove the *cause,* rather than treating or masking the signs and symptoms. When a person has a health problem that is physical, the physician, where possible, attempts to identify and treat the *cause* rather than just treating the signs and symptoms. To treat the *cause* would then *get rid of* the signs and symptoms. It is the same with demonic causes. To treat the signs and symptoms with medication, therapy, and so on, will *not* remove the demon. It may mask the effects and perhaps go some way towards helping the person maintain a somewhat 'normal' life, but they are still spiritually sick.

THE NAME

Originally, the first humans—Adam and Eve, were not vulnerable to demonic indwelling because their hearts were open to the Spirit of God, but were at the same time *sealed* by His Spirit, which was directly connected to Him.

> **Seal**—*n. . . . 3 substance or device used to close a gap etc. . . . —v. 1 close securely hermetically. 2 stamp, fasten, or fix with a seal.*[2]

A believer who has put his or her faith in Jesus Christ will have the seal of the Holy Spirit on his or her heart. A seal is something that blocks an opening and will not let something past it. If the person has the Holy Spirit indwelling his or her heart, it would follow that the *heart* would be guarded from demonic possession. At the moment of coming to faith, the demon or demons may come out of the person. Having said this, it is possible for believers to have been indwelt by a demon or demons *prior* to coming to faith and to still require deliverance from these spirits. Even a demon that was dwelling in the heart of a person could remain, but move to another part of that person. It is also possible for a believer to open themselves to demonic entry *after* coming to faith, especially through sinful practices. Additionally, without actually entering a person, demons can cause oppression, affecting a believer's health and wellbeing.

What is the solution? An account is given in the New Testament of a "man possessed by a demon, an evil spirit. He cried out at the top of his voice, 'Ha! What do you want with us, Jesus of Nazareth? Have you come to destroy us? I know who you are—the Holy One of God!'" (Luke 4:33-34 NIV). Demons know who Jesus is and the power that He has over them. In the book of Acts, we read that "God anointed Jesus of Nazareth with the Holy Spirit and with power. He went about doing good and healing all who were oppressed by the devil, for God was with him" (Acts 10:38). There are many accounts in the New Testament of demonic indwelling, and these demons were ordered to come out of the person *only* in the name of Jesus, as that is the *only* name that demons will submit to.

God has given to some believers the ability to distinguish between spirits and the ministry of driving out demons in the name of Jesus. This ministry, referred to as a 'deliverance ministry', is both needed and practised today, and there are some churches and individuals whose gifting it is to minister to those who are troubled by this spiritual problem.

How do demons leave a person who has been possessed? Often with a scene! Demons usually come out in the same way they came in to a person—often through the breath with protests and shrieks. In the gospel of Mark, we read of a demon coming out of a man, whereby "the evil spirit shook the man violently and came out of him with a shriek" (Mark 1:26 NIV). Sometimes, demons will throw the person down. They may exit through the eyes, ears, or the body's orifices; even through the finger tips or the top of the head. Sometimes the exit of demons may be accompanied by visible signs such as vomiting, coughing, shaking, or fluttering of the eyes. Sometimes there will be little or no audible sounds or visible signs.

There is an account in Luke's gospel of a man who was possessed by a large number of demons. He lived in the tombs and ran around naked. He was so violent that he had to be chained hand and foot and kept under guard, but he kept breaking the chains. Jesus commanded the demons to leave the man and gave them permission to go into a herd of pigs who then "rushed down the steep bank into the lake and were drowned" (Luke 8:33). That certainly did not mean the end of the demons. They would look for another body to inhabit. Interestingly, the demons begged Jesus "repeatedly not to command them to depart into the Abyss" (Luke 8:31). In the abyss is the lake of fire that is being reserved until the end of time. The demons were clearly aware that Jesus had the power to send them into eternal punishment by His word. They knew that their time roaming the earth was limited and thought that Jesus might send them to their demise then and there, and they were afraid.

After the demons had left the man, what happened to him? The people from the town who had known this man found him "sitting at the feet of Jesus, clothed and in his right mind" (Luke 8:35). His 'right mind' would be his *own* mind. The demons had held him in a state where he was definitely not in his right mind. He had been delivered from the demons, set free, and was now following the Lord.

If a person is delivered of a demon and they *do not* enter into faith in the Lord, they have a very high risk of becoming 'repossessed', perhaps with even more demons than they originally had. Jesus tells us that:

> "When the unclean spirit has gone out of a person, it passes through waterless places seeking rest, but finds none. Then it says, 'I will return to my house from which I came.' And when it comes, it finds the house empty, swept, and put in order. Then it goes and brings with it seven other spirits more evil than itself, and they enter and dwell there, and the last state of that person is worse than the first."
>
> —Matt. 12:43-45

Just have a look at the garden! If you weed a patch in your garden but do not then cover that patch with mulch, what is likely to happen? In place of those weeds that were pulled out, more have sprung up; often even more than was originally there! The heart of the person from whom the demon, or demons, have been commanded to come out, needs to be *sealed* with the Holy Spirit through faith because, if the 'house' is unoccupied by the indwelling presence of the Holy Spirit, it is as good as putting out a 'welcome' mat! Furthermore, if a person received the demon, or demons, through sinful practices and continues in these practices or recommences these practices, they are very vulnerable to the re-entry of demons because they are continuing to give these demons the 'right' to enter.

Demon possession is an age-old problem with an age-old cure! Neither the problem nor the cure has changed!

HERE'S WHAT WE NEED:

What we need is an end to Satan's temptations, his accusations, his destructive influence on relationships, and his lies and deceit. We need someone more powerful than Satan to destroy his work and to defeat his hold over the *power* of death, which in turn holds people in slavery over their *fear* of death. We need someone who is able to render Satan powerless for ever.

Part Three

God.

Chapter Seven
The Creator

It is not the purpose of this book to prove the existence of God, nor is it necessary, for "the heavens declare the glory of God, and the sky above proclaims his handiwork. Day to day pours out speech, and night to night reveals knowledge. There is no speech, nor are there words, whose voice is not heard. Their voice goes out through all the earth, and their words to the end of the world" (Ps. 19:1-4). The witness of Creation is evidence for a Creator.

THE ORIGIN

God is eternal. God is the great 'uncaused cause' by whom all things have been brought into existence. He has always existed and He always will. "Behold, God is great, and we know him not; the number of his years is unsearchable" (Job 36:26). He "alone has immortality, who dwells in unapproachable light" (1 Tim. 6:16). King David, in a psalm of praise to his Creator wrote: "Before the mountains were brought forth, or ever you had formed the earth and the world, from everlasting to everlasting you are God" (Ps. 90:2).

There is no one *like* God. In His own words, "I AM" (Exod. 3:14). The prophet Isaiah asks: "To whom then will you liken God, or what likeness compares with him?" (Isa. 40:18). "From of old no one has heard or perceived by the ear, no eye has seen a God besides you" (Isa. 64:4). God said: "Before me no god was formed, nor shall there be any after me. I, I am the LORD, and besides me there is no saviour" (Isa. 43:10-11).

There is only *one* God. "The LORD our God, the LORD is one" (Deut. 6:4). Yet God exists eternally in Father, Son, and Holy Spirit. In the first verse in the Bible, "In the beginning, God created the heavens and the earth" (Gen. 1:1), the Hebrew word that is used for 'God' is *Elohiym*. This is a *plural* word with a *singular* meaning. In other words, it means that God is one, yet more than one. The whole undivided essence of God exists eternally in, and belongs equally to, Father, Son, and Holy Spirit.

What do we know about God? The Bible tells us that "God is spirit" (John 4:24). In several passages, the Bible tells us that God has a Soul, as well as a mind and a heart. God is portrayed as having senses. For example, when Noah sacrificed a burnt offering to the Lord, "the LORD smelled the pleasing aroma" (Gen. 8:21). God is described as having a face, eyes, ears, arms, feet, and hands. Daniel is given a vision of God the Father at the time of the judgement. He gives Him the title 'Ancient of Days' and says that "his clothing was white as snow, and the hair of his head like pure wool; his throne was fiery flames; its wheels were burning fire. A stream of fire issued and came out from before him" (Dan. 7:9-10).

God speaks. Ezekiel described God's voice as "like the roar of rushing waters" (Ezek. 43:2 NIV). Another time he heard God speak in a "low whisper" (1 Kings 19:12). When God spoke from heaven to glorify His Son for the benefit of the people listening so that they would know that He truly was the Son of God, the crowd said that it sounded like thunder and the land became radiant with His Glory.

Heaven is the dwelling place of God. He "sits above the circle of the earth, and its inhabitants are like grasshoppers; who stretches out the heavens like a curtain, and spreads them like a tent to dwell in" (Isa. 40:22). There is a temple and a throne in heaven. God said: "Heaven is my throne, and the earth is my footstool" (Isa. 66:1) and David wrote: "The LORD is in his holy temple; the LORD's throne is in heaven" (Ps. 11:4).

God is surrounded by a multitude of angels. Immediately surrounding the throne are angels with wings, called cherubim and seraphim, who are always giving glory, honour, and praise to God. In the book of Revelation, John is shown a glimpse of the throne room in heaven and describes the following:

> Behold, a throne stood in heaven, with one seated on the throne. And he who sat there had the appearance of jasper and carnelian, and around the throne was a rainbow that had the appearance of an emerald . . . From the throne came flashes of lightning, and rumblings and peals of thunder, and before the throne were burning seven torches of fire, which are the seven spirits of God, and before the throne there was as it were a sea of glass, like crystal.
>
> —Rev. 4:2-3, 5-6

God the Son dwelt in heaven in eternity past. Two thousand years ago, God the Son *took on* a *body of flesh* and dwelt on earth for more than thirty years. By taking on humanity, the Son did not become *less* God. He has always been, and always will be, *fully* God and since being conceived in Mary, *fully* human. The Son returned to heaven and is once again seated at the right hand of God the Father.

The Holy Spirit dwells in unity with both God the Father *and* God the Son and proceeds from both the Father and the Son. Through the Holy Spirit then, God is *everywhere.*

THE NATURE OF GOD

Although there are records in the Bible of people being given *visions* of God, "no-one has ever seen God, but God the One and Only, who is at the Father's side, has made him known" (John 1:18 NIV). Although the Bible tells us a little about God, there is much that we do not know and, at least for now, cannot know. One of the reasons the Son came into the world was so that, *through Him,* we can know the Father. The Son is the likeness of the Father. What we know about the *nature* of God, applies to God the Father, Son, and Holy Spirit.

God is all-powerful. He can do anything. Job says of God: "I know that you can do all things, and that no purpose of yours can be thwarted" (Job 42:2). Job tells us that:

He is wise in heart and mighty in strength—who has hardened himself against him, and succeeded? He who removes mountains, and they know it not, when he overturns them in his anger, who shakes the earth out of its place, and its pillars tremble; who commands the sun, and it does not rise; who seals up the stars; who alone stretched out the heavens and trampled the waves of the sea; who made the Bear and Orion, the Pleiades and the chambers of the south; who does great things beyond searching out, and marvellous things beyond number.

—Job 9:4-10

God is all-seeing. "Do I not fill heaven and earth?" (Jer. 23:24) declares the Lord. "The LORD looks down from heaven; he sees all the children of man; from where he sits enthroned he looks out on all the inhabitants of the earth, he who fashions the hearts of them all and observes all their deeds" (Ps. 33:13-15). God is always watching over His Creation. He has no need for sleep, for He "does not faint or grow weary" (Isa. 40:28).

God is all-knowing. He knows everything that has ever happened and He knows everything that is yet to happen. He is "majestic in holiness, awesome in glorious deeds, doing wonders" (Exod. 15:11). He is "wonderful in counsel and excellent in wisdom" (Isa. 28:29).

God is good and holy. There is no evil in Him. It is not in God's nature to do evil or to be evil, therefore, He cannot. "Far be it from God that he should do wickedness, and from the Almighty that he should do wrong . . . Of a truth, God will not do wickedly, and the Almighty will not pervert justice" (Job 34:10, 12). "This God—his way is perfect; the word of the LORD proves true" (2 Sam. 22:31). David wrote that God is "not a God who delights in wickedness; evil may not dwell with you" (Ps. 5:4). This should fill us with peace and reassurance because the One who is *good and holy* is in control of this world and of our destiny.

Bad things happen in the world because we live in a *fallen* world. Creation is under a temporary curse because of sin. That is why there are so many natural and manmade disasters. Evil is rampant in the world because Satan is active. This too is temporary. Sometimes people blame God for the wrong that *man* does, but God asks: "Would you condemn me to justify yourself?" (Job 40:8 NIV).

God is just and fair. Abraham asks of God: "Shall not the Judge of all the earth do what is just?" (Gen. 18:25). God "is not partial and takes no bribe" (Deut. 10:17). "His work is perfect, for all his ways are justice. A God of faithfulness and without iniquity, just and upright is he" (Deut. 32:4). We cannot fully understand God's ways, for He says: "My thoughts are not your thoughts, neither are your ways my ways . . . as the heavens are higher than the earth, so are my ways higher than your ways and my thoughts than your thoughts" (Isa. 55:8 NIV).

God can, and does, punish people for their sins. "God is a righteous judge, a God who expresses his wrath every day" (Ps. 7:11 NIV). That is a part of the just and fair attributes of God's nature. In speaking to Moses about the people of Israel who were sinning against Him, God said that "when the time comes for me to punish, I will punish them for their sin" (Exod. 32:34 NIV). "The hand of our God is for good on all who seek him, and the power of his wrath is against all who forsake him" (Ezra 8:22).

God has feelings and emotions. "God is love" (1 John 4:16). His love is unfailing. God loves those He has created, as a Father loves a child. God grieves. He grieves over those who have no regard for His love and He has compassion towards them. He grieves over those who go astray. Our sin grieves His heart. Before the flood, when He saw how wicked man had become, "the LORD regretted that he had made man on the earth, and it grieved him to his heart" (Gen. 6:6). God has a sense of humour—He laughs. He can also be angry and, throughout history, He has brought His wrath upon individuals and nations.

God is forgiving. He is "merciful and gracious, slow to anger, and abounding in steadfast love and faithfulness, keeping steadfast love for thousands, forgiving iniquity and transgression and sin" (Exod. 34:6-7), but God is also "a consuming fire, a jealous God" (Deut. 4:24). The Israelites, God's chosen people, were not to make any kind of idol or worship the 'gods' of other nations. Doing so would provoke God to anger and result in punishment for the people, often by sending them into exile in other countries. God, being just and fair, repeatedly warned the people of the consequences of their unfaithfulness so that if, and when, they did this, they would have no excuse. In the time of their unfaithfulness, God punished the Israelites for their own good in order to bring them back to Himself. God is forgiving and loving and when the people repented and turned away from these idols and returned to Him, if from their place of exile they sought Him with all their heart and obeyed Him, He then showed mercy to them, forgave them, comforted them, restored them to a right relationship with Him, and returned them to their land.

God is faithful to His own. He kept His covenant with the nation of Israel even though they were often unfaithful. Nehemiah, in chapter seven, tells us that He keeps His promises because He is righteous.

God requires accountability. He sets conditions for His people. He makes it very clear to them that there are consequences for their actions. He holds them accountable; that is, they must do something and then He will bless them, or they are *not* to do something, otherwise He will send a curse upon them by cursing their blessings. God said to His people: "If you will not listen, if you will not take it to heart to give honour to my name . . . then I will send the curse upon you and I will curse your blessings" (Mal. 2:2).

In God there is absolute truth. The writer of Hebrews assures us that "it is impossible for God to lie" (Heb. 6:18). Jesus said that He *is* the Truth and that the words that He speaks are truth and life.

God is the protector of His people. During the wanderings of the Israelites in the desert, they were instructed to keep the camp holy so that God would not see anything indecent, as "the LORD your God walks in the midst of your camp, to deliver you and to give up your enemies before you" (Deut. 23:14). God's role as protector is likened in Scripture to the protectiveness of a mother hen sheltering her chicks under her wings. God watches over His people today as in times of old. "Behold, the eye of the LORD is on those who fear him, on those who hope in his steadfast love, that he may deliver their soul from death and keep them alive in famine" (Ps. 33:18-19). "The eyes of the LORD are towards the righteous and his ears towards their cry" (Ps. 34:15).

God reveals the future. There are things that, at present, we cannot know about God and His plans. God does not keep us totally in the dark over the future however, for "the secret things belong to the LORD our God, but the things that are revealed belong to us" (Deut. 29:29). Although God does not reveal *all* that the future holds, particularly specific times and dates, He does allow us a glimpse into His plans through the prophets as foretold in His Word. God says: "Behold, the former things have come to pass, and new things I now declare; before they spring forth I tell you of them" (Isa. 42:9).

A significant part of the Bible is prophetic, some of which is still to take place, particularly in relation to the Second Coming of Christ. God always knows what will take place before it happens and He ordains and plans events before they come to pass. He said in His Word: "Have you not heard that I determined it long ago? I planned from days of old what now I bring to pass" (2 Kings 19:25).

How do we know if a message is, or is not, from the Lord? The book of Deuteronomy tells us that "when a prophet speaks in the name of the LORD, if the word does not come to pass or come true, that is a word that the LORD has not spoken; the prophet has spoken it presumptuously" (Deut. 18:22). All prophecies that originate from God come to fulfilment and "not one word of all the good promises that the LORD had made to the house of Israel had failed; all came to pass" (Josh. 21:45). There were, in Old Testament times, and there are today, imposters who *claim* to be speaking words from the Lord. Of these, the Lord says: "The prophets are prophesying lies in my name. I did not send them, nor did I command them or speak to them. They are prophesying to you a lying vision, worthless divination, and the deceit of their own minds" (Jer. 4:14). "Woe to the foolish prophets who follow their own spirit and have seen nothing" (Ezek. 13:3). What was the danger of these false prophets? God said of them: "You have disheartened the righteous falsely, although I have not grieved him, and you have encouraged the wicked, that he should not turn from his evil way to save his life" (Ezek. 13:22).

God wants us to know Him and to know about Him. He speaks to us through His Word, in our hearts, through other people, and through the circumstances in our lives. Through His Word, He has revealed to us His plans, His thoughts, and the reason why we exist. He has revealed to us the right way to live our lives and the only way to eternal life. The Bible is full of wisdom which has been given to us to help us on our life journey.

It is not possible for a person *without* faith to understand the depth of meaning in Scripture because the meaning of God's Word is revealed by the Holy Spirit who works in the heart of the *believer*. The Bible says that "the LORD confides in those who fear him; he makes his covenant known to them" (Ps. 25:14 NIV). God's Word has layers of meaning. If you seek, through faith, to know God and understand His Word, you will. The more you study God's Word and seek to know Him, the more meaning God will reveal to you. God will honour you with understanding.

We can know God and develop a closer relationship with God through prayer. God wants us to have a conversation with Him. He wants us to tell Him our fears, concerns, joys, and doubts. Do our prayers make a difference and does God ever change His mind because of our prayers or because we change our ways? God knows everything before it happens. Nothing surprises Him. The Bible though, makes it clear that our prayers *do* make a difference to what happens. For example, King Hezekiah was ill and at the point of death and was told by God that he was going to die and he was to 'put his house in order'. He wept and reminded God of his faithfulness to Him. God then said, through the prophet Isaiah, that He had heard Hezekiah's prayer and had seen His tears and that He would heal him and add fifteen years to his life. Another similar example from Scripture is found in chapters eighteen and twenty-six of the book of Jeremiah, where there are references to God relenting of the doom that He had intended to bring upon people because they had repented and turned from their ways.

God speaks to man, not only through His written Word and through His prophets, but also through dreams and visions:

> For God speaks in one way, and in two, though man does not perceive it. In a dream, in a vision of the night, when deep sleep falls on men, while they slumber on their beds, then he opens the ears of men and terrifies them with warnings, that he may turn man aside from his deed and conceal pride from a man; he keeps back his soul from the pit, his life from perishing by the sword.
> —Job 33:14-18

God also speaks through other people by giving them a word of revelation, or a message, or advice for them to pass on.

God is our provider. "The Lord is compassionate and merciful" (James 5:11). "He executes justice for the fatherless and the widow, and loves the sojourner, giving him food and clothing" (Deut. 10:18). If we are giving to the work of the Lord, we are only giving back what He has already given us, for "everything comes from you, and we have given you only what comes from your hand" (1 Chr. 29:14 NIV). God owes us nothing, we deserve nothing from the hand of God, and it is only through His loving mercy that He continues to provide for us. He said to Job: "Who has first given to me, that I should repay him? Whatever is under the whole heaven is mine" (Job 41:11).

THE CREATION

There is a Hebrew word that is only used to describe *God's* action of creating. This word is *bara*. It means the calling into existence something that has had no previous existence—creating something from nothing. God brought the world into being by His Word. He spoke and it came to be.

God the Son is called 'The Word' by the apostle John. John tells us that the world was made through the Son: "In the beginning was the Word, and the Word was with God, and the Word was God. He was with God in the beginning. Through him all things were made; without him nothing was made that has been made . . . the world was made through him" (John 1:1-2, 10 NIV), "for by him all things were created, in heaven and on earth, visible and invisible, whether thrones or dominions or rulers or authorities—all things were created through him and for him. And he is before all things, and in him all things hold together" (Col. 1:16-17).

In the beginning, God called into existence the space-time-matter universe. Over four days, He prepared the earth for man to dwell on. He created light, separating day from night. He separated the waters to create the atmosphere, seas, and dry land, and He gave form to the earth which had been formless and empty. He brought forth all kinds of plants and vegetation from the earth. He created the sun, moon, and stars to give light on the earth and to be signs for days, years, and seasons. He brought forth all kinds of living things—sea creatures, birds, and animals. All this was in preparation for the pinnacle of His Creation—man:

> Then God said, "Let us make man in our image, after our likeness. And let them have dominion over the fish of the sea and over the birds of the heavens and over the livestock and over all the earth and over every creeping thing that creeps on the earth." So God created man in his own image, in the image of God he created him; male and female he created them. And God blessed them. And God said to them, "Be fruitful and multiply and fill the earth and subdue it, and have dominion over the fish of the sea and over the birds of the heavens and over every living thing that moves on the earth."
>
> —Gen. 1:26-28

When God said: "Let *us* make man" (Gen 1:26), this was the Father, Son, and Holy Spirit creating together in unity.

As angels were created by God *before* He created man, at the end of day six of Creation, we have all the major players on the scene—God the Father, Son, and Holy Spirit, the angels, and mankind, "and God saw everything that he had made, and behold, it was very good" (Gen. 1:31). All of Creation was living in perfect peace and harmony under the loving care of its Creator. Heaven—God's dwelling place, was so near to earth that God would walk in the Garden of Eden in the cool of the day. Perhaps heaven even *came down* to earth. All relationships were as they were intended to be. God loved those He had created and they loved and obeyed Him.

ANCIENT WORDS – NEW DISCOVERIES

The Bible contains scientific information about the earth that, when written, had not yet been proven or discovered. For example, one of the oldest books in the Old Testament tells us that God "stretches out the north over the void and hangs the earth on nothing" (Job 26:7), and in the book of Isaiah, we read that God "sits above the circle of the earth" (Isa. 40:22). In 1650, thousands of years after the books of Job and Isaiah were written, man 'discovered' that the earth was a sphere suspended in space, not flat and carried on the back of a giant turtle! Amazingly, there are still some people who believe that the earth is flat. Now that's faith!

God asked Job: "Have you entered into the springs of the sea or walked in the recesses of the deep?" (Job 38:16). It is only a relatively recent discovery that there are hot fresh water springs, or vents, deep in the ocean floor, but here it is plainly written in this ancient Book.

When the Bible was written, only about eleven hundred stars were visible to the naked eye; and yet the Bible states that there are "countless" (Jer. 33:22 NIV) stars. The invention of the telescope confirms that there really *are* billions of stars which cannot be numbered.

The book of Genesis tells us that God gave Noah the exact plans and dimensions to build the ark that withstood the torrential rain, massive waves, and tonnes of debris battering it during the flood. In 1609 in Holland, a ship was built based on the same proportions, that is, 30:5:3. This revolutionized the building of large ships and since then has been used as the general proportions of every large ship travelling on the high seas, as this was discovered to be the most stable ratio.

Many of God's laws given to the Israelites were health related. For example, in the book of Leviticus, the Israelites were told not to eat the fat of animals. We now know that a high intake of saturated fats in the diet leads to many health problems including an increased risk of some cancers and coronary artery disease, leading to strokes and heart attacks. The Israelites did not need a Heart Foundation to give them that bit of advice! The health regulations given by God to the Israelites also included laws to prevent the spread of infectious diseases by quarantining those affected outside of the camp. The practice of isolation in hospitals is only a relatively recent practice.

THE PLAN

In our examination of our origin and of angels, Satan and demons, we have established that one third of the angels rebelled against God, led in that rebellion by Satan, and that Adam and Eve also disobeyed God and became separated from their Creator spiritually and were now subject to physical death. Because of sin, their hearts became closed to God and they were no longer connected to the Spirit of life. This must have been absolutely devastating for Adam and Eve; like a small child being ripped away from its loving father. It must also have caused great sorrow to God, who created people to lavish His love and care on and to enjoy a loving relationship with them as their Father. Through Adam, sin and death entered the world and a disconnected spirit and sinful nature has been passed down through the generations. We are, by default, under the law of sin and death instead of the law of the Spirit of life. Cut off from our Creator we have no hope of eternal life.

The Scriptures tell us that "the wages of sin is death" (Rom. 6:23). Sin must be paid for by the losing of a life. Right at the very beginning, when sin entered the world, God demonstrated this payment for sin by the killing of an animal and He used the skin from that animal to make garments for Adam and Eve to cover their nakedness and shame. The 'rules' haven't changed. The payment for sin is still the same—death. By default, we are destined to pay this price ourselves.

We are in desperate need of a new spirit and a new heart. Without these we will die and, tragically, we will be separated from God for all eternity. We are in desperate need of saving from an eternal destiny in the lake of fire. In addition to that, we have the problem of physical death—the death of our bodies. Prospects are looking pretty grim for mankind!

God, who knows everything, knew that this would happen. This is a relief because, *despite* knowing what would happen, He chose to make mankind anyway. You see, He had a plan to restore mankind to a right relationship with Him and He told Adam and Eve of this plan straight after they had sinned so that they would have hope.

God's plan was that He would send a *Redeemer*—a Saviour; someone who would rescue us from our fate. Genesis tells us of One who would come who would destroy the work of Satan. This would be someone who was the offspring of the woman only, not of the man. In other words, the one to come would not have an *earthly* father and therefore He would not inherit a disconnected and fallen spirit and a sinful nature. This would mean that He would be *unique* in *not* being subject to the law of sin and death. It meant that this promised Redeemer, who would defeat Satan, would not need to pay for His *own* sins as He would be without sin Himself. This would uniquely qualify Him to pay for the sins of *others*.

God gave Adam and Eve a little glimpse into His plan—enough to give them hope. Throughout history and through the words of the prophets, we see God's plan being revealed and unfolded in the ensuing years leading to its fulfilment.

THE FAMILY TREE

Adam and Eve had many sons and daughters born to them, although only three are specifically named in the Genesis record. In that generation, brothers and sisters would have married and produced offspring together. The laws that forbid marriage between close relatives were not given until the time of Moses.

When Adam and Eve were created they were physically perfect. They did not have any genetic mutations or abnormalities. These only began to occur *after* sin entered the world. Being the first generation to be born, Cain, Seth, and their brothers and sisters would have had very little, if any, genetic mistakes because genetic mistakes are cumulative, that is, more have occurred with each successive generation since The Fall. Their offspring, unlike the potential offspring of close relatives today, would have been extremely unlikely to have had any deformities.

THE FLOOD

After the creation and subsequent fall of man, people began to drift further and further away from God. From walking in the cool of the day in the Garden of Eden with his loving Creator, man became more and more sinful and distant from God, even forgetting Him altogether, resulting in an increase in wickedness on the earth.

Because of man's wickedness, God decided to wipe everything off the face of the earth by sending a great flood. Every living thing that walked the face of the earth died, except Noah and his family, and the animals that God directed to board the ark. "Noah found favour in the eyes of the LORD . . . Noah was a righteous man, blameless in his generation. Noah walked with God" (Gen. 6:8-9). James Ussher (Pierce & Pierce 2003) places the date of the commencement of the great flood at Sunday 7th of December in the year 2349 BC.

Evidence of this worldwide flood is everywhere. Just what would we expect this evidence to be? Millions of dead animals, people, trees, birds, and so on, buried in mud and debris all over the earth. Many living things that were buried were preserved relatively intact in layers over a very short space of time due to massive shifts of sand, soil, and rock. The evidence of this is the many fossils where the imprint of them is whole. These fossils could not have been buried over millions of years, or even a few years, because the natural elements such as the sun, wind, and rain, as well as predators and scavengers would have destroyed them before they had a chance to be completely immersed. The earth is covered by vast amounts of sedimentary rock—evidence of the fact that, at some stage, the whole earth was covered in water.

All that was left on the earth were Noah's family and the animals that God had saved to repopulate the earth. All people on the earth today are therefore descendants of, not only Adam and Eve, but also of Noah and his wife, and one of their three sons and three daughters-in-law. After the flood, God made a covenant with Noah which was for all generations to come, to never again send a flood that would wipe out all those who lived on the earth. The sign of this covenant was the rainbow, which symbolises God's mercy.

What happened after this flood? Did everyone behave a bit better? Perhaps not! The population grew rapidly and "the whole world had one language and a common speech" (Gen. 11:1 NIV), but mankind became proud and they only wanted to bring glory to themselves, not to their Creator:

> They said, "Come, let us build ourselves a city and a tower with its top in the heavens, and let us make a name for ourselves, lest we be dispersed over the face of the whole earth." And the LORD came down to see the city and the tower, which the children of man had built. And the LORD said, "Behold,

they are one people, and they have all one language, and this is only the beginning of what they will do. And nothing that they propose to do will now be impossible for them. Come, let us go down and there confuse their language, so that they may not understand one another's speech." So the LORD dispersed them from there over the face of all the earth, and they left off building the city. Therefore its name was called Babel, because there the LORD confused the language of all the earth. And from there the LORD dispersed them over the face of all the earth.

—Gen. 11:4-9

There are a number of instances recorded in the Bible of the Holy Spirit bodily transporting people, and it may be that this is what happened in this instance. Alternatively, God may have employed the angels on this particular mission. No doubt angels can scatter just as easily as they can gather!

This is the origin of all the tribes, nations, and languages in the world, for God "made from one man every nation of mankind to live on all the face of the earth, having determined allotted periods and the boundaries of their dwelling place, that they should seek God, and perhaps feel their way toward him and find him. Yet he is actually not far from each one of us" (Acts 17:26-27).

It is likely that there was a remnant of people on the earth that were faithful to God at this time who were *not* dispersed and who retained their original language, likely the Hebrew language.

THE CALL

To begin to bring His plan of redemption into reality, God made a covenant or agreement with a righteous man called Abram.

> **Covenant—/kuv-uh-nuhnt/—*n.* 1 agreement; contract. 2 *Law* sealed contract, esp. a deed of covenant. 3 (Covenant) *Bibl.* Agreement between God and the Israelites. —*v.* agree, esp. by legal covenant. (French: related to CONVENE)**[1]

The covenant that God made with Abram was that He would greatly increase his numbers and that he would be the father of many nations. According to James Ussher (Pierce & Pierce 2003), the call of Abram was in 1922 BC. Abram was called out of a city called Ur of the Chaldeans, which was located in Mesopotamia, to go into the land that God would show him. He left his home where he was comfortable and settled, put his trust in God, took his family, and travelled to the land of Canaan. When God called Abram to follow Him, He made Abram a promise saying: "I will make of you a great nation, and I will bless you and make your name great, so that you will be a blessing. I will bless those who bless you, and him who dishonours you I will curse, and in you all the families of the earth shall be blessed" (Gen. 12:2-3). He also promised Abram that his descendants would inherit the land. God said to him:

"No longer shall your name be called Abram, but your name shall be Abraham, for I have made you the father of a multitude of nations. I will make you exceedingly fruitful, and I will make you into nations, and kings shall come from you. I will establish my covenant between me and you and your offspring after you throughout their generations for an everlasting covenant, to be God to you and to your offspring after you. And I will give to you and to your offspring after you the land of your sojournings, all the land of Canaan, for an everlasting possession, and I will be their God."

—Gen. 17:5-8

The Lord told Abraham that his "Seed shall possess the gate of his enemies . . . in your Seed shall all the nations of the earth be blessed" (Gen. 22:18 GIB). Who was this 'Seed' who would come through Abraham? It was the promised Messiah—the one spoken of by God to Adam and Eve; the one who would be the Seed of the woman only.

Abraham "believed the LORD, and he credited it to him as righteousness" (Gen. 15:6 NIV). What did Abraham believe? He believed that the forgiveness of sins was only possible through God's mercy and that God would send a Saviour who would save the people, including him, from their sins. Even though Abraham was not living on the earth at the time when the Messiah came, he still put his faith in the *coming* Messiah. Throughout history, this has always been the same; the difference being that some have looked *forward* to the time of the Messiah and some look *back*. We have no righteousness of our own. We are sinners. Like Abraham, to whoever believes and has faith, God gives *His* righteousness.

From the beginning of the repopulation of the earth until the calling of Abraham, and during the time of Abraham's travels, it appears that there were other people on the earth who had faith in God. For example, we read of the account where Abraham was blessed by the king of Salem (later known as Jerusalem) after returning from the defeat of kings of other nations and this king is described as 'priest of God Most High'. Abraham then gives him a tenth (a tithe) of all his plunder.

Through Abraham, God called for Himself a people out of the nations of the earth and promised them a land of their own in which to live. As a sign of this covenant between God and Abraham and his descendants, through his son Isaac and grandson Jacob, all males were to be circumcised. This circumcision represented the putting off of the 'flesh life'—the things of the world, and the identifying of themselves with a holy God. The sign of circumcision was to show that a person was identifying himself with the God of the Israelites.

The people were not to enter into this covenant lightly. This was an *everlasting* covenant, one which the people of Israel are still under today. They are still God's chosen people and the land that God has given them is still their land by covenant with God. God never breaks His promises. He will "remember his covenant forever, the word that he commanded, for a thousand generations, the covenant that he made with

Abraham, his sworn promise to Isaac, which he confirmed to Jacob as a statute, to Israel as an everlasting covenant" (1 Chr. 16:15-17).

God miraculously gave Abraham and Sarah, his wife, a son—Isaac, in their old age. Through Isaac, God's promises would be passed on to the next generation. Isaac and his wife Rebecca had two sons—Jacob and Esau. It was through the line of Jacob that God's promise would be fulfilled. Jacob, also known as 'Israel', married two women—Leah and Rachel. To Jacob was born twelve sons from whom came the twelve tribes of Israel.

Joseph was the favoured son of Jacob. His brothers were jealous of him and plotted to kill him out in the fields. Instead of killing him however, they sold him to some passing merchants and he was carried away by them into Egypt where he was sold as a slave to Potiphar, the captain of Pharaoh's guard.

Potiphar's wife told lies about Joseph and had him thrown into jail. God had given Joseph the gift of interpreting dreams. After Joseph had been in prison for two years, Pharaoh sent for him to interpret his *own* dreams that his own wise men were unable to interpret. Joseph told Pharaoh that his dreams meant that there would be seven years of plenty throughout the country followed by seven years of famine. Pharaoh was impressed with Joseph's wisdom and made him governor of the whole kingdom.

Joseph began to lay up an enormous supply of grain that would see the kingdom through the seven years of famine that was to come. This storage of grain not only sustained Egypt through the famine but also helped neighbouring countries to survive. Many came from far and wide to buy grain from Egypt, including Joseph's brothers. At first they did not recognize him and he pretended not to know them. On the second visit though, he revealed to his brothers who he was and forgave them for selling him as a slave all those years ago, comforting them by telling them that what they did was part of God's plan to provide for them in the time of famine.

Joseph's brothers went back to get their father and they brought him and their whole household to Egypt where they were given land, and where Joseph took care of all their needs. Jacob lived out the remainder of his life in Egypt. Before he died, he blessed his twelve sons with the revelation that he had received from God, telling them what the future would hold for them and their descendants. His blessing upon Judah foretold that the promised Messiah would come through *his* line of descent:

> The sceptre shall not depart from Judah, nor the ruler's staff from between his feet, until tribute comes to him; and to him shall be the obedience of the peoples. Binding his foal to the vine and his donkey's colt to the choice vine, he has washed his garments in wine and his vesture in the blood of grapes. His eyes are darker than wine, and his teeth whiter than milk.
>
> —Gen. 49:10-12

The twelve tribes of Israel multiplied rapidly in the land of Egypt:

Then Joseph died, and all his brothers and all that generation. But the people of Israel were fruitful and increased greatly; they multiplied and grew exceedingly strong, so that the land was filled with them.

Now there arose a new king over Egypt, who did not know Joseph. And he said to his people, "Behold, the people of Israel are too many and too mighty for us. Come, let us deal shrewdly with them, lest they multiply, and, if war breaks out, they join our enemies and fight against us and escape from the land." Therefore they set taskmasters over them to afflict them with heavy burdens. They built for Pharaoh store cities, Pithom and Raamses. But the more they were oppressed, the more they multiplied and the more they spread abroad. And the Egyptians were in dread of the people of Israel. So they ruthlessly made the people of Israel work as slaves.

—Exod. 1:6-13

The king of Egypt ordered the Hebrew midwives to kill all the baby boys as they were born, but they feared God and did not do as the king said, telling Pharaoh that the Hebrew women were 'vigorous' and gave birth before the midwives arrived! Pharaoh then ordered his own people to throw every baby Hebrew boy that was born into the Nile River.

A woman from the tribe of Levi gave birth to a son. Desperate not to have him killed by the Egyptians, she placed him in a basket lined with tar and pitch, and placed it among the reeds by the river. The baby's sister Miriam hid nearby to watch. Pharaoh's daughter came down to the river to bathe and heard the cries of the baby. She felt sorry for him and decided to take him to the palace to raise him as her own son. She needed a nursemaid for the baby and Miriam stepped out from the reeds and offered to get one of the Hebrew women. She fetched the baby's own mother. His mother nursed him until he was old enough to live in the palace and then he was raised by the princess as royalty. The baby's name was Moses.

Moses grew up in the palace but, one day, when he went out to where his own people were slaving away making bricks for the buildings of the Egyptians, "he saw an Egyptian beating a Hebrew, one of his people. He looked this way and that, and seeing no one, he struck down the Egyptian and hid him in the sand" (Exod. 2:11-12). Unbeknown to Moses however, he *was* seen, and what he did became known. Because of this, Pharaoh tried to kill Moses and he fled out into the desert of Midian where he married the daughter of a priest.

Eventually the king of Egypt died and "the people of Israel groaned because of their slavery and cried out for help. Their cry for rescue from slavery came up to God. And God heard their groaning, and God remembered his covenant with Abraham, with Isaac, and with Jacob" (Exod. 2:23-25).

Moses became a shepherd and tended the flocks of his father-in-law, Jethro, for forty years. One day as he was tending his flock, he came to Horeb, the mountain of God. "The angel of the LORD appeared to him in a flame of fire out of the midst of a bush. He looked, and behold, the bush was burning, yet it was not consumed... When the LORD saw that he turned aside to see, God called to him out of the bush, 'Moses, Moses!' And he said, 'Here I am'" (Exod. 3:2, 4). God told Moses that He was sending him to bring His people, the Israelites, out of Egypt.

Moses was not too keen on that idea, but God promised that He would be with him and give him the words to say. Pharaoh refused to let the Israelites go and God sent plagues and pestilences upon the Egyptian people, the livestock, and the land. None of these disasters came near the camp of the Israelites. Not until God sent one final plague—the plague of death, to all the firstborn sons of the Egyptians, did Pharaoh finally let the people go. During this plague, the firstborn sons of the Israelites were spared because God instructed the people to kill a lamb and paint the blood on the posts of their doorways so that the angel of death would pass over them. All the generations to follow were to celebrate the Passover as an annual reminder of how God saved them from death by the blood of the lamb.

After Pharaoh finally let the people go, he then changed his mind and sent the army of Egypt in hot pursuit. The Israelites came to the Red Sea and Moses raised his staff over the sea. God parted the waters and the Israelites were able to cross over on dry ground. The Egyptian army who were pursuing them, drowned as the sea collapsed on them. The Israelites, who had been in slavery for four hundred years, were at last freed. There were about 600, 000 men, plus women and children. The total number of Israelites would have likely numbered at least several million. That's a lot of slaves to lose in one day! No wonder Pharaoh was reluctant to let them go!

THE CHOSEN

Moses and the Israelites set out from the Red Sea through the desert. Along the way, the people had many complaints, particularly about the food, or lack of it, but God took care of their needs by providing water for them to drink and manna and quail for them to eat. They travelled until they came to Mount Sinai and made camp at the foot of the mountain. When Moses went up the mountain to talk to God, God declared to Moses that He would renew His covenant with the Israelites:

> The LORD called to him out of the mountain, saying, "Thus you shall say to the house of Jacob, and tell the people of Israel: You yourselves have seen what I did to the Egyptians, and how I bore you on eagles' wings and brought you to myself. Now therefore, if you will indeed obey my voice and keep my covenant, you shall be my treasured possession among all peoples, for all the earth is mine; and you shall be to me a kingdom of priests and a holy nation. These are the words that you shall speak to the people of Israel."
>
> —Exod. 19:3-6

When Moses told the people what God said, they promised that they would do everything He commanded. The people were to consecrate themselves to God and then three days later were to go to the foot of the mountain to meet with God.

Now Mount Sinai was wrapped in smoke because the LORD had descended on it in fire. The smoke of it went up like the smoke of a kiln, and the whole mountain trembled greatly. And as the sound of the trumpet grew louder and louder, Moses spoke, and God answered him in thunder. The LORD came down on Mount Sinai, to the top of the mountain. And the LORD called Moses to the top of the mountain, and Moses went up.

—Exod. 19:18-20

On the top of the mountain, God gave Moses the Ten Commandments as well as many other laws and regulations. These laws were written in the Book of the Covenant which Moses gave to the people. When Moses came down from the mountain, he read to the people the words of the Book of the Covenant and they agreed to keep this covenant. They built an altar and offered sacrifices for sin and as a thanksgiving to the Lord.

Moses returned to the mountain top and received many other instructions from God, including plans for the construction of a tabernacle, or tent meeting place, priestly garments, and rules and regulations concerning sacrifices. He remained on the mountain for forty days and forty nights. At the end of this time, God gave Moses two tablets of stone on which were carved the Ten Commandments by God's own finger. The giving of the Law was in the year 1491 BC (Pierce & Pierce 2003).

God instructed Moses to build a tabernacle so that He could "dwell in their midst" (Exod. 25:8), for this is the reason that God had brought them out of Egypt. God said to the Israelites: "I will make my dwelling among you . . . I will walk among you and will be your God, and you shall be my people" (Lev. 26:11-12).

Work commenced on the tabernacle according to the plans that God had given Moses. Within the tabernacle was the Ark of the Covenant which contained the Ten Commandments. This was in the Most Holy Place where God's presence was, and was shielded by a curtain. God would meet with Moses above the mercy seat in the Most Holy Place. Priests from the tribe of Levi were consecrated to serve in the tabernacle. Moses' brother Aaron and Aaron's four sons were also later consecrated as priests. When the tabernacle was finished, "the cloud covered the tent of meeting, and the glory of the LORD filled the tabernacle . . . Throughout all their journeys, whenever the cloud was taken up from over the tabernacle, the people of Israel would set out. But if the cloud was not taken up, then they did not set out till the day that it was taken up. For the cloud of the LORD was on the tabernacle by day, and fire was in it by night, in the sight of all the house of Israel throughout all their journeys" (Exod. 40:34, 36-38).

The presence of God went before or behind the Israelites throughout their journey through the desert to The Promised Land, appearing as a pillar of cloud by day and a pillar of fire by night. A 'pillar' gives the impression that this cloud or fire was visible to *all* the Israelites, a sign that God was with them. As the Israelites were very numerous and their camp would have extended far across the desert, for the pillar to be visible to the whole community, its top would have had to reach far up into the sky. The presence of God on the earth in the midst of the Israelites was *connected* to God in His dwelling place in heaven. This was not *two* manifestations of God's presence in two separate locations, but rather a *joining* of heaven to earth by the presence of God. As the pillar of fire or smoke was the presence of God, God's presence in the tabernacle was an extension of His presence from His dwelling place in heaven. He says: "Heaven is my throne, and the earth is my footstool" (Isa. 66:1). The book of Amos tells us that God "builds his lofty palace in the heavens and sets its foundation on the earth" (Amos 9:6). God does not disconnect part of Himself from heaven in order to also be on the earth. Nor does He come *out of* heaven to be present on the earth. God is indivisible. His presence can be in *both* places simultaneously.

The Israelites made their way across the desert from Mount Sinai towards The Promised Land with the presence of God guiding them. When they were close to part of the land that God was to give them—the hill country of the Amorites, they were to take possession of it from the current occupants. They sent twelve spies into the land that brought back samples of the luscious fruit that grew there and reported that the land was very good. They also brought back with them a report that made the people afraid. They said that the people currently living there were stronger and taller than they were and they would not be able to defeat them. Because of this report, the people did not trust God to help them. God was very angry with them and swore to them that that generation would not set foot in the land. The only ones of that generation that would cross into the land that God was giving them would be Caleb, who followed the Lord 'wholeheartedly' and did not give this disheartening report, and Joshua, Moses' assistant, who had maintained his faith in God. He would be the one who would lead Israel into the land to inherit it. Apart from these two men only the 'little ones', who were not to be held accountable for the sin and lack of faith of the people, were allowed to enter. The remainder of the Israelites (those over twenty years old), including Moses, would eventually perish in the desert.

"The LORD's anger was kindled against Israel, and he made them wander in the wilderness forty years, until all the generation that had done evil in the sight of the LORD was gone" (Num. 32:13). During all this time though, God provided for them. Their clothes and shoes did not wear out and they had food to eat and water to drink. The Israelites wandered around the desert, stopping to camp when the presence of the Lord stopped over a place. They settled in some places for many months, even years, before moving on. In all they camped in about seventeen places. Did the people learn their lesson? Perhaps not! Many times during their wanderings, the people rebelled against God and many times He disciplined them, sending disasters upon them.

Towards the end of their journeying, Moses climbed Mount Nebo and beheld the land of promise that God was giving to the Israelites, but he did not enter into it. He died at the age of one hundred and twenty years on this mountain and God moved his body to a valley in the land of Moab and buried him there. Joshua, Moses' assistant, became the leader of the Israelites and they crossed over into the land of Canaan in the year 1451 BC (Pierce & Pierce 2003).

God had promised the Israelites land of their own, land which was to be their possession for ever. This land was already occupied by nations who were exceedingly wicked. With God's help, the Israelites battled the people that were occupying the land of Canaan, driving them out. Eventually, God overthrew "seven nations in the land of Canaan" (Acts 13:19) to give the people their inheritance. Moses told the Israelites that it is "because of the wickedness of these nations that the LORD is driving them out before you" (Deut. 9:4). These nations were very violent, worshipped idols, and practised all kinds of vile things. The Lord cautioned the Israelites:

> There shall not be found among you anyone who burns his son or his daughter as an offering, anyone who practices divination or tells fortunes or interprets omens, or a sorcerer or a charmer or a medium or a necromancer or one who inquires of the dead, for whoever does these things is an abomination to the LORD. And because of these abominations the LORD your God is driving them out before you.
>
> —Deut. 18:10-12

Battles were fought under the leadership of men such as Joshua and King Saul. Eventually, during the reign of King David, the whole land of Israel belonged to them and, for a time, they were to enjoy peace in the land under the reign of David's son, Solomon. The people prospered and King Solomon built a temple in place of the tabernacle for the people to worship God in. After King Solomon died, the country divided into two. The land the northern tribes occupied became known as Israel and the southern tribes formed the country of Judah. The people of Judah became known as 'Jews'. Generally, a native Jewish person is considered to be someone whose mother is Jewish.

Although the Israelites were God's chosen people for a purpose, other people were not excluded from God's love and care: "Let no foreigner who has bound himself to the LORD say, 'the LORD will surely separate me from his people'" (Isa. 56:3). There were people from other nations who had faith in God and identified themselves with the God of the Israelites. God said:

> When a foreigner, who is not of your people Israel, comes from a far country for your name's sake (for they shall hear of your great name and your mighty hand, and of your outstretched arm), when he comes and prays toward this house, hear in heaven your dwelling place and do according to all for which the foreigner calls to you, in order that all the peoples of the earth may know your name and fear you, as do your people Israel, and that they may know that this house that I have built is called by your name.
>
> —1 Kings 8:41-43

These foreigners who had faith in, and identified with, the God of the Israelites, were able to be 'grafted in' to 'the vine'.

Although the *nation* of Israel was God's chosen people and they were in covenant relationship with Him, the *individual* was still accountable to God. The Israelites were warned that if anyone of them turned away from the Lord to worship the gods of other nations, "the LORD will not be willing to forgive him, but rather the anger of the LORD and his jealousy will smoke against that man, and the curses written in this book will settle upon him, and the LORD will blot out his name from under heaven" (Deut. 29:20).

God's relationship with His people Israel is spoken of in Scripture as, not only that of a Father (and they were often referred to as a daughter), but that of a Husband: "For your Maker is your husband, the LORD of hosts is his name" (Isa. 54:5). God's covenant with Israel was a covenant of love. God said: "I will make an everlasting covenant with you, my faithful love promised to David" (Isa. 55:3 NIV). The people were to obey God to fulfil *their* part of the covenant. Often though, instead of obeying God they were "following the stubbornness" (Jer. 16:12 NIV) of their own evil hearts. During Israel's times of rebellion and backsliding, God likens them to an unfaithful wife or sometimes a prostitute, asking: "Have I been a wilderness to Israel, or a land of thick darkness? Why then do my people say, 'We are free, we will come no more to you'? Can a virgin forget her ornaments, or a bride her attire? Yet my people have forgotten me days without number" (Jer. 2:31-32), "for they are all adulterers, a company of treacherous men" (Jer. 9:2). Many times they deserted God and turned to the gods of other nations and set up idols in their hearts.

God promised the people that, at the end of time, when He regathers them to the land: "You will call me 'my husband'; you will no longer call me 'my master'" (Hosea 2:16 NIV). Israel's covenant with God will be fulfilled. God promised the people of Israel: "I will betroth you to me forever. I will betroth you to me in righteousness and in justice, in steadfast love and in mercy" (Hosea 2:19).

Because God is faithful to all His promises, the Israelites remained His chosen people despite many times turning away from God, including following the idolatrous practices of the nations around them. In the book of Jeremiah, God asks: "Has a nation changed its gods, even though they are no gods? But my people have changed their glory for that which does not profit . . . my people have committed two evils: they have forsaken me, the fountain of living waters, and hewed out cisterns for themselves, broken cisterns that can hold no water" (Jer. 2:11, 13).

God continued to show His love for them, but many times that love had to be 'tough love' and the people paid for their disobedience by bringing upon themselves and the land, plagues and disasters, being defeated in battle, and being taken into exile away from their own land. God warned the people: "I will scatter you among the nations, and I will unsheathe the sword after you, and your land shall be a desolation, and your cities shall be a waste" (Lev. 26:33). Once, for example, God delivered them into the hands of a pretty rough crowd—the Philistines, for forty years because of the evil they had done in His eyes. The tribes of Israel were also sent into lengthy exile in

Assyria and the tribes of Judah into exile in Babylon, many of whom chose to stay there. The *Diaspora* is the name given to Jews who are living in countries other than their homeland of Israel.

In the book of Amos, God expresses frustration that His people have not returned to Him despite Him bringing disaster after disaster upon them because of their unfaithfulness. He says:

"I gave you cleanness of teeth in all your cities, and lack of bread in all your places, yet you did not return to me. . . I also withheld the rain from you when there were yet three months to the harvest; I would send rain on one city, and send no rain on another city; one field would have rain, and the field on which it did not rain would wither; so two or three cities would wander to another city to drink water, and would not be satisfied; yet you did not return to me. . . I struck you with blight and mildew; your many gardens and your vineyards, your fig trees and your olive trees the locust devoured; yet you did not return to me. . . I sent among you a pestilence after the manner of Egypt; I killed your young men with the sword, and carried away your horses, and I made the stench of your camp go up into your nostrils; yet you did not return to me, I overthrew some of you, as when God overthrew Sodom and Gomorrah, and you were as a brand plucked out of the burning; yet you did not return to me."

—Amos 4:6-11

Once, after repeated warnings through the prophets, which the people ignored, and many disasters, the LORD told the people He would deliver up the city, stir up a nation against them, and again send them into exile. "'The time is ripe for my people Israel; I will spare them no longer. In that day,' declares the Sovereign LORD, 'the songs in the temple will turn to wailing. Many, many bodies – flung everywhere! Silence!'" (Amos 8:2-3 NIV).

When the people were in exile or being punished because of their unfaithfulness, God was willing to forgive them, but *they* had a part to play. It was *not* one-sided. Once, when the Ark of the Covenant was captured by the Philistines and the people mourned for it, as it was the place where God's presence dwelt in the tabernacle, Samuel told them: "If you are returning to the LORD with all your heart, then put away the foreign gods and the Ashtoreth from among you and direct your heart to the LORD and serve him only, and he will deliver you out of the hand of the Philistines" (1 Sam. 7:3). It was generally: 'If you do this, then I will do that'. God's *love* for them was unconditional, but they had to take responsibility for their disobedience and lack of faith. They had to make some changes and turn back to God in order for Him to deliver them.

The temple built by King Solomon was burnt down in 586 BC and another one built in 516 BC. This temple was later destroyed and rebuilt by King Herod in 20 BC, but was then destroyed by Titus in AD 70. During Titus' reign of terror, 1, 100, 000

Jews were killed and many scattered over the face of the earth. The Jewish people were again in exile. There has not been another temple built. In the book of Deuteronomy, God specifically told the people that the place where He would dwell would be in the temple in Jerusalem and that is where He would put His name. Jews scattered around the world have continued to meet in synagogues up to the present day, believing that, one day, they will rebuild the temple in Jerusalem. All that remains of the temple in Jerusalem is the Western Wall, where the Jewish people continue to go to pray and mourn for the loss of the temple, placing prayers written on small pieces of paper between the stones.

In the history of the Israelites, there was always a remnant of people, no matter how small, who remained faithful to God. God's message of love and forgiveness and of the hope of the promised Messiah would be carried through the generations by those who were faithful to Him, and His written Word would be preserved and passed on.

THE LAW

On Mount Sinai, God gave Moses special laws called the Ten Commandments. He inscribed them on two tablets of stone with His finger and Moses placed these in the Ark of the Covenant, which journeyed with the Israelites in the desert and resided in the Most Holy Place in the Tabernacle, or Tent of Meeting during the times they made camp. Later when they were established in the land, the Ark of the Covenant was housed in the Most Holy Place in the temple that King Solomon built.

The Ten Commandments begin with four duties to God:

"I am the LORD your God, who brought you out of the land of Egypt, out of the house of slavery.

"You shall have no other gods before me.

"You shall not make for yourself a carved image, or any likeness of anything that is in heaven above, or that is in the earth beneath, or that is in the water under the earth. You shall not bow down to them or serve them, for I the LORD your God am a jealous God, visiting the iniquity of the fathers on the children to the third and the fourth generation of those who hate me, but showing steadfast love to thousands of those who love me and keep my commandments.

"You shall not take the name of the LORD your God in vain, for the LORD will not hold him guiltless who takes his name in vain.

"Remember the Sabbath day, to keep it holy. Six days you shall labour, and do all your work, but the seventh day is a Sabbath to the LORD your God. On it you shall not do any work, you, or your son, or your daughter, your male servant, or your female servant, or your livestock, or the sojourner who is within your gates. For in six days the LORD made heaven and earth, the sea, and all that is in them, and rested on the seventh day. Therefore the LORD blessed the Sabbath day and made it holy."

—Exod. 20:1-11

The Sabbath was to be observed by the Israelites as a sign between God and them for ever.

The last six commandments concern the duty of the Israelites to their fellowman:

"Honour your father and your mother, that your days may be long in the land that the LORD your God is giving you.

"You shall not murder.

"You shall not commit adultery.

"You shall not steal.

"You shall not bear false witness against your neighbour.

"You shall not covet your neighbour's house; you shall not covet your neighbour's wife, or his male servant, or his female servant, or his ox, or his donkey, or anything that is your neighbour's."

—Exod. 20:12-17

The Ten Commandments are summed up in this: "What does the LORD require of you but to do justice, and to love kindness, and to walk humbly with your God" (Mic. 6:8). Jesus said: "In everything, do to others what you would have them do to you, for this sums up the Law and the Prophets" (Matt. 7:12 NIV). God also gave the people the greatest commandment: "You shall love the LORD your God with all your heart and with all your soul and with all your might" (Deut. 6:5).

Through Moses, God gave the people of Israel the Law. This formed part of the covenant that He entered into with the Israelites. It is also known as the 'Old Covenant' or the 'Old Testament'. The Law was very lengthy and detailed, covering many aspects of daily life and relationships, particularly how the Israelites were to relate to God and their fellowman. The Law also contained many health regulations, regulations regarding food, and laws of justice.

The observing of God's commands and decrees was not for the benefit of God but for the people's own good. Job's friend Elihu said to him:

"Do you think this to be just? Do you say, 'It is my right before God,' that you ask, 'What advantage have I? How am I better off than if I had sinned?' I will answer you and your friends with you. Look at the heavens, and see; and behold the clouds, which are higher than you. If you have sinned, what do you accomplish against him? And if your transgressions are multiplied, what do you do to him? If you are righteous, what do you give to him? Or what does he receive from your hand? Your wickedness concerns a man like yourself, and your righteousness a son of man."

—Job 35:2-8

Moses told the people that these laws and commandments "are not just idle words for you—they are your life" (Deut. 32:47 NIV). According to Psalm nineteen, by the Law, statutes, precepts, and commands of the Lord we are warned, as they are a guide for avoiding what is wrong and doing what is right, and in keeping them there is great reward. The Law then, served as a 'fine-tuner' of the conscience.

Many times the people strayed from God's commands and many times they had to be brought back and reminded of what the Lord expected of them. King Josiah, who began his reign as an eight year old and reigned thirty-one years in Jerusalem, brought the people back from a very dark period in the history of Israel when idol worship was rife and unfaithfulness to God abounded. He read to the people "all the words of the Book of the Covenant that had been found in the house of the LORD. And the king stood by the pillar and made a covenant before the LORD, to walk after the LORD and to keep his commandments and his testimonies and his statutes with all his heart and all his soul, to perform the words of this covenant that were written in this book. And all the people joined in the covenant" (2 Kings 23:2-3).

Why so many rules, regulations, and laws?
— God knew that the people needed these laws to maintain justice, live in peace, and to make sure that the poor and needy were cared for;
— They were to remind the Israelites of their covenant with God. In the observance of the Law, the people would be remembering the Lord their God;
— There were many benefits for the people in keeping God's commands, including good health, prosperity in their land, and long life. Although God's *love* for the people was unconditional, God's *promises* were conditional on the people doing *their* part in the agreement; that is, *I* will do this, if *you* will do that. There were blessings for obedience and curses for disobedience. Usually the people's part was simply that of faithfulness and obedience. For example, God told the people: "If you will diligently listen to the voice of the LORD your God, and do that which is right in his eyes, and give ear to his commandments and keep all his statutes, I will put none of the diseases on you that I put on the Egyptians, for I am the LORD, your healer" (Exod. 15:26). They were to "serve the LORD your God, and he will bless your bread and your water, and I will take sickness away from among you. None shall miscarry or be barren in your land; I will fulfil the number of your days" (Exod. 23:25-26). The Israelites were to "walk in all the way that the LORD your God has commanded you, that you may live, and that it may go well with you, and that you may live long in the land that you shall possess" (Deut. 5:33);
— God wanted a holy nation—a people set apart from the wicked and ungodly nations that surrounded them. God promised them: "Obey my

voice and keep my covenant, you shall be my treasured possession among all peoples, for all the earth is mine; and you shall be to me a kingdom of priests and a holy nation. These are the words that you shall speak to the people of Israel" (Exod. 19:5-6). Through His chosen people, God would give His written Word and, through them, He would bring the promised Messiah; and

— The Law served the purpose of convicting the people of sin. The Law was given as an adjunct to the conscience, not as a substitute. They worked hand in hand. If the people were aware of these laws and they did not do what the laws required of them, they would have a guilty conscience. They would then know that they had sinned and they would feel the need to seek forgiveness from God. According to David, there are sins that are *wilful sins*—those that he is aware of and that cause guilt in his heart, for which he not only asks forgiveness, but also asks for God's help that they might not rule over him. There are others that are *hidden faults*—those that he is not aware of committing, for which he also asks forgiveness, because in doing these things, he is also breaking God's Law. He knows that only through God's forgiveness will he be "blameless and innocent of great transgression" (Ps. 19:13).

Did following the Law make the people holy in God's eyes? Did keeping the Law lead to eternal life? Well for a start, none of the Israelites ever kept the *whole* Law. It was virtually impossible and "whoever keeps the whole law and yet stumbles at just one point is guilty of breaking all of it" (James 2:10 NIV). The people were *all* sinners and under the law of sin and death. The apostle Paul tells us that, "whatever the law says it speaks to those who are under the law, so that every mouth may be stopped, and the whole world may be held accountable to God. For by works of the law no human being will be justified in his sight, since through the law comes knowledge of sin" (Rom. 3:19-20).

At this stage in history then, we have:
1. Those who sin within the boundaries of the conscience; and
2. Those who sin within the boundaries of the conscience *and* The Law; this group being the Israelites and those who have been 'grafted in' with God's chosen people.

The law of sin and death requires that sin is paid for by death. Under the Old Covenant, the Israelites were required to sacrifice an animal as a payment for their sins. They needed to:
1. *Confess their sins* to the priest who, under the Old Covenant, was the mediator between God and the Israelites;
2. *Repent of their sins* by being truly sorry for doing wrong;
3. *Ask for forgiveness for their sins* from God, whose law they had broken; and

4. *Bring an animal for sacrifice to pay for their sins*—often a lamb or a goat without defect or blemish. The guilt of the person, because of their sin, was symbolically transferred by the laying of hands on the animal and the penalty of God's wrath for sin—death—the shedding of blood, was inflicted on the animal.

By instruction from God and under the leadership of Moses, a system of sacrifices was instituted, including burnt offerings which were offered every morning and evening and guilt or sin offerings presented for intentional and unintentional sins. The offerings and sacrifices needed to be accompanied by repentance and then God would forgive the people their sins. These offerings were effective only if offered *in faith*. In other words, *faith* was more important than the actual offering. The people had to have faith that God would forgive their sins once they had repented, asked for forgiveness, and paid the required sacrifice, that is, the death of an animal, which was a substitute for themselves. The people also had to have faith in the promised Messiah—the one who was to come and put an end to all these sacrifices.

Animal sacrifice was a *shadow* of the things to come. It was a 'type' pointing the way to the 'once and for all' sacrifice that was to be made by the Messiah. Like Abraham, the people believed in the Lord and He credited it to them as righteousness. They had faith in God for the forgiveness of sins. Because of *their faith*, He gave them *His righteousness*.

The Bible says: "Blessed is the one whose transgression is forgiven, whose sin is covered. Blessed is the man against whom the LORD counts no iniquity" (Ps. 32:1-2). By the confession of sins and repentance from those sins, and through the people's faith in God for the forgiveness of sins followed by the substitutionary sacrifice of the animal, the people's sins were 'covered'.

This ceremony of sacrifice was something that was required to be repeated over and over. The people continually sinned. Sacrifices were continually offered. In addition to the many burnt offerings and sacrifices, once a year the high priest would enter the Most Holy Place in the inner sanctuary of the temple with a blood sacrifice, offered for the sins of himself and also on behalf of the people. The writer of the letter to the Hebrews describes such sacrifices as "an annual reminder of sins, because it is impossible for the blood of bulls and goats to take away sins" (Heb. 10:3 NIV).

Sacrifice was *not* a substitute for obedience. Although God required the Israelites to sacrifice, He required obedience first and foremost: "Does the LORD delight in burnt offerings and sacrifices as much as in obeying the voice of the LORD? To obey is better than sacrifice" (1 Sam. 15:22-23 NIV). God said: "I desire steadfast love and not sacrifice, the knowledge of God rather than burnt offerings" (Hosea 6:6).

The peoples' faith and love for God was demonstrated by their obedience to God. Moses told the people that, if they were "careful to obey all this law before the LORD our God, as he has commanded us, that will be our righteousness" (Deut. 6:25

NIV). Their obedience in following the Law was a *demonstration of,* and *evidence of,* their faith.

THE WHOLE WORLD IN HIS HANDS

At the end of the six days of Creation, God may have finished creating, but He did not just sit back and watch what went on from a distance. Throughout history, as documented in the Scriptures, it is evident that God was and is, involved in and has full control over, His Creation and is able to override physical processes and the laws of physics and use these laws and processes in His Creation for His own purposes.

King David writes: "Your word O LORD is eternal; it stands firm in the heavens. Your faithfulness continues through all generations; you established the earth, and it endures. Your laws endure to this day, for all things serve you" (Ps. 119:89-90 NIV). God doesn't serve all things. *All things serve God!* He is *outside* the physical laws—the laws of 'nature'.

There are many examples in Scripture where we see evidence of this. For example, there is an account in the book of Joshua when "the sun stood still, and the moon stopped, until the nation took vengeance on their enemies . . . The sun stopped in the midst of heaven and did not hurry to set for about a whole day" (Josh. 10:13). This was to allow a victory in battle for God's people. Yet another instance where God influenced time was as a sign to King Hezekiah when "he brought the shadow back ten steps, by which it had gone down on the steps of Ahaz" (2 Kings 20:11).

In the book of Judges, we read of God causing a fleece of wool to have dew covering it when all the ground around was dry, and of the reverse happening too. The story of Elijah tells of how Elijah challenged the prophets of Baal. God sent down fire from heaven to burn up a sacrifice, as well as the wood, stones, and the soil around it. He also burned up the water that had been poured over and around the sacrifice to prove to the priests of the false god Baal and the people who worshipped this 'god', who was the one true Living God.

God says: "I bring prosperity and create disaster" (Isa. 45:7 NIV). The writer of Lamentations asks: "Is it not from the mouth of the Most High that both calamities and good things come?" (Lam. 3:38). Throughout the Bible, there are records of earthquakes, floods, wind, and fire caused by God, who can bring about disasters for His purposes. In the book of Genesis, we read about a worldwide flood that wiped out all the inhabitants of the earth except for Noah and his family, and prophecy written in the book of Revelation tells of a great earthquake and many other disasters that will kill many people in the end times.

God can cause animals to do what He wants them to do. He directed two of every kind of animal to board the ark and seven of every kind of 'clean' animal. He provided a great fish to swallow Jonah, made a vine grow up over Jonah, provided a worm to chew the vine, and a scorching east wind to blow on Jonah. God ordered ravens to feed the prophet Elijah with meat when he was out in the desert, and He caused Balaam's donkey to speak.

God caused drought, plagues, and pestilence but at other times sent rain upon the land and prevented the spoiling of crops. In the book of Malachi, He promised the Israelites that *if* they were faithful to Him, He would "prevent pests from devouring your crops, and the vines in your fields will not cast their fruit" (Mal. 3:11 NIV).

When Elijah struck a stream with his cloak, God caused the water in it to be divided, just as He had divided the Red Sea by driving the waters back with a strong east wind, forming a path of dry land so that the Israelites could cross over to flee from the Egyptian army who were pursuing them.

God can multiply food to feed crowds of people. The book of Second Kings records a miracle of food being multiplied to feed one hundred men. In the Gospels there were two recorded instances of Jesus feeding four thousand and five thousand with only a small amount of food.

God uses miracles over nature even in everyday problems that may seem insignificant. One of the men working with the prophet Elisha had dropped an axe-head into water and was most alarmed because it was borrowed. When he showed Elisha the place it had dropped, Elisha "cut off a stick and threw it in there and made the iron float" (2 Kings 6:6).

God used part of His Creation to guide the wise men to His Son after His birth. "The star they had seen in the east went ahead of them until it stopped over the place where the child was" (Matt. 2:9 NIV). He also caused a total eclipse and an earthquake at the time when Jesus died and another earthquake when He rose from the dead.

THE HOLY SPIRIT IN THE OLD TESTAMENT

We first read of the Holy Spirit right at the very beginning of Creation. Genesis tells us that the Spirit of God hovered over the waters covering the earth. The Holy Spirit was also active in Old Testament times in a number of other ways and for a number of purposes:

Life. God's Spirit was breathed into Adam, giving him life.

Connections. God the Father and God the Son are one with the Holy Spirit; the Holy Spirit proceeding from both the Father and the Son. The Holy Spirit connected Adam and Eve to God's presence when they were created.

Prophecy. The Holy Spirit sometimes 'rested' on people causing them to prophesy.

Help in fulfilling a role. The Holy Spirit guided people and gave them wisdom in their roles as judges, leaders, or kings in Israel. When Saul was anointed king by Samuel, Samuel told him that "the Spirit of the LORD will rush upon you, and you will . . . be turned into another man" (1 Sam. 10:6). In the latter part of Saul's reign however, he was disobedient to God and the Spirit of the Lord departed from him.

Power. After the reign of King Saul, David reigned as king of Israel, and "the Spirit of the LORD came upon David in power" (1 Sam. 16:13 NIV). The power of the Holy

Spirit also enabled miracles to happen, such as the raising of a boy from the dead through Elisha.

Understanding God's plans. The Spirit put into David's mind the plans of the temple that his son Solomon was later to build. David said: "All this . . . I have in writing from the hand of the LORD upon me, and he gave me understanding in all the details of the plan" (1 Chr. 28:19 NIV).

Transporting from one place to another. Ezekiel had a vision of God in heaven. He said that the "Spirit entered into me and set me on my feet" (Ezek. 2:2). Later, the Spirit lifted Ezekiel up and carried him to some exiles that were living by the river. At another time, the Spirit lifted him up "between earth and heaven and brought me in visions of God to Jerusalem" (Ezek. 8:3), and later "into Chaldea, to the exiles" (Ezek. 11:24). After the fall of Jerusalem, the Spirit took him into the city.

A closer and deeper relationship with God. David, for example, had the Holy Spirit indwelling His heart and was very close to God.

In Old Testament times, the Holy Spirit was not given individually to *all* who had faith in God, only to a select few for God's purposes. The spiritual connections formed by the Holy Spirit between God and these people were temporary. Having the Holy Spirit dwelling within their hearts whilst they lived on earth, did not mean that they would *not* depart to the abode of the dead once they had departed their bodies. They were still under the law of sin and death. On the death of the person to whom the Holy Spirit had been given, the Holy Spirit, along with the person's spirit, would depart from them and return to God, and the person would journey to the abode of the dead to 'rest with their fathers'.

HERE'S WHAT WE NEED:

We need a way of fulfilling all the requirements of the Law and satisfying the payment for sin; or at least we need someone who is willing to do this on our behalf.

A better sacrifice is needed—a perfect one that does not require repeating over and over—one sacrifice that would take away the guilt of our sins once and for all. We need someone to put an end to sacrifices; someone who will make sacrifices *obsolete*.

We need a new and better city, one that is safe and peaceful; a city for *all* nations to enjoy under the protection and rule of a fair and just leader; a city that will never be destroyed.

We need a New Covenant. We need to be able to come directly to God ourselves without needing to go through an earthly priest. We need a restored relationship with our Creator—the God of the universe.

Chapter Eight
The Promise
The Son in Eternity Past

God—Father, Son, and Holy Spirit, has existed eternally. The Holy Spirit proceeds from the Father and the Son. Being one in Spirit, God the Father is never separated from God the Son, even if they 'manifest' in two different locations, for example in heaven and on the earth.

A father will have a son that is equal in position and standing to himself. A human father, for example, will bring forth a son that is equally human. The Son is equal with the Father.

There are several passages in the Old Testament that refer to 'the Son'. David, in the book of Psalms, speaks a number of times about the Son, confirming that the Son already existed *before* coming to the earth in human form as a small baby. For example, he writes: "Kiss the Son, lest he be angry, and you perish in the way, for his wrath is quickly kindled. Blessed are all who take refuge in him" (Ps. 2:11-12).

In the New Testament, John tells us that Jesus is "the only Son from the Father" (John 1:14), that "God sent his only Son into the world" (1 John 4:9) and that "He gave His only begotten Son" (John 3:16 NKJV). Jesus was already the 'only Son' *before* He came in the flesh to dwell among us. God the Father was sending *His Son* into the world, not one who was to *become* His Son by being born of a woman. He already *was* 'the Son'. The Son is eternal in His Sonship. The Sonship-Fatherhood relationship had no beginning.

As the Son of God, He is "appointed the heir of all things" (Heb. 1:2). All things belong to God the Father; therefore all things belong to God the Son. The glory of the Father belongs to the Son. Before He died, Jesus prayed: "And now, Father, glorify me in your own presence with the glory that I had with you before the world existed" (John 17:5).

THE SON IN THE OLD TESTAMENT

The world was made *through* the Son—the Living Word, and it was made *for* the Son. John wrote: "In the beginning was the Word, and the Word was with God, and the Word was God. He was in the beginning with God . . . He was in the world, and the world was made through him, yet the world did not know him" (John 1:1-2, 10), "for by him all things were created, in heaven and on earth, visible and invisible, whether thrones or dominions or rulers or authorities—all things were created through him and for him. And he is before all things, and in him all things hold together" (Col. 1:16-17).

Throughout the Old Testament, we read of the involvement of the Son in the formation and history of Israel. This is the period of time between the creation of the world and when He entered the world as a tiny baby in the stable in Bethlehem. It is generally agreed by scholars that, whenever God appears in the Old Testament in visible form, that it is in the person of God the Son. His appearance in visible form in 'Old Testament times' though, is not the same as the Son coming in the flesh and taking on humanity as He did two thousand years ago. It is, rather, in a similar way to which angels take on visible form, or materialize, to appear to mankind.

The Bible tells us that no one has ever seen the Father. There was a time however, when Moses was shielded by God and allowed to see His back only. This particular instance is likely to have been God the Father, for He said to Moses: "You cannot see my face, for man shall not see me and live" (Exod. 33:20).

Usually, the Lord would speak to Moses "face to face, clearly and not in riddles; he sees the form of the LORD" (Num. 12:8 NIV), "as a man speaks to his friend" (Exod. 33:11). It is likely, therefore, that most of the time Moses saw God, he was seeing God the Son.

Sometimes in Scripture, the Son is referred to as 'the angel of the Lord', such as when He appeared to Moses in the burning bush to call him to go to Egypt to free the Israelites from slavery. When the Israelites were finally let go from Pharaoh's cruel bondage in Egypt, the 'angel of God' went ahead of them, or accompanied them. They were told to "pay careful attention to him and obey his voice; do not rebel against him, for he will not pardon your transgression, for my name is in him" (Exod. 23:21). This was God the Son being spoken of by God the Father. Paul confirms that the Israelites "drank from the spiritual rock that followed them, and the rock was Christ" (1 Cor. 10:4).

When God appeared to Moses, Aaron, Nadab, Abihu, and the seventy leaders of Israel, they "went up, and they saw the God of Israel. There was under his feet as it were a pavement of sapphire stone, like the very heaven for clearness. And he did not lay his hand on the chief men of the people of Israel; they beheld God, and ate and drank" (Exod. 24:9-11). This was likely to have been an appearance of God the Son.

Another time, He appeared to the maidservant of Abraham's wife Sarah in the desert. She said: "You are a God of seeing . . . Truly here I have seen him who looks after me" (Gen. 16:13). He also appeared to Abraham on a number of occasions, once in the company of two angels. Abraham prepared a meal for them and they ate in his presence.

In the book of Genesis, we read the account of Jacob, son of Isaac, son of Abraham, who wrestled with a man one night until daybreak. This 'man' is likely to have been God the Son, for "Jacob called the name of the place Peniel, saying, 'For I have seen God face to face, and yet my life has been delivered'" (Gen. 32:30). The 'man' blessed him and changed his name from Jacob to Israel because he had "struggled with God and man and have overcome" (Gen. 32:28 NIV).

In the book of Judges, we read the account of a man named Gideon, to whom the angel of the Lord appeared. Later in the passage, this angel is referred to as 'the Lord' and Gideon offers a sacrifice to Him which the 'angel' burns up with flames.

The angel of the Lord also appeared to a man and his wife who were to become the parents of Samson. The 'angel' told them that His name was 'beyond understanding'. Upon realising whom they had seen and spoken to, the man was most alarmed and said to his wife: "We shall surely die, for we have seen God" (Jud. 13:22).

The Lord also appeared to a young child. When the boy Samuel, who was later to become a prophet, grew up in the temple, the Lord came and stood near him calling him.

Job believed in the promised Messiah and he knew that He already existed, even though He had not yet come on the earth in the flesh. He said: "Even now, behold, my witness is in heaven, and he who testifies for me is on high. My friends scorn me; my eye pours out tears to God, that he would argue the case of a man with God, as a son of man does with his neighbour" (Job 16:19-22). Job is speaking of the Son of God interceding on his behalf to God the Father in heaven, and he puts his faith in Him. When God questioned Job after the great disasters that befell him, it is likely that this was God the Son because Job actually *saw* Him. Job said: "I had heard of you by the hearing of the ear, but now my eye sees you" (Job 42:5).

The book of Daniel tells of three young men of faith who followed God and obeyed Him. They were thrown into a fiery furnace for defying the king's command, but when King Nebuchadnezzar looked into the fire he saw "four men unbound, walking in the midst of the fire, and they are not hurt; and the appearance of the fourth is like a son of the gods" (Dan. 3:25). This fourth man is likely to have been the Son of God.

Daniel also disobeyed the king's orders by praying to God and was thrown into a den of lions only to be saved by God the Son; for when the king came to check on him expecting him to be long dead, Daniel called out to the king: "My God sent his angel and shut the lion's mouths" (Dan. 6:22).

Daniel later saw in a vision a "man clothed in linen, with a belt of fine gold from Uphaz around his waist. His body was like beryl, his face like the appearance of lightning, his eyes like flaming torches, his arms and legs like the gleam of burnished bronze, and the sound of his words like the sound of a multitude" (Dan. 10:5-6). Even though Daniel was the only one to see this vision, likely of God the Son, the other men with him became overwhelmed with terror and fled and hid themselves. The vision caused Daniel himself to be sapped of strength, his face to pale, and he felt helpless. The 'man' told Daniel that he had been sent to him in response to Daniel's words, to his desire to gain understanding, and because he had humbled himself before God. He touched Daniel's lips enabling him to speak and he gave him strength. Daniel calls him 'my lord'.

The prophet Ezekiel had a vision in which he saw an 'expanse sparkling like ice'. Above this expanse there was "the likeness of a throne, in appearance like sapphire; and seated above the likeness of a throne was a likeness with a human appearance. And upward from what had the appearance of his waist I saw as it were gleaming metal, like the appearance of fire enclosed all around. And downward from what had the appearance of his waist I saw as it were the appearance of fire, and there was brightness around him. Like the appearance of the bow that is in the cloud on the day of rain, so was the appearance of the brightness all around. Such was the appearance of the likeness of the glory of the LORD" (Ezek. 1:26-28). As the Son is the likeness of the Father, it is likely that it was the Son that Ezekiel saw. Later, Ezekiel again saw the Lord and said that "he put out the form of a hand and took me by a lock of my head" (Ezek. 8:3).

THE PROMISE OF THE MESSIAH

Approximately one quarter of the Bible is prophetic. Why? Because God knows the future and He wants to let us know of some things before they happen. The reasons that God has given us this prophecy include:

1. So that we know that the Bible *is* the Word of God. If prophecy that was given in Scripture is fulfilled, then we know that it has come from God, because only God knows the future;
2. So that we can be prepared for some things *before* they happen. God wants to warn and protect His people;
3. To warn the unrighteous of the coming wrath of God so that they might turn from their sins;
4. To give the people of God hope. God gave the people hope for their salvation through the promised Messiah. He gives those who belong to Him hope in the promise of eternal life, in the return of the Lord Jesus, and in the renewal of all things; and
5. Because the people in Old Testament times knew, through prophecy, of the promised Messiah who would come to save them from their sins, they were able to put their faith in Him *then* for the forgiveness of sins, even though this event had not yet happened. They were looking *forward* in faith to this event. Since the Messiah came to dwell in the flesh upon the earth, people have looked *back* at this event in faith.

The Scriptures contain many prophecies foretelling the coming of the Son as Saviour. In addition, many passages contain prophecies about His *Second* Coming as King. This chapter however, will only concentrate on those prophecies relating to the coming of the Son as *Saviour*.

Right from the beginning in the Garden of Eden when Adam and Eve first sinned, God promised to send someone who would be the Seed of the woman only and who would defeat the devil. He said to Satan: "I will put enmity between you and the woman, and between your offspring and her offspring; he shall bruise your head, and you shall bruise his heel" (Gen. 3:15). Right from the giving of that very first prophecy, God wanted sinful man to know that there was hope.

Throughout the Old Testament period, there were signs of the coming Messiah—prophecy, appearances of the Son, events, symbolism, and people whose character and life echoed the character and life of the coming Messiah. This is called a *type*.

> **Type—*Theol*. A foreshadowing in the Old Testament of a thing, person or event in the New Testament *(Jonah in the whale's belly is a type of Christ in the tomb)*.**[1]

God also let the people know in advance what would *immediately* precede the coming of the Messiah, so that they would be in no doubt as to the fact that He is the one of whom the prophets wrote. Isaiah tells of one who would come to prepare the way of the Messiah:

> A voice cries: "In the wilderness prepare the way of the LORD; make straight in the desert a highway for our God. Every valley shall be lifted up, and every mountain and hill be made low; the uneven ground shall become level, and the rough places a plain. And the glory of the LORD shall be revealed, and all flesh shall see it together, for the mouth of the LORD has spoken."
>
> —Isa. 40:3-5

Malachi also foretold the coming of the one who would prepare the way of the Lord: "Behold, I send my messenger, and he will prepare the way before me. And the Lord whom you seek will suddenly come to his temple; and the messenger of the covenant in whom you delight" (Mal. 3:1).

Throughout the Old Testament, God revealed to His prophets details of the future coming of His Son who would be the Saviour for whom they had been waiting, so that when He came they would recognize Him as the One whom God had sent. We will now look at some of those prophecies given to, and recorded by, men of God such as King David, Isaiah, and Jeremiah.

All living things that were originally created were given God's creative blessing to reproduce after their own kinds and fill the earth, the skies, and the seas. Through the prophet Jeremiah though, God told the people that "the LORD will create a new thing on earth—a woman will surround a man" (Jer. 31:22 NIV). The last time God created, He did the exact opposite—a man (Adam) surrounded a woman (Eve). All people that had been on the earth since the time of Adam and Eve had been brought into being by the uniting of physical seed from both parents, and spiritual seed that originated from Adam's spirit which had been passed down through the generations. Now God was telling them of something that was to happen that was totally different. The Son of God was to come into the world and be born of a woman only. This would be the beginning of a *new* Creation and the ushering in of the kingdom of God.

God gave the people specific details regarding where the Messiah was to be born, through which line of descent, and from which tribe He would come. God told His people that the Messiah would be born in the town of Bethlehem and would descend from the line of Judah. The prophet Micah prophesied: "But you, O Bethlehem Ephrathah, who are too little to be among the clans of Judah, from you shall come forth for me one who is to be ruler in Israel, whose coming forth is from of old, from ancient days" (Mic. 5:2). The One who would come would be One who existed *before* He was born and He would be coming *for* God, to *fulfil the purposes of God*.

When Jacob was giving the traditional blessing over his sons before he died, he gave a prophetic blessing over Judah, from whose lineage the Messiah was to come. He said:

> The sceptre shall not depart from Judah, nor the ruler's staff from between his feet, until tribute comes to him; and to him shall be the obedience of the peoples. Binding his foal to the vine and his donkey's colt to the choice vine, he has washed his garments in wine and his vesture in the blood of grapes. His eyes are darker than wine, and his teeth whiter than milk.
>
> —Gen. 49:10-12

The prophet Zechariah foretold the triumphant entry of The Messiah into Jerusalem riding on a donkey on the day that we know as 'Palm Sunday'. He wrote: "Behold, your king is coming to you; righteous and having salvation is he, humble and mounted on a donkey, on a colt, the foal of a donkey" (Zech. 9:9). A donkey is an animal that symbolises peace. It is a beast of burden, not an animal of war like a horse.

There are many prophecies in Isaiah that speak of the coming of the Messiah. Isaiah promised that "the Redeemer will come to Zion, to those in Jacob who repent of their sins" (Isa. 59:20 NIV). God said through Isaiah:

> "But now hear, O Jacob my servant, Israel whom I have chosen! Thus says the LORD who made you, who formed you from the womb and will help you: Fear not, O Jacob my servant, Jeshurun whom I have chosen. For I will pour water on the thirsty land, and streams on the dry ground; I will pour my Spirit upon your offspring, and my blessing on your descendants. They shall spring up among the grass like willows by flowing streams . . . Thus says the LORD, the King of Israel and his Redeemer, the LORD of hosts: 'I am the first and I am the last; besides me there is no god. Who is like me? Let him proclaim it. Let him declare and set it before me, since I appointed an ancient people. Let them declare what is to come, and what will happen.'"
>
> —Isa. 42:1-4, 6-7

Isaiah also wrote of the Messiah: "The Spirit of the Sovereign LORD is on me, because the LORD has anointed me to preach good news to the poor. He has sent me to bind up the broken-hearted, to proclaim freedom for the captives and release from darkness for the prisoners" (Isa. 61:1 NIV). The Messiah would bring salvation, healing, and freedom.

In the following prophecy, Isaiah gives great detail about the coming of the promised Messiah, His death, and the reason He had to die:

> For he grew up before him like a young plant, and like a root out of dry ground; he had no form or majesty that we should look at him, and no beauty that we should desire him. He was despised and rejected by men; a man of sorrows, and acquainted with grief; and as one from whom men hide their faces he was despised, and we esteemed him not. Surely he has borne our griefs and carried our sorrows; yet we esteemed him stricken, smitten by God, and afflicted. But he was pierced for our transgressions; he was crushed for our iniquities; upon him was the chastisement that brought us peace, and with his wounds we are healed. All we like sheep have gone astray; we have turned—every one—to his own way; and the LORD has laid on him the iniquity of us all. He was oppressed, and he was afflicted, yet he opened not his mouth; like a lamb that is led to the slaughter, and like a sheep that before its shearers is silent, so he opened not his mouth. By oppression and judgment he was taken away; and as for his generation, who considered that he was cut off out of the land of the living, stricken for the transgression of my people? And they made his grave with the wicked and with a rich man in his death, although he had done no violence, and there was no deceit in his mouth. Yet it was the will of the LORD to crush him; he has put him to grief; when his soul makes an offering for guilt, he shall see his offspring; he shall prolong his days; the will of the LORD shall prosper in his hand. Out of the anguish of his soul he shall see and be satisfied; by his knowledge shall the righteous one, my servant, make many to be accounted righteous, and he shall bear their iniquities. Therefore I will divide him a portion with the many, and he shall divide the spoil with the strong, because he poured out his soul to death and was numbered with the transgressors; yet he bore the sin of many, and makes intercession for the transgressors.
>
> —Isa. 53:2-12

Again in Isaiah, when God told of the coming Messiah, He said: "See, I lay a stone in Zion, a tested stone, a precious cornerstone for a sure foundation; the one who trusts will never be dismayed . . . your covenant with death will be annulled; your agreement with the grave will not stand" (Isa. 28:16, 18 NIV). The Messiah will wipe out the 'covenant' of death! That is the best news possible! This 'covenant' is the law of sin and death that all who have ever lived have been under since Adam sinned.

In yet another passage, Isaiah wrote of the coming of the Saviour and of His death on the cross:

> See, my servant will act wisely; he will be raised and lifted up and highly exalted. Just as there were many who were appalled at him—his appearance

was so disfigured beyond that of any man and his form marred beyond human likeness—so he will sprinkle many nations, and kings will shut their mouths because of him. For what they were not told, they will see, and what they have not heard, they will understand.

—Isa. 52:13-15 NIV

Describing the events leading up to the crucifixion, as well as the crucifixion itself that would take place hundreds of years after David reigned as king in Jerusalem, David described the scene of the cross which was later fulfilled in detail. He wrote:

I am poured out like water, and all my bones are out of joint; my heart is like wax; it is melted within my breast; my strength is dried up like a potsherd, and my tongue sticks to my jaws; you lay me in the dust of death. For dogs encompass me; a company of evildoers encircles me; they have pierced my hands and feet—I can count all my bones—they stare and gloat over me; they divide my garments among them, and for my clothing they cast lots.

—Ps. 22:14-18

David prophesied that the Son would not be in the grave long enough for His body to decay. He wrote of the Father: "You will not let your Holy One see decay" (Ps. 16:10 NIV). He also prophesied that the Messiah would redeem from Sheol the souls of the righteous who had died and would lead them into heaven, writing: "He leads forth the prisoners with singing" (Ps. 68:6 NIV) and: "When you ascended on high, you led captives in your train" (Ps. 68:18 NIV).

The prophet Micah also had faith that this rescue from the abode of the dead would happen. He said of his own future time in Sheol: "But as for me, I will look to the LORD; I will wait for the God of my salvation; my God will hear me. Rejoice not over me, O my enemy; when I fall, I shall rise; when I sit in darkness, the LORD will be a light to me. I will bear the indignation of the LORD because I have sinned against him, until he pleads my cause and executes judgment for me. He will bring me out to the light; I shall look upon his vindication" (Mic. 7:7-9).

There are many other passages of prophecy in the Old Testament telling of the coming of the Messiah. Since the beginning of time, God prepared the people for the time when He would come and dwell among them in the flesh. Two thousand years ago He came . . .

Chapter Nine
The Way—Two Worlds Collide

> In the beginning was the Word, and the Word was with God, and the Word was God. He was in the beginning with God. All things were made through him, and without him was not any thing made that was made. In him was life, and the life was the light of men . . . And the Word became flesh and dwelt among us, and we have seen his glory, glory as of the only Son from the Father, full of grace and truth . . . He was in the world, and the world was made through him, yet the world did not know him. He came to his own, and his own people did not receive him. But to all who did receive him, who believed in his name, he gave the right to become children of God.
> —John 1:1-4, 14, 10-12

How can we know God? The Bible tells us that "the Son is the radiance of God's glory and the exact representation of his being" (Heb. 1:3 NIV). The Son is "the image of the invisible God, the firstborn over all creation" (Col. 1:15 NIV). "No one knows the Father except the Son and anyone to whom the Son chooses to reveal him" (Matt. 11:27). *The way to the Father is through the Son.*

All things were made through the Son. He is "the author of life" (Acts 3:15). In the Garden of Eden He breathed life into Adam, giving life to all mankind. Thousands of years later, to a world filled with darkness, to a people lost in their sin and under the curse of death, God sent His Son that we might have *new* life—eternal life, and that through Him all might believe. To fulfil God's plan of redemption, the Son took on human flesh. He became incarnate.

Incarnate—*adj.* /in-kah-nuht/ v. embodied in flesh, esp. in human form.[1]

PREPARING THE WAY OF THE LORD

The account of the life of Jesus was recorded by four men. Two were disciples of Jesus—Matthew and John. One was a close follower of Jesus—Mark, who later travelled with Paul and Barnabas. One was a doctor named Luke—a very meticulous historian. Matthew, Mark, and John were eyewitnesses to the life of Jesus and recorded the events soon after they took place. Luke, whose account is a record of the evidence given by eyewitnesses, explained that his gospel was written to record events that "were handed down to us by those who from the first were eyewitnesses and servants of the word. Therefore, since I myself have carefully investigated everything from the beginning, it seemed good also to me to write an orderly account" (Luke 1:2-3 NIV). The gospels were in wide circulation amongst many who were eyewitnesses to the life and death of Jesus, and were upheld to be a true account of the facts.

As foretold by the prophets long ago, God sent a messenger to prepare the way of the Lord. There was a man called Zechariah who had a wife named Elizabeth, both of whom were "righteous before God, walking blamelessly in all the commandments and statutes of the Lord" (Luke 1:6). They were both well advanced in years and had no children. In fact, Elizabeth was past the age of childbearing. They were chosen to become the parents of a son who was the one whom God had chosen to prepare the way of the Messiah.

The angel Gabriel appeared to Zechariah to tell him the news of the impending birth of this child. He told Zechariah that his son, who was to be called John, would "be great before the Lord. And he must not drink wine or strong drink, and he will be filled with the Holy Spirit, even from his mother's womb. And he will turn many of the children of Israel to the Lord their God, and he will go before him in the spirit and power of Elijah, to turn the hearts of the fathers to the children, and the disobedient to the wisdom of the just, to make ready for the Lord a people prepared" (Luke 1:15-17). That was John's purpose—to prepare the hearts of the people to receive the Lord.

After John's birth, his father Zechariah said of him: "And you, child, will be called the prophet of the Most High; for you will go before the Lord to prepare his ways, to give knowledge of salvation to his people in the forgiveness of their sins, because of the tender mercy of our God, whereby the sunrise shall visit us from on high to give light to those who sit in darkness and in the shadow of death, to guide our feet into the way of peace" (Luke 1:76-79). The scene was now set for God's beloved Son to come down to earth.

MARY AND JOSEPH ARE PROUD TO ANNOUNCE THE BIRTH OF A SON . . .

As promised long ago, God sent His Son into the world, and this is how it came to be:

A few months after visiting Zechariah to tell him that he and Elizabeth would have a son who was the one who would prepare the hearts of the people for the coming of the Messiah, the angel Gabriel was again sent by God on a mission. This time it was to the town of Nazareth in Galilee "to a virgin betrothed to a man whose name was Joseph" (Luke 1:26-27). Mary was a cousin of Elizabeth. She was also a descendant of King David, as was her husband-to-be, Joseph.

"The angel said to her, 'Do not be afraid, Mary, for you have found favour with God. And behold, you will conceive in your womb and bear a son, and you shall call his name Jesus. He will be great and will be called the Son of the Most High. And the Lord God will give to him the throne of his father David, and he will reign over the house of Jacob forever, and of his kingdom there will be no end'" (Luke 1:30-33). Mary, obviously aware of the usual process by which new life comes about, asked the angel: "'How will this be . . . since I am a virgin?' The angel answered, 'The Holy Spirit will come upon you, and the power of the Most High will overshadow you. So the holy one to be born will be called the Son of God . . . for nothing is impossible with God'" (Luke 1:34-35 NIV). Mary was honoured to be chosen by God to be the mother of His Son and said to the angel: "I am the servant of the Lord's . . . let it be to me according to your word" (Luke 1:38).

Later, an angel appeared to Joseph in a dream and said to him: "'Joseph, son of David, do not fear to take Mary as your wife, for that which is conceived in her is from the Holy Spirit. She will bear a son, and you shall call his name Jesus, for he will save his people from their sins.' All this took place to fulfil what the Lord had spoken by the prophet: 'Behold, the virgin shall conceive and bear a son, and they shall call his name Immanuel' (which means, God with us)" (Matt. 1:20-23).

The genealogy of Jesus is recorded in Luke chapter three. It is the genealogy of the line of Joseph—Jesus' adoptive father, but Mary, His mother, was also descended from King David. Jesus was descended from Adam, through Adam's son Seth, Enoch whom God translated live to heaven, Methuselah the oldest man to have lived on earth, Noah and his son Shem, the patriarchs—Abraham, Isaac, and Jacob, Judah from whom came one of the twelve tribes of Israel, King David, and many generations between.

From the time of the birth of Cain, the firstborn son of Adam and Eve, until the birth of Christ, every life began the same way, with the uniting of DNA from both parents and the passing on of spirit from the father, which, when united with the physical matter of the new person, forms the soul.

What makes Jesus different from us? Firstly let us look at the physical:

It is biologically possible with two parents that all the genetic information could come solely from the mother, although it would be extremely rare for this to happen. The genes from the mother would have to be all dominant and those from the father all recessive. The father, of course, would still have to contribute spirit.

For a child to result from only the genetic contribution from the mother and spirit from a source other than from a human father *is* possible. For example, Adam was created having his own DNA, rather than combined DNA from two sources, and was given spirit by an outside source—his Creator. Another example is the instance of the procreation of angels with human women before the flood. The source of the physical seed came solely from the human mother, and the spiritual seed came from the fallen angels.

Scripture tells us that Joseph was *not* Jesus' biological father and that Jesus had *no* human father as Mary was a virgin. Additionally, she did not have any physical relations with a man until *after* Jesus was born. This means that Jesus' DNA, and therefore His genetic information, had to come solely from His mother, Mary. Although the female normally contributes two X chromosomes, and therefore the offspring resulting from the genetic contribution coming solely from the mother would likely be female, in very rare cases—"one in five million women"[2], the female contributes both an X and a Y chromosome, and male offspring would result.

In light of the above, it seems possible that *all* of the physical matter needed for a new life *can* come from the female, and *can* result in male offspring, as happened at the conception of Jesus. Mary could not however, provide spirit. It is not possible for a new life to form without the contribution of spirit.

The Bible tells us that the Holy Spirit 'came upon' Mary in power. The Holy Spirit gave life or Spirit to the *physical* seed from Mary. Jesus received this life or Spirit as a *spiritual* seed which would increase, forming His Spirit as He grew.

In addition to the scientific reasoning supporting the feasibility of the virgin birth, the involvement of the Holy Spirit meant that this event was indeed a miracle—an event brought about by the power of God. King David writes: "Your laws endure to this day, for all things serve you" (Ps. 119:90 NIV). God is *outside* the physical laws—the laws of 'nature'. Regardless of any scientific reasoning, the virgin birth is in the realm of the miraculous!

It is clear from Scripture that the Holy Spirit *is, and always has been,* the Spirit of the Son. The apostle Peter confirmed this when he wrote to believers: "The prophets who prophesied about the grace that was to be yours searched and inquired carefully, inquiring what person or time the Spirit of Christ in them was indicating when he predicted the sufferings of Christ and the subsequent glories" (1 Pet. 1:10-11). In other words, the Spirit in the hearts of the prophets *was the same* as the Spirit of the Son.

The Son, in becoming incarnate, was receiving as His Spirit the Spirit that was *already His* in His deity. The Spirit of Jesus, Son of Man, *is* the Holy Spirit, and is the *same* Spirit as the Spirit of the Son of God. Thus, in Jesus, the divine Spirit and the human Spirit are one and the same, and this Spirit is connected to the Father, unlike the disconnected spirit that has been passed down through the generations from Adam. The Spirit of Jesus was pure and untainted by the effects of sin. It was perfect—the way the spirit of Adam was perfect in the beginning. Jesus' Spirit was connected to God as His heart was open to God, having no guilt of sin.

The action of the Spirit on His physical substance formed the human heart and soul of Jesus. Jesus was therefore, fully man with a spirit, soul, and body, but He was without sin, as was Adam at the beginning of Creation. This is why the Bible calls Jesus the 'second Adam'.

Like the Father, God the Son has a divine Soul, and this divine Soul simultaneously began to dwell in the body of Jesus in the womb of Mary with the fullness of the Holy Spirit. Therefore, in Christ, "the whole fullness of deity dwells bodily" (Col. 2:9). The Son is the likeness, or image, of the Father, sharing all attributes and the divine nature that the Father has.

The Holy Spirit connects the Father to the Son and the humanity of Jesus to the deity of Jesus. In other words, as the Holy Spirit is the Spirit of Jesus, Son of Man, and that *same* spirit is the Spirit of the Son of God—the deity of Jesus, Jesus is fully God and fully man but is one person. Through the Spirit, the Son of Man and the Son of God are one, and the Father and the Son are one.

Because Jesus is fully God *and* fully man, He has the mind of God *and* the mind of a man, the nature of God *and* the nature of a man. In coming to the earth in the form of a man, He did not lose the fullness of God, but He took upon Himself the lowliness of man for our sake. Jesus was "in very nature God . . . but made himself nothing, taking the very nature of a servant, being made in human likeness" (Phil. 2:6-7 NIV). In taking on the form and life of a man, He did not become two *separate* persons. He remained *one* person—the divine who took on humanity.

In summary, Jesus has a human body and both human and divine souls. He has one Spirit—the Holy Spirit. The Holy Spirit unites His deity with His humanity. The Holy Spirit also unites the Father with the Son (both in His deity and in His humanity). Jesus is Son of God and Son of Man. He is fully God and fully man.

John the Baptist told the people that "he who comes from heaven is above all. He bears witness to what he has seen and heard" (John 3:31-32). "No-one has ever seen God, but God the One and Only, who is at the Father's side, has made him known" (John 1:18 NIV). We can know about God and about heaven because that is who Jesus is and where He came from.

Jesus said that He is the "one whom the Father set apart as his very own and sent into the world" (John 10:36 NIV). He humbled himself and "for a little while was made lower than the angels" (Heb. 2:9). He became as one of us, coming down from His home with His loving Father in heaven where angels worshipped and honoured Him, to the earth below to show us that love. He came to restore us to God.

It is not possible to fully understand the way in which the Son of God became man. It is, in part, a mystery. Paul says that Christ is "the mystery of God" and in Him "are hidden all the treasures of wisdom and knowledge" (Col. 2:3). God the Son becoming flesh is one of God's mysteries. God is allowed to have mysteries! He is not under any obligation to tell us everything for "the secret things belong to the LORD our God" (Deut. 29:29). Some things, like the Son of God becoming the Son of Man, we can perhaps only understand in part.

There is a passage in Paul's letter to Timothy where he is writing about Eve sinning and he says that "the woman will be saved through childbearing" (1 Tim. 2:15). Through the line of the woman, originally Eve, salvation was to come. Right from the beginning in the Garden of Eden, God had a plan to send His Son to save people from their sins. Genesis chapter three tells us that there would be one who would come from the woman's seed who would crush the head of Satan. It was an amazing plan that would involve God the Son coming into the world in the form of a tiny baby. God had made it possible for this plan to be carried out by designing the process of procreation so that His Son would not have to inherit the spirit of fallen mankind. Furthermore, even though Mary was a sinner, her own fallen spirit could not be passed on to Jesus in the womb, as a mother's circulation is totally separate from the foetal circulation.

Jesus was unique in His sinless nature by *not* inheriting the spirit that has been passed down through the generations since Adam. No other person can claim this—not Buddha, Muhammad, nor the Dalai Lama. Not Mother Theresa or the Pope. Not Abraham, Moses, or David. Not even Mary. This is very important to understand when considering that Jesus came to give *life*, for "as the Father has life in himself, so he has granted the Son also to have life in himself" (John 5:26). Spirit is life and "in him was life" (John 1:4). *Only* Jesus was, and is, qualified to *give* that life, as only Jesus had a spirit that was *not* under the curse of the law of sin and death.

As prophesied, Jesus was born in the town of Bethlehem in Judea. According to *The Annals of the World* (Pierce & Pierce 2003), the year of the Lord's birth was in the autumn (of the northern hemisphere) of the year 5 BC. He came into the world in humble surroundings—a shelter for animals at the back of an inn, and was laid in a manger—a feeding trough for animals. God chose some lowly shepherds to be the first to hear the good news that the Messiah, for whom they had been waiting, had been born:

> And an angel of the Lord appeared to them, and the glory of the Lord shone around them, and they were filled with great fear. And the angel said to them, "Fear not, for behold, I bring you good news of great joy that will be for all the people. For unto you is born this day in the city of David a Saviour, who is Christ the Lord. And this will be a sign for you: you will find a baby wrapped in swaddling cloths and lying in a manger." And suddenly there was with the angel a multitude of the heavenly host praising God and saying, "Glory to God in the highest, and on earth peace among those with whom he is pleased!"
>
> —Luke 2:9-14

The Son of God had become the Son of Man, and "in him all the fullness of God was pleased to dwell" (Col. 1:19). This humble entry of the Creator of the universe into our sinful world would have to be the most incredible event ever. The reason He came, and what He did to bring us back to Him, is the ultimate demonstration of love.

THE LIFE AND TEACHINGS OF THE MESSIAH

Jesus grew up in Nazareth with His mother Mary, His adoptive father Joseph, half-brothers (James, Joseph, Simon, and Judas), and a number of half-sisters. Luke tells us that, as Jesus grew and became strong, He was "filled with wisdom. And the favour of God was upon him" (Luke 2:40).

He was brought up as the son of Joseph, who was a carpenter. It was the tradition in those days that the trade or occupation of the father would be passed on to the son. Jesus would therefore have been trained in the skills of carpentry. As His parents followed the Jewish law, Jesus was circumcised on the eighth day. They regularly attended the temple and made offerings and sacrifices as was required of them by Law.

Even as a boy, Jesus knew that God was His Father. Every year, His parents went to Jerusalem for the feast of the Passover. One year, when Jesus was twelve years old, He stayed behind at the temple when the family group had left for home. After travelling for some time they noticed that He was not with the group. Mary and Joseph went back to look for Him and found Him in the temple discussing the Scriptures with the teachers of the Law who were "amazed at his understanding and his answers" (Luke 2:47). When Mary told Jesus that they had been searching for Him, He said to them: "Did you not know that I must be in my Father's house?" (Luke 2:49).

Before Jesus began His ministry at about thirty years of age, John the Baptist prepared the people for His coming. John lived out in the desert and ate wild locusts and honey and the people came to listen to him preach of the coming of the kingdom of God. He told the people that they needed to confess and repent of their sins. The confession and repentance of sins would cleanse the hearts of the people from the guilt of their sins and prepare their hearts to accept the Word of the Lord. John came to show the people "the way of righteousness" (Matt. 21:32 NIV).

John baptised the people in the River Jordan. It was a baptism for the forgiveness of sins. It symbolized the washing clean of their hearts and the putting off of the things of the flesh. The change brought about in the hearts of those who were baptised by John, and then later heard the words of Jesus, was that "all the people, even the tax collectors, when they heard Jesus' words, acknowledged that God's way was right . . . But the Pharisees and experts in the law rejected God's purpose for themselves, because they had not been baptised by John" (Luke 7:29-30 NIV). The hearts of the people who had been baptised were open to the message of Jesus whereas the hearts of the 'religious' leaders were not. They had an impressive head knowledge of the Scriptures but their hearts were hard. They were depending on their *own* righteousness to save them and did not understand that they, like the tax collectors, were in need of a Saviour. Being God the Son, Jesus "knew all people . . . he himself knew what was in a man" (John 2:24-25) and in His Spirit He knew what they were thinking in their hearts.

Jesus came to make the Father known to us and also so that we might know the words of God the Father, "for he whom God has sent utters the words of God" (John 3:34). The man who accepts the words and testimony of Jesus "has certified that God is truthful" (John 3:33 NIV).

Jesus had a heart for the poor, the destitute, and the lost. He likened the 'tax collectors and sinners' to little children, and said: "I thank you, Father, Lord of heaven and earth, that you have hidden these things from the wise and understanding and revealed them to little children; yes, Father, for such was your gracious will" (Luke 10:21).

John the Baptist made it very clear to the people that he himself was not the one whom they were waiting for. "As the people were in expectation, and all were questioning in their hearts concerning John, whether he might be the Christ, John answered them all, saying, 'I baptize you with water, but he who is mightier than I is coming, the strap of whose sandals I am not worthy to untie. He will baptize you with the Holy Spirit and fire'" (Luke 3:15-16). John likened himself to a friend who waits and listens for the bridegroom to come, the bridegroom being Jesus. In Jewish tradition, it was the role of the friend, or attendant of the bridegroom, to announce the coming of the bridegroom.

One day, while John was baptising, "Jesus came from Galilee to the Jordan to John, to be baptized by him. John would have prevented him, saying, 'I need to be baptized by you, and do you come to me?' But Jesus answered him, 'Let it be so now, for thus it is fitting for us to fulfil all righteousness'" (Matt. 3:13-15). Jesus, being without sin, was not baptised for His *own* sins. He was baptised for *our* sins, on *our* behalf. The cleansing of the heart from the guilt of sin as represented by the act of water baptism was to be applied to the hearts of sinful man *through* Jesus.

"When Jesus was baptized, immediately he went up from the water, and behold, the heavens were opened to him, and he saw the Spirit of God descending like a dove and coming to rest on him; and behold, a voice from heaven said, 'This is my beloved Son, with whom I am well pleased'" (Matt. 3:16-17). God was acknowledging, in front of many witnesses, that this Jesus of Nazareth was His Son. It was at that moment that God "anointed Jesus of Nazareth with the Holy Spirit and with power" (Acts 10:38). As the Son of God, Jesus already had power and authority, but this was the anointing of the *humanity* of Jesus—the man from Nazareth—the Son of Man, with power.

The next day, John saw Jesus coming towards him and said:

> "Behold, the Lamb of God, who takes away the sin of the world! This is he of whom I said, 'After me comes a man who ranks before me, because he was before me.' I myself did not know him, but for this purpose I came baptizing with water, that he might be revealed to Israel." And John bore witness: "I saw the Spirit descend from heaven like a dove, and it remained on him. I myself did not know him, but he who sent me to baptize with water said to me, 'He on whom you see the Spirit descend and remain, this is he who baptizes with the Holy Spirit.' And I have seen and have borne witness that this is the Son of God."
>
> —John 1:29-34

Whatever Jesus did on earth, He did in order to fulfil the will of His Father. Jesus said: I came to "do the will of him who sent me and to finish his work" (John 4:34 NIV). He said that: "The very work that the Father has given me to accomplish, and which I am doing, testifies that the Father has sent me" (John 5:36). God had total faith and confidence in His Son to do this work, for "the Father loves the Son and has given all things into his hand" (John 3:35).

Jesus had the knowledge and wisdom of God. He was an itinerant preacher, who travelled around from village to village. He also occasionally taught in the synagogue, "and many who heard him were amazed. 'Where did this man get these things?' they asked. 'What's this wisdom that has been given him, that he even does miracles?'" (Mark 6:2 NIV). Jesus explained that "the Son can do nothing by himself; he can do only what he sees his Father doing, because whatever the Father does the Son also does. For the Father loves the Son and shows him all he does" (John 5:19-20 NIV). On one occasion, when He was in the synagogue, He stood up to read from the scroll of the prophet Isaiah:

> "The Spirit of the Lord is upon me, because he has anointed me to proclaim good news to the poor. He has sent me to proclaim liberty to the captives and recovering of sight to the blind, to set at liberty those who are oppressed, to proclaim the year of the Lord's favour." And he rolled up the scroll and gave it back to the attendant and sat down. And the eyes of all in the synagogue were fixed on him. And he began to say to them, "Today this Scripture has been fulfilled in your hearing." And all spoke well of him and marvelled at the gracious words that were coming from his mouth.
> —Luke 4:18-22

"People were amazed at his teaching, because he taught them as one who had authority, not as the teachers of the law" (Mark 1:22 NIV). Jesus explained to them: "My teaching is not mine, but his who sent me. If anyone's will is to do God's will, he will know whether the teaching is from God or whether I am speaking on my own authority. The one who speaks on his own authority seeks his own glory; but the one who seeks the glory of him who sent him is true, and in him there is no falsehood" (John 7:16-18).

Being fully human—having human flesh and a human soul, Jesus was *able* to be tempted to sin but He did not *yield* to that temptation. After His baptism for example, He was led by the Spirit into the desert where "for forty days he was tempted by the devil" (Luke 4:2 NIV). Jesus did not eat during those forty days and the devil tempted Him first with food (same old tricks as in the Garden of Eden!). That didn't work! Then he tempted Him with earthly power if Jesus would worship him. Jesus knew Scripture. After all, He is 'The Word'! He replied: "It is written: 'You shall worship the Lord your God, and him only shall you serve'" (Luke 4:8). So that didn't work either! As a last ditch effort, Satan tried to tempt Jesus into throwing Himself down from the highest point of the temple. Satan thought that he could use Scripture in his favour and quoted: "For it is written, 'He will command his angels concerning you, to guard you,' and 'On their hands they will bear you up, lest you strike your foot against a stone'" (Luke 4:10-11). He must have felt pretty smug using Scripture against Jesus! Jesus however, was not perturbed by this and replied: "It is said, 'You shall not put the Lord your God to the test'" (Luke 4:12). Satan, defeated and outwitted, gave up and left!

One day, when Jesus was standing on the shore of Lake Gennesaret, He got into the boat of one of the fishermen who had been out fishing all night but who had not caught anything. He said to Simon Peter: "'Put out into the deep and let down your nets for a catch.' And Simon answered, 'Master, we toiled all night and took nothing! But at your word I will let down the nets.' And when they had done this, they enclosed a large number of fish, and their nets were breaking" (Luke 5:4-6).

These fishermen were the first of twelve men that Jesus called to follow Him. They were a mixed and motley crew—fishermen, tax collectors, and so on. They were to be His core group of followers and were called 'disciples'. They were commissioned to go and preach the kingdom of God and spread the good news of the gospel. Jesus also gave them "authority over unclean spirits, to cast them out, and to heal every disease and every affliction" (Matt. 10:1). They spent three years travelling with Jesus. The message they preached was that: "The time is fulfilled, and the kingdom of God is at hand; repent and believe in the gospel" (Mark 1:15); and many people did. The disciples were told at this stage "not to go among the Gentiles . . . go rather to the lost sheep of Israel" (Matt. 10:5-6 NIV). Jesus explained: "I was sent only to the lost sheep of the house of Israel" (Matt. 15:24). It was not until *after* the death and resurrection of Jesus that the disciples were then commissioned to go and bring the good news to the Gentiles.

Jesus, being fully God, had full command and authority over Creation—both the physical *and* the spiritual world. For example, once, when Jesus was in a boat with the disciples, a huge storm arose. Jesus "rebuked the wind and said to the sea, 'Peace! Be still!' And the wind ceased, and there was a great calm" (Mark 4:39). Matthew's gospel tells of a fig-tree that Jesus immediately caused to wither from the roots as a lesson to the disciples.

Jesus performed many miracles during the time He dwelt on the earth. The miracles were evidence that Jesus was who He said He was. He said that "anyone who has seen me has seen the Father . . . I am in the Father and the Father is in me . . . at least believe on the evidence of the miracles" (John 14:9-11 NIV). The first miracle He performed was the turning of water into wine at a wedding. "This, the first of his signs, Jesus did at Cana in Galilee, and manifested his glory. And his disciples believed in him" (John 2:11).

"Jesus went throughout all the cities and villages, teaching in their synagogues and proclaiming the gospel of the kingdom and healing every disease and every affliction. When he saw the crowds, he had compassion for them, because they were harassed and helpless, like sheep without a shepherd" (Matt. 9:35-36). Many people were healed by the power of Jesus and put their faith in Him, and the dead were brought back to life. He walked on water, turned five loaves and two fish into enough food to feed five thousand people (with leftovers), and later fed four thousand with a similar miracle.

Many people put their faith in Jesus. Many others though, especially the teachers of the Law—the religious leaders, rejected Him. He was not what they had in mind for their Messiah. They wanted a king who would overthrow the prevailing power of Rome—an earthly king. Jesus made it clear however, that at this time, He "did not come to bring peace, but a sword" (Matt. 10:34 NIV). He would come again to bring peace on the earth, "but first he must suffer many things and be rejected by this generation" (Luke 17:25).

Speaking of His Father, Jesus said to those who doubted who He was:

"You have never heard his voice nor seen his form, nor does his word dwell in you, for you do not believe the one he sent. You diligently study the Scriptures because you think that by them you possess eternal life. These are the Scriptures that testify about me, yet you refuse to come to me to have life . . . I know you. I know that you do not have the love of God in your hearts . . . if you believed Moses, you would believe me, for he wrote about me. But since you do not believe what he wrote, how are you going to believe what I say?"

—John 5:37-42, 46-47 NIV

He also said to those who did not believe:

"I told you that you would die in your sins, for unless you believe that I am he you will die in your sins . . . He who sent me is with me. He has not left me alone, for I always do the things that are pleasing to him." As he was saying these things, many believed in him. So Jesus said to the Jews who had believed him, "If you abide in my word, you are truly my disciples, and you will know the truth, and the truth will set you free."

—John 8:24, 29-32

Jesus said to the Pharisees: "If God were your Father, you would love me, for I came from God and I am here. I came not of my own accord, but he sent me" (John 8:42). The Pharisees, who were the religious leaders of the day, studied the Scriptures to try to determine when the kingdom of God would come. Jesus knew that they did not understand that He had come to usher the kingdom of God into the *hearts* of men. They were expecting the Messiah to rule an *earthly* kingdom and they did not understand that Jesus had to come twice. He had come the first time to restore people to God *spiritually*. He said to them: "The kingdom of God does not come with observation; nor will they say, 'See here!' or 'See there!' For indeed, the kingdom of God is within you." (Luke 17:20-21 NKJV).

Jesus knew that the Jewish people of the day would, on the whole, reject Him as the Christ, that they would experience a hardening of their hearts, and that their spiritual eyes would be blinded. Most of them would not accept the truth until the time when He returned. He warned them: "A little while longer the light is with you. Walk while you have the light, lest darkness overtake you; he who walks in darkness does not know where he is going. While you have the light, believe in the light, that you may become sons of light." (John 12:35-36 NKJV).

Jesus did not come to do away with the Old Testament teachings altogether. He said that "every teacher of the law who has been instructed about the kingdom of heaven is like the owner of a house who brings out of his storeroom new treasures as well as old" (Matt. 13:52 NIV).

One day, one of the teachers of the Law asked Jesus which of the commandments was the most important. Jesus answered him: "The first of all the commandments is: 'Hear, O Israel, the LORD our God, the LORD is one. And you shall love the LORD your God with all your heart, with all your soul, with all your mind, and with all your strength.' This is the first commandment. And the second, like it, is this: 'You shall love your neighbour as yourself.' There is no other commandment greater than these." (Mark 12:29-31 NKJV). In other words, love God with all you have got and show that love to others. This is the Ten Commandments in a nutshell! Jesus went on to say: "Do this, and you will live" (Luke 10:28). He also said: "Blessed are those who hear the word of God and obey it" (Luke 11:28 NIV). It was not enough to just *hear* God's Word. Anyone can do that! In fact, one could go to church twice on a Sunday, Bible study during the week, and read the Bible every night, but still not *obey* God's Word. God requires *obedience.* To obey God's Word is a *demonstration* of faith in God and of love for Him. Faith in God and love for God manifests in obedience.

Jesus also gave the disciples a *new* commandment. He said: "Love one another; as I have loved you, that you also love one another. By this all will know that you are My disciples, if you have love for one another" (John 13:34-35 NKJV). Jesus was the *demonstration* of love. They were to follow His example!

Jesus told many stories to the people who came to listen to Him. They were called *parables.*

> **Parable—/pa-ruh-buhl/ n. 1 story used to illustrate a moral or spiritual lesson.[3]**

He loved to present the truth of the gospel by telling the people stories that involved everyday things that they were familiar with, but that had a message in them about the kingdom of God or about how they should treat each other. He often likened the people to sheep. He told them that He is the Good Shepherd and said to the Jewish listeners: "Other sheep I have which are not of this fold; them also I must bring, and they will hear My voice; and there will be one flock and one shepherd" (John 10:16 NKJV). He was speaking of Gentile believers and Jewish believers becoming one through Him.

I AM...

Jesus said: "**I am the way, and the truth, and the life**. No-one comes to the Father except through me" (John 14:6). Jesus is the *only* way, the *absolute* truth, and the *source* of life.

Jesus said: "**I am the bread of life**. He who comes to me will never grow hungry, and he who believes in me will never be thirsty . . . All that the Father gives me will come to me, and whoever comes to me I will never drive away" (John 6:35, 37 NIV). "No-one can come to me unless the Father who sent me draws him . . . everyone who listens to the Father and learns from him comes to me" (John 6:44-45 NIV).

Jesus said: "**I am the gate**; whoever enters through me will be saved. He will come in and go out, and find pasture" (John 10:9 NIV). There is only one gate that leads to safe pastures; only one way to eternal life. You cannot jump the fence, find another gate, or knock the fence down! You can only enter through 'the gate'.

Jesus said: "**I am the good shepherd**. The good shepherd lays down his life for the sheep . . . I know my sheep and my sheep know me—just as the Father knows me and I know the Father—and I lay down my life for the sheep" (John 10:11, 14-15 NIV).

Jesus said: "**I am the resurrection and the life**. He who believes in me will live, even though he dies; and whoever lives and believes in me will never die" (John 11:25-26 NIV). Jesus, of course, said this *before* His death and resurrection. He was giving this reassurance to two groups of people. Those who would die *before* His death and resurrection, believing in Him, would go to Sheol, the abode of the dead, but even though they would taste death, they would be raised to life. Those who lived on earth *beyond* Jesus' death and resurrection and believed in Him, would *not* die and go to Sheol; they would simply pass from their bodies immediately into heaven—eternal life.

God has granted Jesus "authority over all flesh, that He should give eternal life to as many as You have given Him. And this is eternal life, that they may know You, the only true God, and Jesus Christ whom You have sent" (John 17:2-3 NKJV). Jesus said: "It is the Spirit who gives life; the flesh profits nothing. The words that I speak to you are spirit, and they are life" (John 6:63 NKJV). Jesus said: "I have come that they may have life, and that they may have it more abundantly" (John 10:10 NKJV). Peter, one of the disciples, said to Jesus: "You have the words of eternal life . . . We have come to believe and know that You are the Christ, the Son of the living God" (John 6:68-69 NKJV). He recognized that there was no-one else who *could* give eternal life, only Jesus.

Jesus said: "**I am the light of the world**. Whoever follows me will not walk in darkness, but will have the light of life" (John 8:12 NIV). "It is the God who commanded light to shine out of darkness, who has shone in our hearts to give the light of the knowledge of the glory of God in the face of Jesus Christ" (2 Cor. 4:6 NIV).

Jesus said: "If anyone thirsts, let him come to Me and drink. He who believes in Me, as the Scripture has said, out of his heart will flow rivers of living water" (John 7:37-38 NKJV).

THE MISSION

Being fully God, Jesus had foreknowledge of what was to come. Right from the beginning of His ministry, Jesus spoke of His imminent death and resurrection. He said: "I have a baptism to undergo, and how distressed I am until it is completed!" (Luke 12:50 NIV). Jesus knew that He would suffer at the hands of men. He was also greatly distressed about the type of 'baptism' that He knew He would soon be undertaking on our behalf.

Jesus knew that after He died He would be raised from the dead. He said to the Jewish leaders: "Destroy this temple, and in three days I will raise it up" (John 2:19). He was speaking of His body being the temple of God in which God's Spirit dwelt. He knew that they would put Him to death but that, through the power of the Holy Spirit, He would be raised bodily from the dead on the third day.

In referring to the kind of death that He knew awaited Him and the reason He had to die, Jesus explained that the Son of Man must "be lifted up, that whoever believes in Him should not perish but have eternal life" (John 3:14-15 NKJV). Jesus also spoke of His ascension back into heaven after He had risen from the dead. He asked the disciples: "What if you were to see the Son of Man ascending to where he was before?" (John 6:62) and explained to them: "I shall be with you a little while longer, and then I go to Him who sent Me. You will seek Me and not find Me" (John 7:33-34 NKJV). Jesus told His disciples these things in advance so that when they happened, they would remember His words and believe, and so that they would have hope in the midst of what, at the time, might just seem to be the tragic end of a good man.

Chapter Ten
The Saviour

The Jewish religious leaders were always on the lookout to find something with which to condemn Jesus. This proved to be quite a challenge. Jesus inherited a sinless nature, not having the spirit passed down from Adam. Furthermore, He never gave in to temptation and sinned, therefore, He was without guilt. On one occasion, Jesus asked them directly: "Can any of you prove me guilty of sin?" (John 8:46 NIV). Needless to say, no one stepped up to the challenge!

They persecuted Him for healing on the Sabbath but He said to them: "'My Father is always at his work to this very day, and I, too, am working'. For this reason the Jews tried all the harder to kill him; not only was he breaking the Sabbath, but he was even calling God his own Father, making himself equal with God" (John 5:17-18 NIV). The Jewish leaders were always accusing Jesus of blasphemy because He said that He was the Son of God and therefore *was* God, but He asked them: "Why do you accuse me of blasphemy because I said, 'I am God's Son'? Do not believe me unless I do what my Father does. But if I do it, even though you do not believe me, believe the miracles, that you may know and understand that the Father is in me, and I am in the Father" (John 10:36-38). Jesus used the title 'I AM', the title God used when He told Moses His name. He said to the Jewish leaders: "Before Abraham was, I am!" (John 8:58).

Jesus knew when "the time had come for him to leave this world and go to the Father. Having loved his own who were in the world, he now showed them the full extent of his love . . . Jesus knew that the Father had put all things under his power, and that he had come from God and was returning to God" (John 13:1, 3 NIV), returning to His home in heaven that He had left when He came down to earth to live among us. Before Jesus died, He prayed: "I have brought you glory on earth by completing the work you gave me to do. And now, Father, glorify me in your presence with the glory I had with you before the world began" (John 17:4-5 NIV).

Jesus, although fully God, was also fully man. Because of this, He was distressed about His imminent death saying: "'Now My soul is troubled, and what shall I say? 'Father, save Me from this hour'? But for this purpose I came to this hour. Father, glorify Your name'. Then a voice came from heaven, saying, 'I have both glorified it and will glorify it again.'" (John 12:27-28 NKJV).

In order that all would be fulfilled, Satan entered one of Jesus' disciples—Judas Iscariot, and prompted him to betray Jesus. Jesus knew who was going to betray Him from the beginning and had said: "Woe to that man by whom the Son of Man is betrayed! It would have been good for that man if he had not been born" (Matt. 26:24 NKJV).

THE NIGHT BEFORE

On the night before Jesus died, which was also the night before the Passover celebration, He gathered His disciples together and broke bread and shared wine with them. This was to be something that they and all believers were to continue to do when they met together—to share in this as a remembrance of the Lord's death until He comes again. The bread represented Christ's body that was to be broken for them for the forgiveness of sins. The cup represented Christ's blood which was to be poured out for them.

On the night before Jesus was arrested He took Peter, James, and John with Him into the Garden of Gethsemane to pray. "He began to be deeply distressed and troubled. 'My soul is overwhelmed with sorrow to the point of death,' he said to them. 'Stay here and keep watch.' Going a little farther, he fell to the ground and prayed that if possible the hour might pass from him. 'Abba, Father,' he said, 'everything is possible for you. Take this cup from me. Yet not what I will, but what you will'" (Mark 14:33-36 NIV). Then an angel appeared to Him and strengthened Him. "Being in anguish, he prayed more earnestly, and his sweat was like drops of blood falling to the ground" (Luke 22:44 NIV).

> There are both ancient and modern accounts on record of people sweating blood—a condition known as *hematidrosis*, where extreme anguish or physical strain causes one's capillary blood vessels to dilate and burst, mixing sweat and blood.[1]

While Jesus and His disciples were in the garden, Judas came, leading a great crowd who were brandishing swords and clubs. They had been sent by the chief priests and the elders to arrest Jesus. Jesus said to them: "Every day I was with you in the temple courts, and you did not lay a hand on me. But this is your hour—when darkness reigns" (Luke 22:53 NIV). Jesus went with them in peace.

The people led Him to Caiaphas the high priest, where the scribes and elders had gathered. They were seeking testimony against Jesus so that they might put Him to death. They found none, even though many false witnesses came forward. To all the accusations, Jesus was silent. Then the chief priest said: "'Tell us if you are the Christ, the Son of God.' Jesus said to him, 'You have said so. But I tell you, from now on you will see the Son of Man seated at the right hand of Power and coming on the clouds of heaven'" (Matt. 26:63-64 NIV).

Jesus was then taken before the governor, but Pilate told the crowd that he found no basis for a charge against Him. "He knew that they had handed Him over because of envy" (Matt. 27:18 NKJV). Those who had plotted against Jesus could see that He had power and authority, that He had wisdom and grace, and certainly that He had a large following; all the things that they themselves did *not* have. Despite Pilate's insistence that Jesus had done nothing to deserve death, because the angry mob were intent on killing Jesus for any reason that they could invent, Jesus was sentenced to death for blasphemy—claiming to be equal to God. "The Jews insisted, 'We have a law, and according to that law he must die because he claimed to be the Son of God'" (John 19:7 NIV). He was only telling them the truth.

THE CRUCIFIXION

"They stripped him and put a scarlet robe on him, and then twisted together a crown of thorns and set it on his head . . . they mocked him . . . they spat on him . . . and struck him on the head again and again" (Matt. 27:28-30 NIV). At about the third hour of the day (around nine in the morning), "when they came to the place called the Skull, there they crucified him, along with the criminals—one on his right, the other on his left. Jesus said, 'Father forgive them, for they do not know what they are doing'" (Luke 23:33-34 NIV).

> Cross—an upright wooden stake or post on which condemned people were executed . . . From the early days of the Roman Republic, death on the cross was used for rebellious slaves and bandits, although Roman citizens were rarely subjected to this method of execution. The practice continued well beyond the New Testament period as one of the supreme punishments for military and political crimes such as desertion, spying, revealing secrets, rebellion and sedition. Following the conversion of the emperor Constantine to Christianity, the cross became a sacred symbol and its use by Romans as a means of torture and death was abolished.[2]

"From the sixth hour until the ninth hour there was darkness over all the land" (Matt. 27:45 NKJV). Evidence of this darkness is found in other ancient manuscripts as well:

> Lucian, the martyr, testified in Rufinus to the darkness at that time by appealing to the writings of the heathen themselves: "Search your writings and you shall find that, in Pilate's time, when Christ suffered, the sun was suddenly withdrawn and a darkness followed".
>
> Phlegon stated that in the 19th year of Tiberius (as Eustathius Antiochus noted in Hexaemeron) and the fourth year of the 202nd Olympiad (that is 33 AD), the following events took place . . . There was the largest and most famous eclipse that had ever occurred. The day was so turned into night at the sixth hour (noon), that the stars were seen.[3]

"About the ninth hour Jesus cried out with a loud voice . . . 'My God, my God, why have you forsaken me?'" (Matt. 27:46) and then He declared "It is finished" (John 19:30), "'Father, into your hands I commit my spirit.' Having said this, He breathed His last" (Luke 23:46 NKJV) and "yielded up His spirit" (Matt. 27:50 NKJV).

Jesus, the Son of God, Son of Man, died on Friday 3rd of April in the year AD 33 (Pierce & Pierce 2003). *The Annals of the World* explains that:

> It is a common belief that Jesus was 33 years old when he died. This is based on the assumption that he started his ministry when he was thirty. *(Luke 3:23)*

Luke was a very precise historian. If Jesus had been thirty years old, he would not have said *about thirty*. Based on that text, the only thing one can say for certain is Jesus was not thirty years old at the start of his ministry. However, he was likely about thirty when he was baptized by John the Baptist in 26 AD. About three years elapsed between his baptism and the start of his public ministry in 29 AD. According to what we know about when he was born, he would have been about thirty-six years old when he died. The 33 AD date is also confirmed by John *(Joh 2:20)* for this establishes the date of the first Passover of Christ at 30 AD, forty-six full years after Herod started to rebuild the temple in 17 BC.[4]

When Jesus died, Matthew noted that "the curtain of the temple was torn in two, from top to bottom" (Matt. 27:51). He also recorded that, at the very moment that Jesus died:

> The earth shook and the rocks split. The tombs broke open and the bodies of many holy people who had died were raised to life. They came out of the tombs, and after Jesus' resurrection they went into the holy city and appeared to many people. When the centurion and those with him who were guarding Jesus saw the earthquake and all that had happened, they were terrified, and exclaimed, "Surely he was the Son of God".
>
> —Matt. 27:51-54 NIV

Other records from this day, such as the account of Phlegon, confirm the earthquake:

> Also, an earthquake in Bithynia destroyed many houses in the city of Nicaea.[5]

The day after the crucifixion was to be a special Sabbath for the Jews. The bodies of those crucified could not remain on the crosses during the Sabbath, so they asked Pilate to have their legs broken to hasten their deaths so that they could take the bodies down before sunset—the beginning of the Jewish day. When they came to Jesus however, Pilate was surprised to find that He was already dead, so there was no need for them to do this to Him. "But one of the soldiers pierced His side with a spear, and immediately blood and water came out" (John 19:34 NKJV)—evidence of a ruptured heart—likely the primary cause of Jesus' death—a physical consequence of extreme anguish.

On the cross, Jesus would have undoubtedly experienced hypovolemic shock (shock caused by severe loss of blood) and asphyxiation (being unable to draw in breath) because of the position that He had to endure during those hours of torture, making it extremely difficult for Him to push Himself up in order to expand His lungs sufficiently.

> Those sentenced to death on a cross in the Roman period were usually beaten with leather lashes—a procedure that often resulted in severe loss of blood. Victims were then generally forced to carry the upper crossbeam to the execution site, where the central stake was already set up. After being

fastened with ropes—or, in rare cases, nails through the wrist—the naked victim was then hoisted with the crossbeam against the standing vertical stake. A block or peg was sometimes fastened to the stake as a crude seat. The feet were then tied or nailed to the stake . . . Death by suffocation or exhaustion normally followed only after a long period of agonizing pain . . . To hasten death, the executioners sometimes broke the victims' legs with a club. Then they could no longer support their bodies to keep blood circulating, and death quickly followed.[6]

Satan thought he had won! Throughout history, Satan has tried to thwart God's plans to send a Saviour. He tried to contaminate the pure line from which Jesus would descend by the blending of the two seeds when fallen angels procreated with human women. Many times he tried to wipe out the people of Israel from whom the Messiah would come. Around the time Moses was born he tried, through Pharaoh, to kill all the baby boys born to the Israelites while they were slaves in Egypt. After Jesus was born he tried to kill Jesus through King Herod, who ordered the death of all the Hebrew baby boys. In Revelation, Satan is portrayed as a red dragon who stands in front of a woman (Israel) who was about to give birth, "so that he might devour her child the moment it was born" (Rev. 12:4 NIV). When Jesus was put to death on the cross, Satan must have thought that the victory was his. He did not understand the way that salvation for mankind had to be purchased. It was a mystery known only to God, yet to be revealed in the fullness of time. If Satan *had* understood God's plan to redeem fallen mankind, it is more likely that he would want to *keep* Jesus from His death, rather than *send* Him to His death.

Jesus' body was taken down from the cross and given to a man named Joseph of Arimathea. "So Joseph bought some linen cloth, took down the body, wrapped it in the linen, and placed it in a tomb cut out of rock. Then he rolled a stone against the entrance to the tomb" (Mark 15:46 NIV).

THE RESURRECTION

The chief priests and the Pharisees recalled that Jesus had said that He would rise from the dead. They were worried that His disciples would try to steal His body and then claim that this had actually happened, thus keeping what they thought to be a 'myth' alive; so Pilate ordered the tomb to be secured by putting a seal on the stone and posting guards at the entrance.

But, despite all the 'best laid plans', death could not hold Jesus down!

> Now after the Sabbath, toward the dawn of the first day of the week, Mary Magdalene and the other Mary went to see the tomb. And behold, there was a great earthquake, for an angel of the Lord descended from heaven and came and rolled back the stone and sat on it. His appearance was like lightning, and his clothing white as snow. And for fear of him the guards trembled and became like dead men. But the angel said to the women, "Do not be afraid,

for I know that you seek Jesus who was crucified. He is not here, for he has risen, as he said. Come, see the place where he lay. Then go quickly and tell his disciples that he has risen from the dead, and behold, he is going before you to Galilee; there you will see him. See, I have told you."
—Matt. 28:1-7

"When they came back from the tomb, they told all these things to the eleven and to all the others . . . but they did not believe the women, because their words seemed to them like nonsense. Peter however, got up and ran to the tomb" (Luke 24:9, 11-12 NIV).

He saw the linen cloths lying there, and the face cloth, which had been on Jesus' head, not lying with the linen cloths but folded up in a place by itself. Then the other disciple, who had reached the tomb first, also went in, and he saw and believed; for as yet they did not understand the Scripture, that he must rise from the dead. Then the disciples went back to their homes.

But Mary stood weeping outside the tomb, and as she wept she stooped to look into the tomb. And she saw two angels in white, sitting where the body of Jesus had lain, one at the head and one at the feet. They said to her, "Woman, why are you weeping?" She said to them, "They have taken away my Lord, and I do not know where they have laid him." Having said this, she turned around and saw Jesus standing, but she did not know that it was Jesus. Jesus said to her, "Woman, why are you weeping? Whom are you seeking?" Supposing him to be the gardener, she said to him, "Sir, if you have carried him away, tell me where you have laid him, and I will take him away." Jesus said to her, "Mary." She turned and said to him in Aramaic, "Rabboni!" (which means Teacher). Jesus said to her, "Do not cling to me, for I have not yet ascended to the Father; but go to my brothers and say to them, 'I am ascending to my Father and your Father, to my God and your God.'" Mary Magdalene went and announced to the disciples, "I have seen the Lord"—and that he had said these things to her.
—John 20:6-18

God, through the power of the Holy Spirit, had raised Jesus from the dead! Not only was He alive *spiritually* but His spiritual body had returned to His *physical* body which was healed and renewed! He had truly conquered death—spiritual *and* physical! Jesus was "the firstborn from the dead" (Rev. 1:5 NKJV). *The Annals of the World* places this incredible event on Sunday 5th April AD 33 (Pierce & Pierce 2003).

That same day, Jesus appeared to two of the disciples who were on their way to a village called Emmaus, but they were initially kept from recognising Him. "Beginning with Moses and all the Prophets, he explained to them what was said in all the Scriptures concerning himself" (Luke 24:27 NIV). When they reached the village, He came in to the house where they were staying and took bread and broke it and gave it to them. "Their eyes were opened and they recognised him, and he vanished from their sight" (Luke 24:31). These two disciples then went back to Jerusalem at once to tell the other disciples that they had seen Jesus.

As Jesus' disciples had just witnessed Him dying an awful death on the cross, imagine their confusion when they heard the report from some of their own that they had seen Jesus alive:

> As they were talking about these things, Jesus himself stood among them, and said to them, "Peace to you!" But they were startled and frightened and thought they saw a spirit. And he said to them, "Why are you troubled, and why do doubts arise in your hearts? See my hands and my feet, that it is I myself. Touch me, and see. For a spirit does not have flesh and bones as you see that I have." And when he had said this, he showed them his hands and his feet. And while they still disbelieved for joy and were marvelling, he said to them, "Have you anything here to eat?" They gave him a piece of broiled fish, and he took it and ate before them.
>
> —Luke 24:36-43

"Again Jesus said, 'Peace be with you! As the Father has sent me, I am sending you.' And with that he breathed on them and said, 'Receive the Holy Spirit'" (John 20:21-22 NIV). He then gave them the authority to forgive sins, saying to them: "Go into all the world and preach the good news to all creation. Whoever believes and is baptised will be saved, but whoever does not believe will be condemned" (Mark 16:15 NIV).

Jesus told the disciples to go to a mountain in Galilee. There He met with them and said to them: "All authority on heaven and earth has been given to me. Therefore go and make disciples of all nations, baptising them in the name of the Father and of the Son and of the Holy Spirit, and teaching them to obey everything I have commanded you. And surely I am with you always, to the very end of the age" (Matt. 28:18-20 NIV). Jesus was anointing them with the authority and power to do the work which He began to do during the time that He lived on earth. The ministry of the apostles was to spread the good news to all men, "open their eyes and turn them from darkness to light, and from the power of Satan to God, so that they may receive forgiveness of sins and a place among those who are sanctified by faith" (Acts 26:18 NIV) in Christ Jesus.

Jesus appeared many times to His disciples after His resurrection. "After his suffering, he showed himself to these men and gave many convincing proofs that he was alive. He appeared to them over a period of forty days and spoke about the kingdom of God" (Acts 1:3 NIV). One day, He was waiting on the shore of the lake where they were fishing. The disciples had been out in the boat for some time and had not caught anything. He called out to them to throw their nets on the other side of the boat. They did, and they were unable to haul the net in because there were so many fish! Jesus had a fire going on the shore and cooked them a breakfast of fish and bread.

Before Jesus left them to return to His Father in heaven, He said to the disciples: "Do not leave Jerusalem, but wait for the gift my Father promised, which you have heard me speak about. For John baptised with water, but in a few days you will be baptised with the Holy Spirit" (Acts 1:4-5 NIV). He promised them: "You will receive power when the Holy Spirit comes on you; and you will be my witnesses in Jerusalem, and in all Judea and Samaria, and to the ends of the earth" (Acts 1:8 NIV).

THE ASCENSION

A little while later, it was time for Jesus to depart and "when He had led them out to the vicinity of Bethany, he lifted up his hands and blessed them" (Luke 24:50 NIV). "After the Lord Jesus had spoken to them, he was taken up into heaven and he sat at the right hand of God" (Mark 16:19 NIV). "They were looking intently up into the sky as he was going, when suddenly two men dressed in white stood beside them. 'Men of Galilee,' they said, 'why do you stand here looking into the sky? This same Jesus, who has been taken from you into heaven, will come back in the same way you have seen him go into heaven'" (Acts 1:11 NIV). "Then the disciples went out and preached everywhere, and the Lord worked with them and confirmed his word by the signs that accompanied it" (Mark 16:20 NIV).

The writer of the letter to the Hebrews tells us that after Jesus had "provided purification for sins, he sat down at the right hand of the Majesty in heaven" (Heb. 1:3 NIV). During the early days of the Church, there was a man called Stephen who became the first Christian martyr. As he was being stoned for his faith, God allowed him a glimpse of heaven. He "looked up to heaven and saw the glory of God, and Jesus standing at the right hand of God. 'Look,' he said, 'I see heaven open and the Son of Man standing at the right hand of God'" (Acts 7:55-56 NIV).

John also saw the glorified Lord in heaven in the vision that was given to him of the time of the end. He records that he saw:

> One like a son of man, clothed with a long robe and with a golden sash around his chest. The hairs of his head were white, like white wool, like snow. His eyes were like a flame of fire, his feet were like burnished bronze, refined in a furnace, and his voice was like the roar of many waters. In his right hand he held seven stars, from his mouth came a sharp two-edged sword, and his face was like the sun shining in full strength.
>
> —Rev. 1:13-16

Later in his vision, John saw the Lord in heaven as "a Lamb, looking as if it had been slain, standing in the centre of the throne" (Rev. 5:6 NIV). The throne was surrounded by angels and elders worshipping Him.

PENTECOST

Jesus ministry did not end at the cross or even when He ascended into heaven. Luke, a doctor who wrote an account of the life, death, and resurrection of Jesus, detailed the events of Jesus' life for a man he referred to as 'most excellent Theophilus'. At the beginning of the book of Acts, the second book written by Luke, which was written as a follow-on from The Gospel of Luke, he writes: "In my former book, Theophilus, I wrote about all that Jesus began to do and to teach until the day he was taken up to heaven, after giving instructions through the Holy Spirit to the apostles he had chosen" (Acts 1:1-2 NIV). Jesus' ministry on earth *began* during the time that He was bodily on the earth and then was to *continue* through the work of the church by the ministry of His indwelling Spirit. His work was *initially* done while He was in His *earthly* body and then it was to continue through His *new* body on earth—the church. Same work, same Spirit, different body.

The day of the giving of the Holy Spirit was during the celebration of *Pentecost* (the Greek name) or *Shavuot* in Hebrew. This is the day during which the Jews commemorated the end of the barley harvest and the beginning of the wheat harvest. From AD 140 it was also celebrated to commemorate the giving of The Law at Mount Sinai which occurred fifty days after the Passover lamb had been sacrifice in Egypt. Before Pentecost, the Holy Spirit had only been given temporarily to a select few for particular purposes. Now *all* believers were to receive the gift of the Holy Spirit, and this is how it came about:

> When the day of Pentecost arrived, they were all together in one place. And suddenly there came from heaven a sound like a mighty rushing wind, and it filled the entire house where they were sitting. And divided tongues as of fire appeared to them and rested on each one of them. And they were all filled with the Holy Spirit and began to speak in other tongues as the Spirit gave them utterance.
>
> —Acts 2:1-4

This drew the attention of many onlookers:

> When they heard this sound, a crowd came together in bewilderment, because each one heard them speaking in his own language. Utterly amazed, they asked: "Are not all these men who are speaking Galileans? Then how is it that each of us hears them in his own native language? . . . We hear them declaring the wonders of God in our own tongues!"
>
> —Acts 2:6-8, 11 NIV

Peter addressed the crowd, explaining to them that this was what was spoken of by the prophet Joel, who wrote: "And it shall come to pass afterward that I will pour out My Spirit on all flesh; Your sons and your daughters shall prophesy, your old men shall dream dreams, your young men shall see visions. And also on My menservants and on My maidservants I will pour out My Spirit in those days" (Joel 2:28-29 NKJV). Peter then went on to explain:

> "Jesus of Nazareth was a man accredited by God to you by miracles, wonders and signs, which God did among you through him, as you yourselves know. This man was handed over to you by God's set purpose and foreknowledge;

and you, with the help of wicked men, put him to death, by nailing him to the cross. But God raised him from the dead, freeing him from the agony of death, because it was impossible for death to keep its hold on him . . . God raised this Jesus to life, and we are all witnesses of the fact. Exalted to the right hand of God, he has received from the Father the promised Holy Spirit and has poured out what you now see and hear".

—Acts 2:22-24, 33 NIV

Peter also explained to the crowd the Scriptures written by King David, foretelling Jesus' death and resurrection so that they might believe and understand. He said:

"Therefore let all the house of Israel know assuredly that God has made this Jesus, whom you crucified, both Lord and Christ." Now when they heard this, they were cut to the heart, and said to Peter and the rest of the apostles, "Men and brethren, what shall we do?" Then Peter said to them, "Repent, and let every one of you be baptized in the name of Jesus Christ for the remission of sins; and you shall receive the gift of the Holy Spirit. For the promise is to you and to your children, and to all who are afar off, as many as the Lord our God will call." . . . Then those who gladly received his word were baptized; and that day about three thousand souls were added to them.

—Acts 2:36-39, 41 NKJV

At Pentecost, the church began. *The Annals of the World* (Pierce & Pierce 2003) puts the date of Pentecost at Sunday 24th May AD 33. Christ is "the head of the body, the church" (Col. 1:18 NKJV) and His Spirit would now dwell within the body of the church, by dwelling within the heart of the individual believer. All true believers have the Spirit of Christ dwelling within them, and together they make up the body of Christ.

Those believers who were not present in Jerusalem at the time of Pentecost to receive the Holy Spirit also needed to do so. For example, the book of Acts tells of the people of Samaria who had earlier accepted the Word of God. After the events of Pentecost and the outpouring of the Holy Spirit, the apostles sent Peter and John to them. "When they arrived they prayed for them that they might receive the Holy Spirit, because the Holy Spirit had not yet come upon any of them; they had simply been baptised into the name of the Lord Jesus. Then Peter and John placed their hands on them, and they received the Holy Spirit" (Acts 8:15-17 NIV). For others, the situation was reversed. Later, for example, a group of Gentiles came to faith through the witness of Peter and they immediately received the Holy Spirit and began speaking in tongues and praising God. Peter *then* baptised them with water in the name of Jesus Christ because they had not yet had this done. All believers needed both the forgiveness of sins from God the Father, through faith in the name of Jesus, *and* to receive the Holy Spirit.

> Through the hands of the apostles many signs and wonders were done among the people . . . And believers were increasingly added to the Lord, multitudes of both men and women, so that they brought the sick out into the streets and laid them on beds and couches, that at least the shadow of Peter passing by might fall on some of them. Also a multitude gathered from the surrounding cities to Jerusalem, bringing sick people and those who were tormented by unclean spirits, and they were all healed.
>
> —Acts 5:12, 14-16 NKJV

The same Holy Spirit that empowered Jesus during His ministry here on earth now indwelt and empowered the believers.

THE SPREADING OF THE GOOD NEWS

One of the most miraculous conversions to faith in Christ was that of a man named Saul. In the early days of Christianity, believers began to be persecuted by the Jews and the ruling people of the time—the Romans. They saw this 'new religion' as a threat and were trying to stamp it out. Saul was a Pharisee, a very learned and zealous Jew who lived by the letter of the Law. He was instrumental in the imprisonment and persecution of many believers, some of whom were put to death. "Saul was . . . breathing out murderous threats against the Lord's disciples" (Acts 9: 1 NIV) and he took many men and women who belonged to what was then being called 'The Way' to Jerusalem to be imprisoned. "The disciples were called Christians first at Antioch" (Acts 11:26 NIV). Jesus however, had other plans for Saul. They were quite the opposite in fact! Saul was about to meet Jesus...

"As he neared Damascus on his journey, suddenly a light from heaven flashed around him. He fell to the ground and heard a voice say to him, 'Saul, Saul, why do you persecute me?' 'Who are you, Lord?' Saul asked. 'I am Jesus, whom you are persecuting,' he replied. 'Now get up and go into the city, and you will be told what you must do'" (Acts 9:3-6 NIV). Saul was blind for three days until his sight was restored to him through a man called Ananias. God told Ananias: "This man is my chosen instrument to carry my name before the Gentiles and their kings and before the people of Israel" (Acts 9:15 NIV).

Saul was baptised and filled with the Holy Spirit. His name was changed to Paul. He was set apart by the Lord to be a servant of the gospel by the commission of God and was to present the Word of God in its fullness—"the mystery that has been kept hidden for ages and generations, but is now disclosed to the saints. To them God has chosen to make known among the Gentiles the glorious riches of this mystery, which is Christ in you, the hope of glory" (Col. 1:26-27 NIV). Paul himself was to suffer much for the name of Jesus as he travelled far and wide spreading the good news of the Kingdom of God. He wrote many of the letters in the New Testament and God used him mightily in the furthering of His Kingdom.

At the time of Pentecost when the Holy Spirit was given to all believers, the church began, and the message of the gospel was then taken out to the nations and the Gentiles were included in the spreading of the gospel of salvation. Paul and Barnabas, his helper in proclaiming the gospel message, addressed the Jews boldly and said:

> "It was necessary that the word of God be spoken first to you. Since you thrust it aside and judge yourselves unworthy of eternal life, behold, we are turning to the Gentiles. For so the Lord has commanded us, saying, 'I have made you a light for the Gentiles, that you may bring salvation to the ends of the earth.'" And when the Gentiles heard this, they began rejoicing and glorifying the word of the Lord, and as many as were appointed to eternal life believed.
>
> —Acts 13:46-48

God "had opened a door of faith to the Gentiles" (Acts 14:27).

Before this time, there were *three* groups of people:
1. Jews who had faith under the Old Covenant. People from other nations were allowed, by faith, to join the Israelites and worship their God, even though not descended from Abraham;
2. Jews by birth who did *not* have faith and were *not* in covenant relationship with God; and
3. Gentile unbelievers.

After this time, there were *four* groups:
1. Jews who *remained* under the Law of Moses, or the Old Covenant, because they did *not* believe that the Lord Jesus *was* the Messiah;
2. Jews by birth who did *not* have faith and were *not* in covenant relationship with God;
3. The church, which was made up of both Jews and Gentiles. They were under the New Covenant; and
4. Gentile unbelievers.

Paul wrote in his letter to the Corinthians that a 'veil' remains over the hearts of the Jewish people when the books of the Old Covenant, written by Moses telling of the coming of the Messiah, are read. Even today this veil remains, for "only in Christ is it taken away . . . whenever anyone turns to the Lord, the veil is taken away" (2 Cor. 3:14, 16 NIV).

The book of Acts is an account of the history of the early church. It is a record of the Acts of the Apostles, who boldly preached the Word of the Lord in Jerusalem, throughout Israel, and further out into the world, spreading the gospel message of salvation. Most of them were imprisoned and killed for their faith, but this did not stop the spread of the good news. Paul said: "I consider my life worth nothing to me, if only I may finish the race and complete the task the Lord Jesus has given me—the task of testifying to the gospel of God's grace" (Acts 20:24 NIV).

Since the time of the early church, many believers have died for their faith, confident that a better life awaited them. Many have also died to preserve the Scriptures so that we can now enjoy the Word of God in many languages and translations.

Chapter Eleven
A Look Behind the Scenes

In the previous chapter, we examined the accounts in the four gospels of the death, resurrection, and ascension of the Lord Jesus, mostly focussing on what occurred in the *physical* world—the world that we can see and hear. If all we knew about the events of those days was a record of what was seen and heard, that is, historical facts, we may be left a little perplexed. It would seem as if some information was missing and we just wouldn't 'get it'. But God, in His Word, has also given us a record of what happened in the *spiritual* world when Jesus died and rose from the dead—a look behind the scenes.

Before we journey behind the scenes of the central event in world history, it would be helpful to review a few points:

THE ORIGIN OF MANKIND:
— God created Adam's physical body from the dust of the earth.
— All DNA is passed down from Adam.
— God breathed the breath of life into Adam.
— Adam's spirit was formed by the Holy Spirit and gave him life.
— Adam's soul was formed by the imprint of the physical on the spirit and is of spiritual substance.
— The spirit and soul form the spiritual body.
— Eve was formed from Adam's side and inherited his spirit.
— A new life is formed by DNA from both parents and spirit which has been passed down through the generations from Adam and is transferred at conception by the father.
— The soul is formed at the moment of conception by the imprint of the physical on the spirit.
— A human being is complete—body, soul, and spirit, at the moment of conception.

THE STATE OF MANKIND:
— When Adam and Eve sinned, their hearts closed to God and they became separated from the Spirit of God—the Spirit of life. They had chosen 'self', or independence, rather than dependence on God.
— Because of sin they were no longer allowed access to the Tree of Life and their lifespan would now be limited.
— Adam's spirit would now be passed on to future generations in a state of separation from the life of God.
— All generations after Adam were born with a sinful nature.

THE DESTINY OF MANKIND:
— Under God's law, the payment for sin is death.

- Because of the law of sin and death, our bodies will age and deteriorate and eventually die. They will then break down to dust.
- When we breathe our last breath, our spirits and souls will depart from our bodies.
- At the point of leaving the body, the spirit, by default, will become disconnected from the soul.
- The spirit will return to its point of origin, that is, to God in heaven who gave it.
- The soul's default interim destiny is the abode of the dead inside the earth where we will await judgement, either in the place of the righteous or in the place of the unrighteous. Where the soul is, that is where we will be aware of being.
- The final default destiny of the sinner is to spend eternity in the lake of fire, forever separated from their Creator.

This is not a prospect that would fill one with hope! And yet, throughout history, God gave the people hope in the coming of a Saviour; one who would save them from their sins and bring them back into a relationship with Him, reconnecting them to His Spirit giving them new life, and saving them from the power of death.

During our examination of the Scriptures regarding the state of man, we discovered what it was that mankind desperately needed.

WHAT WE NEEDED:
- Renewed and restored physical bodies.
- The ability for those renewed bodies to live forever.
- A new spirit—one that reconnects us to God, the eternal source of life; one that would stay united with the soul upon physical death so that the soul would also return to God and not go to the abode of the dead to await judgement. This new spirit would therefore need to be *exempt* from the law of sin and death. It would need to be a spirit that had *not* been passed down through the generations from Adam, but rather be from a source in which there was *no* sin.
- A new spiritual heart for this new spirit to dwell in—one that is cleansed from the guilt of sin and open to God.
- A way for our souls to be redeemed so that we *don't* have to pay the price for our sins ourselves—eternal separation from God; the final consequence of this being eternal condemnation in the lake of fire. We need someone who can make the payment for sin on our behalf.
- Someone to defeat Satan and break the power of death, freeing us from the fear of death.

Does Jesus Christ of Nazareth qualify as the one who can fulfil our needs? Well, firstly let us recall who Jesus is.

JESUS IS:
- God the Son. As the Son and heir He has all the power and attributes of God.
- He is fully God, having the fullness of the Holy Spirit and the eternal Soul of God the Son.
- He is eternal, therefore, within Him is eternal life.
- He is the only one who has been born of the seed of a woman *only* and the only one who has *not* inherited a fallen spirit.
- He lived a sinless life and therefore did not need to die for His *own* sins.
- He was fully man, having taken on a body of flesh and having a human soul. This meant that His body and soul were able to suffer as a man.
- The Holy Spirit was both His human spirit *and* the divine fullness of the Spirit that had been His eternally, uniting His humanity and His deity in one person.
- The Holy Spirit also united Jesus, in His deity and His humanity, with His Father in heaven, unifying Father, Son, and Holy Spirit as one.
- He became flesh and dwelt among us fulfilling *all* of the prophecies written in the Old Testament writings about the coming of the Messiah, and about His life, death, and resurrection.

Jesus is, in fact, the *only* one who qualifies to give new life, for "in him was life" (John 1:4). No other person in heaven or on earth qualifies. We will now examine exactly what Jesus did in the *spiritual realm* to give us new life and to reconnect us to God.

A LOOK AT THE DEATH AND RESURRECTION OF JESUS CHRIST WITH SPIRITUAL EYES

Based on the timeline of events detailed in the previous chapter, we are now going below the surface, both metaphorically *and* literally.

THE THIRD HOUR OF THE DAY:

"**They stripped him and put a scarlet robe on him, and then twisted together a crown of thorns and set it on his head . . . they mocked him . . . they spat on him . . . and struck him on the head again and again**" (Matt. 27:28-30 NIV). At about the third hour of the day (around nine in the morning), "**when they came to the place called the Skull, there they crucified him, along with the criminals—one on his right, the other on his left. Jesus said, 'Father forgive them, for they do not know what they are doing'**" (Luke 23:33-34 NIV).

From the description of the crucifixion, little probably needs to be said about the incredible physical agony that Jesus went through for six hours on the cross. He had already been stripped, beaten, and flogged, and a crown of thorns had been forced down onto His head mocking Him as 'King of the Jews'. He had to struggle to carry the heavy beam of His cross until it was given to another to carry. He then had large nails driven into His hands and His feet which were to suspend His body as He hung on the cross.

Breathing took great effort, as to breathe required that He had to heave Himself upward by pushing up on His nailed feet to allow His chest, and therefore His lungs, to expand. This would have caused absolute exhaustion. With His arms suspended circulation would be very poor and this would cause great agony. His joints would be pulled out of place because of the weight they had to support in this unnatural position causing even greater pain. He would have already lost a lot of blood through the flogging and beating and the forcing down onto His head the crown of thorns, and further blood would have been lost from the nail wounds in His hands and feet causing severe weakness and a lack of oxygen.

Jesus also went through great mental and emotional stress and agony before His crucifixion, knowing ahead of time what He had to go through, not only physically, but also spiritually during the hours that He hung on the cross. He had already sweated great drops of blood in the Garden of Gethsemane and had told His disciples that His soul was "overwhelmed with sorrow to the point of death" (Mark 14:33 NIV). He was mocked and spat upon and rejected and deserted by all but a few faithful followers.

Why would an innocent man allow Himself to go through this? Being fully God He could have saved Himself, and yet He didn't. He willingly endured the cross, even forgiving those who crucified Him.

FROM THE SIXTH HOUR TO THE NINTH HOUR:

"From the sixth hour until the ninth hour there was darkness over all the land" (Matt. 27:45 NKJV). At the sixth hour, God laid upon Jesus the sins of the world. God "made Him who knew no sin to be sin for us" (2 Cor. 5:21 NKJV).

The payment for sin can only be met with a blood sacrifice. Our sin was laid upon Jesus by His Father in a similar way that, under the Old Covenant, the priest would lay his hand on the head of the animal to be sacrificed for the sins of the people. The animal could never take away their sins but was a 'type' leading the way to the perfect sacrifice—"The Lamb of God, who takes away the sin of the world" (John 1:29).

When God laid our sins upon Jesus, He transferred the *guilt* of our sins to the pure heart of Jesus. Jesus had never sinned; therefore, He had never felt the guilt of sin in His heart. The result of sin is a separation from God and a closing of the heart. This is what happened immediately to Adam and Eve when *they* sinned and this is what happened to the human heart of Jesus when *our* sins were laid upon *Him*.

Under the Old Covenant, when the wrath of God for sinful man was symbolically transferred to the sacrificial animal, the animal's life was taken. God's wrath for our sins was placed upon the perfect *human* soul of Jesus as He hung on the cross. The wrath of God was not placed upon the *divine* Soul of the Son, because God's wrath could not be placed upon Himself. Only the soul of a *man* could suffer the wrath of God and only the *perfect* soul of a man, undeserving of God's wrath, could be a substitute for another.

This was *our* punishment which Jesus willingly took upon Himself when "God presented him as a sacrifice of atonement" (Rom. 3:25 NIV) for our sins. He suffered the fate to which we as sinners were condemned, by substituting His own *perfect* soul for our *sinful* soul.

It was during these dark and agonizing hours on the cross that Jesus, in His humanity, was forsaken by His Father. God cannot abide with sinful man. When Jesus had our sins laid upon Him, the Father turned away from His only Son. Jesus, in His humanity, was separated for the very first time in His life from His Father, and at the ninth hour Jesus cried out **"with a loud voice . . . 'My God, my God, why have you forsaken me?'" (Matt. 27:46).**

THE NINTH HOUR OF THE DAY:

At the ninth hour, Jesus declared: **"It is finished" (John 19:30).** "Christ, our Passover lamb, has been sacrificed" (1 Cor. 5:7). Jesus *completed* the work that the Father had sent Him to do, that is, to bear our sins *and* pay the price for our sins, *while He was on the cross*. He suffered in His body through the physical agony of crucifixion and by the shedding of His blood, and in His soul by being forsaken by His Father. The curse that was placed upon us when Adam and Eve sinned, that is, spiritual separation from God and the condemnation of the soul, had been willingly suffered by Jesus in our place. At the ninth hour, His work of salvation was complete. Mission accomplished!

Later in John's narrative, he relates that **"one of the soldiers pierced His side with a spear, and immediately blood and water came out" (John 19:34 NKJV).** In the book of Psalms, when David writes of the crucifixion, he says of Christ: "My heart is like wax; it is melted within my breast" (Ps. 22:14) and "reproaches have broken my heart" (Ps. 69:20), confirming that the immediate cause of the Saviour's death was a broken heart through the anguish caused by the Father turning His face away from His only Son and because of the reproach, shame, guilt, and dishonour borne for us through the bearing of our sins.

At the ninth hour, Jesus, the Son of God as priest, presented to the Father in the heavenly tabernacle in the sanctuary of God, the human soul of His Son—the perfect sacrifice. Because Jesus in His divinity was one with, and connected to, the Father, He was able to, in effect, enter the heavenly inner sanctuary while He was still on the cross. Under the Old Covenant, the high priest would enter the inner room of the tabernacle or temple once a year to bring a blood sacrifice as an offering for the sins of himself and the people. Jesus Christ—the perfect sacrifice, entered the Most Holy Place of the heavenly tabernacle by His *own* blood, "once for all, having obtained eternal redemption" (Heb. 9:12 NKJV). Christ "did not enter heaven to offer himself again and again, the way the high priest enters the Most Holy Place every year with blood that is not his own . . . he has appeared once for all . . . to do away with sin by the sacrifice of himself" (Heb. 9:25-26 NIV).

God sent "his own Son in the likeness of sinful man to be a sin offering" (Rom. 8:3 NIV) and an "offering for guilt" (Isa. 53:10). When Jesus' divine Soul as priest, presented to His Father at the altar in heaven a sacrifice—His perfect human soul, "he offered up himself" (Heb. 7:27). "When this priest had offered for all time one sacrifice for sins, he sat down at the right hand of God" (Heb. 1:3 NIV). Jesus, Son of Man, was found 'not guilty'. His heart was free from the guilt of sin, His soul was accepted as a perfect sacrifice on our behalf, and He was then "vindicated by the Spirit" (1 Tim. 3:16).

Vindicate—/vin-duh-kayt/ *v.* (-ting) 1 clear of blame or suspicion[1]

After Jesus had paid the price for our sins in those few terrible hours separated from His Father, His human spiritual heart was again open to the Holy Spirit because, even though He had paid the ransom for us by having our sins laid upon Him, He Himself was innocent. He had triumphed over the law of sin and death because, once that price was paid, He no longer *needed* to be separated from God and therefore from the Holy Spirit—the Spirit of life. He was again connected to the life of His Father.

Sacrifice accepted! Position of the Son restored! The 'first Adam' was found guilty, the 'second Adam'—not guilty.

At the ninth hour, Jesus said: **"'Father, into your hands I commit my spirit.' Having said this, He breathed His last" (Luke 23:46 NKJV).** Only Jesus, being God the Son, had power over His own Spirit. Before He went to the cross He said: "I lay down My life that I may take it again. No one takes it from Me, but I lay it down of Myself. I have power to lay it down, and I have power to take it again. This command I have received from My Father" (John 10:17-18 NKJV).

Matthew writes that **"when Jesus had cried out again in a loud voice, he gave up his spirit" (Matt 27:50 NIV).** The fact that Jesus 'gave up' His Spirit confirms that Jesus was always fully in control. He *willingly* laid down His life. Only Jesus had the power to give up His Spirit and He knew that God would accept His sacrifice and that His Spirit would remain in His soul upon the death of His body. As the final breath of Jesus left His body He departed from His body to Sheol, the place where all righteous disembodied souls went. Imagine the angelic escort!

At this moment, **"the curtain of the temple was torn in two, from top to bottom" (Matt. 27:51).** This signified that there was no longer a need for separation between God and man. Jesus had made a way for man to enter the presence of God. The writer of Hebrews tells us that, because of Jesus' sacrifice, "we have confidence to enter the Most Holy Place by the blood of Jesus, by a new and living way opened for us through the curtain, that is, his body" (Heb. 10:19 NIV). Animal sacrifices were no longer necessary. The sacrificial system under the Old Covenant had been made obsolete. God had accepted the *perfect* sacrifice and this sacrifice was in our place.

"**The earth shook and the rocks were split**" **(Matt. 27:51).** The ground shook when Jesus descended into the abode of the dead. "**The tombs broke open and the bodies of many holy people who had died were raised to life. They came out of the tombs, and after Jesus' resurrection they went into the holy city and appeared to many people**" **(Matt. 27:52-53 NIV).** It appears that, during the earthquake that occurred at the very moment Jesus departed from His body and descended into Sheol, some of the Old Testament saints were immediately bodily raised to life. They had been given new life at the very moment Jesus arrived in Sheol and their bodies were resurrected but they did not appear in the city until two days after this event. This will be discussed further, later in this chapter.

FROM THE NINTH HOUR OF THE DAY OF THE CRUCIFIXION UNTIL THE DAWN OF THE FIRST DAY OF THE WEEK—THE DAY AFTER THE SABBATH:

Unlike all others who had died before, Jesus' Spirit (the fullness of the Holy Spirit in His case) remained within Him at His last breath and the death of His body. Jesus was the "firstborn of the dead" (Rev. 1:5). He is the first to retain the spirit of life on physical death. At the very moment that He was "put to death in the flesh" (1 Pet. 3:18), He was "made alive in the spirit" (1 Pet. 3:18).

With the Spirit of life that indwelt Him, Jesus entered the abode of the dead. What did Jesus do in the abode of the dead? Something very similar to what He had done in the realm of the living—He preached. He had a message to bring!

Jesus proclaimed His victory to the righteous souls who had died and who had been waiting in the abode of the dead. Jesus was not preaching to the *unrighteous*, only the righteous. It was too late for the unrighteous to repent of their sins. Peter explained that "the gospel was preached even to those who are now dead, so that they might be judged according to men in regard to the body, but live according to God in regard to the spirit" (1 Pet. 4:6 NIV). The righteous dead, as with all who had died, had already experienced judgement 'according to men in regard to the body' (physical death). Jesus was in Sheol to impart *life* to them so they could 'live according to God in regard to the spirit'.

Jesus preached the good news to the righteous, announcing to them that *He* was the Messiah of whom the prophets had spoken and for whom they had long awaited. No doubt His preaching would have been along similar lines as when He later spoke to two of the disciples on the road to Emmaus: "Beginning with Moses and all the Prophets, he explained to them what was said in all the Scriptures concerning himself" (Luke 24:27 NIV). Jesus was there to tell them that *He* was the fulfilment of the Covenant, the payment for their sins, the perfect sacrifice, and the ransom for their souls.

Although those who died in faith under the Old Covenant, and even *before* the Covenant was given, believed in the *promised* Messiah who would save them from their sins, they were now seeing Him *face to face*. It is likely that, when Jesus descended into the abode of the dead, He did not, in appearance, stand out from anyone else there (apart from perhaps a more impressive angelic escort!). It was His *message* that was the difference rather than His *appearance*. The righteous in Sheol were now being given the opportunity to believe in *Jesus Christ of Nazareth* as this Messiah who had been promised. They were being given the opportunity to believe on *His name* to save them from the power of death.

The righteous dead still had free will and the ability to choose to believe in Jesus Christ as Messiah and Saviour or not. These righteous either had to accept or reject His Word. They had to decide *personally* if Jesus *was* the Messiah and if what He said was the truth. If they rejected His Word they did not receive His life and they would *remain* in the abode of the dead until a later judgement and resurrection.

This opportunity to believe in Jesus as the Messiah does *not* imply that people were given a 'second chance' in Sheol. These were people who had already died *in faith*. Their names were *already* in the book of life. They had already put their faith in the *coming* Messiah. Now they were given the opportunity to translate their faith in the *coming* Messiah into faith in the *person* of Jesus Christ of Nazareth *as* that Messiah and to receive His Spirit. This was a unique event.

Jesus had told the disciples of His journey to the abode of the dead ahead of time. He said that "a time is coming and has now come when the dead will hear the voice of the Son of God and those who hear will live. For as the Father has life in himself, so he has granted the Son to have life in himself" (John 5:25-26 NIV). In this case, to 'hear' refers to hearing in a *spiritual* sense. The spiritual hearts of those who heard and *accepted* Jesus' message would then be ready to receive His Spirit.

The 'voice of the Son of God' is the voice that Job was looking forward to when he said: "If only you would set a time and then remember me! If a man dies will he live again? All the days of my hard service I will wait for my renewal to come. You will call and I will answer you; you will long for the creature your hands have made. Surely then you will count my steps but not keep track of my sin. My offences will be sealed up in a bag; you will cover over my sin" (Job 14:13-17 NIV). Job was at last hearing that voice.

Isaiah prophesied hundreds of years before Jesus died: "I will keep you and will make you to be a covenant for the people and a light for the Gentiles, to open eyes that are blind, to free captives from prison and to release from the dungeon those who sit in darkness" (Isa. 42:6-7 NIV). Those who had been in 'prison' were about to be released!

The prophet Micah also had faith that this release would happen. He prophesied: "I watch in hope for the LORD, I wait for God my Saviour; my God will hear me. Do not gloat over me, my enemy! Though I have fallen, I will rise. Though I sit in darkness, the LORD will be my light. Because I have sinned against him, I will bear the LORD's wrath, until he pleads my case and establishes my right. He will bring me out into the light; I will see his righteousness" (Mic. 7:7-9 NIV). Those who 'sat in darkness' were about to be brought out into the light!

God promised His people, through the prophet Isaiah, that one day the Messiah would come and "your covenant with death will be annulled; your agreement with the grave will not stand" (Isa. 28:18 NIV). As promised, He came.

After Jesus had preached the good news to the righteous in the abode of the dead, He imparted His Spirit to those who believed on Him. Jesus gave them the Spirit of life—the Holy Spirit, likely by breathing on them, giving them new spiritual hearts in which His Spirit could dwell. The receiving of the Holy Spirit set them free from the power of death that was keeping them captive.

Jesus was *willing* to impart His life to the spiritually dead because of His great love for them. Jesus was *able* to impart life to the spiritually dead because He had the Holy Spirit within Him. His Spirit, which He imparted to others, came from, but at the same time *remained in,* His perfect sinless human heart and soul and in His divine Heart and Soul. This same Spirit was also connected to, and one with, God the Father.

It was only *after* Jesus had paid the price for our sins that the Spirit was *able* to give this new life to others. Because Jesus' soul had suffered in place of the sinner, He had a soul which had *already* paid the price for sin. If the Spirit in Him that had conquered death was to give life to another, that other person would share the Spirit of life that Jesus had in Him, and Jesus' death would become *their* death. To receive this Spirit, would therefore mean that the person now had eternal life—connection with God, the source of life. They would no longer be awaiting judgement and condemnation. For them that event had already taken place—through the sacrifice of the Lord Jesus Christ.

The book of Hosea foretells the imparting of the Spirit of Jesus to those Old Testament saints who had died in faith and were waiting for the appearing of the Saviour in the place of the dead. He prophesied that "after two days he will revive us; on the third day he will restore us, that we may live in his presence. Let us acknowledge the LORD; let us press on to acknowledge him. As surely as the sun rises, he will appear; he will come to us like the winter rains, like the spring rains that water the earth" (Hosea 6:2-3 NIV). Hosea was as sure of this happening as he was of the sun rising. Jesus was two days in Sheol after He died, and at the end of those two days, He 'revived', or gave life to, those who believed on His name. They were about to be 'restored' to 'live in his presence'.

Going back in time two days, Matthew's gospel tells us that there was a bodily resurrection from the dead of 'many holy people' at the moment of Jesus' death. He wrote that **"the tombs broke open and the bodies of many holy people who had died were raised to life. They came out of the tombs, and after Jesus' resurrection they went into the holy city and appeared to many people" (Matt. 27: 52-53 NIV).**

From this account it seems that, upon Jesus entering the abode of the dead, some who were there instantly recognized that He was the Messiah and believed in

His name, and therefore received His Spirit immediately, but in *this* case, it appears that they were given the Spirit throughout their hearts *and* their entire souls and their souls were reunited with their bodies which were resurrected and renewed. The action of the Holy Spirit within their souls which then re-united with their bodies caused their bodies to immediately reassemble from the dust they had become, reversing the curse on their physical bodies and resurrecting them to perfection.

Others, who were given the Spirit of life in their hearts, may have only believed *after* Jesus had preached to them for two days. In a similar way, Mary Magdalene believed that she was seeing the risen Lord almost immediately, but the two disciples on the road to Emmaus did not recognize Jesus until He had walked with them some distance, explained to them the Scriptures about Himself, and had broken bread with them. Similarly, some people believe and put their faith in Jesus having only heard the basic gospel message, whereas others may feel that they need to know more and may take years or even a lifetime to believe. Some, despite the evidence, never come to faith in Jesus.

These holy people, who had been bodily resurrected, later ascended into heaven. Not all 'holy people' in Sheol were *bodily* resurrected. The others to whom Jesus imparted life had only their *souls* given life but not their *bodies* resurrected and renewed. It was likely that the reason God bodily resurrected a number of saints was as evidence that His Son was able to impart life to departed souls *and* bring those souls back into resurrected and renewed bodies—visual evidence to those on earth who would witness this amazing event. It was also proof that, not only did *Jesus* return from the dead, He also conquered death on behalf of *others*—sinners, in fact.

DAWN ON THE THIRD DAY:

David wrote of God: "You will not let your Holy One see decay" (Ps. 16:10 NIV). David is referring to the fact that, when Jesus died, His body was not in the grave long enough to decay. At the end of those two days in Sheol, through the power of the Holy Spirit, Jesus ascended up out of the abode of the dead. He also led out those who now had a new heart and a new spirit in their hearts. They had been imprisoned in the depths of the earth awaiting their redemption. That must have been the most exciting prison-break in the history of the universe! Imagine waiting down in that shadowy place for the coming of the Messiah and the triumphant joy you would feel when your Saviour appeared and declared that He had defeated death and that you were free! Imagine breaking forth from the depths of the earth and into the light!

When Jesus arose triumphantly from the depths of the earth, **"there was a violent earthquake, for an angel of the Lord came down from heaven and, going to the tomb, rolled back the stone and sat on it" (Matt. 28:2 NIV).** On ascension from Sheol, Jesus' spiritual body returned to His physical body which had been laid in the tomb. His body was instantly transformed with new life through the power of the Holy Spirit and was resurrected, healed, and renewed.

Jesus then appeared to many people over forty days, as did the 'many holy people' who had been bodily resurrected at the moment of His death—proof that Jesus had defeated death both spiritually and physically, not only for Himself but also for others; proof also that He had life within Him, and that life, He could impart to others. It is likely that those whose souls rose from Sheol but who did *not* receive renewed bodies, also remained on the earth during those forty days. Disembodied souls do not normally dwell on the earth, but these were unique circumstances.

THE GIVING OF AUTHORITY TO THE DISCIPLES:

Jesus spent forty days on the earth after His resurrection. In addition to many miraculous events, as proof to the disciples that He really was Jesus Christ and was alive again, He performed the same miracle that He did when He called the first disciples. Seven of the disciples decided to go fishing:

> Just as the day was breaking, Jesus stood on the shore; yet the disciples did not know that it was Jesus. Jesus said to them, "Children, do you have any fish?" They answered him, "No." He said to them, "Cast the net on the right side of the boat, and you will find some." So they cast it, and now they were not able to haul it in, because of the quantity of fish . . . Simon Peter went aboard and hauled the net ashore, full of large fish, 153 of them. And although there were so many, the net was not torn. Jesus said to them, "Come and have breakfast." Now none of the disciples dared ask him, "Who are you?" They knew it was the Lord.
>
> —John 21:4-6, 11-12

To His disciples Jesus said: "'**Peace be with you! As the Father has sent me, I am sending you.' And with that he breathed on them and said, 'Receive the Holy Spirit'" (John 20:21-22 NIV).** He gave the disciples the same authority that He had had on earth and commissioned them with these words: "All authority in heaven and on earth has been given to me. Therefore go and make disciples of all nations, baptising them in the name of the Father and of the Son and of the Holy Spirit, and teaching them to obey everything I have commanded you. And surely I am with you always, to the very end of the age" (Matt. 28:18-20 NIV).

He also told His disciples: "Do not leave Jerusalem, but wait for the gift my Father promised, which you have heard me speak about. For John baptised with water, but in a few days you will be baptised with the Holy Spirit" (Acts 1:4-5 NIV). He said to them: "You will receive power when the Holy Spirit comes on you; and you will be my witnesses in Jerusalem, and in all Judea and Samaria, and to the ends of the earth" (Acts 1:8 NIV).

THE ASCENSION:

At the end of these forty days, **"after the Lord Jesus had spoken to them, he was taken up into heaven and he sat at the right hand of God" (Mark 16:19 NIV).** Jesus—Son of God, Son of Man, ascended into the throne room of heaven to His Father. The power and mighty strength of God through the working of the Holy Spirit was "exerted in Christ when he raised him from the dead and seated him at his right hand in the heavenly realms" (Eph. 1:19-20 NIV). He was once again to dwell in heaven, this time in both the fullness of deity *and* the fullness of humanity, as the Lord and Saviour, Jesus Christ.

David prophesied of the Saviour: "He leads forth the prisoners with singing" (Ps. 68:6 NIV) and "when you ascended on high, you led captives in your train" (Ps. 68:18 NIV). When Jesus ascended into heaven, those who had received new life when He was in Sheol also ascended—some bodily, others their soul only, yet to await a future bodily resurrection.

The apostle John had a vision, as recorded in the book of Revelation, where he sees Israel portrayed as a woman who had given birth to a male child (Jesus). He sees Satan portrayed as a red dragon waiting to devour the child by the power of death. This does not happen as the child is "caught up to God and to his throne" (Rev. 12:5). Death was not able to hold Jesus, who rose from the dead and ascended into heaven, triumphing over death and the power of Satan.

THE OUTPOURING OF THE SPIRIT:

A short time later, after Jesus had ascended into heaven, there was an outpouring of the Spirit in power upon believers:

> **When the day of Pentecost arrived, they were all together in one place. And suddenly there came from heaven a sound like a mighty rushing wind, and it filled the entire house where they were sitting. And divided tongues as of fire appeared to them and rested on each one of them. And they were all filled with the Holy Spirit and began to speak in other tongues as the Spirit gave them utterance.**
>
> **—Acts 2:1-4**

Spirit is imparted through the breath of God. That was one big breath—like a 'mighty rushing wind'! Jesus had, as promised, given His Spirit to those who believed—those who had put their faith in Him, whose hearts were open, and whose sins were forgiven. The Spirit proceeds *from* the Father *through* the Son. By giving His Spirit, the believers were now connected to the life of God through His Son. They received new spiritual hearts and they now had the Spirit of the 'new Adam'—the Spirit of life, indwelling their new hearts. Even though they were still living here on earth, they were now part of the kingdom of heaven through the Holy Spirit that flowed from the Lord Jesus Christ. They had been 'born again', having been given the deposit of a new Spirit—new life, and they now belonged to the kingdom of God.

When the Jews who witnessed this outpouring of the Spirit realised that Jesus *was* who He said He was and that they had crucified their Messiah, they were greatly distressed. Peter told them that what they needed to do was to repent of their sins and they would receive this new life—the gift of the Holy Spirit. This gift of life was not only for them, but for "all who are far off" (Acts 2:39) who would put their faith and trust in Jesus—those who lived in other parts of the earth, those who belonged to other nations, and those who had not yet been born. The gift of life is for all who repent and believe in Jesus' name for the forgiveness of sins; for all are invited to be a part of God's kingdom.

Part Four

You (Again)

Chapter Twelve
The Life

WHAT REALLY MATTERS ... A MESSAGE TO THE READER

When you consider your life and analyse what is really important, you may come to the realisation that possessions, wealth, career, social standing, and worldly happiness are not really as important as you thought, or certainly as the world would *have* you think. All these things are temporary and will one day fade away. All earthly possessions and positions are on loan. Even your family, whom you may love very much, cannot give you the real joy, peace, and fulfilment that you yearn for.

Jesus told this parable:

> "The land of a rich man produced plentifully, and he thought to himself, 'What shall I do, for I have nowhere to store my crops?' And he said, 'I will do this: I will tear down my barns and build larger ones, and there I will store all my grain and my goods. And I will say to my soul, 'Soul, you have ample goods laid up for many years; relax, eat, drink, be merry.'' But God said to him, 'Fool! This night your soul is required of you, and the things you have prepared, whose will they be?' So is the one who lays up treasure for himself and is not rich toward God."
>
> —Luke 12:16-21

"This is what the LORD says: 'Let not the wise man boast of his wisdom or the strong man boast of his strength or the rich man boast of his riches, but let him who boasts boast about this: that he understands and knows me, that I am the LORD, who exercises kindness, justice and righteousness on earth, for in these I delight'" (Jer. 9:23-24 NIV). Only being restored to your heavenly Father can bring real joy, true and lasting peace, and fulfilment of your purpose in life. If you have peace with God, you have hope for the future—eternal life. The psalmist asked: "Whom have I in heaven but you? And there is nothing on earth that I desire besides you" (Ps. 73:25), and Paul said: "I consider everything a loss compared to the surpassing greatness of knowing Christ Jesus my Lord" (Phil. 3:8 NIV).

Knowing that your future is safe in God's hands relieves you of the unnecessary worry over everything else in life—the drive to accumulate wealth, the need to climb the social or corporate ladder, the disappointment of relationships, the uncertainty and frailty of health, and the inevitability of ageing. None of that really matters in the light of eternity and would pale in comparison with the knowledge that you have eternal life!

EATING FRUIT

There was a tree in the Garden of Eden called the Tree of the Knowledge of Good and Evil. When Adam and Eve ate from this tree, they chose to sin by disobeying God. They were deceived. They thought that they could be independent from God and rely on themselves. There is a reference in the book of Hosea to 'eating the fruit of deception'. The people of Israel were told that this is what they were doing in their wickedness by depending "on their own strength" (Hosea 10:13 NIV). Just as Adam and Eve did this, so did the people of Israel and so do people today, deceiving themselves into thinking that they do not *need* God; that they only need themselves. They choose independence from God. They choose to 'eat from the tree' and their hearts remain full of the guilt of sin. As a consequence of this, they remain disconnected from the Spirit of life and they remain under the sentence of death.

The restoration of our relationship with God is only able to be initiated while we are in our earthly bodies. Once we die, there will not be another chance to do this and the Bible makes this very clear: "For what is the hope of the godless when God cuts him off, when God takes away his life?" (Job 27:8). There is no possibility of negotiating your way into heaven after you have died; no chance of being taken to heaven because of the prayers of loved ones you have left behind. Your eternal destiny is determined *before* you depart the earth, so "seek the LORD while He may be found, call upon Him while He is near. Let the wicked forsake his way, and the unrighteous man his thoughts; let him return to the LORD, and He will have mercy on him; and to our God, for He will abundantly pardon" (Isa. 55:6-7 NKJV). At the point of departure from your body it will be *too late to be pardoned.*

WHAT WE NEEDED:

When we examined what the Word of God said about our spirit, our heart, and our soul, we discovered three things that we needed:

1. *A new spirit.* The old spirit we inherited from Adam was in a state of separation from God and was subject to the law of sin and death. It would not remain with the soul when we die and therefore the soul would go to the abode of the dead;
2. *A new heart,* cleansed from the guilt of sin; and
3. *A redeemed soul,* freed from the power of death.

THE OPTIONS

King David said of God: "With you the wicked cannot dwell" (Ps. 5:4 NIV). God cannot abide sin, so sinful man cannot dwell with God in heaven. This should apply to us all, for *all* have sinned. The payment for sin is death and "why should a living man complain, a man for the punishment of his sins?" (Lam. 3:39 NKJV) After all, this *is* the penalty of the Law.

Death is a very high price to pay; so let's look at a few possible payment options to see if there is an alternative:

OPTION NUMBER ONE:

You can pay the price yourself. It is not even necessary to *choose* this option. It is your *default* option. If you do *not* choose another option, by default you *will* be paying the price for your own sins. There are plenty of people who will remain in 'default' on option number one.

OPTION NUMBER TWO:

Is it possible to earn salvation and somehow 'purchase' for yourself an exemption from the payment of death? No! Paul explains that salvation "does not depend on man's desire or effort, but on God's mercy" (Rom. 9:16 NIV). Salvation cannot be earned by going to church, praying, giving to the poor, or doing good deeds. While these are good and worthwhile things to do, you cannot substitute *any* of these things for the payment of death. If salvation *could* be earned, there would be no assurance of life, no peace of mind. After all ... how good is good? How much would you have to give? How often would you have to pray? What if you missed going to church a few times?

OPTION NUMBER THREE:

How about another religion or faith? No. God said: "There is no other God besides Me, a just God and a Saviour; There is none besides Me. Look to Me, and be saved, all you ends of the earth! For I am God, and there is no other" (Isa. 45:21-22 NKJV). Unlike other 'religions', "our God is a God who saves; from the Sovereign LORD comes escape from death" (Ps. 68:20). Isn't that exactly what man desires—escape from death? Who really wants to die?

There are many 'religions' out there; hundreds in fact. Man has an inbuilt need to worship, the need to be accountable to someone, the need for forgiveness, the need to be loved and to belong, the need to have something to live for, the need for meaning and purpose, the need to know one's origin and destiny, and the need for peace of mind. Many people spend their time searching for answers to the big questions in life, but life here on earth is short. There is no time to waste looking for life in all the wrong places. Other 'religions' cannot give you forgiveness from sins. Nor do they lead to eternal life. There are many religions made up by man and many religions have demonic forces behind them. In contrast, Paul gives this reassurance: "The gospel which was preached by me is not according to man. For I neither received it from man, nor was I taught it, but it came through the revelation of Jesus Christ" (Gal. 1:11-12 NKJV).

That's three options so far that have had a dead end (pun intended). So, apart from the undesirable option of paying for your sin yourself, the *only* other option for the payment of sin that God will accept is...

OPTION NUMBER FOUR:

THE RANSOM

Someone else *could* pay the price for your sins. If you could find someone who was perfect enough to have *never* sinned then perhaps, if they were willing, *they* could pay the price for *your* sins. If they had not sinned themselves, they wouldn't need to pay the price for their own sins, so their death could be a substitute for your death; their soul for your soul. Is it possible to find someone who qualifies and, if so, would they willingly lay down *their* life so that *you* could live?

We are estranged from God in our sinful state and will *remain* estranged, or banished, from God forever if we pay the price of sin ourselves.

> **Banish—/ban-ish/** *v.* **1 condemn to exile. 2 dismiss (esp. from one's mind).**[1]
>
> **Estrange—/uh-straynj/** *v.* **(-ing) 1 (usu. In *passive*; often foll. by *from*) alienate; make hostile or indifferent. 2 (as estranged *adj.*) (of a husband or wife) no longer living with his or her spouse.**[2]

Good News! Scripture tells us that God "devises ways so that a banished person may not remain estranged from him" (2 Sam. 14:14 NIV). That can only mean one thing—there *is* someone who can pay the price for our sins. A substitute has been found!

The word *gospel* means 'good news'. The good news of the gospel is that God *has* devised a way so that we do not have to remain estranged from Him. According to the apostle Paul, the gospel is "that Christ died for our sins according to the Scriptures, and that He was buried, and that He rose again the third day according to the Scriptures" (1 Cor. 15:3-4 NKJV). Paul further explains that the gospel of God is that which "He promised before through His prophets in the Holy Scriptures, concerning His Son Jesus Christ our Lord, who was born of the seed of David according to the flesh, and declared to be the Son of God with power according to the Spirit of holiness, by the resurrection from the dead" (Rom. 1:2-4 NIV). Jesus *is* the good news!

Jesus explained that "salvation is from the Jews" (John 4:22). Salvation is *only* found in Jesus Christ who, in His humanity, descended from the line of Abraham, Isaac, and Jacob. "There is no other name under heaven given among men by which we must be saved" (Acts 4:12 NKJV).

Jesus said that He came "to give His life as a ransom for many" (Matt. 20:28) and "to seek and to save the lost" (Luke 19:10). The way that God has devised to bring us back into a right relationship with Himself is through His Son's death, paid as a ransom for our souls.

> **Ransom—/ran-suhm/ —***n.* **1 money demanded or paid for the release of a prisoner. 2 liberation of a prisoner in return for this. —***v.* **1 buy the**

freedom or restoration of; redeem . . . 3 release for a ransom (Latin: related to REDEMPTION).[3]

According to God's Law, "without the shedding of blood there is no forgiveness" (Heb. 9:22 NIV) of sins. The ransom for your life was costly. It cost God the life of His beloved Son: "The man Christ Jesus . . . gave himself as a ransom for all" (1 Tim. 2:5-6). God sent "his own Son in the likeness of sinful man to be a sin offering" (Rom. 8:3 NIV) and He gave His life as "a guilt offering" (Isa. 53:10 NIV). *His* blood was shed to cover *our* sins. With His blood, Jesus "ransomed people for God from every tribe and language and people and nation" (Rev. 5:9).

That is amazing! God the Son *Himself* has willingly laid down His life for us! "Scarcely for a righteous man will one die; yet perhaps for a good man someone would even dare to die. But God demonstrates His own love toward us, in that while we were still sinners, Christ died for us" (Rom. 5:7-8 NKJV). Did we deserve this sacrifice? No! "He saved us, not because of the righteous things we had done, but because of his mercy" (Titus 3:5 NIV). Jesus died because of God's love for us, "for God so loved the world, that he gave his only Son, that whoever believes in him should not perish but have eternal life" (John 3:16).

If a person does *not* have forgiveness of sins through faith in Jesus as Lord and Saviour, by default he stands condemned. By the grace of God, this death sentence can be reversed. Eternal life is a gift that is received through faith in Jesus for the forgiveness of sins. It is *only* through Jesus that a person can be saved from the consequences of sin—eternal separation from God and eternal condemnation in the lake of fire.

The forgiveness of sins through faith in Jesus removes a person's condemnation—the sentence of death. *It's all about the Son.* "He who believes in the Son has everlasting life; and he who does not believe the Son shall not see life, but the wrath of God abides on him" (John 3:36 NKJV). Paul writes that "there is now no condemnation for those who are in Christ Jesus, because through Christ Jesus the law of the Spirit of life set me free from the law of sin and death" (Rom. 8:1 NIV).

So, what does it mean to be 'in Christ Jesus'?

THE IMPORTANCE OF BEING 'IN'

We are all born 'in Adam' having the spirit that was passed down from Adam. Because this spirit is disconnected from the life of God, it will *not* lead to eternal life. It is subject to the law of sin and death. To have eternal life, we need to be *reborn* 'in Christ Jesus', in whom is the Spirit of life.

Jesus spoke to the people of this *new* birth—of being born again. He said that "unless one is born again, he cannot see the kingdom of God" (John 3:3 NKJV) and that to enter the kingdom of God they must be "born of water and the Spirit . . . That which is born of the flesh is flesh, and that which is born of the Spirit is spirit" (John 3:5-6 NKJV). The people understood that they were born once 'of water' and that they were given the life of the flesh through their parents, but what was Jesus talking about when He said that they must be *born again*, this time of the Spirit?

Jesus told the people that "whoever drinks the water I give him will never thirst. Indeed, the water I give him will become in him a spring of water welling up to eternal life" (John 4:14 NIV). Out of the heart flow the 'springs of life'—the spirit. Imagine if your heart was filled with a spirit that 'welled up' to *eternal* life. This is the living water that Jesus said only *He* can give. To be born again means to receive a new Spirit—to be reborn 'in Christ'—to become part of a *new* creation.

TO BELIEVE ... A NEW HEART AND A NEW SPIRIT

We are all sinners according to God's Law and our conscience, for "whoever commits sin also commits lawlessness, and sin is lawlessness" (1 John 3:4 NKJV) and "whoever knows the right thing to do and fails to do it, for him it is sin" (James 4:17). We have inherited a sinful nature. That is why we are separated from God, for "your iniquities have separated you from your God; and your sins have hidden His face from you" (Isa. 59:2 NKJV).

The first chapter of the book of James explains the process of sin:
1. There exists an *evil desire* in us (our inherited sinful nature);
2. Because of this desire we are enticed and *tempted* to sin;
3. This conceives a desire in us to *give in* to that temptation; then
4. The desire to give in gives birth to the *sinful act*.

Nobody is immune to the temptation of sin or the consequences of giving in to temptation. Sin causes guilt in our hearts. At times this guilt may feel like a heavy burden that you just cannot shake; a shadow hanging over your life and sapping your joy. It is God whom we have sinned against; God's laws that we have broken, and it is *only* God who can forgive our sins, cleanse our hearts, and free us from the guilt of sin.

King David cried out to the Lord: "Have mercy upon me, O God, according to Your lovingkindness; according to the multitude of Your tender mercies, blot out my transgressions. Wash me thoroughly from my iniquity, and cleanse me from my sin . . . Against You, You only, have I sinned, and done this evil in Your sight" (Ps. 51:1-2, 4 NKJV). David knew what it was like to feel the wretchedness of sin and a guilty conscience. He had committed adultery with a married woman and then arranged for her husband to be placed in the front line on the battlefield where he was bound to be killed. In great remorse, David pleaded with God for mercy and forgiveness and asked God to create in him a "clean heart" (Ps. 51:10). Sin causes a guilty conscience and an *unclean* heart.

David said: "When we were overwhelmed by sins, you forgave our transgressions" (Ps. 65:3 NIV). If *you* feel overwhelmed by sins, God's forgiveness is for you. Even if you think you are one of the worst sinners there is, God *can* forgive your sins and blot them out if you come to Him in repentance. Those who repent of their sins and ask God for forgiveness *will be forgiven*. God does not pick and choose the sins to forgive or the sinner. *All* have sinned and His forgiveness and grace are available to *all*. God promises that "everyone who calls on the name of the LORD shall be saved" (Joel 2:32). 'Everyone' excludes no one, for "God our Saviour . . . desires all people to be saved and to come to a knowledge of the truth" (1 Tim. 2:4).

God wants everyone to have life! "'Do I take any pleasure in the death of the wicked?' declares the Sovereign LORD, 'Rather, am I not pleased when they turn from their ways and live? . . . I will judge you each one according to his ways . . . Repent! Turn away from all your offences; then sin will not be your downfall. Rid yourself of all the offences you have committed, and get a new heart and a new spirit . . . repent and live!'" (Ezek. 18:23, 30-32 NIV).

It is the Holy Spirit who convicts us of sin and of the need for repentance, and we come to faith *only* through God's grace.

Grace—*n*. . . . the unmerited favour of God.[4]

The Bible described believers in the New Testament as "those who through grace had believed" (Acts 18:27). God is graciously choosing *you* to return to Him. Like the people of Israel, you can be one of God's chosen people. He *wants* to forgive you and restore you to Himself. He loves you! He *wants* to be your Father and to lavish His love and forgiveness upon you. If you have never been part of a family that loves you, or even if you have, until you experience the love of God you have not known *perfect* love. God is a "father to the fatherless, a defender of widows . . . God sets the lonely in families" (Ps. 68:5-6 NIV)—His family.

In the book of Acts, we read of a jailer who asked the apostles: "'Sirs, what must I do to be saved?' And they said, 'Believe in the Lord Jesus, and you will be saved'" (Acts 16:30). To repent of your sins requires faith. Paul said that we must have "repentance toward God and faith toward our Lord Jesus Christ" (Acts 20:21 NKJV). If you believe that the Lord Jesus Christ died to pay the price for your sins, then put your faith in Him—faith that God will accept *His* death as the payment for *your* sins. To come into God's family requires that you:

1. *Recognize* that you are a sinner;
2. *Confess* to God that you are a sinner;
3. *Repent* of your sins to God;
4. *Have faith* in the blood of Jesus which was shed on the cross to pay the price for your sins; and
5. Ask God to *forgive* you.

How do you do this? To ask someone to forgive you of something requires that you *talk* to them. You can talk to God anywhere, at any time; either out loud or in the quietness of your heart. He is everywhere. He is always listening and He knows what is in your heart. You can kneel beside your bed and whisper to Him, climb a mountain and shout to Him, sit in the garden and converse with Him, or talk to Him in the company of some of His family—those who already have faith in the Lord Jesus

Christ. Use the words that come into your heart. God wants you to pour out your heart to Him. Ask God for forgiveness for your sins and tell Him, in your own words, what it is that you believe about His Son and why you believe that He is the only one who can give you life, then ask Him to give you the Spirit of His Son.

Faith opens your heart to God and He will breathe into you His Spirit through His Son. This will cleanse your heart from the guilt of sin and give you a *new* heart. By receiving a new spiritual heart, the old is gone. Along with the old goes all the guilt of your past sins. They are part of your *old* heart and, if you no longer have that old heart, you no longer have the guilt from those sins in your heart. In fact, in God's eyes, they are no longer even associated with your name. They are "blotted out" (Acts 3:19 NKJV). He tells us that: "I, even I, am He who blots out your transgressions for My own sake; and I will not remember your sins" (Isa 43:25 NKJV). It is as if the sins of the past were committed under a totally different name. Your new heart is clean—free from guilt and the stain of sin, and if God does not remember your past sins, why should you? Let them go!

It is in your new heart that the Holy Spirit—the Spirit of life—the Spirit of Christ, will dwell. God will "put his Spirit in our hearts as a deposit, guaranteeing what is to come" (2 Cor. 1:22 NIV).

> **Deposit—/duh-poz-uht/—payment made as a pledge for a contract or as an initial part payment for a thing bought . . . pay (a sum) as part of a larger sum or as a pledge for a contract.[5]**

A deposit of something generally means that what is to come will be more (usually a larger quantity) of the same thing. When you come to faith, God will give you the Holy Spirit in your *heart*. This means that, if you pass from your body with this new Spirit of life in your heart, your soul will be redeemed from death as a result of having this 'deposit' and will return to God with your spirit. This guarantees that, one day, you will receive 'what is to come'—the Holy Spirit throughout your entire soul, redeeming and renewing your body.

Ephesians chapter one describes the Holy Spirit as a *seal*. As your open heart receives the Holy Spirit, which is connected to Christ, it is sealed. Just as the cloud or the pillar of fire was the presence of God that connected the Israelites to the presence of God in heaven, so the Holy Spirit indwelling the believer's heart connects the believer to the life of the Lord Jesus Christ in heaven.

When you have the Spirit of life in you, you are no longer under the curse of the spirit passed down from Adam. The Spirit that now dwells in your heart is the Spirit that has conquered death! Jesus' death was the *only* way that we could receive this new life. Jesus said that "unless a grain of wheat falls to the ground and dies, it remains only a single seed. But if it dies, it produces many seeds" (John 12:24 NIV). He *had* to die in order to give us His spiritual Seed—His life. His death was the only way to make this possible. When we receive His spiritual 'Seed', we are "born of him" (1 John 2:29 NKJV). We are 'in Christ'—part of the kingdom of God.

Jesus assures us that "whoever hears my word and believes him who sent me has eternal life and will not be condemned; he has crossed over from death to life" (John 5:24 NIV). When a person comes to faith in Christ he dies with Christ who took the guilt of our sins upon His heart and suffered the wrath of God for our sins upon His soul. Through faith, Christ's death becomes our death. This means that we are no longer awaiting death and judgement. Through Christ Jesus, we have *already* died and been judged. Christ's death sets us free because He was accepted as a perfect sacrifice in our place. Through His death, we have been found 'not guilty'. When we put our faith in Him, we are indwelt with a Spirit that has *already* passed from death to life.

Adam's spirit brought the consequences of sin with it—death and separation from God. Jesus' Spirit brings life. He overcame the law of sin and death by being resurrected to life by the power of the Holy Spirit. In Jesus Christ, we become spiritually alive, "for since by man came death, by Man also came the resurrection of the dead. For as in Adam all die, even so in Christ all shall be made alive" (1 Cor. 15:22 NKJV). It is at the point of belief in Christ that a person crosses over from death to life—the turning point! "If anyone is in Christ, he is a new creation; old things have passed away; behold, all things have become new" (2 Cor. 5:17 NKJV).

As we died in Christ, we also live in Christ. Because He lives, His Spirit gives *us* life. His life becomes our life. Only Jesus has the power to give life to those who are spiritually dead, for "as the Father has life in himself, so he has granted the Son also to have life in himself" (John 5:26). "The Son gives life to whom he is pleased to give it" (John 5:21 NIV). If we receive the life of Christ—His Spirit, we will be 'in Christ' because His Spirit is not only in Him, but will also be in us. We will share *His* life. His Spirit will be in our heart and in the hearts of all who believe. That makes us family—God's family!

... OR NOT TO BELIEVE

Why would someone choose not to believe? In the face of all the evidence that God's Word is the truth and that Jesus is the only way to the Father—the only way to forgiveness and eternal life, why would anyone choose to remain under condemnation and pay the price for their own sins?

The Bible tells us that those who are perishing do so because "they refused to love the truth and so be saved" (2 Thess. 2:10). "The light has come into the world, and men loved darkness rather than light, because their deeds were evil. For everyone practicing evil hates the light and does not come to the light, lest his deeds should be exposed. But he who does the truth comes to the light, that his deeds may be clearly seen, that they have been done in God" (John 3:19-21 NKJV).

Each person, during his or her lifetime, will need to decide if Jesus *is* who He says He is. He said to the Pharisees, who were the religious leaders of the day: "I said to you that you will die in your sins; for if you do not believe that I am He, you will die in your sins" (John 8:24 NKJV).

Not only do the hearts of men refused to love the truth but they are deceived, for Satan, "the god of this age has blinded the minds of unbelievers, so that they cannot see the light of the gospel of the glory of Christ, who is the image of God" (2 Cor. 4:4 NIV).

There are those who, no matter how many opportunities they have or how much light they are given, choose *not* to repent of their sins and believe, but this is at their own peril, for "how shall we escape if we neglect such a great salvation?" (Heb. 2:3). In the story Jesus told of the rich man and Lazarus, who had both died, Lazarus, the poor beggar, went to Abraham's side—the place of the righteous and the rich man was in hell. The rich man called out to Abraham: "'I beg you therefore, father, that you would send him to my father's house, for I have five brothers, that he may testify to them, lest they also come to this place of torment.' Abraham said to him, 'They have Moses and the prophets; let them hear them.' And he said, 'No, father Abraham; but if one goes to them from the dead, they will repent.' But he said to him, 'If they do not hear Moses and the prophets, neither will they be persuaded though one rise from the dead.'" (Luke 16:27-32 NKJV). Well ... someone did rise from the dead and still people do not believe!

Turning away from your sins and identifying with Christ has a cost. It means changing your ways, your priorities, standing out in the crowd, defending the truth, maybe even being persecuted for what you believe, but the benefits are eternal.

If you have gotten to this stage of the book and are still 'in Adam' rather than 'in Christ', I have not given up on you and neither has God! Just follow this instruction:

'GO BACK AND READ FROM THE BEGINNING OF THE BOOK'

Hopefully this will not leave any readers stuck in a loop for too long! Let's read on...

FAMILY NEWS...

Jesus told the people that, because they were sinners, they were *slaves* to sin, so they were *not* free. He told them that being a slave meant that they had "no permanent place in the family, but a son belongs to it forever. So if the Son sets you free, you will be free indeed" (John 8:35-36). You will have a place in God's family. Belonging to God's family is *only* possible if you have the Spirit of God's Son. If you do *not* have His Spirit, you are *not* a part of God's family. You remain 'in Adam'. When we put our faith in Jesus and receive His Spirit, we receive the "Spirit of adoption by whom we cry out, 'Abba, Father.' The Spirit Himself bears witness with our spirit that we are children of God" (Rom. 8:15-16 NKJV).

Those who put their faith and trust in the Lord Jesus Christ are chosen in Him to be children of God. "He chose us in Him before the foundation of the world, that we should be holy and without blame before Him in love, having predestined us to adoption as sons by Jesus Christ to Himself, according to the good pleasure of His will

. . . In Him we have redemption through His blood, the forgiveness of sins, according to the riches of His grace" (Eph. 1:4-5, 7 NKJV). Before the world was created, God knew that we would need a Saviour, and His plan was that those who would be 'in Christ' would become children of God.

Not only are we God's children, but children of Abraham, because "those who are of faith are sons of Abraham. And the Scripture, foreseeing that God would justify the Gentiles by faith, preached the gospel to Abraham beforehand, saying, 'In you all the nations shall be blessed.' So then those who are of faith are blessed with believing Abraham . . . Christ has redeemed us from the curse of the law, having become a curse for us . . . that the blessing of Abraham might come upon the Gentiles in Christ Jesus, that we might receive the promise of the Spirit through faith" (Gal. 3:7-9, 13-14 NKJV). "The promises were spoken to Abraham and his seed. The Scripture does not say 'and to seeds,' meaning many people, but 'and to your seed,' meaning one person, who is Christ" (Gal. 3:16 NIV). Because this promise was for Christ (Abraham's Seed), and we receive His Spirit, then the promise is for those who are 'in Christ'! This promise is given "by faith in Jesus Christ . . . to those who believe . . . For you are all sons of God through faith in Christ Jesus. For as many of you as were baptized into Christ have put on Christ. There is neither Jew nor Greek, there is neither slave nor free, there is neither male nor female; for you are all one in Christ Jesus. And if you are Christ's, then you are Abraham's seed, and heirs according to the promise" (Gal. 3:22, 26-29 NKJV).

It does not matter what nationality you are, you can be one of God's chosen people, for "God shows no partiality. But in every nation whoever fears Him and works righteousness is accepted by Him" (Acts 10:34-35 NKJV). The apostle John said of Jesus that, "as many as received Him, to them He gave the right to become children of God, to those who believe in His name" (John 1:12 NKJV). A 'right' implies a legal claim. You are now *legally* God's child because you have received the Spirit of Christ. You have *inherited* His Spirit. You have new birth into a new family—God's family. You are a child of God—joint heirs with the Son. You now belong to the kingdom of God!

BEING THE CHOSEN

What are the differences and similarities between being under the Old Covenant and being under the New Covenant? The apostle Paul tells us that:

> Whatever the law says it speaks to those who are under the law, so that every mouth may be stopped, and the whole world may be held accountable to God. For by works of the law no human being will be justified in his sight, since through the law comes knowledge of sin.
>
> But now the righteousness of God has been manifested apart from the law, although the Law and the Prophets bear witness to it—the righteousness of God through faith in Jesus Christ for all who believe. For there is no

distinction: for all have sinned and fall short of the glory of God, and are justified by his grace as a gift, through the redemption that is in Christ Jesus, whom God put forward as a propitiation by his blood, to be received by faith. This was to show God's righteousness, because in his divine forbearance he had passed over former sins.

—Rom. 3:19-25

We can be "justified by faith apart from the deeds of the law . . . since there is one God who will justify the circumcised by faith and the uncircumcised through faith" (Rom. 3:28, 30 NKJV). Both Jews and Gentiles can be put right with God through faith in Christ Jesus. We are the chosen, 'in Him'.

"What does the Scripture say? 'Abraham believed God, and it was credited to him as righteousness'" (Rom. 4:3 NIV). Under the Old Covenant and even before the Old Covenant, people believed in the Lord and He credited it to them as righteousness. In other words, in exchange for their faith, God gave them *His* righteousness. Like us, they had no righteousness of their own. "The words 'it was credited to him' were written not for him alone, but also for us, to whom God will credit righteousness—for us who believe in him who raised Jesus our Lord from the dead" (Rom. 4:23-24 NIV).

Under the New Covenant, the concept of faith and righteousness remains the same, "for in the gospel a righteousness from God is revealed, a righteousness that is by faith from first to last, just as it is written: 'The righteous will live by faith'" (Rom. 1:17 NIV). Righteousness then, comes from God, and is given to us because of our faith in Jesus Christ. Through faith in Jesus we are given *His* righteousness; for "He made Him who knew no sin to be sin for us, that we might become the righteousness of God in Him" (2 Cor. 5:21 NKJV).

One of the reasons Jesus came was to destroy the barrier between Jew and Gentile and to reconcile *both* to God through the cross. Paul says that Gentiles are no longer foreigners but "fellow citizens with the saints and members of the household of God . . . fellow heirs, of the same body, and partakers of His promise in Christ through the gospel" (Eph. 2:19, 3:6 NKJV).

What is the difference between those under the Old and New Covenants at the point of physical death? Those who *remain* under the Law will go to the place of the dead to await judgement. Those under the New Covenant have received the life or Spirit of Jesus into their hearts. This means that they have *already* "passed out of death into life" (1 John 3:14). Because of this, when they leave their bodies they will go immediately to heaven where they will await a bodily resurrection. The Spirit of Jesus will always return to where He is.

THE HELPER

Before Jesus died, He made a promise to the disciples and to all believers. He said:

"I will pray the Father, and He will give you another Helper, that He may abide with you forever—the Spirit of truth, whom the world cannot receive, because it neither sees Him nor knows Him; but you know Him, for He dwells with you and will be in you. I will not leave you orphans; I will come to you . . . A little while longer and the world will see Me no more, but you will see Me. Because I live, you will live also. At that day you will know that I am in My Father, and you in Me, and I in you. He who has My commandments and keeps them, it is he who loves Me. And he who loves Me will be loved by My Father, and I will love him and manifest Myself to him . . . If anyone loves Me, he will keep My word; and My Father will love him, and We will come to him and make Our home with him . . . But the Helper, the Holy Spirit, whom the Father will send in My name, He will teach you all things, and bring to your remembrance all things that I said to you . . . You have heard Me say to you, 'I am going away and coming back to you.'"

—John 14:16-21, 23, 26, 28 NKJV

Jesus promised His disciples that when He returned to His Father He would send them the Holy Spirit—His Spirit, to live in their hearts, and that through His indwelling Spirit He would still be with them.

Under the Old Covenant, God's presence was in the Most Holy place within the temple. When Jesus died, He made a way for the Holy Spirit to dwell within the hearts of men. The Holy Spirit proceeds from the Father through the Son to the hearts of believers. Paul asks believers: "Do you not know that you are the temple of God and that the Spirit of God dwells in you?" (1 Cor. 3:16 NKJV). In fact, "he who is joined to the Lord is one spirit with Him" (1 Cor. 6:17 NKJV). The same Spirit of life that raised Christ from the dead would now dwell in the hearts of believers, guaranteeing them eternal life.

WHAT THE HOLY SPIRIT DOES IN A BELIEVER'S LIFE:

Testifies about Jesus: Jesus said that "when the Helper comes, whom I shall send to you from the Father, the Spirit of truth who proceeds from the Father, He will testify of Me" (John 15:26 NKJV). "No one can say that Jesus is Lord except by the Holy Spirit" (1 Cor. 12:3 NKJV).

Reveals truth and prophecy, counsels and teaches: The Spirit would reveal truth to them, would be Counsellor to them, and would teach them and remind them of what Jesus had taught them. Jesus said that the Holy Spirit will "guide you into all truth; for He will not speak on His own authority, but whatever He hears He will speak; and He will tell you things to come" (John 16:13 NKJV).

Convicts of sin: The Holy Spirit convicts the believer of the need for repentance. When we initially come to faith we receive forgiveness for all our past sins. We will however, still struggle with sin and will need to continually come to God and ask for forgiveness, but Jesus will intercede on our behalf to the Father, and through the Holy Spirit our hearts will then be cleansed from the guilt of sin.

Sanctifies: The Holy Spirit works through the heart of the believer to purify and make holy. The state of our heart affects the state of our spirit which flows throughout our soul. Because of the Holy Spirit in our hearts, our whole being, including our mind will be transformed to be more like Christ and our nature will become more Christ-like. This is called *sanctification*.

>   **Sanctify—/sangk-tuh-fuy/** *v.* **(-ies, -ied) 1 consecrate; treat as holy. 2 free from sin. 3 justify.**[6]

Sanctification is a lifelong process.

Anoints: In the Old Testament, kings and leaders were anointed with authority and wisdom to help them to carry out their role. Jesus, before He ascended into heaven, anointed the disciples with the same authority that He had had on earth and commissioned them with these words: "All authority has been given to Me in heaven and on earth. Go therefore and make disciples of all the nations, baptizing them in the name of the Father and of the Son and of the Holy Spirit, teaching them to observe all things that I have commanded you; and lo, I am with you always, even to the end of the age" (Matt. 28:18-20 NKJV). These words of Jesus are for all believers everywhere.

Empowers: The Holy Spirit gives the believer power. Paul prayed for the Ephesians that, out of the Father's glorious riches, they may "be strengthened with might through His Spirit in the inner man, that Christ may dwell in your hearts through faith" (Eph. 3:16-17 NKJV). He also assured them that the Father is "able to do exceedingly abundantly above all that we ask or think, according to the power that works in us" (Eph. 3:20 NKJV).

When we *initially* come to faith in the Lord, our hearts become *indwelt* with the Holy Spirit. As we walk along the path of faith, we are to be *continually filled* with the Holy Spirit. "God gives the Spirit without limit" (John 3:34 NIV). By having the Holy Spirit in your heart, the Lord is "with your spirit" (2 Tim. 4:22), and the Holy Spirit continually renews and refreshes our spirits as He indwells our hearts, for "even though our outward man is perishing, yet the inward man is being renewed day by day" (2 Cor. 4:16 NKJV).

Paul said that the signs that a person is filled with the Spirit are: "Addressing one another in psalms and hymns and spiritual songs, singing and making melody to the Lord with your heart, giving thanks always and for everything to God the Father in the name of our Lord Jesus Christ, submitting to one another out of reverence for Christ" (Eph. 5:19-20). In other words, Spirit-filled believers will exude great joy and thankfulness because that is what is in their hearts. They will be thankful because the Lord Jesus, through His own death, took away *their* death sentence. They were like prisoners waiting on 'death row' for their sentence to be carried out, and they are now pardoned. They will be full of great joy because they are now part of God's family—

they have eternal life. The person who is filled with the Holy Spirit will also put others before themselves because of their desire to honour and obey the Lord. Paul says that you can be continually filled with the Spirit by letting "the word of Christ dwell in you richly" (Col. 3:16).

YOUR NEW DESTINY—THE HOPE OF HEAVEN

God anointed us and "set his seal of ownership on us, and put his Spirit in our hearts as a deposit, guaranteeing what is to come" (2 Cor. 1:22 NIV)—the promise of the fullness of the Holy Spirit throughout our souls, resurrecting and renewing our bodies. As we are joint heirs with the Son, our inheritance is eternal life and all the riches of the kingdom of heaven and the blessings of the life to come.

If you have the Spirit of the Lord Jesus dwelling in your heart when you die, you will return to where He is because His Spirit will *always* return to Him. Your soul will *not* depart to the abode of the dead. At your last breath, when your spirit and soul leave your body, the Holy Spirit—the Spirit of life which is in your heart and is connected to Christ, will *remain* in your heart and you will return to God in heaven with *His* Spirit. You will pass from your mortal body into the presence of God in heaven. Peter simply describes what will happen as "the putting off of my body" (2 Pet. 1:14).

God has promised a place in heaven for all those who believe and we have "this hope . . . as an anchor of the soul, both sure and steadfast" (Heb. 6:19 NKJV). In fact, those 'in Christ' are *already* part of the kingdom of God, for "our citizenship is in heaven" (Phil. 3:20).

In heaven, we will dwell in a beautiful city called the 'New Jerusalem'. The writer of the letter to the Hebrews tells believers that they have come to "Mount Zion, to the heavenly Jerusalem, the city of the living God . . . to thousands upon thousands of angels in joyful assembly, to the church of the firstborn, whose names are written in heaven . . . to God, the judge of all men, to the spirits of righteous men made perfect, to Jesus the mediator of a new covenant" (Heb. 12:22-24 NIV).

Jesus gave this assurance to the disciples:
> "Do not let your hearts be troubled. Trust in God; trust also in me. In my Father's house are many rooms; if it were not so, I would have told you. I am going there to prepare a place for you. And if I go and prepare a place for you, I will come back and take you to be with me that you also may be where I am. You know the way to the place where I am going . . . I am the way, the truth and the life. No-one comes to the Father except through me."
> —John 14:1-4, 6 NIV

According to Jesus then, the following would happen:
1. *"I am going there"*. After Jesus' death and resurrection, He ascended into heaven to His Father's house where there were already 'many rooms'.

2. *"to prepare a place for you"*. In heaven, Jesus will prepare a place in His Father's house for the rest of the family—believers in Christ.
3. *"I will come back"*. He will come back to live with them by sending His Spirit into their hearts.
4. *"and take you to be with me"*. When they pass from their earthly bodies, Jesus, by His Spirit that indwells their hearts, will take them into heaven to be with Him.
5. *"that you also may be where I am"*. Believers will then dwell in heaven where Jesus is.

The apostle Paul certainly believed that when he departed his earthly body he would *immediately* be with the Lord. He told the Philippian believers that he had "a desire to depart and be with Christ, which is far better. Nevertheless to remain in the flesh is more needful for you" (Phil. 1:23-24 NKJV). He said that "if we have died with Christ, we believe that we will also live with him" (Rom. 6:8).

Let us now have a look at the 'what's what' and the 'who's who' of heaven . . .

Where is heaven? In the Bible, heaven is referred to as being 'to the North'. The book of Job says of God: "He comes from the north as golden splendour; with God is awesome majesty" (Job 37:22 NKJV).

Heaven is the place where God dwells. He has a throne and a sanctuary on which the earthly tabernacle, or temple, which God instructed Moses and later David, through his son Solomon, to build, is a "copy and shadow of the heavenly things" (Heb. 8:5 NKJV). John saw in the temple in heaven "the ark of his covenant" (Rev. 11:19). This is the *heavenly* Ark of the Covenant of which the earthly one is a copy.

Christ is seated at the right hand of God in heaven: "When this priest had offered for all time one sacrifice for sins, he sat down at the right hand of God" (Heb. 1:3 NIV). He is our high priest, the mediator between us and the Father, and serves in "the sanctuary and of the true tabernacle which the Lord erected, and not man" (Heb. 8:2 NKJV).

There are multitudes of angels in heaven praising and worshipping God, reporting to God, receiving instruction from God, and continually going between heaven and earth.

Those who believe, even though they are bodily here on this earth, are already with Christ in heaven. They are joined with Him through His Spirit. The church is His body and He is the head of the body. Jesus said: "Where I am, there will my servant be also" (John 12:26). We are connected 'in Christ' to the heavenly dwelling by the Holy Spirit who indwells our hearts.

There are multitudes of people from many tribes and nations in heaven who have died having faith. Some have died in faith under the Old Covenant or before the Old Covenant was given and have been released from Sheol and led into heaven by the Lord Jesus; some bodily, some their souls only. Others have died under the New Covenant and, on departure from their bodies, they have gone straight to heaven with the Holy Spirit that indwelt their hearts. Of these multitudes, there are countless children and babies who died before they had knowledge of good and evil.

It was on the apostle Peter, whom Jesus referred to as 'the rock', that Jesus said He would build His church. Peter was to begin to build the church from all nations, and Jesus told Peter that "the gates of Hades shall not prevail against it" (Matt. 16:18 NKJV). Anyone who is part of the body of Christ, the true church of believers, will *never* pass through the gates of hades. When they leave the earth they will be immediately welcomed through the gates of heaven. In heaven there is a book called the "Lamb's book of life" (Rev. 21:27). Those whose names are written in this book will inherit eternal life because they have life from the Son. They belong to "the church of the firstborn who are registered in heaven" (Heb. 12:23 NKJV).

Some people in heaven have physical bodies. Jesus has a resurrection body. Many Old Testament saints were bodily raised when Jesus was raised from the dead and therefore have resurrection bodies. These resurrection bodies would be of the same perfection as Adam and Eve's bodies originally were. Elijah and Enoch have physical bodies.

As there are people in heaven with physical bodies then heaven must, at least in part, be a physical place. The New Jerusalem that, at the end of time and the beginning of eternity, comes down out of heaven to the new earth, as seen by John in his vision recorded in the book of Revelation, must be of a physical nature as it will be coming to the new earth which is physical, and will be lived in by people with physical bodies.

Paul, when he spoke of being caught up to the 'third heaven', also referred to as 'paradise', was not sure whether this experience was of the nature of a *bodily* transportation to heaven or whether he was taken *in spirit*. This would suggest that, if he was unsure whether this was physically or spiritually, the experience must have at least *felt* like it was physical, because that is the mode of 'being' that he was most familiar with.

In light of the above, heaven, or at least part of heaven if we were close enough to see it, must be visible to our physical eyes. Heaven must currently exist at a distance in the universe that is not accessible by space travel or visible through the most powerful telescope, because the Bible tells us that "the Almighty is beyond our reach" (Job 37:23 NIV).

Heaven may have once been closer than this in the early stages of the history of mankind. In fact, heaven may well have been *on* the earth at the beginning of Creation. When God banished Adam and Eve from the Garden of Eden after The Fall, He put cherubim with a flaming sword to guard the entrance so that they could not eat from the Tree of Life and live forever. This prevented them from going into the Garden, which may well have been the *same* as preventing them from going into heaven. The entrance to the Garden and the entrance to heaven may have been one and the same. Heaven may then have moved further away from the earth but still remained very close to earth, and then perhaps moved further away still as man's wickedness increased upon the earth.

When men tried to build the Tower of Babel, they tried to build it to 'reach into heaven'. It may have been that they could actually *see* heaven from earth at this stage of history and that it later moved further away from the earth. Just as the earth and planets rotate, there is no reason why heaven cannot move. It will certainly do this at the end of the ages when heaven descends to the new earth and God will dwell amongst men. If this was the original plan, then it would make sense that this was how things were in the beginning—heaven on or near the earth, before sin entered the world.

There is a passage in the book of Job that seems to allude to heaven being at a distance further than the eye can see. It speaks of the origin of wisdom. Wisdom, being from God who dwells in heaven, originates in heaven:

> From where then does wisdom come? And where is the place of understanding? It is hidden from the eyes of all living, and concealed from the birds of the air. Destruction and Death say, "We have heard a report about it with our ears." God understands its way, and He knows its place. For He looks to the ends of the earth, and sees under the whole heavens.
>
> —Job 28:20-24 NKJV

Just because the current location of heaven is likely to be a great distance away, that does not mean that God does not involve Himself with what happens here on earth. "He observes the sons of men; his eyes examine them" (Ps. 11:4 NIV), He "looks down from heaven on the children of man" (Ps. 14:2), and "it is He who sits above the circle of the earth, and its inhabitants are like grasshoppers, who stretches out the heavens like a curtain, and spreads them out like a tent to dwell in" (Isa. 40:22 NKJV). His Spirit is active on the earth, His Spirit indwells the hearts of believers, and there are angels all around who have direct access to heaven. We are never out of God's sight for a moment!

Heaven, whilst perhaps not functioning under the same laws of time as earth, appears to have time of some sort. For example, in Revelation, John observed that on the opening of the seventh seal, "there was silence in heaven for about half an hour" (Rev. 8:1).

Heaven is a beautiful place and God gives us just a glimpse of it in the Scriptures. King David, for example, tells us that there is a river in heaven "whose streams shall make glad the city of God, the holy place of the tabernacle of the Most High" (Ps. 46:4 NKJV). Heaven will be full of light because God is "resplendent with light" (Ps. 76:4 NIV). There are rainbows. There is peace, love, and joy. There is singing, worship, and beautiful music. There is food. There are celebrations and joyous reunions.

The splendour of heaven is beyond our imaginings, for "eye has not seen, nor ear heard, nor have entered into the heart of man the things which God has prepared for those who love Him" (1 Cor. 2:9 NKJV).

Chapter Thirteen
The Path

What is our purpose? Paul writes that "for us there is but one God, the Father, from whom all things came and for whom we live; and there is but one Lord, Jesus Christ, through whom all things came and through whom we live" (1 Cor. 8:6 NIV). We live *for* God the Father *through* our Lord Jesus Christ. Our purpose in life is to bring glory and honour to the One who created us and who redeemed us by His blood. Paul said: "I have been crucified with Christ and I no longer live, but Christ lives in me. The life I live in the body, I live by faith in the Son of God, who loved me and gave himself for me" (Gal. 2:20-21 NIV). We have been bought with a price, therefore, "those who live should live no longer for themselves, but for Him who died for them and rose again" (2 Cor. 5:15 NKJV).

STONE BUILDINGS

Jesus is referred to in Scripture as a 'capstone' and a 'cornerstone'. Picture two buildings. One is the building of those under the Old Covenant on which Jesus is the *capstone* that completes the building because, through Jesus, all the requirements of the Law were fulfilled. Jesus ushered in the commencement of a *new* building under a New Covenant. Jesus is the *cornerstone* of this new building, upon which the remainder of the building is fashioned. We are like "living stones . . . being built up a spiritual house" (1 Pet. 2:5 NKJV), "Christ Jesus himself being the cornerstone, in whom the whole structure, being joined together, grows into a holy temple in the Lord. In him you also are being built together into a dwelling place for God by the Spirit" (Eph. 2:19-22). If you are 'in Christ', you are part of this building—a unique 'living stone'.

Let's look at the differences in the architecture of these two distinct buildings that have this one stone in common. Through Moses, God gave the Law—the Old Covenant. Through Jesus Christ, He gave the New Covenant, which is superior to the Old Covenant as it is "founded on better promises . . . By calling this covenant 'new', he has made the first one obsolete" (Heb. 8:6, 13 NIV). Jesus "cancelled the written code, with its regulations, that was against us and that stood opposed to us; he took it away, nailing it to the cross" (Col. 2:14 NIV). Jesus *fulfilled* the requirements of the Law on *our* behalf.

Under the Old Covenant, "the gifts and sacrifices being offered were not able to clear the conscience of the worshipper. They are only a matter of food and drink and various ceremonial washings—external regulations applying until the time of the new order" (Heb. 9:9-10 NIV), for "it is impossible for the blood of bulls and goats to take away sins" (Heb. 10:3), but the blood of Christ, through the *New* Covenant, is able to "cleanse our consciences from acts that lead to death, so that we may serve the living

God" (Heb. 9:14 NIV). "A man is not justified by the works of the law but by faith in Jesus Christ" (Gal. 2:16 NKJV).

FREEDOM

Those who are 'in Christ' are not bound by hundreds of rules and regulations. Paul referred in particular to the observing of certain days and the eating of meat for those now under the New Covenant. He said that "one man considers one day more sacred than another; another man considers every day alike. Each one should be fully convinced in his own mind. He who regards one day as special, does so to the Lord. He who eats meat, does so to the Lord, for he gives thanks to God; and he who abstains, does so to the Lord and gives thanks to God" (Rom. 14:5-6 NIV). We are not to judge others by *our* conscience with regard to matters such as these. Paul said: "Do not let anyone judge you by what you eat or drink, or with regard to a religious festival, a New Moon celebration or a Sabbath day. They are a shadow of the things that were to come; the reality, however, is found in Christ" (Col. 2:16-17 NIV).

"If you are led by the Spirit, you are not under the law" (Gal. 5:18). In other words, if you allow the Spirit to lead you, you will not *need* to follow the Law. Being led by the indwelling Holy Spirit makes the Law obsolete. This does not mean 'anything goes' though! The New Covenant gives freedom with responsibility. Under the New Covenant, Paul says that "'everything is permissible for me'—but not everything is beneficial. 'Everything is permissible for me'—but I will not be mastered by anything . . . 'Everything is permissible'—but not everything is constructive" (1 Cor. 6:12, 10:23 NIV). In other words:
1. Avoid that which is not beneficial, pursue that which is of benefit;
2. Avoid that which has the potential to master you, exercise self-control; and
3. Avoid that which may be destructive, pursue that which is *con*structive.

These guidelines are for your own good, not God's. They are wise guidelines to use when making a judgement on whether to do something or not. Peter advises believers to "abstain from sinful desires, which wage war against your soul" (1 Pet. 2:11 NIV).

The Holy Spirit works through the *heart* of the believer. The conscience is one of the functions of the heart. Therefore, the Holy Spirit will speak to the believer through their conscience. If your conscience tells you not to do something, don't do it. Paul cautions believers to "be careful . . . that the exercise of your freedom does not become a stumbling block to the weak" (1 Cor. 8:9 NIV), for "nobody should seek his own good, but the good of others" (1 Cor. 10:24 NIV).

LOVE AND OBEDIENCE

If you have faith, you will love God. If you love God, you will obey Him, for "this is love for God: to obey his commands" (1 John 5:3 NIV). Paul said that "obedience . . . comes from faith" (Rom. 1:5 NIV). John writes that the evidence that we have truly come to know Jesus is "if we obey his commands. The man who says, 'I know him,' but does not do what he commands is a liar, and the truth is not in him. But if anyone obeys his word, God's love is truly made complete in him. This is how we know we are in him: Whoever claims to live in him must walk as Jesus did" (1 John 2:3-6 NIV).

If we love God, we will also love others. "This is His commandment: that we should believe on the name of His Son Jesus Christ and love one another" (1 John 3:23 NKJV). Paul goes as far as to say that we are to "let no debt remain outstanding, except the continuing debt to love one another, for he who loves his fellow-man has fulfilled the law. The commandments . . . are summed up in this one rule: 'Love your neighbour as yourself'. Love does no harm to its neighbour. Therefore love is the fulfilment of the law" (Rom. 13:8-10 NIV). He says that "the only thing that counts is faith expressing itself through love" (Gal. 5:6 NIV).

How, in God's eyes, is love for your neighbour demonstrated? James writes that "religion that God our Father accepts as pure and faultless is this: to look after orphans and widows in distress" (James 1:27 NIV). In New Testament times, orphans and widows depended on others for charity. Today 'orphans and widows' would encompass the poor, the destitute, the needy, and the lonely, not only locally, but globally. At the heart of caring for those less fortunate lies the sacrifice of doing something for those who are unable to give anything in return. This is a true demonstration of 'love for your neighbour'.

How do we live a life of love? By being "imitators of God" (Eph. 5:1). Jesus is the exact representation of the Father. Follow His example.

Salvation is through faith alone and by the grace of God. Nothing can be added to this. God exchanges *our* faith for *His* righteousness. However, the *evidence* that someone has faith will be shown by his deeds—his obedience in doing the will of God. The people were to "repent and turn to God and prove their repentance by their deeds" (Acts 26:20 NIV). That is why James said that "faith by itself, if it is not accompanied by action, is dead" (James 2:17 NIV).

SIN AND HOLINESS

Even though we have repented of sin and God has given us a new heart cleansed from the guilt of sin and a new spirit—His Spirit, to dwell in our hearts, we will still sin. In this, Paul's frustration is evident. He asks: "We died to sin; how can we live in it any longer?" (Rom. 6:2 NIV). We don't *want* to sin, but we do. This is because, even though we have the Holy Spirit indwelling our hearts, we still have our original fallen spirit inherited from Adam in us as well, and therefore a sinful nature. This creates conflict within. We know what we *should* be doing and yet we are still drawn to sin.

When we initially come to faith we are born again. Our old life is past, our sins are forgiven. We are a 'new creation'. But, Paul warns believers not to slip back into their old lifestyle of wickedness. He says that "we are the temple of the living God" (2 Cor. 6:16) and asks: "Do you not know that your bodies are members of Christ himself? Shall I then take the members of Christ and unite them with a prostitute? Never! . . . Do you not know that your body is a temple of the Holy Spirit, who is in you, whom you have received from God? You are not your own; you were bought at a price. Therefore honour God with your body" (1 Cor. 6:19 NIV). Paul is likening those who have originally come to faith but are later unfaithful to God and subsequently 'backslide' resulting in unclean hearts, to prostitutes. He is saying that it would be unthinkable to unite, through the sharing in the Spirit that indwells all believers, those with faith and clean hearts with those who are no longer faithful and have unclean hearts. Paul is warning them of the danger of continuing in that lifestyle of wickedness; that danger being the possibility of no longer remaining part of the body of Christ.

The book of Jude warns the believer that the grace of God is not a "licence for immorality" (Jude 1:4 NIV) and on that topic Paul writes to the church in Corinth: "You, my brothers, were called to be free. But do not use your freedom to indulge in the sinful nature" (Gal. 5:13 NIV).

The apostle Paul wrestled with the problem of the conflict between the sinful nature and the Spirit. He said:

> For I know that nothing good dwells in me, that is, in my flesh. For I have the desire to do what is right, but not the ability to carry it out. For I do not do the good I want, but the evil I do not want is what I keep on doing. Now if I do what I do not want, it is no longer I who do it, but sin that dwells within me.
>
> So I find it to be a law that when I want to do right, evil lies close at hand. For I delight in the law of God, in my inner being, but I see in my members another law waging war against the law of my mind and making me captive to the law of sin that dwells in my members. Wretched man that I am! Who will deliver me from this body of death? Thanks be to God through Jesus Christ our Lord! So then, I myself serve the law of God with my mind, but with my flesh I serve the law of sin.
>
> —Rom. 7:18-25

Paul's advice with regard to this constant struggle is to:

> Walk in the Spirit, and you shall not fulfil the lust of the flesh. For the flesh lusts against the Spirit, and the Spirit against the flesh; and these are contrary to one another, so that you do not do the things that you wish . . . Now the works of the flesh are evident, which are: adultery, fornication, uncleanness, lewdness, idolatry, sorcery, hatred, contentions, jealousies, outbursts of wrath, selfish ambitions, dissensions, heresies, envy, murders, drunkenness, revelries, and the like; of which I tell you beforehand, just as I also told you in time past, that those who practise such things will not inherit the kingdom of God. But the fruit of the Spirit is love, joy, peace, longsuffering,

kindness, goodness, faithfulness, gentleness, self-control. Against such there is no law. And those who are Christ's have crucified the flesh with its passions and desires.

—Gal. 5:16-17, 19-24 NKJV

Having the Holy Spirit in our hearts, means that we are connected to the mind of Christ. This means that we "have become partakers of the divine nature" (2 Pet. 1:4). *This* is the nature that should rule us—the nature that displays those fruits of the Spirit that Paul talks about; not the *sinful* nature.

Paul makes it clear that the wicked will *not* inherit the kingdom of God. He says: "Do not be deceived: Neither the sexually immoral nor idolaters nor adulterers nor male prostitutes nor homosexual offenders nor thieves nor the greedy nor drunkards nor slanderers nor swindlers will inherit the kingdom of God" (1 Cor. 6:9-10 NIV). This does not mean that there is no one in God's kingdom who has *not* been one of these though, and Paul goes on to explain to the Corinthians: "And that is what some of you were. But you were washed, you were sanctified, you were justified in the name of the Lord Jesus Christ and by the Spirit of our God" (1 Cor. 6:11 NIV). That 'lifestyle' belonged to their *past* and that is where they were to leave it. They were *not* to take it up again, for it was not compatible with the Spirit of God in their hearts.

Paul cautions: "Be very careful, then, how you live—not as unwise but as wise, making the most of every opportunity, because the days are evil" (Eph. 5:15-16 NIV). Set others "an example by doing what is good . . . for the grace of God that brings salvation has appeared to all men. It teaches us to say 'No' to ungodliness and worldly passions, and to live self-controlled, upright and godly lives" (Titus 2:7, 11-12 NIV). Paul says to "conduct yourselves in a manner worthy of the gospel of Christ" (Phil. 1:27 NIV). We are to live in a way which honours Christ.

While we are to set an example to others, we are not to judge unbelievers by what *they* do—their lifestyle, their language, their relationships, their choices, and their indulgences. We cannot expect *them* to live godly lives without the help of the indwelling Holy Spirit. Paul asks: "What business is it of mine to judge those outside the church? . . . God will judge those outside" (1 Cor. 5:12-13 NIV).

We are to set ourselves apart from the world and its desires. James tells believers that friendship with the world is hatred towards God and likens this to being adulterous, saying that "the spirit he caused to live in us envies intensely" (James 4:5 NIV). This does not mean that we are not to associate with unbelievers however, only the 'things of this world'. John describes the things of the world that we are to avoid as being "the cravings of sinful man, the lust of his eyes and the boasting of what he has and does" (1 John 2:16 NIV). These things do not originate from the Spirit but come from the sinful nature. In Galatians chapter six, Paul says that we can sow either to please the sinful nature or to please the Spirit. The former reaps destruction and the latter reaps eternal life.

Even though the Holy Spirit dwells in the believer's *heart*, the change that comes about in their heart sanctifies their spirit and therefore their soul and mind. This is not something that happens instantly upon coming to faith. Sanctification is a lifelong process.

When you become a believer, Paul says that you are to "put off your old self, which is being corrupted by its deceitful desires; to be made new in the attitude of your minds; and to put on the new self, created to be like God in true righteousness and holiness" (Eph. 4:22-24 NIV). You are also to take "captive every thought to make it obedient to Christ" (2 Cor. 10:5 NIV). Paul writes: "Do not conform any longer to the pattern of this world, but be transformed by the renewing of your mind. Then you will be able to test and approve what God's will is—his good, pleasing and perfect will" (Rom. 12:2 NIV).

According to Paul, what you set your mind on determines whether you live according to the sinful nature or the Spirit. He writes:

> For those who live according to the flesh set their minds on the things of the flesh, but those who live according to the Spirit, the things of the Spirit. For to be carnally minded is death, but to be spiritually minded is life and peace. Because the carnal mind is enmity against God; for it is not subject to the law of God, nor indeed can be. So then, those who are in the flesh cannot please God. But you are not in the flesh but in the Spirit, if indeed the Spirit of God dwells in you. Now if anyone does not have the Spirit of Christ, he is not His. And if Christ is in you, the body is dead because of sin, but the Spirit is life because of righteousness . . . For if you live according to the flesh you will die; but if by the Spirit you put to death the deeds of the body, you will live. For as many as are led by the Spirit of God, these are sons of God.
>
> —Rom. 8:5-10, 13-14 NKJV

Paul prayed for the Philippian believers that "the peace of God, which transcends all understanding, will guard your hearts and your minds in Christ Jesus . . . whatever is true, whatever is noble, whatever is right, whatever is pure, whatever is lovely, whatever is admirable—if anything is excellent or praiseworthy—think about such things" (Phil. 4:7-8 NIV).

In his letter to the believers in Ephesus, Paul spoke of the problem of sin in their lives and encouraged them to live holy lives so that they would not "give the devil a foothold" (Eph. 4:27 NIV). It was essential that the believers did not become complacent and slip back into their old sinful habits. This of course is exactly what Satan, or 'the devil', would be hoping for.

Were the believers on their own in resisting sin and the devil's schemes? No! They had the Holy Spirit to help them. Paul encourages them to:

> Be strong in the Lord and in the strength of his might. Put on the whole armour of God, that you may be able to stand against the schemes of the

devil. For we do not wrestle against flesh and blood, but against the rulers, against the authorities, against the cosmic powers over this present darkness, against the spiritual forces of evil in the heavenly places. Therefore take up the whole armour of God, that you may be able to withstand in the evil day, and having done all, to stand firm.

—Eph. 6:10-13

Paul also exhorts them to "take up the shield of faith, with which you can extinguish all the flaming arrows of the evil one" (Eph. 6:16 NIV), and James' advice to believers is: "Submit yourselves, then, to God. Resist the devil, and he will flee from you" (James 4:7 NIV). Faith and submission to God will help the believer to resist Satan.

Believers are very vulnerable to temptation. In fact, they are highest on Satan's hit list. His aim is to tempt the believer into sinning in order to bring shame to them and discredit them in the eyes of others in the hope that this will cause them to give up on their faith and that it will also discredit *God* in the eyes of unbelievers and keep *them* from coming to faith. He often uses temptation to try to lure believers off the path of salvation. The most common areas of temptation that Satan will use are:

— *Money and possessions*—wanting more than you have;
— *Pleasures and indulgences*—doing things that you hope will make you feel good;
— *Making a name for yourself*—the desire for recognition from other people; and
— *Power*—within the home, the workplace, the community, and the church.

Not only do these temptations place 'you' at the centre of your life instead of God, but behind all of these areas of temptation lies the same underlying cause—envy—dissatisfaction with what you have; wanting what you do not have; wanting what other people have. Satan knows that temptation in these areas works. It certainly worked in the Garden of Eden! In *God's* kingdom however, "godliness with contentment is great gain" (1 Tim. 6:6 NIV). The gain of these positions and possessions will ultimately prove unsatisfactory. The antidote to envy is to be content with what you have and to live an upright and godly life with God at the centre. Treasures in heaven far outweigh and outlast treasures on earth!

Believers have the assurance that "the Lord is faithful, and he will strengthen and protect you from the evil one" (2 Thess. 3:3 NIV). The apostle Peter tells believers that their "enemy the devil prowls around like a roaring lion looking for someone to devour. Resist him, standing firm in the faith, because you know that your brothers throughout the world are undergoing the same kind of sufferings" (1 Pet. 5:8-9 NIV). Paul says that "if you think you are standing firm, be careful that you don't fall! No temptation has seized you except what is common to man. And God is faithful; he will not let you be tempted beyond what you can bear. But when you are tempted, he will also provide a way out so that you can stand up under it" (1 Cor. 10:12-13 NIV). You

are not alone, for Jesus Himself "suffered when he was tempted . . . he is able to help those who are being tempted" (Heb. 2:18 NIV). When you are tempted to sin:
1. There will *always* be a way out;
2. You *can* resist the devil; and
3. Jesus *is* able to help you.

The guilt of sin is foreign to the temple of the Holy Spirit—the heart of the believer. Paul gives this advice about sin: "Do not let sin reign in your mortal body so that you obey its evil desires. Do not offer parts of your body to sin, as instruments of wickedness, but rather offer yourselves to God, as those who have been brought from death to life; and offer the parts of your body to him as instruments of righteousness . . . Now that you have been set free from sin and have become slaves to God, the benefit you reap leads to holiness, and the result is eternal life" (Rom. 6:12-13, 22 NIV).

How do you live a life that pleases God?
1. *Read the Scriptures* to find out what God requires of you;
2. *Follow the example of Jesus*;
3. *Listen to your heart*, for therein dwells the Holy Spirit. Paul says that "the requirements of the law are written" (Rom. 2:15 NIV) on our hearts; and
4. *Listen to your conscience.* Your thoughts are either telling you *not* to do something or that it is *okay* to do something. According to Hebrews chapter five, maturity in the faith through knowledge of the Lord leads to a greater ability to distinguish between good and evil.

God chose us to be saved through "the sanctifying work of the Spirit and through belief in the truth" (2 Thess. 2:13 NIV). In other words, we are saved by:
1. Faith in the Lord Jesus Christ for the forgiveness of sins; and
2. The washing clean of our hearts by the Holy Spirit, allowing the Holy Spirit to indwell our hearts—a deposit which guarantees eternal life.

We have been "sanctified in Christ Jesus and called to be holy" (1 Cor. 1:2 NIV). "It is God's will that you should be sanctified . . . for God did not call us to be impure, but to live a holy life . . . He who rejects this instruction does not reject man but God, who gives you his Holy Spirit" (1 Thess. 4:3, 7-8 NIV). In other words, the rejection of this instruction to live a holy life equates to the rejection of God, which will consequently result in the rejection of God's gift of the Holy Spirit. "We must purify ourselves from everything that contaminates body and spirit, perfecting holiness out of reverence for God" (2 Cor. 7:1 NIV). Living a holy life honours God. God calls His people to be holy, for "without holiness no-one will see the Lord" (Heb. 12:14 NIV).

IDENTIFYING WITH CHRIST

Under the Old Covenant, the Israelites were required to keep many annual feasts of remembrance such as the Passover, which reminded them of the night that the angel of death passed over the camp of the Israelites, killing only the first born sons of the Egyptians. There were also other observances associated with food, clothing, and so on. The keeping of these feasts and other observances was not a pre-requisite for receiving the righteousness of God; faith was, and this faith was only by the grace of God. The people kept these feasts out of love and obedience to God to remind themselves and the generations to come of His love and mercy towards them. The feasts and ceremonies were a physical representation of something that was spiritual in meaning.

Under the New Covenant, there are two observances which the Lord Jesus asks believers to partake of. One of these is baptism and the other is The Lord's Table. These are to be observed *out of obedience* to Christ and *to identify with* Christ.

BAPTISM—The moment a person comes to faith in Christ and repents of their sins, they are identifying with the Son in His death and resurrection and they will receive the Holy Spirit. This is the *spiritual* baptism in the name of the Father, and of the Son, and of the Holy Spirit. It is this *spiritual* baptism that saves.

Physical baptism by immersion in water represents what has happened to you *spiritually*. It is to be done *once only* by the believer, as a public witness that you are identifying yourself with the Lord Jesus Christ. It is a sign of your faith. A person must believe *before* being baptised. The act of physical baptism is in obedience to Jesus' command *because* a person believes. The account of baptism in the book of Acts records that the people "believed and were baptised" (Acts 18:8). They believed *first*. It was not the act of physical baptism that *caused* them to believe.

1. We believe and are credited with the righteousness of Christ and receive the Holy Spirit when we are still *unbaptised physically*; then
2. We are to undergo physical baptism as a *sign* of our faith.

It is God's will that those who believe undergo the physical act of baptism as a sign of their faith. Being baptised is an act of obedience to Christ who commanded His disciples to "go and make disciples of all nations, baptising them in the name of the Father and of the Son and of the Holy Spirit, and teaching them to obey everything I have commanded you" (Matt. 28:19 NIV).

Although spiritual and therefore physical baptism in the name of the Father, Son, and Holy Spirit is a single act, we will now examine what this means by breaking it down into the three parts of this act, focussing on the *spiritual* side of baptism which physical baptism represents.

Being baptised in the name of the Father is the **"baptism of repentance"** (Acts 19:4) from sins. It is the "pledge of a good conscience towards God" (1 Pet. 3:21 NIV). This is the baptism that John was doing—preparing the hearts of the people for the message of Jesus. The cleansing of the heart from sin is necessary in order that the Holy Spirit may dwell within the person's heart.

Being baptised into the name of the Son is the **identifying with Jesus in His death, and putting your faith in Him and in what He has done for you**. Jesus' soul underwent a baptism of suffering unto death on our behalf and we are identifying with this as, through faith, His death becomes our death, His soul the substitute for our soul. Paul says:

> Do you not know that all of us who have been baptized into Christ Jesus were baptized into his death? We were buried therefore with him by baptism into death, in order that, just as Christ was raised from the dead by the glory of the Father, we too might walk in newness of life.
>
> For if we have been united with him in a death like his, we shall certainly be united with him in a resurrection like his. We know that our old self was crucified with him in order that the body of sin might be brought to nothing, so that we would no longer be enslaved to sin. For one who has died has been set free from sin.
>
> —Rom. 6:2-7

When you are baptised into Christ you are acknowledging that your old life has gone. It has been buried. It is in the past along with your past sins and you are now identifying with *His* name. We have been given "fullness in Christ . . . in him you were also circumcised, in the putting off of the sinful nature, not with a circumcision done by the hands of men but with the circumcision done by Christ, having been buried with him" (Col. 2:10-11 NIV).

Being baptised in the Holy Spirit is to have your heart **filled with the Holy Spirit**—Spirit that gives life and connects the believer to God. It is identifying with the resurrection of Jesus by the power of the Holy Spirit. You are "raised with him through your faith in the power of God, who raised him from the dead. When you were dead in your sins and in the uncircumcision of your sinful nature, God made you alive with Christ" (Col. 2:12-13 NIV). "It saves you by the resurrection of Jesus Christ, who has gone into heaven and is at God's right hand" (1 Pet. 3:22 NIV). It is the taking on of newness of life—the life of Jesus.

The Holy Spirit indwells the hearts of those who repent and believe, for God "saved us through the washing of rebirth and renewal by the Holy Spirit, whom he poured out on us generously through Jesus Christ our Saviour, so that, having been justified through his grace, we might become heirs having the hope of eternal life" (Titus 3:5-7 NIV).

In New Testament times, it was the normal practice that physical baptism in water occurred immediately after the person came to faith. The person baptising them would take them down to the nearest body of water. The physical baptism, in accurately representing the spiritual baptism, is a single event, going down under the water and coming forth into new life. The taking of a breath and then going under the water is symbolic of taking the 'spirit of Adam' into Christ's death and burial. When you come up out of the water, your first breath is symbolic of the newness of life that the Holy Spirit gives. Because physical baptism is a visible sign, it shows others that the believer is willing to be identified with Christ and they are not ashamed of His name. It is a witness to fellow believers and also to unbelievers.

THE LORD'S TABLE—The second observance the Lord requires the believer to partake of is The Lord's Table or The Lord's Supper.

The first time that this was observed was on the night before Jesus died. He gathered His disciples together and broke bread and shared wine with them. This was to be something that they and all believers were to continue to do when they met together as a remembrance of the Lord's death until He comes again. The bread represents Christ's body that was broken for them for the forgiveness of sins. The cup represents Christ's blood that was poured out for them.

In churches today all over the world, this remembrance of Christ's death is shared amongst believers with reverence and solemnity.

SEEKING

How do you develop a closer relationship with your heavenly Father? "Come near to God and he will come near to you" (James 4:8 NIV). We come near to God through faith, for "without faith it is impossible to please God, because anyone who comes to him must believe that he exists and that he rewards those who earnestly seek him" (Heb. 11:6 NIV). Paul asked God to give the Ephesian believers "the Spirit of wisdom and revelation, so that you may know him better" (Eph. 1:17 NIV), for "the Spirit searches all things, even the deep things of God" (1 Cor. 2:10 NIV), therefore the Spirit helps us to understand "what God has freely given us" (1 Cor. 2:12 NIV).

What does it mean to earnestly seek God? There was a group of people called the Bereans who "received the message with great eagerness and examined the Scriptures every day to see if what Paul said was true" (Acts 17:11 NIV). Paul advises us to "test everything; hold fast to what is good" (1 Thess. 5:21).

"Faith comes by hearing, and hearing by the Word of God" (Rom. 10:17 NKJV), and it is the "knowledge of the truth that leads to godliness" (Titus 1:1 NIV). But James warns: "Do not merely listen to the word, and so deceive yourselves. Do what it says. Anyone who listens to the word but does not do what it says is like a man who looks at his face in a mirror and, after looking at himself, goes away and immediately forgets what he looks like. But the man who looks intently into the perfect law that gives freedom, and continues to do this, not forgetting what he has heard but doing it—he will be blessed in what he does" (James 1:22-25 NIV).

Devote time to studying the Scriptures "which are able to make you wise for salvation through faith which is in Christ Jesus. All Scripture is given by inspiration of God, and is profitable for doctrine, for reproof, for correction, for instruction in righteousness, that the man of God may be complete, thoroughly equipped for every good work" (2 Tim. 3:15-17 NIV).

Do not be swayed or misled by those teaching things that are *not* from God's Word. Examine carefully what you hear and read, using the Scriptures as your authority and guide to discerning truth. Paul warned the Colossians: "See to it that no-one takes you captive through hollow and deceptive philosophy, which depends on human tradition and the basic principles of this world rather than on Christ" (Col. 2:8 NIV). If you possess a thorough knowledge of the Scriptures, you are less likely to be misled by those who distort the truth. Paul warned that "the time will come when men will not put up with sound doctrine. Instead, to suit their own desires, they will gather around them a great number of teachers to say what their itching ears want to hear. They will turn their ears away from the truth and turn aside to myths" (2 Tim. 4:3-4 NIV).

God would have all believers:
1. Eagerly receive His Word;
2. Examine the Scriptures;
3. Test everything;
4. Hold fast to the truth;
5. Know what they believe; and
6. Do what God's Word says.

According to the writer of the letter to the Hebrews, the elementary or foundational teachings about Christ are: "Repentance from acts that lead to death, and of faith in God, instruction about baptisms, the laying on of hands, the resurrection of the dead, and eternal judgement" (Heb. 6:1-2 NIV). We are to know the 'elementary' teachings well and then build on this foundation.

THE WRITTEN WORD

The Bible is a collection of sixty-six books by about forty authors who were inspired and directed by the Holy Spirit to write down the Word of God. The Old Testament contains books of history, law, prophecy, psalms, poetry, philosophy, and proverbs. It was written over a period of approximately 1500 years. The New Testament begins with the four gospels which give an account of the life of Jesus, followed by the book of Acts which is a history of the early church. This is followed by letters to individual believers and churches on holy living, explaining the life and teachings of Jesus, and the truth of the kingdom of God. Finally, the New Testament ends with the book of Revelation, which contains letters to seven churches and a prophetic vision of end times.

The Old Testament was originally written in Hebrew and the New Testament in Greek. Since then, the Scriptures have been translated into many languages. There are also different Bible versions. For example, some are 'thought for thought translations, such as the *New International Version* (NIV). Some are literal or 'word for word' translations, such as the original *King James Version* (KJV) which reads in 'old-style' English, the *New King James Version* (NKJV) which is similar but in 'modern' English, and the *English Standard Version* (ESV). Some are interlinear, such as *The Interlinear Bible—Hebrew Greek English* by Jay P. Green Snr., where the English translation is written below the Hebrew or Greek.

Where is the best place to start reading the Bible? Generally, books are read from front to back. The Bible however, being a collection of many books of various genre, is a little different. It is helpful to have a study guide to accompany your Bible reading that will walk you through the reading of Scripture in a logical sequence, perhaps starting with the story of The Creation, The Fall, and The Flood in the first few chapters of Genesis, then a little bit of the history of the Israelites, perhaps a selection of prophecies about the coming of the Messiah, particularly from the book of Isaiah, followed by the gospels telling about the life of Jesus. Interspersed with these, you might like to read a few Psalms and Proverbs. Read a little of the history of the early church in the book of Acts, followed by some of the teachings of Paul and the other writers of the letters of the New Testament. One day, you might even like to 'tackle' the book of Revelation!

There are plenty of good books available through Christian book stores that are written as an aid to understanding God's Word, and a pastor or mature believer should be able to point you in the direction of some of these, or even lend them to you. It is a good idea to have a daily devotional book also, and you can even get these mailed to your address every month or two via a subscription. Alternatively, you can have an online daily devotion sent straight to your inbox!

Think about joining a Bible study or home group through your local church. This will give you the perspective of fellow believers on God's Word. There are even groups that are set up specifically to cater for new believers.

Above all, ask God for guidance and understanding. It is the Holy Spirit who teaches us the things of God and helps us to understand His Word.

PRAISING

We serve a great and glorious God who is worthy of our praise. He has done great things for us by redeeming us through the sacrifice of the life of His Son and setting us free from the power of death.

You can praise God through songs, prayer, and acts of service. God can be glorified through music, art, banners, and creative avenues such as writing and poetry. Allow God to use you for His glory. Paul writes: "Offer your bodies as living sacrifices, holy and pleasing to God—this is your spiritual act of worship" (Rom. 12:1 NIV).

Read the book of Psalms. King David knew how to give praise to the Lord! "Speak to one another with psalms, hymns and spiritual songs. Sing and make music in your heart to the Lord, always giving thanks to God the Father for everything, in the name of our Lord Jesus Christ" (Eph. 5:19-20 NIV).

Tune in to a Christian radio station for uplifting music, inspirational and encouraging teaching, and a sense of community. Look in the local Christian bookstore or an online Christian bookstore for music that you can listen to in the car or at home. Bursting into songs of praise lifts the spirit, gladdens the heart, and brings God glory.

PRAYING

Prayer is simply talking to God. We can talk to Him anywhere, any time. Prayers can be short or long, plain or fancy, out loud or in the quietness of your heart, on any topic, for any reason. Prayer can also be in conjunction with fasting.

Pray with a fellow believer. Jesus said that "if two of you on earth agree about anything you ask for, it will be done for you by my Father in heaven. For where two or three come together in my name, there am I with them" (Matt. 18:19-20 NIV).

Paul writes: "Do not be anxious about anything, but in everything, by prayer and petition, with thanksgiving, present your requests to God" (Phil. 4:6 NIV). Peter tells us that to pray effectively, we must be "clear minded and self-controlled" (1 Pet. 4:7 NIV) and James assures us that "the prayer of a righteous person has great power as it is working" (James 5:16).

"Pray in the Spirit on all occasions with all kinds of prayers and requests" (Eph. 6:18 NIV). Paul says that "we do not know what we ought to pray for but the Spirit himself intercedes for us with groans that words cannot express. And he who searches our hearts knows the mind of the Spirit, because the Spirit intercedes for the saints in accordance with God's will" (Rom. 8:26-27 NIV). Furthermore, "Christ Jesus . . . is at the right hand of God and is also interceding for us" (Rom. 8:34 NIV). Through Jesus, we have direct access to God, for "in him and through faith in him we may approach God with freedom and confidence" (Eph. 3:12 NIV). The writer of the letter to the Hebrews assures us that "we have confidence to enter the Most Holy Place by the blood of Jesus, by a new and living way opened for us through the curtain, that is, his body" (Heb. 10:19 NIV). The Holy Spirit in our hearts flows through the body of Christ (the open curtain) to the very heart of the Father!

Through prayer we can:
— *Praise and thank God* for what He has done, what He is doing, and who He is. Paul tells us to "be joyful always; pray continually; give thanks in all circumstances" (1 Thess. 5:16 NIV). He also tells us that it is the Holy Spirit who gives joy.
— *Intercede on behalf of others*, such as those who are sick, those who are unbelievers, our friends, colleagues, and loved ones.
— *Intercede for those in positions of authority* such as those in government. Pray for "kings and all those who are in high positions" (1 Tim. 2:2).
— *Intercede for those in the church*. Pray for the church leaders. Pray for fellow believers. "Always keep on praying for all the saints" (Eph. 6:18 NIV). "Is any one of you in trouble? He should pray . . . Is any one of you sick? He should call the elders of the church to pray over him and anoint him with oil in the name of the Lord. And the prayer offered in faith will make the sick person well; the Lord will raise him up. If he has sinned, he will be forgiven. Therefore confess your sins to each other and pray for each other so that you

may be healed. The prayer of a righteous man is powerful and effective" (James 5:13-16 NIV).

— *Confess and repent of sins and ask God for forgiveness.* Even though when a person comes to faith in Christ their past sins are forgiven and the guilt from these sins is removed when a new heart is created in them, they continue to sin. The result of this sin is that our hearts condemn us and we will have a guilty conscience. Because of this, we need to continually come to God in prayer, confessing our sins and asking God for forgiveness. John reassures us that "if we confess our sins, he is faithful and just and will forgive us our sins and purify us from all unrighteousness" (1 John 1:9 NIV) and "if anybody does sin, we have one who speaks to the Father in our defence—Jesus Christ, the Righteous One" (1 John 2:1 NIV). When we have confessed our sins, repented and have been forgiven, our hearts will be cleansed from guilt and will no longer condemn us. This, in turn, has a marked effect on the result of prayer, for "if our hearts do not condemn us, we have confidence before God and receive from him anything we ask, because we obey his commands and do what pleases him" (1 John 3:21-22 NIV).

— *Ask God for things for yourself.* Like King Solomon, ask God for wisdom: "If any of you lacks wisdom, he should ask God, who gives generously to all without finding fault, and it will be given to him. But when he asks, he must believe and not doubt" (James 1:5-6 NIV). "The wisdom that comes from heaven is first of all pure; then peace-loving, considerate, submissive, full of mercy and good fruit, impartial and sincere" (James 3:17 NIV). James warns believers though, that "when you ask, you do not receive, because you ask with wrong motives, that you may spend what you get on your pleasures" (James 4:3 NIV). He also explains the reason that believers may be lacking in what they need: "You do not have because you do not ask God." (James 4:3 NIV). God *wants* us to ask Him for what we need, but with the right motives.

Do we deserve the Lord to answer the requests that we bring to Him in prayer? No! Daniel says: "We do not make requests of you because we are righteous, but because of your great mercy" (Dan. 9:18 NIV). We need God's help! Do our prayers reach God? Yes! Daniel related this experience of prayer: "While I was seeking and praying, confessing my sin . . . while I was still in prayer, Gabriel, the man I had seen in the earlier vision, came to me in swift flight . . . he instructed me and said to me, 'Daniel, I have now come to give you insight and understanding. As soon as you began to pray, an answer was given, which I have come to tell you, for you are highly esteemed'" (Dan. 9:20-23 NIV). Having an angel come to tell you this of course is an exception! Nevertheless, our prayers are *always* heard by God.

Notice that Daniel was seeking God through prayer and confessing his sin. He wasn't only asking God for things. Through the confession of sin, God would give him a clean heart, free from guilt. He was seeking to know God and to develop his relationship with God and he was also putting his concerns and requests before God.

Our prayers go up to God like incense—a pleasing aroma. John had a vision of heaven in which he saw an angel at the altar with a golden censer. "He was given much incense to offer, with the prayers of all the saints, on the golden altar before the throne. The smoke of the incense, together with the prayers of the saints, went up before God from the angel's hand" (Rev. 8:3-4 NIV).

Answers to prayer depend largely on faith. When Jesus was travelling through the towns and villages, He performed many miracles healing the sick and disabled. In His home town of Nazareth however, He did not do many miracles "because of their lack of faith" (Matt. 13:58 NIV). Faith makes things happen!

When Jesus travelled through the towns and the villages, people were often healed just by touching the hem of His cloak. Later, when the disciples were sent out into the world, people were healed just by the shadow of Peter falling on them. Why? Because the people had faith that they *would* be healed! Jesus told His disciples: "If you have faith as small as a mustard seed, you can say to this mountain, 'Move from here to there' and it will move. Nothing will be impossible for you" (Matt. 17:20 NIV).

After the disciples had received the Holy Spirit, they went throughout the towns and villages healing the sick. Early in their ministry, when the people were surprised after seeing a man healed, Peter explained to them: "By faith in the name of Jesus, this man whom you now see and know was made strong. It is Jesus' name and the faith that comes through him that has given this complete healing to him, as you can all see" (Acts 3:16 NIV). Jesus said, "Whatever you ask in prayer, believe that you have received it, and it will be yours" (Mark 11:24). That is faith!

Receiving answer to prayer, including healing then, depends on:
1. What you pray for being within God's will;
2. The power of the name of Jesus; and
3. Faith in His name.

How can we have greater faith? Jesus told a man who had brought his son to Him to drive out an evil spirit that "'everything is possible for him who believes.' Immediately the boy's father exclaimed, 'I do believe; help me overcome my unbelief!'" (Mark 9:23-24 NIV). The disciples said to Jesus: "Increase our faith!" (Luke 17:5). Like this father and like Jesus' disciples, we can ask God for greater faith. The increase of faith is a gift from God.

GIVING

Money, in itself, is not evil. Money is a commodity that we use to trade for the necessities of life and a means by which to bless others. It is the 'love of money' that is wrong. The writer of the book of Hebrews cautions us to "keep your lives free from the love of money and be content with what you have" (Heb. 13:5 NIV).

Paul said that those who are rich in this present world should not "be arrogant nor . . . put their hope in wealth, which is so uncertain, but . . . put their hope in God, who richly provides us with everything for our enjoyment . . . do good . . . be rich in good deeds, and . . . be generous and willing to share. In this way they will lay up treasure for themselves as a firm foundation for the coming age, so that they may take hold of the life that is truly life" (1 Tim. 6:17-19 NIV).

God has given us many blessings. He expects us to be good stewards, being generous to others and giving to help further His kingdom. What we have is not ours to keep. Everything belongs to God and no material possessions can be taken with us when we leave this earth. God's Word tells us that good stewards will be entrusted with more. This means more to share and bless others with; not just so we can buy more things for ourselves.

With regards to giving, Paul writes that "each man should give what he has decided in his heart to give, not reluctantly or under compulsion, for God loves a cheerful giver" (2 Cor. 9:7 NIV). Giving not only involves money, but also our time, our talents, and other resources.

God blesses those who give generously. He said to the Israelites: "Will a man rob God? Yet you rob me. But you ask, 'How do we rob you?' In tithes and offerings . . . Bring the whole tithe into the storehouse, that there may be food in my house. Test me in this . . . and see if I will not throw open the floodgates of heaven and pour out so much blessing that you will not have room enough for it" (Mal. 3:10-11 NIV).

We are to give out of love for God and compassion for others, without thought of reward. In the book of Acts, Luke writes of a man named Cornelius. "He and all his family were devout and God-fearing; he gave generously to those in need and prayed to God regularly" (Acts 10:2 NIV). Cornelius had a vision in which he saw an angel of God who came to him and told him that his prayers and gifts to the poor had "come up as a special memorial offering before God" (Acts 10:4 NIV). Giving to others is giving to God. It is an act of worship and evidence of our faith.

Jesus said that it is better to give, pray, and fast in secret, than to make sure that everyone sees what you are doing, for "your Father, who sees what is done in secret, will reward you" (Matt. 6:4 NIV. Those who like to make sure that their deeds are noticed by others "have received their reward in full" (Matt. 6:2 NIV) by the acknowledgement and approval of others.

STAYING ON THE PATH

To *begin* on the path of life, you must enter through The Gate—Jesus. When you first come to faith in the Lord Jesus, you are at the *beginning* of the path. You then must *stay on* the path that leads to salvation. Jesus explained that we must "enter through the narrow gate. For wide is the gate and broad is the road that leads to destruction, and many enter through it. But small is the gate and narrow the road that leads to life, and only a few find it" (Matt. 7:13-14 NIV).

The writer of Hebrews describes believers as those "who will inherit salvation" (Heb. 1:14 NIV), rather than describing them as being 'already saved'. While we are living here on the earth in our mortal bodies, Paul says we are "being saved" (1 Cor. 1:18). It is a *process* that we have commenced; a path that we have begun to walk on. He encourages believers to "continue to work out your salvation with fear and trembling, for it is God who works in you to will and to act according to his good purpose" (Phil. 2:12-13 NIV) and Jude writes: "Keep yourselves in God's love as you wait for the mercy of our Lord Jesus Christ to bring you to eternal life" (Jude 1:21 NIV).

The eleventh chapter of the book of Hebrews is often referred to as the 'faith chapter'. It honours and uses as an example to us, some of the Old Testament men and women who lived by faith. What is important to note is that "all these people were still living by faith when they died" (Heb. 11:13 NIV). You can *start* on the path of faith but, just as importantly, you must *remain* on that path and be still *on* that path when you die in order to inherit eternal life.

John cautions: "See that what you have heard from the beginning remains in you. If it does, you also will remain in the Son and in the Father. And this is what he promised us—even eternal life . . . remain in him . . . continue in him" (1 John 2:24-25, 27-28 NIV).

If we believe in Jesus for the forgiveness of sins, God takes our faith and credits us with His righteousness. This makes us holy in His eyes. The names of the righteous are written in the 'Lamb's book of life'. Under the New Covenant, believers in the Lord Jesus have their names written in this book along with those who died in faith *before* the Old Covenant was given and those who died in faith *under* the Old Covenant. The Lamb's book of life is a list of those whose sins have been forgiven and who have righteousness through faith in Jesus Christ. They have *life* through the Lamb of God—Jesus Christ.

It is possible that a name can be written in this book and then blotted out. Moses alluded to this when he said to God: "But now, please forgive their sin—but if not, then blot me out of the book you have written" (Exod. 32:32 NIV). David also believed that this was possible. Of his enemies he said: "Do not let them share in your salvation. May they be blotted out of the book of life and not be listed with the righteous" (Ps. 69:27-28 NIV). In the book of Revelation, Jesus said of him who overcomes, that He "will never blot out his name out of the book of life" (Rev. 3:5). 'Overcomers' are those who *endure faithfully to the end*. If having your name blotted out of this book was not a possibility, then Jesus would not have made this statement and, as it is His book, He would know.

It is God's will that, once a person believes and comes to faith in Christ, he or she *continues* in that faith and does not turn away, so that he or she will be raised to life. Jesus said: "This is the will of him who sent me, that I shall lose none of all that he has given me, but raise them up at the last day. For my Father's will is that everyone who looks to the Son and believes in him shall have eternal life, and I will raise him up at the last day" (John 6:39-40 NIV). Peter encourages believers to be "eager to make your calling and election sure" (2 Pet. 1:10 NIV). In this way they would be fulfilling God's will that they inherit eternal life.

How can a believer fulfil God's will and inherit eternal life? How can a believer endure faithfully to the end? Jesus said that "the one who feeds on me will live because of me" (John 6:57 NIV). Believers must *continue* to 'feed' on the bread from heaven—the Lord Jesus Christ; not have a quick snack and then go on a diet!

Salvation does not occur immediately upon coming to faith in the Lord here on this earth, but is later *brought to fruition*. When a person repents of their sins and believes in the Lord, they *begin the journey* on the path to salvation. While living here on earth in relationship with God you are in the *process* of being saved; but only "the one who endures to the end will be saved" (Matt. 10:22). The goal of our faith, according to Peter, is the "salvation of your souls" (1 Pet. 1:9) and this is what will be brought to fruition when we depart our earthly bodies. Once the saving of our souls has been brought to fruition, we are assured of the full redemption of soul *and* body. King David understood this when he said at the end of his life: "Will he not bring to fruition my salvation?" (2 Sam. 23:5 NIV).

Once a person's salvation has been 'brought to fruition', no one can snatch that person out of God's hands. Jesus told His disciples that "he who stands firm to the end will be saved" (Matt. 10:22 NIV), because "by standing firm you will gain life" (Luke 21:19 NIV). There is no promise of salvation to those who do not stand firm to the end; no promise of 'gaining life'. 'Standing firm to the end' is the condition by which salvation will be brought to fruition; the condition by which we will gain eternal life.

The Bible often speaks of faith as being weak or strong. Weak faith is in danger of dying and needs to be strengthened. To the Church in Sardis, Jesus warned: "Wake up! Strengthen what remains and is about to die . . . Remember, therefore, what you have received and heard; obey it, and repent" (Rev. 3:2-3 NIV). Through faith, we are "shielded by God's power until the coming of the salvation that is ready to be revealed in the last time" (1 Pet. 1:5 NIV), but we must *continue in* that faith.

Paul did not consider that he himself had *already* taken hold of salvation, but rather that he was 'pressing on' towards the goal. He said that his desire was to:

> Know him and the power of his resurrection, and . . . share his sufferings, becoming like him in his death, that by any means possible I may attain the resurrection from the dead. Not that I have already obtained this or am already perfect, but I press on to make it my own, because Christ Jesus has made me his own. Brothers, I do not consider that I have made it my own. But one thing I do: forgetting what lies behind and straining forward to what lies ahead, I press on toward the goal for the prize of the upward call of God in Christ Jesus.
>
> —Phil. 3:10-14

Paul said that God has "reconciled you by Christ's physical body through death to present you holy in his sight, without blemish and free from accusation—if you continue in your faith, established and firm, not moved from the hope held out in the gospel" (Col. 1:22-23 NIV). The condition is *if you continue in your faith.* He writes: "Just as you received Christ Jesus as Lord, continue to live in him, rooted and built up in him, strengthened in the faith as you were taught" (Col. 2:6-7 NIV). He separates the initial event of *receiving* Christ as Lord to the ongoing journey of *continuing to live* in Christ.

Paul writes: "Here is a trustworthy saying: If we died with him, we will also live with him; if we endure, we will also reign with him. If we disown him, he will also disown us; if we are faithless, he will remain faithful, for he cannot disown himself" (2 Tim. 2:11-13 NIV). To be disowned by Jesus would mean the loss of eternal life—the greatest tragedy. Paul is saying that if we lose our faith (are faithless), the Spirit of Jesus will remain faithful *to Jesus* and to the body of Christ (believers) rather than to the person who no longer has faith. The Holy Spirit will *depart from the faithless person* in order to *remain part of the body of Jesus,* "for he cannot disown himself (2 Tim. 2:13 NIV).

Paul writes that "the Lord knows those who are his . . . Everyone who confesses the name of the Lord must turn away from wickedness" (2 Tim. 2:19 NIV). If, through continual sin (wickedness) and disregard for God *after* initially coming to faith, the heart becomes so unclean that the Holy Spirit can no longer dwell there, the Holy Spirit may depart. The writer of the letter to the Hebrews warns that, "if we deliberately keep on sinning after we have received the knowledge of the truth, no sacrifice for sins is left, but only a fearful expectation of judgement and of raging fire that will consume the enemies of God" (Heb. 10:26-27 NIV).

Furthermore, if a person no longer has faith, his or her heart will 'turn away' from God, close to God, and the Holy Spirit will depart. The writer of the letter to the Hebrews addressed this warning to believers: "See to it, brothers, that none of you has a sinful, unbelieving heart that turns away from the living God. But encourage one another daily, as long as it is called Today, so that none of you may be hardened by sin's deceitfulness. We have come to share in Christ if we hold firmly to the end the confidence we had at first" (Heb. 3:12-14 NIV). He is saying that there are two things that can lead to the turning away of the person from God after they initially come to faith:
1. A sinful heart; and
2. An unbelieving heart.

'Holding firmly' to our faith to the end is the condition by which we share in Christ. 'Sharing in Christ' means to share in His Spirit along with the body of believers who also share in His Spirit. Our walk of faith is likened to the Israelites on their journey to the Promised Land, when God declared that those whose hearts had gone astray would not enter, and the writer explains that "they were unable to enter because of unbelief" (Heb. 3:19).

Scripture prophesies that the abandonment of faith will increase towards the time of the end. Paul wrote that "in later times some will abandon the faith and follow deceiving spirits and things taught by demons" (1 Tim. 4:1 NIV). Clearly, those that abandon the faith had faith to begin with. Jesus told the disciples that "because of wickedness, the love of most will grow cold, but he who stands firm to the end will be saved" (Matt. 24:12-13 NIV).

Jesus warned that "anyone who speaks against the Holy Spirit will not be forgiven, either in this age or the age to come" (Matt. 12:32 NIV) and Paul also warns believers: "Do not grieve the Holy Spirit of God, with whom you were sealed for the day of redemption" (Eph. 4:30 NIV). This is also described in Hebrews as 'insulting the Spirit of grace', and is what a person is said to do if he deliberately keeps on sinning after receiving the knowledge of truth. The writer says that this is like "trampling the Son of God under foot" and treating "as an unholy thing the blood of the covenant that sanctified him" (Heb. 10:29 NIV). What is the danger of doing that? If the Holy Spirit were grieved to the point of departing from the heart of the person, that person would *not* inherit eternal life. John speaks of the grieving of the Holy Spirit as "sin that leads to death" (1 John 5:16). This is because by the grieving of, and subsequent departing of, the Holy Spirit, the person no longer has connection to Jesus—the source of eternal life, and therefore will again be on the road that leads to death with only the disconnected spirit passed down from Adam.

Jesus is the mediator between believers and God the Father. He intercedes with God on our behalf for the forgiveness of our sins because He died to free us from the guilt of sin by taking our sin upon Himself on the cross. If someone grieves the Holy Spirit to the point of departure, that person will no longer have the Spirit of Jesus dwelling in his or her heart. Without His Spirit, the person is no longer connected to the only One who can be the mediator, or High Priest, between his or herself and God. If the person is no longer connected to Jesus by His Spirit, then that person no longer has this mediator acting on his or her behalf and therefore a sin or sins, no matter what they are, that cause the Holy Spirit to depart, *will* lead to death because the person will be disconnected from the source of life and will again be under the law of sin and death with no mediator.

In the letter to the Hebrews, the writer warns that "it is impossible for those who have once been enlightened, who have tasted the heavenly gift, who have shared in the Holy Spirit, who have tasted the goodness of the word of God and the powers of the coming age, if they fall away, to be brought back to repentance, because to their loss they are crucifying the Son of God all over again and subjecting him to public disgrace" (Heb. 6:4-6 NIV). However, he reassures the recipients of the letter by saying: "Even though we speak like this, dear friends, we are confident of better things in your case—things that accompany salvation" (Heb. 6:9 NIV). He implores them to continue in their work, show love and help fellow believers, be diligent *to the end* to make their hope sure, and to not become lazy but rather to "imitate those who through faith and patience inherit what has been promised" (Heb. 6:12 NIV).

The people of Israel, on many occasions, were unfaithful to God. They corrupted their ways and their sins were many. God told them through the prophet Hosea to "return, O Israel, to the LORD your God. Your sins have been your downfall! . . . Say to him: 'Forgive all our sins and receive us graciously'" (Hosea 14:1-2 NIV). When the people returned to the Lord He said: "I will heal their waywardness and love them freely, for my anger has turned away from them" (Hosea 14:4 NIV). In the book of Zechariah, God says: "Return to me . . . and I will return to you" (Zech. 1:3). If someone has turned away from God, He *will* return to that person *if* the person returns to Him. If someone returns to God, He is able to restore that person to a right relationship with Him.

Jesus said:
> "I am the true vine, and my Father is the gardener. He cuts off every branch in me that bears no fruit. While every branch that does bear fruit he prunes so that it will be even more fruitful . . . Remain in me, and I will remain in you. No branch can bear fruit by itself; it must remain in the vine . . . If a man remains in me and I in him, he will bear much fruit; apart from me you can do nothing. If anyone does not remain in me, he is like a branch that is thrown away and withers; such branches are picked up, thrown into the fire and burned . . . now remain in my love. If you obey my commands, you will remain in my love"
>
> —John 15:1-2, 4-5, 9-10 NIV

If branches are cut off vines, it means that they are no longer attached to the *life* of the vine. The gardener eventually throws these detached branches into the fire.

There would be no need for Jesus to exhort believers to 'remain in me' and 'continue in me', if there was no other possibility. The promise that Christ will remain in them is made only to those who *remain* 'in Christ'. Paul, many times in his letters to the churches, implores them to remain in Christ, to hold firmly to their faith, and not depart from it. He said to the Corinthians: "By this gospel you are saved, if you hold firmly to the word I preached to you. Otherwise, you have believed in vain . . . be on your guard; stand firm in the faith" (1 Cor. 15:2, 16:13 NIV).

Paul likened the Israelites to an olive tree, with the Gentile believers being a wild olive shoot that had been grafted in. He explained that some of the original branches were "broken off because of their unbelief" (Rom. 11:20), and he cautioned the Gentile believers to *continue* in God's kindness otherwise they too will be cut off. He also said that if the Israelites who *had* been cut off do *not* persist in their unbelief, they will "be grafted in, for God is able to graft them in again" (Rom. 11:23 NKJV).

We are to remain 'in Christ'. If we stray from the path, we must repent of our sins and return to God, asking Him for forgiveness and restoration, for He is able to forgive us and restore us to Himself.

God does not force us to remain 'in Christ'. We have freewill. We can choose either to remain in Him or to depart from Him. One choice gives life, the other leads to death. But *if* we remain in Christ then nothing can separate us from the love of God—"neither death nor life, nor angels nor principalities nor powers, nor things present nor things to come, nor height nor depth, nor any other created thing, shall be able to separate us from the love of God which is in Christ Jesus our Lord" (Rom. 8:38-39 NKJV).

The walk of faith requires patience and perseverance. The writer to the Hebrews encourages the believer to "throw off everything that hinders and the sin that so easily entangles, and let us run with perseverance the race marked out for us. Let us fix our eyes on Jesus, the author and perfector of our faith, who for the joy set before him endured the cross, scorning its shame, and sat down at the right hand of the throne of God. Consider him who endured such opposition from sinful men, so that you will not grow weary and lose heart' (Heb. 12:1-3 NIV).

Paul implores believers to:
> Be strong in the Lord and in the strength of his might. Put on the whole armour of God, that you may be able to stand against the schemes of the devil. For we do not wrestle against flesh and blood, but against the rulers, against the authorities, against the cosmic powers over this present darkness, against the spiritual forces of evil in the heavenly places. Therefore take up the whole armour of God, that you may be able to withstand in the evil day, and having done all, to stand firm. Stand therefore, having fastened on the belt of truth, and having put on the breastplate of righteousness, and, as shoes for your feet, having put on the readiness given by the gospel of peace. In all circumstances take up the shield of faith, with which you can extinguish all the flaming darts of the evil one; and take the helmet of salvation, and the sword of the Spirit, which is the word of God, praying at all times in the Spirit, with all prayer and supplication. To that end keep alert with all perseverance, making supplication for all the saints.
>
> —Eph. 6:10-18

We are not alone in our journey of faith. God helps us in our daily walk of faith through the indwelling Holy Spirit. The Holy Spirit helps us to remain on the path to salvation. God "gives strength to the weary and increases the power of the weak. Even youths grow tired and weary, and young men stumble and fall; but those who hope in the LORD will renew their strength. They will soar on wings like eagles; they will run and not grow weary, they will walk and not be faint" (Isa. 40:29-30 NIV).

JOINING OTHERS ON THE PATH

If we are believers in Christ, we are part of His body. This is because we share the one Spirit—the Spirit of Christ—the Holy Spirit. Christ is the head of His body—the church. The church began at the time of Pentecost, after Jesus had ascended into heaven. God poured out the Holy Spirit on believers and about three thousand were added to their number because of the bold witness of Peter. What did these new believers do after that?

> They devoted themselves to the apostles' teaching and the fellowship, to the breaking of bread and the prayers. And awe came upon every soul, and many wonders and signs were being done through the apostles. And all who believed were together and had all things in common. And they were selling their possessions and belongings and distributing the proceeds to all, as any had need. And day by day, attending the temple together and breaking bread in their homes, they received their food with glad and generous hearts, praising God and having favour with all the people. And the Lord added to their number day by day those who were being saved.
>
> —Acts 2:42-47

The book of Acts is a history of the early church. It contains a record of the way in which the early believers lived and fellowshipped together. Even though they did things such as selling their homes and possessions, it does not mean that God would have *all* believers do this. There may well be those of whom God *does* ask this sacrifice. Others may be asked to leave their families, their countries, or give up secure jobs. What God asks of one is different from what He asks of another.

Because we are all members of the one body, we belong to each other. We have been given different spiritual *gifts* through the Holy Spirit. Paul says that some examples of gifts are: prophesying, serving, teaching, encouraging, contributing to the needs of others, leadership, and showing mercy. Whilst God is the *giver* of these spiritual gifts, it is up to the recipient to *nurture* them. Paul encourages the recipients of these gifts to "try to excel in gifts that build up the church" (1 Cor. 14:12 NIV). "Each one should use whatever gift he has received to serve others, faithfully administering God's grace in its various forms" (1 Pet. 4:10 NIV).

Paul also says that there are different kinds of service and different kinds of working but "to each one the manifestation of the Spirit is given for the common good" (1 Cor. 12:7 NIV). The *manifestations* of the Spirit according to Paul include: the message of wisdom, the message of knowledge, faith, healing, miraculous powers, prophecy, distinguishing between spirits, speaking in different kinds of tongues, and the interpretation of tongues. These are given as God determines and in the measure that God determines.

In the church, God has appointed "apostles . . . prophets . . . teachers . . . workers of miracles . . . those having gifts of healing . . . those able to help others . . .

those with gifts of administration . . . and those speaking in different kinds of tongues" (1 Cor. 12:28 NIV).

The way God calls us to serve Him depends on:
— Our *spiritual gifts*;
— Our *abilities*—the natural gifting that we have;
— Our *heart's desire*—our dreams and ambitions;
— Our *personality*; and
— Our *life experience*—our tragedies and triumphs, our culture, education, and career path.

Of far greater importance than any of the gifts and manifestations of the Spirit is love. Peter tells us to "love each other deeply, because love covers over a multitude of sins" (1 Pet. 4:8 NIV), and Paul says that, even with all of the spiritual gifts, without love he is nothing! "Love is patient, love is kind. It does not envy, it does not boast, it is not proud. It is not rude, it is not self-seeking, it is not easily angered, it keeps no record of wrongs. Love does not delight in evil but rejoices with the truth. It always protects, always trusts, always hopes, always perseveres. Love never fails . . . And now, these three remain: faith, hope and love. But the greatest of these is love" (1 Cor. 13:4-8, 13 NIV).

The early church began meeting regularly with one another on the first day of the week, rather than on the Jewish Sabbath. Luke confirms this in the book of Acts when he says that "on the first day of the week . . . the disciples came together to break bread" (Acts 20:7 NKJV). The first day of the week was also the first day of Creation and the day that the Lord Jesus was raised from the dead.

Being a part of the body of Christ means that God wants you to meet with fellow believers to encourage them and support them in their walk and show them love and acceptance; and they are to reciprocate. Local church members often meet for Bible studies, meals, outings, and recreational activities. They run groups for all ages and nurture believers at all stages of their Christian walk.

The writer of the letter to the Hebrews was concerned that some of the believers were no longer meeting together and implored them: "Let us not give up meeting together, as some are in the habit of doing, but let us encourage one another" (Heb. 10:25 NIV). Meeting with fellow believers is a habit that must be *nurtured*. It is for our own good and for the good of others that we gather together to encourage one another and build one another up in faith. How do you form this habit? The same as any other habit—do it and keep on doing it!

Will fellow believers always be easy to get along with? No. Will they be perfect? No. They will be just like you! Sometimes they will do or say things that will upset you and likewise you will do the same. You will never find a perfect church or perfect fellow believer. Before Jesus died on the cross, however, He prayed for the unity of believers. He asked His Father to protect them by the power of His name so "that they may be one as We are" (John 17:11 NKJV).

GOING AND TAKING THE PATH WITH YOU

All believers are called to be witnesses to the world, for through them God spreads the "fragrance of His knowledge" (2 Cor. 2:14 NKJV)—the knowledge of Christ. For some, this might mean witnessing within their family, local community, workplace, school, or university. Others may be called by God to take the good news of salvation into the wider world, perhaps overseas to another culture. They may be required to give up much that they hold dear in their lives—family, friends, career, and worldly possessions.

Jesus said: "Any of you who does not give up everything he has cannot be my disciple" (Luke 14:33 NIV), and "if anyone would come after me, he must deny himself and take up his cross and follow me" (Mark 8:34 NIV). To one rich young man, Jesus said: "'One thing you lack: Go your way, sell whatever you have and give to the poor, and you will have treasure in heaven; and come, take up the cross, and follow Me.' But he was sad at this word, and went away sorrowful, for he had great possessions" (Mark 10:21-22 NKJV). His worldly wealth was more important to him than following Jesus.

There is great reward for those who have been called to give up much in this life for the sake of the gospel. Jesus said that "everyone who has left houses or brothers or sisters or father or mother or children or fields for my sake will receive a hundred times as much and will inherit eternal life" (Matt. 19:29 NIV). He also said: "If anyone serves me, the Father will honour him" (John 12:26).

Jesus told His disciples that they would be ridiculed for speaking the truth; perhaps even arrested or persecuted, but He reassured them: "When they arrest you, do not worry about what to say or how to say it. At that time you will be given what to say, for it will not be you speaking, but the Spirit of your Father speaking through you" (Matt. 10:19-20 NIV). He told them that being arrested and persecuted by "kings and governors" will "result in your being witnesses to them" (Luke 21:13 NIV). They were not to "be afraid of those who kill the body but cannot kill the soul. Rather be afraid of the One who can destroy both soul and body in hell" (Matt. 10:28 NIV). In other words, the worst that man can do to them is to destroy their body. That is nothing compared to the losing of the soul.

"If you are insulted as a Christian, do not be ashamed, but praise God that you bear that name . . . those who suffer according to God's will should commit themselves to their faithful Creator and continue to do good" (1 Pet. 4:19 NIV), "for our light and momentary troubles are achieving for us an eternal glory that far outweighs them all. So we fix our eyes not on what is seen, but on what is unseen. For what is seen is temporary, but what is unseen is eternal" (2 Cor. 4:17-18 NIV).

TELLING OTHERS ABOUT THE PATH

Our lives as believers should demonstrate to others that we belong to the Lord. We are called to represent Jesus to others. People come to faith through the work of the Holy Spirit who convicts a person of their sins and of their need for a Saviour. Often, the Holy Spirit will work through the witness of other people. Jesus said: "You are the light of the world . . . let your light shine before men, that they may see your good deeds and praise your Father in heaven" (Matt. 5:16 NIV).

Know the reason for what you believe. Know the basic truths of the faith well so that you will always be confident in sharing your faith with others. "In your hearts set apart Christ as Lord. Always be prepared to give an answer to everyone who asks you to give the reason for the hope that you have. But do this with gentleness and respect" (1 Pet. 3:15 NIV).

It is important to "tell people the full message of this new life" (Acts 5:20 NIV). Although people can and do repent and believe through avenues such as a small tract, an evangelistic crusade, and so on, people are more likely to understand the *reason* for repentance and belief if they are given the 'full message', and new believers are more likely to *remain* on the path of salvation if they have a more thorough introduction to faith than if they are only told that they are sinners and need to 'repent and believe'. This does not mean that they have to know and understand *everything* before coming to faith, and indeed they cannot. It is important however, that people have at least a rudimentary understanding of Creation, their origin, The Fall, the nature of God and His love for them, the promise of the Saviour through the prophets, the uniqueness of Christ and His life, death and resurrection and how that can be applied to them, the truth of their eternal destiny, and the hope of heaven and a new creation.

God wants us to tell others the good news of salvation. Don't hide something that can change someone's life. Someone has shared this with you. Now go and tell others. "No-one lights a lamp and puts it in a place where it will be hidden, or under a bowl. Instead he puts it on its stand, so that those who come in may see the light" (Luke 11:33 NIV).

King David said: "I do not hide your righteousness in my heart; I speak of your faithfulness and salvation. I do not conceal your love and your truth from the great assembly" (Ps. 40:10 NIV), "my mouth will tell of your righteousness, of your salvation all day long" (Ps. 71:6 NIV). The prophet Jeremiah is another great example of one whose passion was to tell others God's Word. He said: "His word is in my heart like a fire, a fire shut up in my bones. I am weary of holding it in; indeed, I cannot" (Jer. 20:9 NIV).

The Holy Spirit enables a believer to speak "the word of God boldly" (Acts 4:31 NIV), "for God did not give us a spirit of timidity, but a spirit of power, of love and of self-discipline" (2 Tim. 1:7 NIV). The disciples, who "were all filled with the Holy Spirit . . . spoke the word of God boldly" (Acts 4:31 NIV), and Apollos, who was a faithful servant of Christ, "vigorously refuted the Jews in public debate, proving from the Scriptures that Jesus was the Christ" (Acts 18:28 NIV). Follow the example of the disciples who "never stopped teaching and proclaiming the good news that Jesus is the Christ" (Acts 5:42 NIV).

Do not be ashamed of the gospel of Christ. When Jesus lived on the earth, many believed in Him but, of these, many were afraid to publicly confess their belief. "Because of the Pharisees they would not confess their faith for fear they would be put out of the synagogue; for they loved praise from men more than praise from God" (John 12:42-43 NIV). However, Jesus said: "If anyone is ashamed of me and my words . . . the Son of Man will be ashamed of him when he comes in his Father's glory with the holy angels" (Mark 8:38 NIV). Do not be afraid to acknowledge God before men. Jesus said: "Whoever acknowledges me before men, I will also acknowledge him before my Father in heaven. But whoever disowns me before men, I will disown before my Father in heaven" (Matt. 10:32-33 NIV). Paul was "not ashamed of the gospel, because it is the power of God for the salvation of everyone who believes" (Rom. 1:16 NIV).

If the message that you have to share will save a life, that is more important than any sense of embarrassment or awkwardness that you may feel. Remember that "he who turns a sinner from the error of his way will save a soul from death and cover a multitude of sins" (James 5:20 NKJV). Witness for the honour and glory of God. Don't preach at people, don't criticize or judge them, just talk with them in a genuine, authentic, and caring way, sharing with them the truth of the gospel. Demonstrate God's love and practise what you believe. People will listen if you speak the truth in love.

Share this book with someone. Buy someone a Bible so that they can read God's Word for themselves. Tell others about how God has given *you* life! Sharing the gospel is like one beggar telling another beggar where to find food! Invite them to go to church with you and most importantly, pray for them.

Jesus gave some good advice about worldly wealth. He said: "Use worldly wealth to gain friends for yourselves" (Luke 16:9 NIV). Does this mean that God wants us to go around shouting beer for people in pubs so that they will like us, or giving them money so they will be our friends? No. What Jesus is saying is that a good use for worldly wealth which has been entrusted to you by the Father, is to use it to help others in such a way that you will be seen to be a genuine friend and a representative of Jesus to them, and in this way you may have the opportunity for witness. For example, maybe you are able to buy food to put together hampers for those who are in need. Through this ministry you will be showing them the love of God and this might lead to the opportunity to speak to them of that love. Perhaps you have a vehicle in which you could offer to take someone to an appointment and in doing so have the opportunity to ask them to church with you. Maybe you can afford to buy someone a Bible and some books that will help them to understand God's Word. Perhaps you could pay for someone to attend a Christian conference or camp, or a breakfast that has an inspiring speaker or evangelist speaking at it. Maybe you could sponsor a child in poverty and bring blessing to a whole family or sponsor and support a missionary.

God entrusts us with wealth not so we can spend it on every luxury we desire for ourselves, but so that we can use it wisely to minister to others and demonstrate to them His love. Material wealth is a test. Jesus said that "whoever can be trusted with very little can also be trusted with much, and whoever is dishonest with very little will also be dishonest with much. So if you have not been trustworthy in handling worldly wealth, who will trust you with true riches?" (Luke 16:10-11 NIV). True riches are the gifts of the Spirit. God observes how you handle worldly wealth and uses that as a standard for determining how you will handle *spiritual* gifts, that is, whether you will use them for the furthering of His kingdom, the blessing of others, and for His glory, or whether you will use them selfishly.

The central message of the gospel that God wants you to share with others is the crucifixion of Christ. Paul describes this as "a stumbling block to Jews and foolishness to Gentiles" (1 Cor. 1:23 NIV). Telling someone else the good news of salvation may not always have the result that you had hoped for, "for the message of the cross is foolishness to those who are perishing, but to us who are being saved it is the power of God" (1 Cor. 1:18 NIV). This means then, that there are two groups of people:
1. Those who are *perishing*; and
2. Those who are *being saved*.

It is therefore at the *point* of being saved that the person realises that the message of the cross is *not* foolishness, but rather, the power of God that can save them. This makes perfect sense. Once they realise that the message of the cross has the power to *save*, they surely would not *remain* in a state of perishing. They would immediately come to faith and repentance. If they are *not* yet at a point of 'being saved', it is because they *still* believe that the message of the cross is foolishness. When you understand this, you will expect that *all* unbelievers with whom you share the good news will, at first, think that your message is foolishness, at least up to a point. At that point, there will again be two groups:
1. Those who cross over from death to life because they have come to the point where they realise that the gospel message has the power to save and they put their faith in Jesus; and
2. Those who *continue* to perish because they continue to believe that the gospel message is foolishness.

Do not expect that those who are *not* believers will understand spiritual truths. Indeed, they cannot. Paul explains that "the man without the Spirit does not accept the things that come from the Spirit of God, for they are foolishness to him, and he cannot understand them, because they are spiritually discerned" (1 Cor. 2:14 NIV).

You need to be patient and start to tell them God's story from the beginning. Share with them the *full* story starting from *before* the Creation. One of the benefits of knowing Scripture well is that you can present the truth of the gospel in sequence and with logic and clarity, without skipping straight to the 'climax' and leaving big gaps in their understanding.

Sometimes, it may seem that your witness to someone does not seem to get through and you do not see the end result that you had hoped for. It may be however, that you have sown a seed. It does not matter whether you sow a seed or water it. God will reward those who witness to others. Paul says that "the man who plants and the man who waters have one purpose, and each will be rewarded according to his own labour" (1 Cor. 3:8 NIV), but it is God who makes things grow because, only from the Creator ... comes life!

Part Five

You (Yet Again), The Others, And God

Chapter Fourteen
Path's End—The New Beginning

About a quarter of the Bible is prophetic. Much of this prophecy has already been fulfilled. All fulfilled prophecy, including that which relates to the coming of the Son of God into humanity, has been fulfilled *accurately*, down to the smallest detail. It is therefore reasonable to assume that the remaining prophesies of events that are yet to come will *also* be fulfilled accurately.

WHAT WE STILL NEEDED:
— An end to Satan's temptations, accusations, destructive influence on relationships, lies, and deceit;
— The destruction of the *work* of Satan;
— Satan to be rendered powerless for ever;
— A removal of the constraints and the consequences of sin;
— The curse on mankind to be broken;
— Renewed bodies—to complete the salvation of our spirit, soul, *and* body;
— The ability for our bodies to endure forever;
— A new earth;
— A return to the original order of Creation as it was in the beginning, when humans were aware of angels and they both lived in harmony in God's beautiful world; and
— A new city in which to dwell; one that will never be destroyed; one where God dwells with mankind.

There are many books on the subject of end-time prophecy; this is not one of them! This chapter will *not* cover every single prophecy in detail, but rather focus mainly on key events. A literal interpretation will be used because Christ's coming to earth two thousand years ago was fulfilled literally, and it would therefore follow that His *Second* Coming and the events associated with it will also be literal. Interpretations vary on some aspects of prophecy, as with various other passages in the Bible. In keeping with the themes of this book however, the interpretations presented will aim to:
— Have the most scriptural support;
— Not be contradicted in Scripture; and
— Be consistent with God's nature.

It is easy to become caught up with the feeling that it is necessary to know and understand *every* aspect of end-time prophecy and one could easily end up with 'interpretation anxiety' followed by 'interpretation fatigue'! That is *not* why God has given us this prophecy. Although He wants us to be *aware* of the things to come, our time is better spent focussing on the work that He has given us to do *now* on earth. We are to:

Continue to proclaim 'The King is coming!'
and
Occupy until He comes!

Regardless of whether or not your interpretation and understanding of prophecy is one hundred percent correct, God will still bring about *what* He has planned, *when* He has planned it, and in the *order* He has ordained it. Differences in the interpretation of end-time prophecy will *not* affect the eternal outcome. God will not 'adjust' His plans to suit our interpretations!

The main *themes* of prophecy that relate to the end are that:
1. God is just and fair and His wrath will fall upon sinful unrepentant mankind, who persist in going their own way and ignoring His grace and salvation, and He does not want *you* to be a part of *this*; and
2. God has plans for the future; plans for better things by far than what has already taken place, and He wants *you* to be a part of *them*.

Prophecy which has not yet taken place relates to the time of the end. The study of this prophecy is encompassed within *eschatology*.

Eschatology /es-kuhtol-uh-jee/ n. the part of theology concerned with death and final destiny.[1]

The Word of God does not give specific times and dates when these end-time events will occur. Jesus said that "no-one knows about that day or hour, not even the angels in heaven, nor the Son, but only the Father" (Matt. 24:36 NIV). Paul writes:

> Now concerning the times and the seasons, brothers, you have no need to have anything written to you. For you yourselves are fully aware that the day of the Lord will come like a thief in the night. While people are saying, "There is peace and security," then sudden destruction will come upon them as labour pains come upon a pregnant woman, and they will not escape. But you are not in darkness, brothers, for that day to surprise you like a thief. For you are all children of light, children of the day. We are not of the night or of the darkness. So then let us not sleep, as others do, but let us keep awake and be sober. For those who sleep, sleep at night, and those who get drunk, are drunk at night. But since we belong to the day, let us be sober, having put on the breastplate of faith and love, and for a helmet the hope of salvation. For God has not destined us for wrath, but to obtain salvation through our Lord Jesus Christ, who died for us so that whether we are awake or asleep we might live with him. Therefore encourage one another and build one another up, just as you are doing.
>
> —1 Thess. 5:1-11

Scripture gives us a fairly good idea of the general condition of humanity leading up to the time of the end. According to Paul, "people will be lovers of themselves, lovers of money, boastful, proud, abusive, disobedient to their parents, ungrateful, unholy, without love, unforgiving, slanderous, without self-control, brutal, not lovers of the good, treacherous, rash, conceited, lovers of pleasure rather than lovers of God—having a form of godliness but denying its power" (2 Tim. 3:2-5 NIV).

Jesus said that leading up to the time of the end, there will be "wars and rumours of wars . . . nation will rise against nation, and kingdom against kingdom. And there will be famines, pestilences, and earthquakes in various places. All these are the beginning of sorrows" (Matt. 24:6-8 NKJV).

Is heaven the final destiny for believers? No. Just as the abode of the dead is not the final destiny for the *unrighteous*, heaven is not where *believers* will spend eternity. The time of the end is the end of the path for believers—the path that leads to their final destiny—a new beginning.

THE DAY OF THE LORD

The time of the end is divided into two distinct periods—one is a seven-year period known as 'The Tribulation' or 'The Day of the Lord', and the second period is a thousand-year period—the Millennium (prophetic years have three hundred and sixty days). After the Millennium will come eternity.

The initial seven-year period has three purposes:
1. God's final offer of salvation to mankind;
2. The outpouring of the wrath of God on sinful unrepentant mankind; and
3. The resuming of God's programme for Israel which will bring them back to Him.

Between Pentecost and The Day of the Lord is the 'Church Age'. Since the time of Pentecost when Israel, on the whole, had rejected Jesus Christ as Messiah and the Holy Spirit was poured out on believers, God's programme for Israel has been on hold. The church age will conclude and God's programme for Israel will recommence when the "full number of the Gentiles has come in" (Rom. 11:25 NIV). The church will therefore be complete *before* Israel is saved.

Even though the chosen people went into exile a number of times in foreign countries and many did not return to their homeland, they have been largely scattered over the face of the earth since the second temple was destroyed by Titus in the year AD 70 when 1, 100, 000 Jews died. The Jewish people have suffered great persecution over the centuries, including during World War II when Hitler's regime killed at least 5, 950, 000 during the Holocaust in 'death camps', and in the notorious gas chambers, as part of his 'final solution'.

Micah prophesied that "Israel will be abandoned until the time when she who is in labour gives birth and the rest of his brothers return to join the Israelites" (Mic. 5:3 NIV). The fulfilment of this prophecy of Israel returning to the land that God has given them and the re-uniting of the twelve tribes of Israel, had the foundation laid for its fulfilment with the rebirth of the nation of Israel in 1948 and the beginning of the return to their land by those who had been scattered throughout many countries. Between 1991 and 2000, for example, nearly one million Jews arrived in Israel from ex-USSR countries after the collapse of the 'Iron Curtain'. In 2010 there were 5, 703, 200 Jews living in Israel. This equates to over forty-two percent of the world Jewish population, now exceeding the number that reside in the United States. This means that in 2010, approximately seventy-five percent of the population of Israel was Jewish. The total Jewish population of Israel *and* the disputed territories of West Bank and Gaza in 2010, equated to over eleven million or approximately fifty-one percent of the total population. God's plans for the people of Israel are coming to fulfilment as more and more exiles return to their land.

The commencement of The Tribulation signals the beginning of the outpouring of God's wrath on sinful man. Jeremiah prophesied: "See, the storm of the LORD will burst out in wrath, a driving wind swirling down on the heads of the wicked. The fierce anger of the LORD will not turn back until he fully accomplishes the purposes of his heart" (Jer. 30:23-24 NIV).

According to Scripture, during the Tribulation God will pour out many judgements on the inhabitants of the earth including a great earthquake, a number of other earthquakes, hail and fire mixed with blood burning up one third of the earth, one third of the sea turning to blood killing all living things in it, rivers and springs of water turning to blood, one third of the rivers and springs turning bitter, and one third of the sun, moon, and stars turning dark. There will be plagues such as a demonic locust-type of creature that rises from the abyss and stings like a scorpion causing agony to people over a period of five months leading them to seek death which will elude them, and plagues of fire, smoke, and sulphur killing one third of mankind. The sun will scorch people with fire and there will be darkness over the earth.

Many of the inhabitants on the earth will die, and many will wish they could, as they will prefer death over what has befallen them, for "it is a fearful thing to fall into the hands of the living God" (Heb. 10:31). Satan will be very active towards the end of time, particularly in his quest to deceive those who are perishing by trying to keep them from turning to God and believing the truth, for "he knows that his time is short" (Rev. 12:12).

In the book of Revelation, the *true* church, which is the body of Christ, is not mentioned as being on the earth during the time of The Tribulation. The Day of the Lord is referred to as the "time of distress for Jacob" (Jer. 30:7) or Israel, not for the church. Whilst God has *not* promised to keep those 'in Christ' from hardships, trials, or even persecution during their lives, He *has* promised to rescue them from His wrath.

> **Wrath /roth/** *n. literary* **extreme anger (Old English: related to WROTH).**[2]

Jesus told the disciples to "be always on the watch, and pray that you may be able to escape all that is about to happen, and that you may be able to stand before the Son of Man" (Luke 21:36 NIV). Paul assures those who belong to Christ that He "delivers us from the wrath to come" (1 Thess. 1:10 NKJV), "for God did not appoint us to wrath, but to obtain salvation through our Lord Jesus Christ" (1 Thess. 5:9 NKJV) and Peter writes that "the Lord knows how to rescue the godly from trials" (2 Pet. 2:9).

Jesus used the example of two men from the Old Testament to parallel how God has rescued godly men in the past. Noah and his family were taken into the safety of the ark and *then* the flood came which destroyed the earth, and Lot, Abraham's nephew, was taken out of Sodom *before* the Lord rained down burning sulphur on the city and destroyed it. Both men were removed from the scene of God's wrath and the resultant devastation *before* God brought these events to pass.

How will God protect believers from the outpouring of His wrath? Paul writes about a future bodily taking up of believers into heaven and, at the same time, a bodily resurrection of those righteous who have already died. Most scholars interpret the passages about the taking up of believers as pertaining to the rescue of those 'in Christ' *before* the devastation that is about to unfold on the earth—the coming wrath of The Day of the Lord. Because the 'Rapture' (as this 'taking up' is known) is part of God's programme for the *church*, there are no prophecies about it in the Old Testament which was written *before* the church existed.

When John was given a vision of the time of the end, which is recorded in the book of Revelation, he was called to "come up here" (Rev. 4:1). He was shown what is to take place on the earth from the perspective of one looking down from heaven, rather than one standing on the earth amidst the devastation; thus paralleling the perspective of those 'in Christ' during the time of The Tribulation.

Paul calls the taking up of believers to heaven "the blessed hope—the glorious appearing of our great God and Saviour, Jesus Christ" (Titus 2:13 NIV), and explains that this is "the redemption of those who are God's possession" (Eph. 1:14 NIV). He writes:

> For this we declare to you by a word from the Lord, that we who are alive, who are left until the coming of the Lord, will not precede those who have fallen asleep. For the Lord himself will descend from heaven with a cry of command, with the voice of an archangel, and with the sound of the trumpet of God. And the dead in Christ will rise first. Then we who are alive, who are left, will be caught up together with them in the clouds to meet the Lord in the air, and so we will always be with the Lord.
>
> —1 Thess. 4:15-17

Paul describes this event as a mystery. He says:

> Behold! I tell you a mystery. We shall not all sleep, but we shall all be changed, in a moment, in the twinkling of an eye, at the last trumpet. For the trumpet will sound, and the dead will be raised imperishable, and we shall be changed. For this perishable body must put on the imperishable, and this mortal body must put on immortality. When the perishable puts on the

imperishable, and the mortal puts on immortality, then shall come to pass the saying that is written: "Death is swallowed up in victory."

—1 Cor. 15:51-54

The 'loud command' from the Lord would be to call out of their graves the bodies of the righteous who have died, in a similar way to when Jesus called Lazarus, the brother of Mary and Martha, out of *his* grave after he had been dead for four days. The 'last trump' or last trumpet is a Roman military term which would be familiar to the people of Corinth who were the recipients of Paul's letter. When an army was to move camp, three trumpets would sound. The last trumpet was the order to move out. It is possible then, that there will be three trumpet blasts in quick succession, the last summoning those 'in Christ' up to heaven—a change in 'camp'.

Those who have already died in faith in the Lord Jesus Christ will come down with Him from heaven and their bodies will rise to re-join their souls in the air. Their souls will be infused with a new spirit and, on joining their resurrected bodies, will cause their bodies to be renewed. Those believers who are living on the earth at that time will rise to meet them in the air. At this very moment, they too will receive the full blessing of the newness of spirit throughout *their* entire souls—complete new spirits. Through the action of this occurring, their bodies will be transformed to be perfect and renewed, completing *their* full salvation of body, soul, and spirit.

In Paul's day, there were rumours that The Day of the Lord had already come because of the intense persecution that believers were under at that time. Paul wrote to the Thessalonians: "Brothers, we beg you by the coming of our Lord Jesus Christ, and of our gathering together to him, for you not to be quickly shaken in the mind, nor to be troubled; . . . as if the Day of Christ has come. Do not let anyone deceive you in any way, because that day will not come unless first comes the falling away, and the man of sin is revealed, the son of perdition, the one opposing and exalting himself over everything being called God" (2 Thess. 2:1-3 GIB). Clearly, the believers were not expecting to still be there on the earth during The Tribulation, and they were concerned that perhaps they had either misunderstood and that they actually *would* have to endure this time of God's wrath rather than being saved from it by being first gathered to Christ, or that the gathering had already occurred and they had missed it. Paul reassured them that this was not the case and that the persecution that they were currently under was not 'The Day of Christ' and that 'The Day of Christ' would *commence* with them being gathered to the Lord.

Paul explained to the Thessalonians that, before The Day of the Lord, there would be a 'falling away'. The Greek word used here is *apostasia;* literally—'The Departure'. It means to 'go away, depart, or remove'. This word is used twelve times in Scripture. Three times it is used to describe a *spiritual* falling away from the truth. Nine times it is used in the context of a *physical* departure from a place or person. In the structure of the sentence in which this word is used in *this* case, it is preceded by the definitive article—'the'. It is speaking of an *event*—*The* Departure, rather than an action done over a period of time (for example, falling away from the truth).

According to Paul, the revealing of the one referred to as 'the man of sin' is currently being held back, or kept in check, by "one who now holds it back" (2 Thess. 2:7 NIV). This 'one' holding it back is widely interpreted as being the indwelling of the Holy Spirit in believers. It is therefore the presence of the *church* on earth that is holding back the revelation of the 'lawless one'. The role of indwelling that the Holy Spirit does in believers will *not* continue during The Tribulation, although the Holy Spirit *will* continue to have a presence on the earth. The return to Christ of the indwelling Holy Spirit further confirms that believers will also be withdrawn from the earth at the same time, as they are Christ's body here on earth and the Holy Spirit dwells within them. The Holy Spirit will not be removed *from* believers but rather, believers will be removed *with* the Holy Spirit.

God is more than able to remove believers from the earth in this way and has done similar things in the past on a smaller scale:
— He bodily transported Elijah and Enoch into heaven;
— By the power of the Holy Spirit, He has taken people places physically, for example Phillip and Ezekiel;
— He reunited Jesus' soul with His body and resurrected and renewed His body;
— He reunited the souls of many Old Testament saints who had died with *their* resurrected bodies and renewed them; and
— Both Jesus and these Old Testament saints rose bodily into heaven.

How do we know that those who have died will bodily rise from the grave? Paul reassures believers that "if the Spirit of him who raised Jesus from the dead is living in you, he who raised Christ from the dead will also give life to your mortal bodies through his Spirit, who lives in you" (Rom. 8:11 NIV). This confirms that those believers who have died will have their bodies resurrected and restored, rather than be given totally new bodies. Paul writes that, "by his power God raised the Lord from the dead, and he will raise us also" (1 Cor. 6:14 NIV). God made Adam from dust. He is more than able to transform the dust that our bodies have *become* upon death into renewed bodies with renewed life through the power of the Holy Spirit. God is a God of miracles!

Our new bodies shall "bear the image of the man from heaven" (1 Cor. 15:49). They will be like the resurrection body of Christ—perfect and renewed with life and vitality. Paul says that "we eagerly await a Saviour from there, the Lord Jesus Christ, who, by the power that enables him to bring everything under control, will transform our lowly bodies so that they will be like his glorious body" (Phil. 3:20-21 NIV). Our flesh will be "renewed like a child's" (Job 33:25 NIV), and we will at last be in the presence of Christ and united with all believers who have ever lived on the earth.

God has called us to Himself by His grace through the working of the Holy Spirit to unite us with His Son; to be the *bride* of the Son. Jesus purchased the church—His Bride, with His own blood. Paul tells us that Christ cares for the church as His own body, "for we are members of his body. 'For this reason a man will leave his father and mother and be united to his wife, and the two shall become one flesh.' This is a profound mystery—but I am talking about Christ and the church" (Eph. 5:30-32 NIV).

> In biblical times, the first step in marriage was taken by the man or his family ... He sealed the agreement by giving gifts (a dowry).[3]

The Son sealed the marriage agreement with the church by giving believers His Spirit to dwell in their hearts as a deposit guaranteeing their inheritance. In Jewish tradition:

> The bridegroom usually came about midnight. Someone in the bridegroom's company would cry, "Behold, the bridegroom cometh!" Then they would go with him to the bride's place and would eventually escort her back to his place.[4]
>
> In Israel, the bride usually went to her husband's home and became part of his family.[5]

The taking of believers to the Father's house in heaven, will signify the consummation of the marriage between Christ and the church when the two shall become one—when we shall inherit a full new spirit, which is Christ's Spirit—the Holy Spirit, which will give full life to our souls *and* our bodies. This event is known as 'The Marriage of the Lamb' and will be a great and joyous celebration. Only those who are part of this redeemed church are the Bride of the Lamb—those who are 'in Christ' at that point in time. The Jewish marriage feast lasted seven days—a parallel to the seven years that the church will be in heaven during the Tribulation.

How will the mass disappearance of people all over the globe be explained? There are a few possible reasons that might be given:

1. Alien abduction. Many people believe openly, or secretly, in the existence of aliens. This has been fuelled by the many television shows and movies that depict 'citizens' from other planets interacting with, or abducting, those from earth. This has conditioned the minds of many sufficiently so that they may actually accept this explanation sparking a mass hysteria, or perhaps a mass following, of all things 'alien'.
2. There may be those who will explain these disappearances by saying that it is the act of God to remove the 'wicked' from the earth, or even the 'false' church, when it will, in fact, be the opposite.
3. Media control and ownership of media by fewer and fewer organisations, means that it is quite possible to have a media 'blackout' or simply a misrepresentation of the facts of an event, even one of this magnitude. This would mean that people would not realise the extent of the disappearances and the resultant chaos.

4. Because of worldwide chaos and the beginning of many disasters, the disappearance of people may actually be fairly minor news in relation to other events, or at least may quickly pale in comparison.
5. Although there are many millions of *professing* Christians in the world, unfortunately the actual number of *true* believers who are indwelt by the Holy Spirit may be significantly less than the statistics would imply, and therefore the number of people who disappear may not be as impacting as the official figures of those who are by name 'Christian', would suggest.

What will believers be doing in heaven during the time of The Tribulation on earth? Apart from celebrating and enjoying being in the presence of our Lord and Saviour and those who love Him, they will come before His judgement seat. Paul tells us that "we will all stand before the judgement seat of God . . . each of us will give an account of himself to God" (Rom. 14:10, 12).

The judgement of believers is *not* a judgement calling into question the genuineness of their faith. The judgement seat here is encircled by a rainbow—the symbol of mercy. If they *are* in heaven, it means that they had died or had been taken up to heaven *in faith* by the indwelling Holy Spirit. Their faith, therefore, is genuine.

This judgement of believers in heaven is a judgement of what they have done in the body—a judgement of works. Works are *not* a prerequisite to faith but rather a *demonstration* of, or *evidence* of, faith. When believers stand before the judgement seat of Christ, their work will be shown for what it is. "It will be revealed with fire, and the fire will test the quality of each man's work. If what he has built survives, he will receive his reward. If it is burned up, he will suffer loss; he himself will be saved, but only as one escaping through the flames" (1 Cor. 3:13-15 NIV). The work that survives is that which is the work of the Lord, not the works of man. Our motives will be examined and rewards will be given. Reward and recognition by the One you serve is part of the fair and just attributes of God's nature.

It is the judgement of works that determines rewards received or lost. The Scriptures speak of four crowns, but this does not necessarily exclude other crowns. Those mentioned are:

— *The crown of life.* "Blessed is the man who perseveres under trial, because when he has stood the test, he will receive the crown of life that God has promised to those who love him" (James 1:12 NIV). With regard to persecution and imprisonment, Jesus said: "Be faithful unto death, and I will give you the crown of life" (Rev. 2:10).
— *The crown of glory.* Peter wrote that "when the Chief Shepherd appears, you will receive the unfading crown of glory" (1 Pet. 5:4).
— *The crown of rejoicing.* Paul asks: "For what is our hope, or joy, or crown of rejoicing? Is it not even you in the presence of our Lord Jesus Christ at His coming?" (1 Thess. 2:19 NKJV).

— *The crown of righteousness.* Towards the end of Paul's ministry, he told Timothy: "I have fought the good fight, I have finished the race, I have kept the faith. Now there is in store for me the crown of righteousness, which the Lord, the righteous Judge, will award to me on that day—and not only to me, but also to all who have longed for his appearing" (2 Tim. 4:7-8 NIV).

A crown is given to a person to bestow honour and dignity on them. The crowns that are awarded are *victor's* crowns. Paul likens the believer's journey to the race of an athlete, saying that "if anyone competes as an athlete, he does not receive the victor's crown unless he competes according to the rules" (2 Tim. 2:5 NIV). The 'rules' are laid out in the Word of God. Paul says that we are in this race to "get a crown that will last forever" (1 Cor. 9:25 NIV)—an incorruptible crown.

There are also other rewards mentioned in the Bible:

— *Reward for witnessing to others.* Paul said that "the man who plants and the man who waters have one purpose, and each will be rewarded according to his own labour" (1 Cor. 3:8 NIV).

— *Reward for doing good.* Paul said that "the Lord will reward everyone for whatever good he does" (Eph. 6:8 NIV) and "whatever you do, work at it with all your heart, as working for the Lord, not for men, since you know that you will receive an inheritance from the Lord as a reward. It is the Lord Christ you are serving" (Col. 3:23-24 NIV).

— *Reward for seeking God.* "Without faith it is impossible to please God, because anyone who comes to him must believe that he exists and that he rewards those who earnestly seek him" (Heb. 11:6 NIV).

The book of Revelation tells of the many rewards and benefits of remaining faithful and overcoming, or enduring, to the end:

> To him who overcomes, I will give the right to eat from the tree of life, which is in the paradise of God . . . He who overcomes will not be hurt by the second death . . . To him who overcomes, I will give some of the hidden manna. I will also give him a white stone with a new name written on it, known only to him who receives it . . . Hold on to what you have until I come. To him who overcomes and does my will to the end, I will give authority over the nations . . . I will also give him the morning star . . . He who overcomes will . . . be dressed in white. I will never blot out his name from the book of life, but will acknowledge his name before my father and his angels . . . Him who overcomes I will make a pillar in the temple of my God. Never again will he leave it. I will write on him the name of my God and the name of the city of my God, the new Jerusalem, which is coming down out of heaven from my God; and I will also write on him my new name . . . To him who overcomes, I will give the right to sit with me on my throne, just as I overcame and sat down with my Father on his throne.
>
> —Rev. 2:7, 11, 17, 25-27, 28, 3:5, 12, 21 NIV

Those who are awarded crowns are later seen in John's vision to be casting this material sign of their reward at the feet of God, giving the glory to Him. John saw twenty-four elders around the throne of God dressed in white and wearing crowns of gold. They fall down and worship Him who sits on the throne and "lay their crowns before the throne and say: 'You are worthy, our Lord and God, to receive glory and honour and power, for you created all things, and by your will they were created and have their being'" (Rev. 4:10-11 NIV).

During the time of the Tribulation, as well as appearing before the judgement seat of Christ, those in heaven will also be preparing for their return to the earth with the Lord.

What does the seven-year Tribulation hold for the Jewish nation? Leading up to the time of the end, God has been preparing the Jewish people for their return to the land He has given them. They have been scattered all over the face of the earth for about two thousand years but, since 1948 when the state of Israel was re-established, Jews have been slowly returning to their homeland—the land that God had promised to Abraham's descendants through his son Isaac and grandson Jacob.

At the beginning of the seven-year Tribulation, there will arise a powerful leader of the revived Roman Empire—a coalition of nations. He will appear to be a man of peace and goodwill, and people, including the leaders of other nations, will trust him and look to him for a solution to the global crisis. This leader will at first appear to be favourable towards the Jewish people. He will sign a covenant—likely a peace treaty, with them, and they will experience a false sense of peace and security, some even believing that this leader is the Messiah that was promised. But he will soon show his true colours and his deceitful nature, and he will turn against God's people. Daniel prophesied that:

> A king of bold face, one who understands riddles, shall arise. His power shall be great—but not by his own power; and he shall cause fearful destruction and shall succeed in what he does, and destroy mighty men and the people who are the saints. By his cunning he shall make deceit prosper under his hand, and in his own mind he shall become great. Without warning he shall destroy many. And he shall even rise up against the Prince of princes, and he shall be broken—but by no human hand.
>
> —Dan. 8:23-25

The Bible refers to this leader as the 'Antichrist'. Up until the time that The Tribulation begins, he will not have been revealed because of the one who was holding back this power of lawlessness—the Holy Spirit indwelling the church. This confirms that the church, because of the indwelling Holy Spirit, is a stronger force than this man of lawlessness and the power that energizes *him*. The 'power' that gives him strength will be from Satan, possibly by the possession of his body, at least for part of this time. Satan gives him "power and his throne and great authority" (Rev. 13:2), and his coming will "be in accordance with the work of Satan displayed in all kinds of counterfeit miracles, signs and wonders, and in every sort of evil that deceives those who are perishing" (2 Thess. 2:9-10 NIV).

The false 'king' will assist the Jewish people in the rebuilding of their temple in Jerusalem, encouraging them to recommence the sacrifices and rituals that they have been unable to do for so long during their dispersion, and because of the lack of a temple in Jerusalem. John says that the nature of the Antichrist is to "deny the Father and the Son" (1 John 2:22 NIV). This man of lawlessness will "oppose and will exalt himself over everything that is called God or is worshipped, so that he sets himself up in God's temple, proclaiming himself to be God" (2 Thess. 2:4 NIV). In the middle of the Tribulation, he will set up an *image* of himself in the temple, desecrating it.

Jesus warned the people of Israel that when they see "standing in the holy place 'the abomination that causes desolation' . . . then let those who are in Judea flee to the mountains. Let no-one on the road of his house go down or take anything out of the house. Let no-one in the field go back to get his cloak" (Matt. 24:15-18 NIV). God's people, who are living in Jerusalem at this time, are to flee to escape persecution and death.

The Antichrist will have an 'offsider', which the book of Revelation refers to as the 'False Prophet. He will try to force the entire inhabitants of the earth to give their allegiance to the leader of this empire, and even to worship him as God. It is likely that this person will claim to be fulfilling the prophecies in the Scriptures that were fulfilled by John the Baptist, who pointed the way to the Messiah. The False Prophet will make:

> The earth and its inhabitants worship the first beast, whose mortal wound was healed. It performs great signs, even making fire come down from heaven to earth in front of people, and by the signs that it is allowed to work in the presence of the beast it deceives those who dwell on earth, telling them to make an image for the beast that was wounded by the sword and yet lived. And it was allowed to give breath to the image of the beast, so that the image of the beast might even speak and might cause those who would not worship the image of the beast to be slain. Also it causes all, both small and great, both rich and poor, both free and slave, to be marked on the right hand or the forehead, so that no one can buy or sell unless he has the mark, that is, the name of the beast or the number of its name.
>
> —Rev. 13:12-18

Under the Antichrist and the False Prophet, a false religious system will be established, as well as a cashless system of trade whereby people can only buy and sell if they have this 'mark'—likely a microchip implant. This will be a *world* power, not just confined to a country or region. *Nobody* will be immune. The Antichrist will seek to control every political and religious system. The false church, which has always existed alongside the true church, will be overthrown during this time of Tribulation. These are those who are 'church' by name only, but have not come to a saving faith in

Christ, and therefore did not have His Spirit indwelling their hearts at the time of the departure of those 'in Christ' from the earth.

The people of Israel will suffer great persecution during The Tribulation. "'In the whole land,' declares the LORD, 'two-thirds will be struck down and perish; yet one-third will be left in it'" (Zech. 13:8 NIV). God warned: "How awful that day will be! None will be like it. It will be a time of trouble for Jacob, but he will be saved out of it" (Jer. 30:7 NIV). A remnant of God's people will remain.

Early in the Tribulation period, the Jews will recognize God's intervention on their behalf to prevent a massive invasion of their land by a coalition army and they will turn to the Lord and repent. God says: "The house of Israel shall know that I am the Lord their God, from that day forward" (Ezek. 39:22). "The Israelites will return and seek the LORD their God . . . they will come trembling to the LORD and to his blessings in the last days" (Hosea 3:5 NIV). God will send four judgements on the invading armies—earthquakes, disunity, disease, and hailstones, and only one sixth of them will escape.

The last half of The Tribulation will be far worse than the first half for *all* who live on the earth, but the Jewish people will be the prime targets of the Antichrist. It is likely that the Antichrist's efforts to eradicate the Jewish people will be stirred up by their turning to the Lord. Satan will try to destroy the people of Israel through the Antichrist, but the book of Revelation tells us that the "woman fled into the desert to a place prepared for her by God, where she might be taken care of for 1,260 days" (Rev. 12:6 NIV) or approximately three and one half years—the latter half of the Tribulation. The 'woman' represents Israel, who is the "woman who gave birth to a son, a male child" (Rev. 12:5 NIV)—Jesus. Satan, being unable to destroy the 'woman', "went off to make war against the rest of her offspring—those who obey God's commandments and hold to the testimony of Jesus" (Rev. 12:17 NIV). These are those Gentiles who, during the Tribulation, become believers in Jesus Christ. They are referred to as 'Tribulation saints'.

Those who are on the earth during these last days will still have the opportunity to repent and turn to the Lord, putting their faith in Jesus Christ as Saviour. Many of the Jewish people will recognize early in the Tribulation that Jesus is the Messiah and they will be used by God as witnesses to spread the gospel throughout the earth. Because they have been dispersed around the earth for so long, they will have the collective ability to speak many languages fluently.

The book of Revelation also tells of 144, 000 witnesses who will go throughout the earth proclaiming the gospel message to all nations. Because the church has been removed, these witnesses will go out into the world in their place. These 144, 000 are from the nation of Israel—12, 000 from each of the twelve tribes. There are two possible identities for these witnesses:

1. They are Jews who are living at the beginning of the Tribulation and have been saved through coming to faith in Jesus during the Tribulation at, or near, the beginning of the seven years; or
2. They are the Old Testament saints who were bodily raised at the time of Jesus' death. These resurrected saints are described in the gospel account as 'firstfruits', as are the witnesses spoken of in the book of Revelation, which describes the witnesses in the end times as "those who did not defile themselves with women, for they kept themselves pure . . . They were purchased from among men and offered as firstfruits to God and the Lamb" (Rev. 14:4-5 NIV). The Bible does not elaborate on the number of saints who were bodily raised at that time, but states that there were 'many'.

These witnesses will be protected from harm by God during the outpouring of His wrath by putting a seal on their foreheads, in much the same way as the Israelites were protected by painting the blood of a lamb over their door lintels in Egypt to save them from the angel of death who passed through, killing the firstborn son of every Egyptian family during the time of Moses. The end time judgements are the outpouring of God's wrath and are administered by angels, just as an angel administered death in the camp of the Egyptians. This would imply that the witnesses who are sealed will be protected from being killed by any of the disasters that fall upon the earth and its occupants. If they are, in fact, the saints who rose bodily when Christ died, they would certainly need to be protected from a *second* death by being sealed, for man is destined to die only once. This protection seems as though it will be a *physical* protection—an 'immunity'.

During the Tribulation, these Jewish witnesses will be supported by Gentile believers with food, clothing, and so on, and Revelation chapter seven tells of a great multitude in heaven who have been saved because of the witness of the 144, 000.

The 144, 000 sealed Jewish witnesses are seen later in John's vision standing on Mount Zion (the heavenly Jerusalem) with the Lamb, after being "redeemed from the earth" (Rev. 14:3). It seems that about halfway through the Tribulation, all of these witnesses are taken up to heaven. Although John sees these witnesses on Mount Zion—the heavenly Jerusalem, the account in Revelation does not actually specify that they were *killed*, thus giving more reason to believe that these witnesses may be those saints who had been bodily resurrected at the time of Jesus' death and who had returned to heaven with Him when He ascended, and that when they had completed their work of witnessing during The Tribulation, they were bodily taken up to heaven again.

Alternatively, if they were Jews who had been living at the time of the beginning of The Tribulation period and had come to faith in Jesus, they may have been bodily removed from the earth later in the Tribulation without dying, and their bodies renewed and transformed by the Holy Spirit in a similar way to those 'in Christ' at the departure of the church prior to The Tribulation.

There are also two witnesses that are clothed in sackcloth and preach repentance:

> "And I will grant authority to my two witnesses, and they will prophesy for 1,260 days, clothed in sackcloth." These are the two olive trees and the two lampstands that stand before the Lord of the earth. And if anyone would harm them, fire pours from their mouth and consumes their foes. If anyone would harm them, this is how he is doomed to be killed. They have the power to shut the sky, that no rain may fall during the days of their prophesying, and they have power over the waters to turn them into blood and to strike the earth with every kind of plague, as often as they desire. And when they have finished their testimony, the beast that rises from the bottomless pit will make war on them and conquer them and kill them, and their dead bodies will lie in the street of the great city that symbolically is called Sodom and Egypt, where their Lord was crucified. For three and a half days some from the peoples and tribes and languages and nations will gaze at their dead bodies and refuse to let them be placed in a tomb, and those who dwell on the earth will rejoice over them and make merry and exchange presents, because these two prophets had been a torment to those who dwell on the earth. But after the three and a half days a breath of life from God entered them, and they stood up on their feet, and great fear fell on those who saw them. Then they heard a loud voice from heaven saying to them, "Come up here!" And they went up to heaven in a cloud, and their enemies watched them.
> —Rev. 11:3-12

'Come up here!' is the same call given to John when he was taken up to heaven to view the Tribulation events unfolding. The identity of these two witnesses is unknown, but it may be that they are:

1. Elijah and Enoch, both of whom were powerful preachers of repentance in their time and who had not died but were bodily translated to heaven. God says: "See, I will send you the prophet Elijah before that great and dreadful day of the LORD comes. He will turn the hearts of the fathers to their children, and the hearts of the children to the fathers; or else I will come and strike the land with a curse" (Mal. 4:5-6 NIV). Some scholars believe that one cannot be identified as Enoch because these two witnesses are referred to as 'olive trees'—a Jewish symbol, and Enoch actually lived *prior* to the formation of Israel. However, that argument certainly does not preclude God from referring to him as an 'olive tree' if He so desires;
2. Elijah and Moses, although Moses has already died a physical death, so it is unlikely that he would be subject to a *second* physical death; or
3. Two godly Jewish men who are living at the time of the Tribulation.

The witness of these two will bring a great many Jews to repentance. After these witnesses are taken up to heaven halfway through the Tribulation, there will be a great earthquake causing a tenth of the city to collapse and killing seven thousand people.

It is after seeing the 144,000 witnesses in heaven, that John records seeing angels proclaiming the gospel. He wrote that he saw an "angel flying in mid-air, and he had the eternal gospel to proclaim to those who live on the earth—to every nation, tribe, language and people. He said in a loud voice, 'Fear God and give him glory, because the hour of his judgement has come. Worship him who made the heavens, the earth, the sea and the springs of water'" (Rev. 14:6-7 NIV). This angelic witness signals mankind's final chance to repent. All of mankind will have, one way or another, heard the eternal gospel message. Jesus said that "the gospel of the kingdom will be preached in the whole world as a testimony to all nations, and then the end will come" (Matt. 24:14 NIV).

Many people will turn to the Lord during this time, but many will continue in their disregard for His salvation and will die in their sins, for despite all these plagues and disasters and the death that they cause, "the rest of mankind that were not killed by these plagues still did not repent of the work of their hands; they did not stop worshipping demons, and idols of gold, silver, bronze, stone, and wood—idols that cannot see or hear or walk. Nor did they repent of their murders, their magic arts, their sexual immorality or their thefts" (Rev. 9:20-21 NIV).

God's wrath will be upon those who worship the beast and receive the mark of the beast. He will cause those who receive the mark to have ugly and painful sores break out on them. But, receiving this mark, a sign of allegiance with the Antichrist and identification with this worldly system, will also have *eternal* consequences:

> If anyone worships the beast and its image and receives a mark on his forehead or on his hand, he also will drink the wine of God's wrath, poured full strength into the cup of his anger, and he will be tormented with fire and sulphur in the presence of the holy angels and in the presence of the Lamb. And the smoke of their torment goes up forever and ever, and they have no rest, day or night, these worshippers of the beast and its image, and whoever receives the mark of its name.
>
> —Rev. 14:9-11

The Holy Spirit will still remain *operative* on the earth during The Tribulation but will not be *resident*, and therefore will not have the role of indwelling the hearts of believers. They will be part of a 'spiritual Israel' in a similar way to those in the New Testament who recognized that Jesus was the Messiah of whom the prophets spoke and put their faith in the Lord Jesus as Saviour *before* the giving of the Holy Spirit. These believers will be acceptable to God and will be redeemed through faith in the blood of the Lamb and through the repentance from sins. Regeneration and indwelling are *different* works or actions of the Holy Spirit. Indwelling is associated with empowerment, as well as with sealing the heart and connecting the believer to God. Salvation during The Tribulation will still be by faith, but the Holy Spirit will be received at a future time. There will be no indwelling or baptism in the Holy Spirit, nor will the hearts of believers be sealed and connected to Christ's Spirit.

Those believers who die during The Tribulation appear to be in heaven for the remainder of the seven years. They are seen in John's vision in Revelation "under the altar" (Rev. 6:9). Because they would not have the indwelling Holy Spirit when they die, it is likely that their souls would have an angelic escort to heaven as the righteous did when escorted to Sheol. It is also likely that, once in heaven, they would receive the Holy Spirit into their hearts as a deposit, and thus would experience the redemption of the soul. Some of these may arrive in heaven in time for the Marriage of the Lamb but only as guests, not as part of the Bride. These Tribulation saints would then await the redemption and renewal of their bodies at the end of the seven years of Tribulation. Many believers will die as martyrs for their faith amidst severe persecution, particularly during the latter half of the seven years.

THE RETURN OF THE KING

The Bible tells us that Jesus "must remain in heaven until the time comes for God to restore everything, as he promised long ago through his holy prophets" (Acts 3:21 NIV). At the end of The Tribulation, John describes hearing "what sounded like the roar of a great multitude in heaven" (Rev. 19:1 NIV). These multitudes shout: "'Hallelujah! For the wedding of the Lamb has come, and his bride has made herself ready. Fine linen, bright and clean, was given her to wear.' (Fine linen stands for the righteous acts of the saints). Then the angel said to me, 'Write: 'Blessed are those who are invited to the wedding supper of the Lamb!''" (Rev. 19:6-8 NIV). The Bride is now ready to return to the earth with the Lord!

Jesus said that immediately prior to His return, "there will be signs in the sun, moon and stars. On the earth, nations will be in anguish and perplexity at the roaring and tossing of the sea. Men will faint from terror, apprehensive of what is coming on the world, for the heavenly bodies will be shaken. At that time they will see the Son of Man coming in a cloud with power and great glory. When these things begin to take place, stand up and lift up your heads, because your redemption is drawing near" (Luke 21:25-28 NIV). In contrast to the glorious meeting of believers in the air to take them to heaven *before* The Tribulation, at the Second Advent of Christ, there will be "a day of wrath . . . distress and anguish . . . trouble and ruin . . . darkness and gloom . . . clouds and blackness" (Zeph. 1:15 NIV), "the sun will be turned to darkness and the moon to blood" (Acts 2:19 NIV).

When Jesus ascended into heaven, two angels appeared to the disciples who were watching. "'Men of Galilee,' they said, 'why do you stand here looking into the sky? This same Jesus, who has been taken from you into heaven, will come back in the same way you have seen him go into heaven'" (Acts 1:11 NIV). The angels were right! "He is coming with the clouds, and every eye will see him, even those who pierced him; and all the peoples of the earth will mourn because of him" (Rev. 1:7 NIV). Jesus "will return to Zion" (Zech. 8:3 NIV).

When Jesus returns to the earth, He will bring the saints with Him—those who have been waiting in heaven. John, in his vision, saw the scene in heaven just prior to the return of the Lord Jesus Christ:

> Then I saw heaven opened, and behold, a white horse! The one sitting on it is called Faithful and True, and in righteousness he judges and makes war. His eyes are like a flame of fire, and on his head are many diadems, and he has a name written that no one knows but himself. He is clothed in a robe dipped in blood, and the name by which he is called is The Word of God. And the armies of heaven, arrayed in fine linen, white and pure, were following him on white horses. From his mouth comes a sharp sword with which to strike down the nations and he will rule them with a rod of iron. He will tread the winepress of the fury of the wrath of God the Almighty. On his robe and on his thigh he has a name written, King of kings and Lord of lords.
> —Rev. 19:11-16

The first coming of the Lord was to "preach good news to the poor . . . to bind up the broken-hearted, to proclaim freedom for the captives and release from darkness for the prisoners" (Isa. 61:1 NIV). The Second Coming of the Lord will be "to proclaim the year of the LORD's favour and the day of vengeance of our God, to comfort all who mourn, and provide for those who grieve in Zion—to bestow on them a crown of beauty instead of ashes, the oil of gladness instead of mourning, and a garment of praise instead of a spirit of despair. They will be called oaks of righteousness, a planting of the LORD for the display of his splendour" (Isa. 61:2-3 NIV).

The Lord will bring with Him His reward: "See, the Sovereign LORD comes with power, and his arm rules for him. See, his reward is with him, and his recompense accompanies him" (Isa. 40:10 NIV).

The Lord will bring with Him judgement. Enoch prophesied: "See, the Lord is coming with thousands upon thousands of his holy ones to judge everyone, and to convict all the ungodly of all the ungodly acts they have done in the ungodly way, and of all the harsh words ungodly sinners have spoken against him" (Jude 1:14-15 NIV).

Towards the end of the seven years of Tribulation, demons will have gone out to summon "the kings of the whole world, to gather them for battle on the great day of God Almighty" (Rev. 16:14 NIV). A "200 million" (Rev. 9:16 NIV) strong army will have gathered in the Middle East by this time, intent on annihilating Israel and ultimately making war against the true King. The scene on earth will now be set for the return of the Lord.

"The beast and the kings of the earth and their armies gathered together to make war against the rider on the horse and his army" (Rev. 19:19 NIV), "but the Lamb will overcome them because he is Lord of lords and King of kings—and with him will be his called, chosen and faithful followers" (Rev. 17:14 NIV). "The LORD will march out like a mighty man, like a warrior he will stir up his zeal; with a shout he will raise the battle cry and will triumph over his enemies" (Isa. 42:13 NIV). With the armies of the earth gathered in one place, God will suddenly bring down His wrath upon them:

> And they assembled them at the place that in Hebrew is called Armageddon. The seventh angel poured out his bowl into the air, and a loud voice came out of the temple, from the throne, saying, "It is done!" And there were flashes of lightning, rumblings, peals of thunder, and a great earthquake such as there had never been since man was on the earth, so great was that earthquake. The great city was split into three parts, and the cities of the nations fell, and God remembered Babylon the great, to make her drain the cup of the wine of the fury of his wrath. And every island fled away, and no mountains were to be found. And great hailstones, about one hundred pounds each, fell from heaven on people; and they cursed God for the plague of the hail, because the plague was so severe.
>
> —Rev. 16:16-21

Armageddon (arm ah GED un) (*mountain of Megiddo*)—the site of the final battle of this age in which God intervenes . . . Scholars disagree about the exact location of this place, but the most likely possibility is the valley between Mount Carmel and the city of Jezreel. This valley (known as the Valley of Jezreel and sometimes referred to as the Plain of Esdraelon) was the crossroads of two ancient trade routes and this was a strategic military site and the scene of many ancient battles.[6]

Ezekiel chapter thirty-eight speaks of this great earthquake in Israel as well as plagues and bloodshed, torrents of rain, hailstones, and burning sulphur falling from the heavens on the armies of the Antichrist and the many nations with him. They will be overthrown and killed and birds and wild animals will feast upon their flesh. "The Sovereign LORD says: Call out to every kind of bird and all the wild animals: 'Assemble and come together from all around to the sacrifice I am preparing for you, the great sacrifice on the mountains of Israel'" (Ezek. 39:17 NIV).

Israel will be under angelic protection during this great battle and devastation, for "at that time Michael, the great prince who protects your people, will arise. There will be a time of distress such as has not happened from the beginning of nations until then." (Dan. 12:1 NIV).

During this battle, the Antichrist will be "captured and with him the false prophet who had performed the miraculous signs on his behalf. With these signs he had deluded those who had received the mark of the beast and worshipped his image" (Rev. 19:20 NIV). The Antichrist "will be destroyed, but not by human power" (Dan. 8:25 NIV). He will be overthrown by the Lord Jesus "with the breath of his mouth" and will be destroyed "by the splendour of his coming" (2 Thess. 2:8 NIV). The

Antichrist and the False Prophet will be "thrown live into the fiery lake of burning sulphur. The rest were killed with the sword that came out of the mouth of the rider on the horse" (Rev. 19:20-21 NIV). As the armies with the Antichrist are *bodily* destroyed by the sword of the Lord Jesus Christ, their souls will go to the unrighteous section in the abode of the dead to await judgement, for "the LORD will punish the powers in the heavens above and the kings on the earth below. They will be herded together like prisoners bound in a dungeon; they will be shut up in prison and be punished after many days" (Isa. 24:21-22 NIV).

After this, John saw an angel come down out of heaven, "having the key to the Abyss and holding in his hand a great chain. He seized the dragon, that ancient serpent, who is the devil, or Satan, and bound him for a thousand years. He threw him into the Abyss, and locked and sealed it over him, to keep him from deceiving the nations any more until the thousand years were ended" (Rev. 20:1-3 NIV).

Once the 'troublemakers' are out of the way, God's programme of resurrection will resume. 'Resurrection' always refers to *bodily* resurrection. The first resurrection is the bodily resurrection of those who are 'in Christ' and those who 'are Christ's'. It is like a harvest that is in three parts:

— *The firstfruits*—Christ and the Old Testament saints who were bodily resurrected with Him;
— *The main harvest*—the rapture of the church before The Tribulation along with the bodily resurrection of those who have been waiting in heaven; and finally
— *The gleanings*—the final stage of the first resurrection. The gleanings occurs in stages and includes the two witnesses, and the tribulation martyrs.

After Satan is imprisoned, the tribulation martyrs who were in heaven "came to life" (Rev. 20:4 NIV). Up until this point, they likely had only a 'deposit' of the Holy Spirit in their *hearts* given to them on their taking up into heaven. Now they would be given the *full* Spirit of life throughout their souls which would cause their bodies to resurrect, renewing and restoring them.

There will also be a resurrection of the remaining righteous who died under the *Old* Covenant and who went to Sheol. They will recognize that Jesus is their Messiah and they will receive the Spirit of life throughout their souls, and *their* bodies will be resurrected and renewed.

At this time, God will gather the Jewish people who remain scattered throughout the earth and bring them to Jerusalem. "He will send his angels with a loud trumpet call, and they will gather his elect from the four winds, from one end of the heavens to the other" (Matt. 24:31 NIV). God said: "I will bring your children from the east and gather you from the west. I will say to the north, 'Give them up!' and to the south, 'Do not hold them back.' Bring my sons from afar and my daughters from the ends of the earth" (Isa. 43:5-6 NIV). "For a brief moment I abandoned you, but with deep compassion I will bring you back. In a surge of anger I hid my face from you for a moment, but with everlasting kindness I will have compassion on you" (Isa. 54:7-8 NIV). "I will take the Israelites out of the nations where they have gone. I will gather them from all around and bring them back into their own land" (Ezek. 37:21 NIV). "I will surely bring together the remnant of Israel. I will bring them together like sheep in a pen, like a flock in its pasture; the place will throng with people. One who breaks open the way will go up before them; they will break through the gate and go out. Their king will pass through before them, the LORD at their head" (Mic. 2:11-13 NIV). "Then they will live in their own land" (Jer. 23:8 NIV).

> "Behold, I will bring them from the north country, and gather them from the ends of the earth, among them the blind and the lame, the woman with child and the one who labours with child, together; a great throng shall return there. They shall come with weeping, and with supplications I will lead them. I will cause them to walk by the rivers of waters, in a straight way in which they shall not stumble; for I am a Father to Israel, and Ephraim is My firstborn. Hear the word of the LORD, O nations, and declare it in the isles afar off, and say, 'He who scattered Israel will gather him, and keep him as a shepherd does his flock.'"
> Thus says the LORD: "Refrain your voice from weeping, and your eyes from tears; For your work shall be rewarded, says the LORD, And they shall come back from the land of the enemy."
> —Jer. 31:8-10, 16 NKJV
>
> "Therefore thus says the Lord GOD: Now I will restore the fortunes of Jacob and have mercy on the whole house of Israel, and I will be jealous for my holy name. They shall forget their shame and all the treachery they have practised against me, when they dwell securely in their land with none to make them afraid, when I have brought them back from the peoples and gathered them from their enemies' lands, and through them have vindicated my holiness in the sight of many nations. Then they shall know that I am the LORD their God, because I sent them into exile among the nations and then assembled them into their own land. I will leave none of them remaining among the nations anymore. And I will not hide my face anymore from them, when I pour out my Spirit upon the house of Israel, declares the Lord GOD."
> —Ezek. 39:25-29

The people of Israel will finally recognize that Jesus Christ is the Messiah spoken of by the prophets: "They will look on me, the one they have pierced, and they will mourn for him as one mourns for an only child, and grieve bitterly for him as one grieves for a firstborn son. On that day the weeping in Jerusalem will be great" (Zech. 12:10-11 NIV) but "the Sovereign Lord will wipe away the tears from all faces; he will remove the disgrace of his people from all the earth . . . In that day they will say, 'Surely this is our God; we trusted in him, and he saved us. This is the Lord, we trusted in him; let us rejoice and be glad in his salvation'" (Isa. 25:8-9 NIV).

Those Israelites who are living on the earth at this time will be judged in Jerusalem. Paul says that "not all who are descended from Israel are Israel" (Rom. 9:6 NIV), but "everyone whose name is found written in the book—will be delivered" (Dan. 12:1 NIV). Those who believe in the Lord Jesus Christ as Saviour will then receive the Holy Spirit into their *hearts*. They will not, at this stage, experience the *fullness* of a new spirit throughout their souls and the renewal of their bodies.

The Gentiles (those not of Jewish descent) who are alive on the earth will then be gathered before the throne of the Son of Man in Jerusalem and separated—the righteous (the 'sheep') from the unrighteous (the 'goats'). The basis for determining which group they are in is how they treated the elect (the Jews) who were witnesses for the Lord during the Tribulation. These are 'the King's messengers'. This is *not* a judgement of works, but the treatment of, and response to, these witnesses is evidence of their salvation.

The unrighteous will be thrown into "the eternal fire prepared for the devil and his angels . . . they will go away to eternal punishment" (Matt. 25:41 NIV). Their bodies will be immediately destroyed in the lake of fire, but their souls will remain in the lake of fire for eternity and they will have full awareness of where they are. Only those who have repented and believed in Jesus as Lord and Saviour will remain on the earth. They will be the ones who belong to the Lord through faith and the forgiveness of sins, and they will receive the Holy Spirit into their hearts and will await a future bodily renewal.

After this bit of 'housework' and 'filing', there will be a great celebration in Jerusalem—'The Wedding Supper of the Lamb'. The Bridegroom has arrived, the Bride has accompanied Him, and the guests are assembled. In biblical times:

> The feast was an important part of the marriage ceremony. It was usually given by the bride's family . . . but the groom's family might give it too . . . Both the bride and groom had attendants to serve them . . . Even though the bride would adorn herself with jewels and beautiful clothing . . . the groom was the centre of attention.[7]

Jesus said that "people will come from the east and west and north and south, and will take their places at the feast in the kingdom of God" (Luke 13:29 NIV). "Blessed are those who are invited to the wedding supper of the Lamb!" (Rev. 19:9 NIV). "The Lord Almighty will prepare a feast of rich foods for all peoples, a banquet of aged wine—the best of meats and the finest of wines" (Isa. 25:6 NIV).

The Lord Jesus Christ has come to set up His earthly kingdom. "'Shout and be glad, O Daughter of Zion. For I am coming, and I will live among you,' declares the LORD. 'Many nations will be joined with the LORD in that day and will become my people. I will live among you and you will know that the LORD Almighty has sent me to you. The LORD will inherit Judah as his portion in the holy land and will again choose Jerusalem'" (Zech. 2:10-13 NIV).

All covenants that God has made, both material and spiritual, have been made with the people of Israel. The covenants that God made with the house of Israel will be fulfilled during Christ's earthly reign, the duration of which will be one thousand years—a millennium. They will also enjoy the blessings of the *New* Covenant. The church, as a branch that has been 'grafted into the vine', has been able to enjoy the *spiritual* blessings of the covenants by being 'in Christ'. Now the people of Israel, with whom these covenants were made, will also enjoy these spiritual blessings as well as the promised material blessings of the kingdom.

In the Millennium, the distinction between the church, the Jew, and the Gentile, will remain. To the Jews, Christ will be 'King of the Jews' and will reign on the throne of David in Jerusalem. To the Gentiles, He will be 'King of kings'—the King over the whole earth. To the church, He is the Bridegroom.

The Lord Jesus will reign on the earth as the rightful King and the saints will reign with Him. Isaiah wrote: "See, a king will rule in righteousness and rulers will reign with justice" (Isa. 32:1 NIV). "The LORD will be king over the whole earth" (Zech. 14:9 NIV). "The sovereignty, power and greatness of the kingdoms under the whole heaven will be handed over to the saints, the people of the Most High. His kingdom will be an everlasting kingdom, and all rulers will worship and obey him" (Dan. 7:27 NIV).

To him who overcomes, or endures in faith to the end, Jesus promised that He would "write on him . . . the name of the city of my God, the new Jerusalem" (Rev. 3:12). As this home of the saints is now in heaven, it will likely move closer to the earth in order for the saints to continue to *dwell* in this heavenly city and also *reign* with Christ on the earth. Jesus was not subject to the same earthly laws of gravity after *His* body was resurrected and restored, so in *their* resurrection bodies, the saints will be able to go between both places.

John was shown by an angel the Holy City—the New Jerusalem, in which the church—the wife of the Lamb, dwells, coming down out of heaven from God. According to the angel's words, the saints and the New Jerusalem—the dwelling place of the saints, are seen as being as if one, as the New Jerusalem is *also* described as 'the wife of the Lamb'. The angel said to John:

> "Come, I will show you the bride, the Lamb's wife." And he carried me away in the Spirit to a great and high mountain, and showed me the great city, the holy Jerusalem, descending out of heaven from God, having the glory of God. Her light was like a most precious stone, like a jasper stone, clear as crystal. Also she had a great and high wall with twelve gates, and twelve angels at the gates, and names written on them, which are the names of the twelve tribes of the children of Israel . . . Now the wall of the city had twelve foundations, and on them were the names of the twelve apostles of the Lamb. The construction of its wall was of jasper; and the city was pure gold, like clear glass. The foundations of the wall of the city were adorned with all

kinds of precious stones: the first foundation was jasper, the second sapphire, the third chalcedony, the fourth emerald, the fifth sardonyx, the sixth sardius, the seventh chrysolite, the eighth beryl, the ninth topaz, the tenth chrysoprase, the eleventh jacinth, and the twelfth amethyst. The twelve gates were twelve pearls: each individual gate was of one pearl. And the street of the city was pure gold, like transparent glass.

But I saw no temple in it, for the Lord God Almighty and the Lamb are its temple. The city had no need of the sun or of the moon to shine in it, for the glory of God illuminated it. The Lamb is its light. And the nations of those who are saved shall walk in its light, and the kings of the earth bring their glory and honour into it. Its gates shall not be shut at all by day (there shall be no night there). And they shall bring the glory and the honour of the nations into it. But there shall by no means enter it anything that defiles, or causes an abomination or a lie, but only those who are written in the Lamb's Book of Life.

And he showed me a pure river of water of life, clear as crystal, proceeding from the throne of God and of the Lamb. In the middle of its street, and on either side of the river, was the tree of life, which bore twelve fruits, each tree yielding its fruit every month. The leaves of the tree were for the healing of the nations. And there shall be no more curse, but the throne of God and of the Lamb shall be in it, and His servants shall serve Him. They shall see His face, and His name shall be on their foreheads. There shall be no night there: They need no lamp nor light of the sun, for the Lord God gives them light. And they shall reign forever and ever.

—Rev. 21:9-12, 14, 18-27, 22:1-5 NKJV

The thousand-year reign of Christ will be an earthly kingdom, but it will be spiritual in character and will be governed from the earthly capital—Jerusalem. In Ezekiel we are told that "the name of the city from that time on will be: THE LORD IS THERE" (Ezek. 48:35 NIV).

The form of government will be that of a theocracy where God has absolute sovereignty. The rights of the individual will be upheld though, as they are in a republican government rather than in a dictatorship. Jesus will be the King. There will be rulers under the King. David will be regent or prince over Palestine, but under the authority of Jesus. There will be governors and nobles under David in Palestine. The disciples will have authority over the twelve tribes of Israel, for Jesus had promised the disciples: "When the Son of Man sits on his glorious throne, you who have followed me will also sit on twelve thrones, judging the twelve tribes of Israel" (Matt. 19:28 NIV). There will also be many lesser authorities and judges. The whole earth will be under the authority of the King of kings and there will be unified government.

There will be forgiveness and restoration for the people of Israel. "Judah will be inhabited for ever and Jerusalem through all generations. Their bloodguilt, which I have not pardoned, I will pardon" (Joel 3:20-21 NIV). God says: (I will) "pour my Spirit upon your offspring, and my blessing on your descendants" (Isa. 44:3). This will be evidenced in righteousness, holiness, and obedience. Israel will no longer be despised but revered among the nations.

In the Millennium, the kingdoms of Israel and Judah will once again be one:

"And I will make them one nation in the land, on the mountains of Israel; and one king shall be king over them all; they shall no longer be two nations, nor shall they ever be divided into two kingdoms again. They shall not defile themselves anymore with their idols, nor with their detestable things, nor with any of their transgressions; but I will deliver them from all their dwelling places in which they have sinned, and will cleanse them. Then they shall be My people, and I will be their God.

David My servant shall be king over them, and they shall all have one shepherd; they shall also walk in My judgments and observe My statutes, and do them. Then they shall dwell in the land that I have given to Jacob My servant, where your fathers dwelt; and they shall dwell there, they, their children, and their children's children, forever; and My servant David shall be their prince forever. Moreover I will make a covenant of peace with them, and it shall be an everlasting covenant with them; I will establish them and multiply them, and I will set My sanctuary in their midst forevermore. My tabernacle also shall be with them; indeed I will be their God, and they shall be My people. The nations also will know that I, the LORD, sanctify Israel, when My sanctuary is in their midst forevermore."

—Ezek. 37:22-28 NKJV

The people of Israel will be restored, as will their land. The Lord said: "I will give you honour and praise among all the peoples of the earth when I restore your fortunes before your very eyes" (Zeph. 3:20 NIV). "They will enter Zion with singing; everlasting joy will crown their heads. Gladness and joy will overtake them, and sorrow and sighing will flee away" (Isa. 51:11 NIV). People will say: "This land that was laid waste has become like the garden of Eden; the cities that were lying in ruins, desolate and destroyed, are now fortified and inhabited" (Ezek. 36:35 NIV). The desert will blossom and rain will fall abundantly on the parched earth. Rivers will flow and there will be springs in the mountains and valleys. God promised the people: "I will repay you for the years the locusts have eaten . . . You will have plenty to eat, until you are full, and you will praise the name of the LORD your God, who has worked wonders for you; never again will my people be shamed. Then you will know that I am in Israel, that I am the LORD your God, and that there is no other" (Joel 2:25-27 NIV).

Houses will be built and vineyards and fruit trees planted, and the fruit of them enjoyed by those who planted them. "Old men and old women shall again sit in the streets of Jerusalem, each with staff in hand because of great age. And the streets of the city shall be full of boys and girls playing in its streets" (Zech. 8:3-5). The Lord will protect His people and tend "his flock like a shepherd: He gathers the lambs in his arms and carries them close to his heart; he gently leads those who have young" (Isa. 40:11 NIV).

There will be no more sickness. "No-one living in Zion will say 'I am ill'; and the sins of those who dwell there will be forgiven" (Isa. 33:24 NIV). Old age will be attained by those in their natural bodies and there will be no miscarriages. The population will increase, as many will be born to those still in their unrestored earthly bodies during the thousand years.

There will be an increase in knowledge, for "now we see but a poor reflection in a mirror; then we shall see face to face. Now I know in part; then I shall know fully, even as I am fully known" (1 Cor. 13:12 NIV). There will be work to do and people will not be idle. At the beginning of the Millennium, there will be much to clean up and rebuild. The earth will have been devastated by wars and disasters.

There will be prosperity. "The wealth of the surrounding nations will be collected—great quantities of gold and silver" (Zech. 14:14 NIV), and these will provide the building materials to rebuild Jerusalem and to build a new temple. The Lord says:

> Behold, I will lay your stones with colourful gems, and lay your foundations with sapphires. I will make your pinnacles of rubies, your gates of crystal, and all your walls of precious stones. All your children shall be taught by the LORD, and great shall be the peace of your children. In righteousness you shall be established; you shall be far from oppression, for you shall not fear; and from terror, for it shall not come near you.
>
> —Isa. 54:11-14, 17 NKJV

The temple will be rebuilt and people will flock to the temple to worship the Lord, "for my house will be called a house of prayer for all nations" (Isa. 56:7 NIV). Ezekiel gives a very detailed description of the millennial temple, including measurements. He also records seeing "the glory of the God of Israel coming from the east. His voice was like the roar of rushing waters, and the land was radiant with his glory" (Ezek. 43:2 NIV), and the *Shekinah* glory filled the temple. "In the last days the mountain of the LORD's temple will be established as chief among the mountains; it will be raised above the hills, and peoples will stream to it. Many nations will come and say, 'Come, let us go up to the mountain of the LORD, to the house of the God of Jacob'" (Mic. 4:1-2 NIV), and "the nations on every shore will worship him, every one in its own land" (Zeph. 2:11 NIV).

In the Millennium, "the survivors from all the nations that have attacked Jerusalem will go up year after year to worship the King, the LORD Almighty, and to celebrate the Feast of Tabernacles" (Zech. 14:16 NIV) or *Sukkot*—traditionally a seven-day gathering to celebrate God's provision and goodness and the completion of the harvest, and also to learn about God's Word—like a big family camp! "Many peoples will come and say, 'Come, let us go up to the mountain of the LORD, to the house of the God of Jacob. He will teach us of his ways, so that we may walk in his paths'" (Isa. 2:3 NIV).

There will still be some sacrifices in the millennial temple by the Jewish people. These will be done in *remembrance* of the blood sacrifice that Jesus Christ made for them for the forgiveness of sins, in the same way that the church was to partake in the Lord's Supper as a remembrance of His death until He came again. The sacrifices will be an expression of faith. The millennial temple has no Ark of the Covenant in which the tablets of the Law were contained, no cherubim, mercy seat, veil, or Most Holy Place inaccessible to the people. The new temple does *not* represent the re-establishment of Judaism.

In Ezekiel's vision of the temple in Jerusalem and of the city surrounding it and beyond, he saw water coming out from under the temple and becoming deeper and flowing into a river, then flowing into the sea. "When it empties into the Sea, the water there becomes fresh; so where the river flows everything will live . . . Fruit trees of all kinds will grow on both banks of the river. Their leaves will not wither, nor will their fruit fail. Every month they will bear, because the water from the sanctuary flows to them. Their fruit will serve for food and their leaves for healing" (Ezek. 47:8, 12 NIV). The water flowing from under the temple from the throne changes the salty water into fresh water. This spot where the river flows into the sea will be a fisherman's paradise: "There will be large numbers of fish . . . fishermen will stand along the shore . . . there will be places for spreading nets . . . the fish will be of many kinds" (Ezek. 47:9-10 NIV). Jesus "will proclaim peace to the nations. His rule will extend from sea to sea and from the River to the ends of the earth" (Zech. 9:10 NIV).

THE BEGINNING IS NIGH

Heaven was not our final destiny, so is this rebuilt earth our final destiny? No—there's more! The Bible tells us that Jesus will reign on the earth for one thousand years, fulfilling God's promise to the Israelites of an earthly king.

During the Millennium, as there will still be people who have their original earthly bodies, many people will be born who will still have the spirit of Adam. They will have to choose to believe in Jesus as their Lord and Saviour or not, and the Scriptures indicate that, despite the truth being blatantly obvious, there will still be many who choose to go their own way. During this time, Satan will be bound in the abyss, so the element of Satan's deception and temptation will have been removed. Deceit and rebelliousness will only come from their own wicked hearts.

It is likely that those who believe during this time will receive the Holy Spirit into their hearts, as believers did *before* the Tribulation. Their hearts will open to the Spirit of God through faith. They will not, at this stage, experience *bodily* redemption and will die a natural death. The Bible does however, promise a full life span in the Millennium for those who are in their original earthly bodies still. It is likely that the spirits and souls of those who die in faith will go to heaven, the dwelling place of God the Father, and the souls of unbelievers to the unrighteous section of the abode of the dead.

At the end of the Millennium, Satan "must be released for a little while" (Rev. 20:3). This will test the genuineness of those in their natural bodies on the earth who have professed faith in the Lord Jesus. Satan will then gather together a rebellion from the nations that will surround Jerusalem in one last effort to defeat the Lord Jesus and His people:

> And when the thousand years are ended, Satan will be released from his prison and will come out to deceive the nations that are at the four corners of the earth, Gog and Magog, to gather them for battle; their number is like the sand of the sea. And they marched up over the broad plain of the earth and surrounded the camp of the saints and the beloved city, but fire came down from heaven and consumed them, and the devil who had deceived them was thrown into the lake of fire and sulphur where the beast and the false prophet were, and they will be tormented day and night forever and ever.
>
> —Rev. 20:7-10

That is finally the end of Satan—his eternal destiny being the lake of fire. The souls of the wicked whose bodies are devoured by fire will go to the unrighteous section of the abode of the dead to await judgement.

Angels will then be judged. Rebellious angels throughout history have deceived, destroyed, infiltrated humanity, possessed the bodies of people, and caused people to worship and sacrifice to them as 'gods'. All of these actions by fallen angels are in direct contradiction to the role that God had created them for and they will *not* escape punishment. "When their judgement comes, they will perish" (Jer. 10:15 NIV). Fallen angels or demons will be cast into the lake of fire for following Satan in his rebellion against God. Faithful angels may possibly receive rewards for service.

After this purge of evil from the earth, there will still be believers on the earth in natural bodies to whom God will give the full Spirit of life, and their bodies will be renewed. There will also be those waiting in heaven who died in faith during the Millennium and God will also give *them* the Spirit of life throughout their souls, resulting in the resurrection and transformation of *their* bodies. It is at this final stage of the resurrection to life, that *all* those who are the Lord's will be fully redeemed. All will finally be 'in Christ'. All will have resurrected and renewed bodies, redeemed souls, and new spirits, ready for eternity.

After this, God will bring up all the unrighteous that are still in the abode of the dead. Their spirits will return to their souls and they will be reunited with their bodies and judged for the deeds done in the body—works. Jesus said: "Do not be amazed at this, for a time is coming when all who are in their graves will hear his voice and come out—those who have done good will rise to live, and those who have done evil will rise to be condemned" (John 5:28-29 NIV). The resurrection of those who 'rise to live' will have already taken place—the first resurrection, which is the harvest of the righteous. This final resurrection is the resurrection of those who are rising 'to be condemned'—the resurrection to damnation. There is *no* rainbow of mercy seen encircling the throne this time. Daniel had this vision of the scene at the time of this judgement:

> As I looked, thrones were set in place, and the Ancient of Days took his seat. His clothing was as white as snow; the hair on his head was white like wool. His throne was flaming with fire, and its wheels were all ablaze. A river of fire was flowing, coming out from before him. Thousands upon thousands attended him; ten thousand times ten thousand stood before him. The court was seated and the books were opened . . . there before me was one like a son of man, coming with the clouds of heaven. He approached the Ancient of Days and was led into his presence. He was given authority, glory and sovereign power; all peoples, nations and men of every language worshipped him. His dominion is an everlasting dominion that will not pass away, and his kingdom is one that will never be destroyed.
>
> —Dan. 7:9-10, 13-14 NIV

Will there be a valid excuse for not being in a right relationship with God? Many on that day standing before the throne of God will try to argue that they knew nothing of God and that they do not deserve to be condemned. There will be all the excuses under the sun on that day:

— No one ever told me.
— I thought everyone went to heaven.
— I thought all religions led to God.
— We had a pastor in our church that was a bad example so I gave up on God.
— Bad things happened in my life so I stopped believing in God.
— My parents did not have faith so I cannot be held responsible.
— I have gone to church all my life.
— I am a good person.
— I am not a sinner.
— I have not done anything bad enough to deserve eternal punishment.

What does the Bible say about these excuses?

> The wrath of God is revealed from heaven against all ungodliness and unrighteousness of men, who by their unrighteousness suppress the truth. For what can be known about God is plain to them, because God has shown it to them. For his invisible attributes, namely, his eternal power and divine nature, have been clearly perceived, ever since the creation of the world, in the things that have been made. So they are without excuse. For although they knew God, they did not honour him as God or give thanks to him, but they became futile in their thinking, and their foolish hearts were darkened.
>
> —Rom. 1:18-21

Even though those in this final resurrection will have been given their spirits again in order for their souls to return to their bodies and their bodies to be resurrected, their wicked and unbelieving hearts will be closed and they will *not* be connected to God. After judgement and sentencing, "the wicked shall return to Sheol, all the nations that forget God" (Ps. 9:17). "He will punish those who do not know God and do not obey the gospel of our Lord Jesus. They will be punished with everlasting destruction and shut out from the presence of the Lord and from the majesty of his power" (2 Thess. 1:8-10 NIV). The wicked will be thrown into the lake of fire.

The eternal redemption of the body only comes through having the fullness of a *new* spirit—the Spirit of life throughout the soul, in connection with the Lord through a clean heart. Eternal life is only 'in Christ'. The bodies of the unrighteous will *not* endure. When their newly resurrected bodies are thrown into the lake of fire they will perish. Their spirits will again separate from their souls and depart, and their souls, in which is their awareness of 'being', will endure an eternity in the lake of fire, forever separated from the source of life.

The first death was spiritual separation from God through the sin of Adam. *Everyone* has a part in the first death. The lake of fire is the *second* death—*eternal* separation from God. The second death is the death that Jesus died to save us from. Many will have a part in the second death. Jesus said that there are only two alternatives: "entering life" or being "thrown into the eternal fire" (Matt. 18:8).

God promised: "I will create new heavens and a new earth. The former things will not be remembered, nor will they come to mind" (Isa. 65:17 NIV). At the completion of judgement and the close of the Millennium, "the heavens will disappear with a roar; the elements will be destroyed by fire, and the earth and everything in it will be laid bare . . . That day will bring about the destruction of the heavens by fire, and the elements will melt in the heat. But in keeping with his promise we are looking forward to a new heaven and a new earth, the home of righteousness" (2 Pet. 3:10-12 NIV).

Heaven—God's dwelling place and the New Jerusalem—earth's new capital city "whose architect and builder is God" (Heb. 11:10 NIV), will join with this new earth. It is likely that all of God's people who would have been protected from the purging of the earth by fire, will descend to the new earth along with the New Jerusalem.

John saw a vision of the new heavens, the new earth, and the New Jerusalem:
> Then I saw a new heaven and a new earth, for the first heaven and the first earth had passed away, and the sea was no more. And I saw the holy city, new Jerusalem, coming down out of heaven from God, prepared as a bride adorned for her husband. And I heard a loud voice from the throne saying, "Behold, the dwelling place of God is with man. He will dwell with them, and they will be his people, and God himself will be with them as their God. He will wipe away every tear from their eyes, and death shall be no more,

neither shall there be mourning, nor crying, nor pain anymore, for the former things have passed away."

And he who was seated on the throne said, "Behold, I am making all things new."

—Rev. 21:1-5

The redeemed will join together in the city of the New Jerusalem and on the new earth for eternity, for "the saints of the Most High will receive the kingdom and will possess it for ever" (Dan. 7:18 NIV). The writer to the Hebrews describes the city that descends from heaven as the home of "the spirits of the righteous made perfect" (Heb. 12:23). In eternity, this will include *all* redeemed mankind.

The angel who had shown John the New Jerusalem had a measuring rod with which to measure the city. "The city was laid out like a square—as long as it was wide. He measured the city with the rod and found it to be 12,000 stadia in length, and as wide and high as it is long. He measured its wall and it was 144 cubits thick" (Rev. 21:15-16 NIV). It is likely that the shape of this city will be a pyramid with a square base. '12,000 stadia' is about 1400 miles or 2200 kilometres, and '144 cubits' is about two hundred feet, or sixty-five metres. This means that, apart from having massively thick walls, this city is huge! A city of those dimensions would just fit inside the moon!

Picture the new earth and the New Jerusalem together—a beautiful garden-city—a return to Eden *and* heaven on earth—a palace in paradise—better by far than the original Creation! The new heavens and the new earth will *never* pass away or be destroyed. God promises that they "will endure before me" (Isa. 66:22 NIV).

Will we be in danger of losing our salvation? No. The Lord says: "My salvation will last for ever, my righteousness will never fail" (Isa. 51:6 NIV).

Jesus said: "Behold, I am coming soon! My reward is with me, and I will give to everyone according to what he has done . . . Blessed are those who wash their robes, that they may have the right to the tree of life and may go through the gates into the city" (Rev. 22:12, 14 NIV).

"I am the Alpha and the Omega, the Beginning and the End. To him who is thirsty I will give to drink without cost from the spring of the water of life. He who overcomes will inherit all this, and I will be his God and he will be my son" (Rev. 21:5-7 NIV).

> "Whoever is thirsty, let him come;
> and whoever wishes,
> let him take the free gift of the water of life"
> (Rev. 22:17 NIV)

Beginnings . . . Endings . . . Beginnings

The author cordially invites you
to visit her at...

www.jrthomas.com.au

for
resources, inspiration,
art, and recommended
reading.

Have your say about this book . . .
How has it impacted your life and the
lives of those
with whom you have shared it?

It would be great to hear from you!

Also by J R Thomas:

Realm of Angels: Light

'Gilliad hovered, weightless, suspended on the timeless eve of eternity past. It was hard to put into words what it felt like to suddenly exist. There was nothing he could compare with the awareness of being that he felt at that moment. He was not, and then in a breath, he was. Simple as that . . . the beginning.'

Witness the incredible unfolding of Creation and the beginnings of mankind through the eyes of the angel Gilliad – gentle protector and faithful servant, not to mention culinary connoisseur, and his friend Latorius – loyal and trustworthy, with a reputation for impulsiveness and pushing the boundaries.

Realm of Angels: Light retells the true events that have shaped the hearts and lives of mankind along with the imaginings of the lives of angels, and the magnificence and splendour of heaven - the King's garden, the children's paradise, the training fields, the sanctuary, The Great Hall, and The New Jerusalem.

Realm of Angels: Light chronicles the lives of those on the earth intertwined with the lives of the hosts of heaven - a tapestry - the weaving together of the warp and the weft - to create the fabric of history. It is a story of paradise lost, of promise, of hope, of beginnings, endings, and beginnings . . . of paradise found.

217 pages

Published 2014

Available as a free eBook or in print

For details visit www.jrthomas.com.au

Notes

Introduction

1. Moore, B (Ed), *Australian Pocket Oxford Dictionary* (Australia: Oxford University Press, 1976, 5th Edition 2002), 1145

Chapter One

1. Strong J, *The New Strong's Exhaustive Concordance of the Bible,* Section— *New Strong's Concise Dictionary of the Words in the Hebrew Bible* (Nashville, Tennessee, USA: Thomas Nelson Publishers 1995,1996), 22
2. Strong J, *The New Strong's Exhaustive Concordance of the Bible,* Section— *New Strong's Concise Dictionary of the Words in the Hebrew Bible,* 8
3. Strong J, *The New Strong's Exhaustive Concordance of the Bible,* Section— *New Strong's Concise Dictionary of the Words in the Hebrew Bible,* 59
4. Moore, B (Ed), *Australian Pocket Oxford Dictionary* (Australia: Oxford University Press, 1976, 5th Edition 2002), 320
5. Moore, *Australian Pocket Oxford Dictionary,* 1028
6. Moore, *Australian Pocket Oxford Dictionary,* 1241

Chapter Two

1. McCall Smith A, *Love Over Scotland* (UK: Polygon, an imprint of Birlinn Ltd. 2006), 301
2. Youngblood, RF (Ed), Bruce, FF (Ed), Harrison, RK (Ed), *New Illustrated Bible Dictionary* (Nashville, Tennessee, USA: Thomas Nelson Publishers, 1995, 1986) 1089

Chapter Three

1. Moore, B (Ed), *Australian Pocket Oxford Dictionary* (Australia: Oxford University Press, 1976, 5th Edition 2002), 574
2. Foster, C, *Wired for God?* (Great Britain: Hodder & Stoughton 2010), 261
3. Miller B F and Keane C B, *Encyclopedia and Dictionary of Medicine, Nursing and Allied Health,* (Philadelphia, PA USA: W. B. Saunders Company 1972, 3rd Edition 1983), 754
4. Miller B F and Keane C B, *Encyclopedia and Dictionary of Medicine, Nursing and Allied Health,* 754
5. Moore, *Australian Pocket Oxford Dictionary,* 1009
6. Moore, *Australian Pocket Oxford Dictionary,* 904
7. Moore, *Australian Pocket Oxford Dictionary,* 916

Chapter Six
1. Moore, B (Ed), *Australian Pocket Oxford Dictionary* (Australia: Oxford University Press, 1976, 5th Edition 2002), 803
2. Moore, *Australian Pocket Oxford Dictionary*, 989

Chapter Seven
1. Moore, B (Ed), *Australian Pocket Oxford Dictionary* (Australia: Oxford University Press, 1976, 5th Edition 2002), 243

Chapter Eight
1. Moore, B (Ed), *Australian Pocket Oxford Dictionary* (Australia: Oxford University Press, 1976, 5th Edition 2002), 1196

Chapter Nine
1. Moore, B (Ed), *Australian Pocket Oxford Dictionary* (Australia: Oxford University Press, 1976, 5th Edition 2002), 554
2. Deem, R, *Is the Virgin Birth Scientifically Impossible?* http://www.godandscience.org/apologetics/virginbirth.html 2005, 1 viewed 15/03/2011
3. Moore, *Australian Pocket Oxford Dictionary*, 783

Chapter Ten
1. *Crossway Bibles English Standard Version Study Bible* (Wheaton, Illinois USA: Good News Publishers 2008), 2007
2. Youngblood, RF (Ed), Bruce, FF (Ed), Harrison, RK (Ed), *New Illustrated Bible Dictionary* (Nashville, Tennessee, USA: Thomas Nelson Publishers, 1995, 1986) 313-314
3. Ussher J, Pierce L (Ed), Pierce M (Ed), *The Annals of the World by James Ussher* (USA: Master Books 2003) 822
4. Ussher J, Pierce, L (Ed), Pierce M (Ed), *The Annals of the World by James Ussher,* 822-823
5. Ussher J, Pierce L (Ed), Pierce M (Ed), *The Annals of the World by James Ussher,* 822
6. Youngblood, RF (Ed), Bruce, FF (Ed), Harrison, RK (Ed), *New Illustrated Bible Dictionary* (Nashville, Tennessee, USA: Thomas Nelson Publishers, 1995, 1986) 314-316

Chapter Eleven
1. Moore, B (Ed), *Australian Pocket Oxford Dictionary* (Australia: Oxford University Press, 1976, 5th Edition 2002), 1233

Chapter Twelve
1. Moore, B (Ed), *Australian Pocket Oxford Dictionary* (Australia: Oxford University Press, 1976, 5th Edition 2002), 76
2. Moore, *Australian Pocket Oxford Dictionary*, 375
3. Moore, *Australian Pocket Oxford Dictionary*, 904
4. Moore, *Australian Pocket Oxford Dictionary*, 474
5. Moore, *Australian Pocket Oxford Dictionary*, 289
6. Moore, *Australian Pocket Oxford Dictionary*, 972

Chapter Fourteen
1. Moore, B (Ed), *Australian Pocket Oxford Dictionary* (Australia: Oxford University Press, 1976, 5th Edition 2002), 373
2. Moore, *Australian Pocket Oxford Dictionary*, 1286
3. Packer, JI (Ed) & Tenney, M C (Ed), *Illustrated Manners and Customs of the Bible* (Nashville, Tennessee, USA: Thomas Nelson Publishers, 1980), 434
4. Capps, C, *End Time Events* (Oklahoma, USA: Harrison House, Inc., 1997), 116
5. Packer, JI (Ed) & Tenney, M C (Ed), *Illustrated Manners and Customs of the Bible* (Nashville, Tennessee, USA: Thomas Nelson Publishers, 1980), 434
6. Youngblood, RF (Ed), Bruce, FF (Ed), Harrison, RK (Ed), *New Illustrated Bible Dictionary* (Nashville, Tennessee, USA: Thomas Nelson Publishers, 1995, 1986) 115-116
7. Packer, JI (Ed) & Tenney, M C (Ed), *Illustrated Manners and Customs of the Bible* (Nashville, Tennessee, USA: Thomas Nelson Publishers, 1980), 434

Bibliography

Alcorn, R 2004, *Heaven*, Tyndale House Publishers Inc., Illinois, USA

Alexander, P (Ed) 1978, *The Lion Encyclopedia of the Bible*, 2nd Edition 1986, Lion Publishing, England

Andrews, E 2009, *Who Made God?* E P Books, England

Barclay, W 1960, *The Promise of the Spirit*, The Epworth Press, London

Beauregard, M & O'Leary, D 2007, *The Spiritual Brain*, Harper Collins, New York, USA

Behrends, K International Continental Scientific Drilling Programme 2009 *Kola Superdeep Borehole (KSDB) 408: "Rocks and Minerals at Great Depths and on the Surface"*, pp 1-2, viewed 30/05/2011 http://www.icdp-online.org/front_content.php?idcat=695

Beverley, JA 2009, *Nelson's Illustrated Guide to Religions*, Thomas Nelson, Nashville, Tennessee, USA

Capps, C 1997, *End Time Events*, Harrison House, Inc., Oklahoma, USA

Carson, DA (Ed), France, RT (Ed), Motyer, JA (Ed), Wenham, GJ (Ed) 1953, *New Bible Commentary 21st Century Edition*, 4th Edition 1994, Inter-Varsity Press, Leicester, UK

Collins, FS 2006, *The Language of God*, Free Press, New York, USA

Colson, C & Fickett, H 2008, *The Faith*, Zondervan, Michigan, USA

Comfort, R 2001, *Scientific Facts in the Bible*, Bridge-Logos, USA

DNA 2011, Wikipedia, viewed 5/04/2011 http://en.wikipedia.org/wiki/DNA

Deem, R, *Is the Virgin Birth Scientifically Impossible?* 2005 http://www.godandscience.org/apologetics/virginbirth.html 2005, viewed 15/03/2011

Driscoll, M & Breshears, G 2010, *Doctrine—What Christians Should Believe*, Crossway, Illinois, USA

Eaton, M 2006, *The Jesus of the Gospels*, New Wine Press, UK

Ecob, JR 2003, *The Bible Prophecy Handbook*, 3rd Edition 2011, Herald of Hope, Australia

Foster, C 2010, *Wired for God?* Hodder & Stoughton, Great Britain

Glasscoe, M, Nasa 1998 *Structure of the Earth*, pp 1-4, viewed 30/05/2011 http://scign.jpl.nasa.gov/learn/plate1.htm

Ham, K, Sarfati, J, Wieland, C, Batten, D (Ed) 1999, *The Answers Book*, Triune Press, Brisbane, Australia

Hodgkin, AM 1907, *Christ in All the Scriptures*, 9th Edition 1943, Pickering & Inglis Ltd., London

Horrobin, P, 2008 *Healing Through Deliverance—The Foundation and Practice of Deliverance Ministry*, Sovereign World Limited, England

Howard, K & Rosenthal, M 1997, *The Feasts of the Lord*, Zion's Hope, Inc., Orlando, Florida USA

Jeffrey, GR 1988, *Armageddon—Appointment with Destiny*, Frontier Research Publications, Toronto, Canada
Jeffrey, GR 1990, *Heaven—The Last Frontier*, Frontier Research Publications, Toronto, Ontario
Jewish Virtual Library, 2010
http://www.jewishvirtuallibrary.org/jsource/Judaism/jewpop.html Source: *American Jewish Year Book, 2006*, (NY: American Jewish Committee, 2006); North American Jewish Databank viewed 27/02/2012
Livingstone Corporation, The 2010, *The Life of Jesus*, Baker Books, USA
McCall Smith, A 2006, *Love Over Scotland*, Polygon, an imprint of Birlinn Ltd, UK
Millard, A 1985, *Discoveries from Bible Times*, 2nd Edition 1997, Lion Publishing, England
Miller, BF & Keane CB 1972, *Encyclopedia and Dictionary of Medicine, Nursing and Allied Health*, 3rd Edition 1983, W. B. Saunders Company, Philadelphia, PA USA
Moody, DL 1880, *Heaven*, Updated Edition 1995, Fleming Revell—A Division of Baker Books (orig), The Moody Bible Institute of Chicago (updated edition), Chicago, USA
Moore, B (Ed) 1976, *Australian Pocket Oxford Dictionary*, 5th Edition 2002, Oxford University Press, Australia
Morris, HM 1971, *The Bible Has the Answer*, Baker Book House, Michigan, USA
Morris, HM 1976, *The Genesis Record*, Baker Books, MI USA
Ovum 2011, Wikipedia, viewed 08/04/2011 en.wikipedia.org/wiki/Ovum
Packer, JI (Ed) & Tenney, M C (Ed) 1980, *Illustrated Manners and Customs of the Bible*, Thomas Nelson Publishers, Nashville, Tennessee, USA
Pawson, D 1997, *Jesus Baptises in One Holy Spirit*, Hodder & Stoughton, London
Pawson, D 1996, *Once Saved Always Saved? A Study in Perseverance and Inheritance*, Hodder & Stoughton Ltd., London
Pawson, D 1992, *The Road to Hell*, Hodder & Stoughton, Great Britain
Pawson, D 1995, *When Jesus Returns*, Hodder & Stoughton, Great Britain
Payne, JB 1973, *Encyclopedia of Biblical Prophecy*, Baker Books, M I, USA
Penney, S 2001, 2008 *World Beliefs and Cultures Judaism*, Heinemann Library, Great Britain
Pentecost, JD 1958, *Things to Come—A Study in Biblical Eschatology*, Zondervan/Dunham Publishing Company, Michigan, US
Pierce, L (Ed), Pierce, M (Ed) 2003, *The Annals of the World by James Ussher*, Master Books, USA
Samples, KR 2004, *Without a Doubt*, Baker Books, Grand Rapids, MI, USA
Schuster, CS & Ashburn, SS 1992, *The Process of Human Development: A Holistic Life-span Approach*, 3rd Edition, Lippincott
Smail, T 1988, *The Giving Gift—The Holy Spirit in Person*, 2nd Edition 1994, Hodder and Stoughton Ltd, London

Spermatogenesis 2011, Wikipedia, viewed 08/04/2011
http://en.wikipedia.org/wiki/Spermatogenesis
Spurgeon, C, Hall, R (Ed) 1993, *What the Holy Spirit Does in a Believer's Life*, Emerald Books, Lynnwood, Washington USA
Strong, J 1995, *The New Strong's Exhaustive Concordance of the Bible*, Thomas Nelson Publishers, Nashville, Tennessee, USA
Tipler, FJ 2007, *The Physics of Christianity*, The Doubleday Publishing Group, New York, USA
Tipler, FJ 1994, *The Physics of Immortality*, Random House, New York & Canada
Viola, F 2009, *From Eternity to Here,* David C. Cook (pub), Colorado springs, CO USA
Wright, NT 2007, *Surprised by Hope*, Society for Promoting Christian Knowledge, Great Britain
Yerbury, RW 1992, *God's Blueprint for Planet Earth*, Cross Publications, Australia
Yerbury, RW 1988, *The Ultimate Event*, Cross Publications, Australia
Youngblood, RF (Ed), Bruce, FF (Ed), Harrison, RK (Ed) 1995, 1986, *New Illustrated Bible Dictionary*, Thomas Nelson Publishers, Nashville, Tennessee, USA

www.ingramcontent.com/pod-product-compliance
Lightning Source LLC
Chambersburg PA
CBHW030135170426
43199CB00008B/77